MCGILLIVRAY
of the CREEKS

SOUTHERN CLASSICS SERIES

John G. Sproat and Mark M. Smith, Series Editors

MCGILLIVRAY
of the CREEKS

JOHN WALTON CAUGHEY

New Introduction by William J. Bauer, Jr.

The University of South Carolina Press

Published in Cooperation with the Institute for
Southern Studies of the University of South Carolina

© 1938 University of Oklahoma Press
New material © 2007 University of South Carolina

First cloth edition published by the University of Oklahoma Press, 1938;
second printing by offset, 1959
Paperback edition published by the University of South Carolina Press,
Columbia, South Carolina 29208

www.sc.edu/uscpress

Manufactured in the United States of America

16 15 14 13 12 11 10 09 08 07   10 9 8 7 6 5 4 3 2 1

Library of Congress Cataloging-in-Publication Data

Caughey, John Walton, 1902–
    McGillivray of the Creeks / John Walton Caughey ; new introduction by William J.
Bauer, Jr. — Pbk. ed.
        p. cm. — (Southern classics series)
    Originally published: Norman : University of Oklahoma Press, 1938.
    With new introd.
    Includes bibliographical references and index.
    ISBN-13: 978-1-57003-692-7 (pbk : alk. paper)
    ISBN-10: 1-57003-692-6 (pbk : alk. paper)
    1. McGillivray, Alexander, ca. 1740–1793. 2. McGillivray, Alexander, ca. 1740–1793–
Correspondence. 3. Creek Indians—Biography. 4. Creek Indians—Government relations.
5. Creek Indians—History—18th century. 6. Southern States—History—18th century.
I. University of South Carolina. Institute for Southern Studies. II. Title.
    E99.C9M343 2007
    975.004'973850092–dc22
    [B]

                                                                              2006100451

This book was printed on a Glatfelter recycled paper with 20 percent postconsumer
waste content.

Publication of the Southern Classics series is made possible in part by the
generous support of the Watson-Brown Foundation.

CONTENTS

Illustrations

x

SERIES EDITORS' PREFACE

John Walton Caughey's 1939 book, *McGillivray of the Creeks,* as the sparkling new introduction by William J. Bauer, Jr., makes clear, continues to address multiple audiences. Caughey's short biography and collection of more than two hundred primary documents concerning the activities of the Creek leader Alexander McGillivray reveal a great deal not only about southern history but also about American Indian and borderlands history. Indeed, as Bauer properly suggests, any student of southern and American Indian history will read these fascinating documents with profit and learn a great deal about federal-Indian relations, the importance of American Indian affairs to the history of the South in the second half of the eighteenth century, and the intriguing and sometimes controversial figure of Alexander McGillivray.

Southern Classics returns to general circulation books of importance dealing with the history and culture of the American South. Sponsored by the Institute for Southern Studies, the series is advised by a board of distinguished scholars who suggest titles and editors of individual volumes to the series editors and help establish priorities in publication.

Chronological age alone does not determine a title's designation as a Southern Classic. The criteria also include significance in contributing to a broad understanding of the region, timeliness in relation to events and moments of peculiar interest to the American South, usefulness in the classroom, and suitability for inclusion in personal and institutional collections on the region.

MARK M. SMITH
JOHN G. SPROAT
Series Editors

INTRODUCTION

AT FIRST GLANCE a book by the historian John Walton Caughey might seem like an odd addition to the Southern Classics series of the University of South Carolina Press. After all, Caughey earned his Ph.D. in history at the University of California, Berkeley (UCB), taught at the University of California, Los Angeles (UCLA), and spent the bulk of his career writing about California and the history of the American West. In other words, Caughey devoted most of his life and research to an area that is geographically far removed from the American South.[1] However, Caughey's early career reflected an interest in history of the Old Southwest and the influence of his mentor, Herbert Eugene Bolton. The dean of the "borderlands" school of American history, Bolton examined areas of Spanish exploration and colonization, including the American South, and passed these interests on to his students—Caughey included. Published in 1939, *McGillivray of the Creeks,* which Bolton helped fund with a research grant, represents one of Caughey's three contributions to southern and borderlands history and remains a relevant work in southern and American Indian history. In it Caughey provides a short biography of the Creek leader Alexander McGillivray as well as more than two hundred primary documents from the period, most of which were written by McGillivray. While this book contains anachronistic, if not deplorable, language, *McGillivray of the Creeks* provides a unique look into southern political history and the early days of federal Indian policy, and it is an important contribution to the base of sources with which scholars write American Indian history.

Caughey was born in Wichita, Kansas, in 1902. His mother was Emily Walton, and his father was a Presbyterian minister named Rudolph Weyerhaeuser Caughey. The family moved several times—first to Marion, Kansas, and then to Pawnee City, Nebraska—before settling in Lincoln, Nebraska. In 1919 Caughey enrolled at the University of Texas, where he majored in English. While at Texas, Caughey took the European history classes offered by the historian Walter Prescott Webb, a then recent addition to the Texas faculty. Norris Hundley, a Caughey student and biographer, wrote, "Webb had not yet discovered those ideas which were to fire his imagination and lead to the publication of his epochal *Great Plains,* and perhaps this is the reason Caughey remembers him conducting rather uninspired discussions in European history."[2] After graduating from Texas, Caughey found a job as a bookkeeper in Roswell, New Mexico, and then taught at the Schreiner Institute in Kerrville, Texas, for two years. Initially Caughey did not appear interested in obtaining a higher degree or pursuing an academic career.[3]

In 1925 Caughey renewed his academic interests and enrolled at UCB to work with Bolton. By the mid-1920s Bolton had already established himself as a leading historian of the American West. Trained at the University of Wisconsin in medieval history, Bolton held his first academic job at the University of Texas. There he taught a course on colonial Texas history. Teaching this class was a watershed moment in Bolton's academic career. The course, and his discovery of previously untapped archival resources in Mexico, convinced Bolton to change his research focus to the Southwest. Bolton eschewed the conventional perspective of American history that focused on British settlements on the East Coast and insisted that other areas were also important to the development of the nation, including the wide swath of territory that Spain colonized and that stretched from Florida to California. Bolton and his students examined the role of Spanish exploration and settlement in the Southeast and Southwest and the impact of institutions (such as the Spanish missions and presidios) on the Spanish frontier. Conventionally, people refer to Bolton and his students as the progenitors of the borderlands school of American history.[4] Indeed, Bolton's most famous book, *The Spanish Borderlands: A Chronicle of Old Florida and the Southwest,* dominated the field for more than fifty years and remains required reading for those interested in writing about the Southeast and Southwest.[5] After leaving Texas, Bolton briefly taught at Stanford University and then moved to UCB, where he remained for the rest of his career. There Bolton trained a generation of scholars who left an indelible imprint on southern and western history.[6]

Under Bolton's tutelage, Caughey wrote a dissertation in the spirit of his mentor: "Louisiana under Spain, 1763–1783." Completed in 1928 and published in 1934 as *Bernardo de Gálvez in Louisiana, 1776–1783,* Caughey's study argued that Bernardo de Gálvez's activities in the Southeast played an important role in the outcome of the American Revolution.[7] After Caughey earned his degree, Bolton used funds from a research fellowship from the Native Sons of the Golden West to send Caughey to Spain to finish some research for Bolton's study of Juan Bautista de Anza.[8] During this trip, Caughey found a cache of McGillivray's letters in Madrid's Archivo General de Indias. The documents provided the foundation for *McGillivray of the Creeks.* Much like his dissertation, the book evinced an interest in leaders and politicians rather than examining the social history of the Old Southwest. After returning to the United States, Caughey briefly taught at San Bernadino Junior College before securing a position at UCLA in 1930, where he remained for the rest of his academic career.[9]

For the next two decades, Caughey's career proceeded smoothly and perhaps in an unsurprising fashion. In 1939 he published *McGillivray of the Creeks,* the third of his eighteen books. At UCLA, Caughey's research interests drifted away from the Old Southwest and toward the New Southwest. He began to write about the history of California and published numerous books and articles on the Gold Rush, the history of Los Angeles, and the historian Hubert Howe Bancroft. In the early 1950s, however, Caughey faced serious academic and personal problems. Influenced by the anti-Communist movements in the 1950s, the University of California's board of regents mandated that all employees sign a loyalty oath that declared that they were not Communists. Caughey and other University of California faculty members refused, and their respective institutions fired them. He faced a difficult time, living on research stipends and enduring criticism from media outlets during a lengthy appeals process. In 1952 the California Supreme Court ruled that the loyalty oath was unconstitutional and violated the tenets of academic freedom, and it decreed that the fired professors could return to their jobs. Caughey returned to UCLA, rebuilt his career, and launched a crusade for civil rights and liberties. He wrote several articles and a book on school desegregation in Los Angeles. Several prominent historical associations recognized Caughey's diligent work in and out of the classroom. In 1958 he served as the president of the Pacific Coast branch of the American Historical Association (he also had a long and distinguished stint as the editor of the *Pacific Historical Review*). Six years later the Organization of American Historians elected Caughey its president. In 1970 Caughey retired from UCLA but remained active in the profession. In 1974 he served as the president of the Western Historical Association. In 1995 Caughey died in his home in Massachusetts. All in all, his was an illustrious career.[10]

Like his biographer, Alexander McGillivray was a controversial and enigmatic figure. McGillivray was born during a transitional moment in Creek and southern history. In the eighteenth century the Creeks had to face profound changes to their way of life. With the arrival of Europeans in the South, the Creeks had entered the political and economic activities of the Atlantic world. Creeks participated in the deerskin and slave trade that marked the region since the arrival of the English in South Carolina and Georgia. Moreover, the Creeks' flexible political organization allowed them to play European powers off against each other. Even though most Creeks sided with the British colonies, they still used imperial rivalries to their advantage. When presented with overtures from the English in the Carolina colonies, the Creeks solicited aid and trade goods from the French in Louisiana, and vice versa. Thus, the historian Joshua Piker concluded, "the effects of the English trade in skins, slaves, and firearms—although threatening—could be kept at arm's length."[11]

The turbulence of the eighteenth century slowly narrowed the distance between the Creek Nation and the colonial powers. By the time of the American Revolution, deer populations had dwindled, and the demand for Indian slaves had long dried up. Between 1760 and 1780 the political opportunities in the South changed as much as the economic ones. In the mid-1760s England defeated France in the Seven Years' War, and France secretly surrendered Louisiana to the Spanish. This did not afford the Creeks the protection they desired because Spain was a shadow of its former imperial self. It had a tenuous hold on Louisiana and Florida, and it failed to replace the economic and military strength of France. The monopoly that England enjoyed in Indian affairs between 1765 and 1776 limited the political options for Creek and other southeastern Indian leaders. The choices were reduced further following the American Revolution. The United States believed it did not need Indian trade for its economic livelihood or Indian allies for imperial conflicts. Rather, the new nation treated the Creeks and other American Indians as conquered peoples and cast an eye toward acquiring Indian land. Thus the Creeks and other southeastern Indians became increasingly dependent economically on the United States and, to a lesser extent, Spain.[12]

Born in the 1750s, McGillivray grew up in this tumultuous political and economic milieu. He received his surname from the Scottish trader Lachlan McGillivray. Lachlan was born in 1719 in the Scottish Highlands. In 1736 he arrived in the fledgling colony of Georgia and began a career as a trader on the Georgia frontier. In 1740 Lachlan moved to Charleston and entered the employ of Archibald McGillivray, a Creek trader. He quickly became conversant in the Creek language and accompanied trade caravans to the Creeks as an interpreter. By 1744 Lachlan was the chief trader between Georgia and the Creeks and remained an important figure on the Georgia frontier for the next thirty years. Like many traders in North America, Lachlan married an American Indian woman, Sehoy Marchand, in order to establish kinship ties with American Indian groups and to facilitate the formation of bonds of reciprocity and exchange between himself and them. Sehoy was the daughter of a Creek woman from the Wind clan and a French officer from the nearby Fort Toulouse. Together Lachlan and Sehoy raised three children: a son, Alexander, and two daughters, Jeannet and Sophia. As a teenager, Alexander attended school in Charleston, South Carolina, where he remained for nearly a decade. During the American Revolution, Lachlan was a Loyalist and had his properties and those of some of his relatives confiscated. He then fled for Scotland, where he died in 1799.[13]

Meanwhile, the young McGillivray returned to Creek country. During the Revolutionary War, British officials hired him as an assistant to David Taitt of the British Southern Indian Department, and he fought against the rebelling colonies. After the American Revolution, McGillivray emerged as a political spokesman for the Creeks. He used his connections to the trading house Panton, Leslie and Company, his ability to read and write English, and his kinship ties with his maternal clan to gain influence among the Creeks. McGillivray negotiated a series of treaties with Spain and the United States and attempted to use the fears of both nations to his advantage. During this period McGillivray led a coterie of Creek leaders to New

York and negotiated a treaty with the United States that is seen as both the highlight and denouement of his political career. After the conference concluded, McGillivray's power and influence within the Creek Nation waned, probably because he surrendered vast quantities of Creek land to the United States, and he faced competition from outside traders. But McGillivray had already amassed quite an estate. When McGillivray passed away in 1793, William Panton reported that the trader owned sixty African American slaves and large numbers of livestock. Even though McGillivray positioned himself as a Creek leader, his economic activities resembled those of a Southern plantation owner rather more than those of a Creek hunter.[14]

McGillivray's political and economic career has generated considerable historical scholarship and debate. Early writers lauded McGillivray for his tactful diplomacy with Spain and the United States. In his work *The Winning of the West*, President Theodore Roosevelt lauded McGillivray for his "masterly diplomacy."[15] The historian Albert J. Pickett said of McGillivray, "We doubt if Alabama has ever produced, or ever will, produce a man of greater ability. . . . We have called him the Talleyrand of Alabama."[16] Yet some assessments of McGillivray depicted the Creek leader negatively. In 1929 Carolyn Thomas Foreman wrote, "McGillivray displayed the greed of the Scotch, the diplomacy of the French and the craft of the Indian."[17] The historian Arthur Whitaker was a more vociferous critic, stating, "The truth is, [McGillivray] committed an unpardonable blunder in being born a half-breed. Without attempting to penetrate the mysteries of racial inheritance, we are on reasonably safe ground when we recognize the disturbing effect of his dual cultural inheritance. . . . For one thing, his emotional instability, a trait common among half-breed Indians, prevented the persistent prosecution of any large design."[18] Influenced by the times, Foreman and Whitaker believed that mixed-blood peoples were cultural pariahs, outcasts in both parents' societies. These authors adopted the ideological baggage of miscegenation, which posited that the children of biethnic or biracial parents were worse off than their "pure blood" parents, having inherited the worst biological and cultural traits of their parents.[19]

Caughey rejected many of the foregoing statements. He wrote,

> The tendency with regard to McGillivray has been, naturally enough, to commiserate him for the bad luck of his racial admixture. Yet the sociologists, to the best of my knowledge, have found no tangible proof that the offspring of mixed unions are physically or mentally inferior. . . . Except with his relations with the white people outside the nation—and even there he was seldom the victim of condescension—McGillivray seems not to have suffered because of his racial make-up.[20]

Rather, Caughey extolled McGillivray as a masterful diplomat and politician: "North America has produced no more extraordinary Indian leader than Alexander McGillivray."[21] Indeed, Caughey seemed impressed that McGillivray fought so diligently for his nation. Norris Hundley, one of Caughey's students, summarized Caughey's argument: "[McGillivray] launched a vigorous program to shield his Indian people from the encroaching white man."[22]

Still, Caughey wrote with some biases and language, common in the 1930s, that are anachronistic and offensive to a modern audience. He called American Indian women "squaws" and wrote of Creek culture in the following terms: "In many other particulars, cultural development among the Creeks had stopped at a rather low level."[23] Further, he described the Creeks as being in constant conflict with Euro-Americans and ultimately falling in the face of a "superior" culture. Caughey wrote that after McGillivray's death in 1793, "it became manifest that he had been fighting against what was inevitable, that his efforts to preserve the Creek lands were doomed to ultimate futility."[24] Caughey's terminology for and arguments about American Indians were part of what has been called "Old Indian history."[25] Until the 1950s, scholars argued that American Indians were a vanishing people. American Indians were part of the frontier phase of American history, and when that period ended, so did American Indian history. Scholars used the Wounded Knee massacre, the promises of assimilation policy, and the shrinking indigenous population to assert that Indians were either assimilating into mainstream American life or dying off. Moreover these scholars posited that American Indians and Euro-Americans have been in perpetual conflict. These historians argued that the frontier marked the border between civilization and savagery, and civilization ultimately triumphed. Three generations of scholarship have rendered these ideas obsolete. Influenced by the civil rights movement, the Vietnam War, and the writings of Vine Deloria Jr. and Dee Brown that excoriated Euro-American exploitation of the American Indian, scholars developed the discipline of ethnohistory, which combined anthropological and historical research methods and sources in an attempt to understand both sides of cultural encounters. Whereas the authors of Old Indian history wrote from a Euro-American perspective, ethnohistorians have endeavored to explore how American Indians envisioned and interpreted their contacts and encounters in a "new world." More recently, some historians have made American Indians the central players and key historical actors in their works. The "New Indian history," which was influenced by the creation of the D'Arcy McNickle Center for the History of the American Indian at Chicago's Newberry Library, "places Indian peoples at the center of the scene and seeks to understand the reasons for their actions."[26] Ethnohistorians and New Indian historians have demonstrated that American Indians and Euro-Americans often cooperated rather than fought and that the outcomes of encounters with the colonies and the early Republic were far from predetermined. Still, despite the dated nature of its language and viewpoint, Caughey's biography of McGillivray remains the standard interpretation of the Creek leader's life.

Reviewers immediately recognized the importance of *McGillivray of the Creeks*. Many lauded Caughey's succinct biography of McGillivray and the inclusion of the letters. M. J. Smith of Oklahoma's Bacone College wrote, "Mr. Caughey presents documents showing that no one could have played the diplomatic game more adroitly, nor with more desire for the good of the Indians themselves, than did Alexander McGillivray."[27] Charles F. Ward agreed: "The result [of Caughey's work], in the opinion of this reviewer, is that this volume affords the clearest picture anywhere available of the Indian sentiment and attitude toward European inthrust in Eastern America."[28] Finally, Roscoe R. Hill of the National Archives wrote that "the collection of documents presents a fairly complete picture of the activity of McGillivray during the short period of his prominence on the Spanish-American frontier."[29] James Leyburn, however, was more critical: "[The letters] are disappointingly concerned almost wholly with politics, marking the wily manoeuvering of the Creek in his dealings with the Americans, the Spanish, and the British. Neither in the correspondence nor in Caughey's introductory essay does the Indian nation live. The volume merely preserves in permanent form a record of the diplomatic skill of an Indian chief."[30] As Leyburn suggests, Caughey's book and the letters tell scholars much about the political machinations of McGillivray, American statesmen, Spanish leaders, and Georgia representatives, but little about the social history of the Creek Nation. Perhaps not surprisingly, Arthur Whitaker also criticized Caughey's treatment of McGillivray and presaged later arguments about McGillivray as a leader: "In my opinion [Caughey] exaggerates McGillivray's devotion to the interests of the Creeks. . . . If the confused story of [McGillivray's] career has a central theme, it is McGillivray's defense not of the Creek tribes but of his own way of life."[31] Whitaker, like later writers, questioned whether McGillivray had the best interests of the Creek Nation in mind or whether he was looking out for himself.

The debate between Caughey and Whitaker raged throughout the twentieth century. Many historians examined McGillivray's life, some taking Caughey's side and others agreeing with Whitaker. The historian J. H. O'Donnell argued that McGillivray's service in the American Revolution, a period of time Caughey did not include in this book, was instrumental to his rise. His assistance to Great Britain during the Revolution trained him for service and permitted him access to Euro-American leaders, which convinced other Creeks he was suitable for leadership.[32] The historian Michael D. Green deems McGillivray an effective leader, considering the circumstances, stating, "Like most reformers, [McGillivray] underestimated the size of his job, but during the late 1780s his efforts to protect his people and their homeland promised some success."[33] Thomas D. Watson concurs with Green and argues that McGillivray protected Creek sovereignty during the 1780s and 1790s.[34] In his fascinating study of pan-Indian Nativist movements, the historian Gregory Evans Dowd writes, "McGillivray could write in the Anglo-American idiom of republican virtue, although he despised republicans. . . . [He] remained dedicated to preserving political autonomy and economic security for [his] people."[35] Recently, Linda Langley has refined our understanding of McGillivray's ethnicity and has argued that McGillivray's ethnic heritage, besides Scottish and French, was Koasati, a Muskogeon-speaking people that lived near the Alabama River and are the ancestors of the contemporary Coushatta nation of Louisiana. Since many Creek identities were local and town oriented rather than the encompassing linguistic or Euro-American-bestowed titles, we may better appreciate McGillivray and see his history in context of his Koasati ethnicity.[36]

Other scholars have raised criticisms of McGillivray. By examining the manifold interests represented at the Treaty of New York in 1790, the historian J. Leitch Wright Jr. concluded that McGillivray could not have negotiated a successful treaty. The differing American, Georgian, Spanish, British, and, of course, Creek interests ensured that the Treaty of New York would fail to placate all involved parties. Wright notes, "McGillivray appears here as something less than the 'Talleyrand of Alabama.'"[37] James Lamar Appleton and Robert David Ward have conducted extensive research into the history of the Treaty of New York and its secret clauses, and they have concluded that McGillivray was duplicitous because he negotiated with the United States while already having a treaty with Spain: "Every part of [McGillivray's] policies, every bit of what he hoped to accomplish for his people, depended on the influence that he could attain and thus the wealth and power that he could command."[38]

Most persuasively, Claudio Saunt argues that McGillivray represented a disruptive force in Creek life. He and other mestizos (people with Creek and European parents) championed a new order of private property accumulation and centralized government that divided the Creeks into those who followed the "new order" and those who adhered to the old. McGillivray, Saunt contends, wanted to centralize power in order to protect private property, helped institute a system of race-based plantation slavery in Creek territory, and duped other Creeks using his ability to write. These values were opposed to the values of the Creeks, who practiced a communal economic system, diffused leadership, and believed in the primacy of oral dialogue. Saunt counters that McGillivray was not the leader of the Creek Nation, as Caughey asserts, because Creek politics were local and headmen had little influence beyond their clan and village. McGillivray could not speak for an entire "nation." Indeed, the term "nation" did not have much meaning among the Creeks in the late eighteenth century.

Creeks were divided as to which path to follow in the wake of international wars of the late eighteenth century. Saunt claims, "Many Creeks objected to McGillivray's authority, and instead turned to Hoboithle Micco for leadership."[39] Indeed, Saunt questions whether McGillivray was, or even considered himself, Creek. "This Scots Indian," Saunt writes, "who may not have even had a Muskogee name, was himself ambivalent about his identity." McGillivray adhered to a different concept of time, did not speak Muskogee very well, and remained ambivalent about his ethnicity in his own writings.[40]

McGillivray was probably something in between "the genius diplomat" that Theodore Roosevelt described and the destructive influence that Saunt discovers. McGillivray closely resembles what ethnohistorians have termed cultural brokers or go-betweens. These frontier people possessed knowledge of both indigenous and Euro-American cultures and the wherewithal to move easily between both. Joshua Piker, for instance, writes of the early-eighteenth-century Creek diplomat, "as someone with friends and relatives in both towns, this man united social worlds; he represented a creative melding of the familial and the political. . . . In a Creek context, then, a Fanni Mico was a fictive relative who functioned as a spokesman for his adopted family or nation in the councils of his original family or nation."[41] Certainly, McGillivray was a shadowy figure in Creek, Spanish, and U.S. circles. And yet he did "unite" these worlds and spoke for the Creeks to the Spanish and U.S. politicians. Moreover, he wrote letters to and for other Creek leaders that conveyed an understanding of traditional Creek diplomatic protocol. This is not to say that all Creeks or Euro-Americans accepted McGillivray or other go-betweens. Indeed, because of the facility with which they traveled between both cultures, cultural brokers engendered resentment and distrust from both American Indians and Euro-Americans. This partly explains why historians have considered McGillivray a duplicitous negotiator, an astute politician, and a man out for himself. The people with whom McGillivray negotiated distrusted him, and this has influenced the scholarship about this singular leader.[42] Still, Caughey's biography remains one of the definitive treatments of McGillivray and remains the closest thing we have to a monograph-length study of McGillivray's life.[43]

The written sources left behind by McGillivray, however, are the valuable part of this book. The letters initially chronicle McGillivray's negotiations with the Spanish officials in Florida and Louisiana. They then detail McGillivray's evolving relationship with the trader William Panton and McGillivray's response to American overtures toward the Creeks. During this period, McGillivray wrote letters to American politicians to discuss frontier encroachments as well as to Spanish politicians avowing his loyalty to Spain. Between 1787 and 1789 tensions between Georgia and the Creek Nation peaked, with conflicts and battles between the two parties. Finally, the letters document McGillivray's participation at the Treaty of New York and the waning years of McGillivray's influence. Throughout, McGillivray strives to play Spanish interests off American ones and to navigate a difficult course for the Creeks in the late eighteenth century.

These letters, which Caughey compiled and transcribed from archives in Madrid and Seville, the Library of Congress, and the Bancroft Library on the UCB campus, are certainly not all the extant letters that McGillivray wrote during his career,[44] but they do provide unique sources and insights into the historian's craft as well as southern, U.S., and American Indian historiography. Since this book includes primary sources, it allows readers to draw their own conclusions regarding these historiographic debates. Did McGillivray strive for Creek sovereignty, or was he looking out for himself? Was McGillivray even a Creek leader?

Caughey's work in compiling McGillivray's letters provides important insights into southern historiography. Southern history has usually been, literally, a black-and-white story, focusing on American slavery. This is logical because slavery seems to be a particularly southern story, especially after the American Revolution. Yet recent scholarship, much of which owes a debt of gratitude to Bolton, Caughey, and other members of the borderlands school, reveals a much more complex story. The southern history that Caughey writes faces west rather than north. In addition to the white and black residents of the South, it includes the various indigenous inhabitants of the region as well as Spanish and French imperial interests. *McGillivray of the Creeks,* then, provides a unique look at southern politics and economics from the other side of the frontier. Certainly we cannot assume that McGillivray spoke for the entire Creek Nation. However, he was an influential and important Creek go-between in the aftermath of the American Revolution because he had the ear of Spain, Georgia, and the United States, and his letters provide insights into how some Creeks viewed their relations with these European and American interests.[45]

This book also examines the question of federal-Indian relations in the aftermath of the American Revolution. After 1783, government officials debated who would negotiate and deal with American Indian nations. Indeed, much of the controversy in which McGillivray is embroiled began when Hoboithle Micco (Tame King) and Neha Micco (Fat King) signed the Treaty of Augusta (1784) with the state of Georgia, ceding eight million acres of land to the state. McGillivray and other Creek leaders repudiated this treaty and opened negotiations with Spain that culminated in the Treaty of Pensacola (1784). Two years later the Creeks and Georgia signed another treaty at Shoulderbone Creek that ceded more land, and again McGillivray opposed this treaty. President George Washington and Secretary of War Henry Knox realized that these negotiations were untenable. First of all, as members of the elite, they distrusted the frontiersmen who signed these treaties with the Creeks. Second, they insisted on federal, not state, primacy in dealing with American Indians in order to stem rivalries and competition between the states. The Treaty of New York of 1790 (which recognized the land cession of the Treaty of Augusta) helped establish the precedent of signing treaties with, and recognizing the sovereignty of, American Indian nations and of federal rather than state predominance in Indian affairs. McGillivray's letters reveal important insights and views into the early days of federal Indian policy and the abilities of an Indian leader to bring federal officials to the bargaining table.[46]

The 214 letters included in this text provide a unique view into post-Revolutionary American Indian and southern politics. Since American Indians did not have writing systems before the arrival of Europeans, historians have long struggled with the dearth of American Indian documentation before the nineteenth centuries. Indeed the lack of archival and written sources was one of the impetuses behind the development of ethnohistorical research methodology in the mid–twentieth century that has increased our understanding of American Indian history. More recently, this question of American Indian sources, especially oral history and intellectual traditions, has generated more controversy.[47] McGillivray's letters, however, provide an opportunity to see eighteenth-century Creek political life from the perspective of a Creek leader. This is not to say that we should necessarily privilege written documents over oral histories.[48] However, documents written by American Indian authors can provide perspectives absent from the papers of American traders, politicians, and their ilk. McGillivray's letters provide a unique look into the workings of Creek politics as well as insight as to how some Creeks attempted to chart a path for the Creek Nation in the new American republic. The letters provide opportunities for readers to draw their own conclusions about American Indian sources, the Creeks, and McGillivray himself. Scholars rarely have the opportunity to handle and use documentary Indian sources from the eighteenth century. These are truly a treasure and are worth a second (or third) look.[49]

Notes

1. Among Caughey's best-known works are *California: A Remarkable State's Life History* (Englewood Cliffs, N.J.: Prentice-Hall, 1970), and *Hubert Howe Bancroft, Historian of the West* (Berkeley: University of California Press, 1946).

2. Norris Hundley and John A. Schutz, eds., *The American West, Frontier & Region: Interpretations* (Los Angeles: Ward Ritchie Press, 1969), ix. Webb's famous book has appeared in several editions; see, for instance, Walter Prescott Webb, *The Great Plains* (Lincoln: University of Nebraska Press, 1981).

3. Stephen Dow Beckham, "John Walton Caughey: Historian and Civil Libertarian," *Pacific Historical Review* 56 (November 1987): 482–83; Hundley, *John Walton Caughey: A Bibliography of His Writings* (Los Angeles: Glen Dawson, 1961), 1–2; Hundley and Schutz, *The American West*, viii–ix; Albert L. Hurtado, "Introduction to the Bison Books Edition," in *The Indians of Southern California in 1852: The B. D. Wilson Report and a Selection of Contemporary Comment*, ed. John Walton Caughey (Lincoln: University of Nebraska Press, 1995), x.

4. Even seventy years after the emergence of the borderlands school, areas of Spanish colonization are ignored in American history textbooks and survey courses. See James A. Hijiya, "Why the West Is Lost," *William and Mary Quarterly* 51 (April 1994): 276–92.

5. Herbert Eugene Bolton's classic book has gone through several editions. See, for example, *The Spanish Borderlands: A Chronicle of Old Florida and the Southwest* (Albuquerque: University of New Mexico Press, 1996).

6. For the impact of Bolton, the borderlands school, and Caughey's place, see . Hurtado, "Introduction," x–xi; Albert L. Hurtado, "Parkmanizing the Spanish Borderlands: Bolton, Turner and the Historians' World," *Western Historical Quarterly* 26 (Summer 1995): 150–51; David Weber, *The Spanish Frontier in North America* (New Haven, Conn.: Yale University Press, 1992), 6–8. In total Bolton trained 104 Ph.D. students.

7. John Walton Caughey, *Bernardo de Gálvez in Louisiana, 1776–1783* (Berkeley: University of California Press, 1934).

8. Herbert Eugene Bolton, *Anza's California Expeditions*, 5 vols. (Berkeley: University of California Press, 1930).

9. Norris Hundley, "John Walton Caughey," *Pacific Historical Review* 65 (May 1996): 176; Beckham, "John Walton Caughey," 485; Hundley, *John Walton Caughey*, 4–5; Hurtado, "Introduction," xi. The original manuscript of *McGillivray of the Creeks* is located in boxes 8, 9, 15, 16, and 17 of the John Walton Caughey Papers, Collection No. 998, Department of Special Collections, Young Research Library, University of California, Los Angeles (hereafter JWCP). This collection contains Caughey's research notes, a draft of the original publications, and letters that he did not include in this volume.

10. Beckham, "John Walton Caughey," 492–93; Hundley, "John Walton Caughey," 175–76; Hundley, *John Walton Caughey*, 8–9; Hurtado, "Introduction," ix–x, quote p. x.

11. Joshua Piker, *Okfuskee: A Creek Indian Town in Colonial America* (Cambridge, Mass.: Harvard University Press, 2004), 18. For early southeastern and Creek history, see Weber, *Spanish Frontier*, 49–55, 60–75, 158–65; Claudio Saunt, *A New Order of Things: Property, Power, and the Transformation of the Creek Indians, 1733–1816* (New York: Cambridge University Press, 1999), 11–63; David H. Corkran, *The Creek Frontier, 1540–1783* (Norman: University of Oklahoma Press, 1967), 3–228; Kathryn E. Holland Braund, *Deerskins & Duffels: The Creek Indian Trade with Anglo-America, 1685–1815* (Lincoln: University of Nebraska Press, 1996); Julie Anne Sweet, *Negotiating for Georgia: British-Creek Relations in the Trustee Era, 1733–1752* (Athens: University of Georgia Press, 2005); Richard White, *The Roots of Dependency: Subsistence, Environment, and Social Change among the Choctaws, Pawnees, and Navajos* (Lincoln: University of Nebraska Press, 1983), 1–68; Alan Gallay, *The Indian Slave Trade: The Rise of the English Empire in the American South, 1670–1717* (New Haven, Conn.: Yale University Press, 2002); James Merrell, *The Indians' New World: Catawbas and Their Neighbors from European Contact through the Era of Removal* (New York: W. W. Norton, 1989), Daniel Usner, *Indians, Settlers, & Slaves in a Frontier Exchange Economy: The Lower Mississippi Valley before 1783* (Chapel Hill: University of North Carolina Press, 1992); James Axtell, *The Indians' New South: Cultural Change in the Colonial Southeast* (Baton Rouge: Louisiana State University Press, 1997).

12. I follow the argument put forth by Jeremy Alderman and Stephen Aron in "From Borderlands to Borders: Empires, Nation-States, and the Peoples in Between in North American History," *American Historical Review* 104 (June 1999): 814–41. Alderman and Aron state, "With states claiming exclusive dominions over all territories within their borders, Indians lost the ability to play off rivalries; they could no longer take advantage of occupying the lands 'in between.' Thus, as colonial borderlands gave way to national borders, fluid and 'inclusive' intercultural frontiers yielded to hardened and more 'exclusive' hierarchies" (816). See also two critiques of this article: Evan Haefeli, "A Note on the Use

of North American Borderlands," *American Historical Review* 104 (October 1999): 1222–25; and esp. John R. Wunder and Pekka Hämäläinen, "Of Lethal Places and Lethal Essays," *American Historical Review* 104 (October 1999): 1229–34. For Creek and southeastern history from 1763 to the aftermath of the American Revolution, see Weber, *Spanish Frontier in North America,* 177–86, 198–203, 265–85; Saunt, *New Order of Things,* 67–135; and Corkan, *Creek Frontier,* 229–325.

13. For Lachlan McGillivray, see Edward J. Cashin, *Lachlan McGillivray, Indian Trader: The Shaping of the Southern Colonial Frontier* (Athens: University of Georgia Press, 1992). For marriage and kinship, see Richard White, *The Middle Ground: Indians, Empires, and Republics in the Great Lakes Region, 1650–1815* (New York: Cambridge University Press, 1991), 60–75, and Gary Clayton Anderson, *Kinsmen of Another Kind: Dakota-White Relations in the Upper Mississippi Valley, 1650–1862* (St. Paul: Minnesota Historical Society Press, 1997).

14. For a biographical sketch of McGillivray, see Michael D. Green, "Alexander McGillivray," in *American Indian Leaders: Studies in Diversity,* ed. R. David Edmunds, 41–63 (Lincoln: University of Nebraska Press, 1980). For information on his wealth, see document 214 below.

15. Cited in Caughey, *McGillivray of the Creeks,* 57.

16. Ibid., 34.

17. Carolyn Thomas Foreman, "Alexander McGillivray," *Chronicles of Oklahoma* 7 (March 1929): 106.

18. Arthur Preston Whitaker, "Alexander McGillivray, 1789–1793," *North Carolina Historical Review* 5 (July 1928): 308. See also Whitaker, "Alexander McGillivray, 1783–1789," *North Carolina Historical Review* 5 (April 1928): 181–203.

19. For ideas about miscegenation, see Michael Omi and Howard Winant, *Racial Formation in the United States: From the 1960s to the 1990s,* 2nd ed. (New York: Routledge Books, 1994), 63–64.

20. Caughey, *McGillivray of the Creeks,* 5–6.

21. Ibid., xxix.

22. Hundley, *John Walton Caughey,* 5.

23. Caughey, *McGillivray of the Creeks,* 7. Caughey also writes, "*Squaws*' work, on the other hand, included 'cultivation of the soil and almost every other domestic drudgery'" (emphasis added). In addition, then, to using a pejorative term to describe Indian women, Caughey repeated the stereotype of the "squaw drudge."

24. Caughey, *McGillivray of the Creeks,* 57.

25. For the development of Old Indian history, ethnohistory, and New Indian history, see R. David Edmunds, "Native Americans, New Voices: American Indian History, 1895–1995," *American Historical Quarterly* 100 (June 1995): 717–40, and Donald L. Fixico, "Ethics and Responsibilities in Writing American Indian History," in *Natives and Academics: Researching and Writing about American Indians,* ed. Devon A. Mihesuah, 84–99 (Lincoln: University of Nebraska Press, 1998). For the themes of cooperation and contingency in colonial and early Republic history, see White, *Middle Ground;* James F. Brooks, *Captives & Cousins: Slavery, Kinship, and Community in the Southwest Borderlands* (Chapel Hill: University of North Carolina Press, 2002); and James Merrell, *Into the American Woods: Negotiators on the Pennsylvania Frontier* (New York: W. W. Norton, 2002). For contingency rather than predestination in Western history, see Richard White, "The Gold Rush: Consequences and Contingencies," *California History* 77 (Spring 1998): 42–55.

26. White, *Middle Ground,* xi.

27. M. J. Smith, review of *McGillivray of the Creeks* by John W. Caughey, *Chronicles of Oklahoma* 17 (March 1939): 99.

28. Charles F. Ward, review of *McGillivray of the Creeks* by John Walton Caughey, *Southwestern Historical Quarterly* 48 (July 1939): 122–23.

29. Roscoe R. Hill, review of *McGillivray of the Creeks* by John Walton Caughey and *Woodward's Reminiscences of the Creek; or, Muscogee Indians, Contained in Letters to Friends in Georgia and Alabama* by Thomas S. Woodward, *Journal of Mississippi History* 1 (October 1939): 266. For other positive reviews of this book, see A. P. Nasatir, review of *McGillivray of the Creeks* by John Walton Caughey, *Hispanic American Historical Review* 19 (August 1939): 328–30; R. S. Cotterill, review of *McGillivray of the Creeks* by John Walton Caughey, *Journal of Southern History* 5 (February 1939): 106–7; Don Russell, review of *The Faithful Mohawks* by John Wolfe Lydekker, *McGillivray of the Creeks* by John Walton Caughey, *Winning Oregon: A Study of the Expansionist Movement* by Melvin Clay Jacobs, and *Southern Plainsmen* by Carl Coke Rister, *Journal of the American Military Institute* 3 (Summer 1939): 124–25.

30. James F. Leyburn, review of *Southern Plainsmen* by Carl Coke Rister, *Between Sun and Sod,* by Willie Newbury Lewis, and *McGillivray of the Creeks,* by John Walton Caughey, *American Sociological Review* 4 (June 1939): 441. E. M. Coulter made a similar critique. See his review of *McGillivray of the Creeks* by John Walton Caughey, *North Carolina Historical Review* 16 (April 1939): 220–23.

31. Arthur P. Whitaker, review of *McGillivray of the Creeks* by John W. Caughey, *Mississippi Valley Historical Review* 26 (June 1939): 83.

32. J. H. O'Donnell, "Alexander McGillivray: Training for Leadership," *Georgia Historical Quarterly* 49 (Summer 1965): 172–86. This article on McGillivray, unfortunately, repeated much of the anachronistic language and many of the anachronistic views of American Indian history. O'Donnell wrote, "When military operations [during the colonial period] were deemed necessary, consideration had to be given to the role played by the numerous bands of *savages* living along the frontiers of the colonies from the Great Lakes to the Gulf," 173 [emphasis added].

33. Green, "Alexander McGillivray," 59–60.

34. Thomas D. Watson, "Striving for Sovereignty: Alexander McGillivray, Creek Warfare, and Diplomacy, 1783–1790," *Florida Historical Quarterly* 58 (Spring 1980): 400–414.

35. Gregory Evans Dowd, *A Spirited Resistance: The North American Indian Struggle for Unity, 1745–1815* (Baltimore: Johns Hopkins University Press, 1992), 90–91.

36. Linda Langley, "The Tribal Identity of Alexander McGillivray: A Review of the Historical and Ethnographic Data," *Louisiana History* 46 (Spring 2005): 231–39.

37. J. Leitch Wright Jr., "Creek-American Treaty of 1790: Alexander McGillivray and the Diplomacy of the Old Southwest," *Georgia Historical Quarterly* 51 (December 1967): 397. Wright also employed anachronistic and insensitive language. First he juxtaposed the apparent "civilization" of McGillivray with the "savagery" of other Creek leaders: "Alexander McGillivray, Creek Indian chief, tall, reserved, dressing and looking like a white man, accompanied by thirty-odd Creeks adorned with feathers, beads, earrings, and silver gorgets, escorted by Revolutionary War veteran Colonel Marinus Willett, made a grand entrance into the city." Furthermore, Wright described McGillivray as the "son of a wealthy Scottish Loyalist merchant and a *half-breed squaw*" [emphasis added]. Wright, "Creek-American Treaty of 1790," 379, 382.

38. James Lamar Appleton and Robert David Ward, "Albert James Pickett and the Case of the Secret Articles: Historians and the Treaty of New York of 1790," *Alabama Review* 51 (January 1998): 3–36, quote p. 32.

39. Saunt, *New Order of Things,* 79. Recently, Joshua Piker has argued for greater understanding of Indian community history to better comprehend colonial era American

history. See Piker, *Okfuskee* and Piker, "'White & Clean' and Contested: Creek Towns and Trading Paths in the Aftermath of the Seven Years' War," *Ethnohistory* 50 (Spring 2003): 315–47.

40. Saunt, *New Order of Things,* 67–135, 186–204, quote p. 83.

41. Piker, *Okfuskee,* 22–23.

42. In this way, I agree with Gregory Evans Dowd's assessment of McGillivray. See *Spirited Resistance,* 90–91. For cultural broker, see Margaret Connell Szasz, ed., *Between Indian and White Worlds: The Cultural Broker* (Norman: University of Oklahoma Press, 1994). James Merrell has recently refined the idea of the cultural broker with the term "go-between." Merrell writes, "If colonists and Indians were ever to look past such fundamentally antithetical ideas of the American woods, if they were to get along at all, someone had to step in in order to downplay differences and play up—or, if need be, make up—areas of common ideology, common interest, and common experience. . . . Negotiators were not, it turns out, denizens of some debatable land between native and newcomer; almost without exception, they were firmly anchored on one side of the cultural divide or the other." Still, Merrell points out, "Colonial leaders who left most of the records tended to mistrust and despise the intermediary, uncomfortable with his importance and uncertain of his loyalties." Merrell, *Into the American Woods,* 27, 37, 32. For letters that McGillivray wrote for and to Creek leaders, see Alexander McGillivray to the Halloing King of the Cowetas, April 14, 1786, and the Fat King to Matthews, August 7, 1787, both in JWCP, box 15: Documents Eliminated, 1786–1787.

43. Michael Green writes, "Though never the subject of a full-length biography, [McGillivray] has been explained, described, analyzed, and dissected in countless biographical sketches." Green, "Alexander McGillivray," 41.

44. A reviewer noted that McGillivray did not consult Spanish archives in Havana, Cuba. See Coulter, review of *McGillivray of the Creeks,* 222. However, the *Georgia Historical Quarterly* and the *East Tennessee Historical Society Publications* printed many of McGillivray's letters that were left out of this book. Moreover, other scholars have found McGillivray's correspondence with British officials during the American Revolution. See O'Donnell, "Alexander McGillivray," 172–86.

45. David Weber writes, "In his own work, and that of many of his students, Bolton focused on the interplay of cultures on both sides of the frontier, be it Spanish and Indian or Spanish and French." See "Turner, the Boltonians, and the Borderlands," *American Historical Review* 91 (February 1986): 73.

46. An insightful look in Henry Knox's view of frontiersman can be found in Alan Taylor, *Liberty Men and Great Proprietors: The Revolutionary Settlement on the Maine Frontier, 1760–1820* (Chapel Hill: University of North Carolina Press, 1990). For the Treaty of New York and the early days of federal Indian policy, see Francis Paul Prucha, *The Great Father: The United States Government and the American Indians* (1984; abridged ed., Lincoln: University of Nebraska Press, 1986), 13–22.

47. For the development of ethnohistory, see Donald L. Fixico, ed., *Rethinking American Indian History* (Albuquerque: University of New Mexico Press, 1997). For criticism of ethnohistory and the New Indian history and a discussion of sources in American Indian studies, see Devon A. Mihesuah, ed., *Natives and Academics: Researching and Writing about American Indians* (Lincoln: University of Nebraska Press, 1998) and Devon A. Mihesuah and Angela Cavender Wilson, eds., *Indigenizing the Academy: Transforming Scholarship and Empowering Communities* (Lincoln: University of Nebraska Press, 2004).

48. Claudio Saunt writes, "Historians have unavoidedly depended on the written word in interpreting the Muskogee past, and especially on McGillivray's voluminous correspondence. . . . Creeks, of course, wanted to hold on to their land and retain their

political autonomy as much as any people, but they concerned themselves with actions, promises, and memory rather than with the meaning of written words" (*New Order of Things,* 68–69).

49. In a different context, the historian Brenda Child has argued for the importance of written documents produced by American Indians. Writing about federal boarding schools, Child notes, "In letters, students described their bouts of homesickness, their regimens of work and study, their instances of rebellion, and often their struggles with serious diseases such as tuberculosis. The letters sent from Indian parents to the schools are just as revealing regarding problems parents confronted: the agony of separation from children, their concerns about health care and diet in the schools, and sometimes their despair when children grew sick or died at school." Brenda J. Child, *Boarding School Seasons: American Indian Families, 1900–1940* (Lincoln: University of Nebraska Press, 1998), 7. Alexander McGillivray is only one of a few American Indian authors from the eighteenth and nineteenth centuries. See Laura J. Murray, ed., *To Do Good to My Indian Brethren: The Writings of Joseph Johnson, 1751–1776* (Amherst: University of Massachusetts Press, 1998); William Apess, *On Our Own Ground: The Complete Writings of William Apess, a Pequot,* ed. Barry O'Connell (Amherst: University of Massachusetts Press, 1992); and Maureen Konkle, *Writing Indian Nations: Native Intellectuals and the Politics of Historiography, 1827–1863* (Chapel Hill: University of North Carolina Press, 2004).

PREFACE TO THE FIRST EDITION

NORTH AMERICA has produced no more extraordinary Indian leader than Alexander McGillivray. Born and reared in the Creek Nation but educated at Charleston and Savannah, he knew the ways of his tribesmen and understood the methods of the whites. Thus doubly equipped, he was the natural choice of the Creeks for the direction of their tribal affairs in the critical decade following the American Revolution.

From the Indian standpoint all American history can be reduced to terms of defending their lands against Caucasian encroachment. For McGillivray even this problem was multiple. The Creeks were virtually surrounded. He had to deal with the frontiersmen of Georgia, with the Cumberland settlers in Tennessee, with the American land speculators, with the Spaniards of Louisiana and the Floridas, and with English intrigues and expeditions. Against these forces he pitted his diplomatic talents.

How well McGillivray did his work is attested by many historians. "The most gifted and remarkable man that ever was born upon the soil of Alabama" is the pronouncement of the foremost historian of that state. Theodore Roosevelt remarked that it was McGillivray's "consummate craft" and "cool and masterly diplomacy" which enabled the Creeks "for a generation to hold their own better than any other native race against the restless Americans." A Georgian writer ranked him "by all odds the foremost man of Indian blood and raising that Anglo-America has ever seen; one who was universally allowed and felt in his day to be the very soul of the Creek nation, which was almost absolutely swayed by his genius and will."

Despite his recognized importance most of the source materials on McGillivray's career have remained inaccessible. The primary purpose of this study, launched some eight or nine years ago, has been to assemble and make conveniently available the essential documents descriptive of the man and his work. As the project developed, the broad significance of his correspondence became increasingly apparent. His letters recount the struggle for the Old Southwest in the period after the Revolutionary War. They depict the trials of the United States in the first years of national existence. They reveal a vigorous Spanish frontier policy, long after Spain had supposedly passed into her dotage as a colonial power. Above all, they voice the Indian sentiment concerning European expansion in America. Delineation of McGillivray's remarkable personality is the central contribution of these documents, but they also epitomize the history of colonial North America.

With pleasure I acknowledge the generous assistance that has been given me in compiling this volume. A Native Sons of the Golden West fellowship enabled me to work in the Spanish archives, and research grants from the University of California made possible the gathering of additional material.

I am particularly obliged to the staff of the Archivo General de Indias for many courtesies and to Miss Irene A. Wright for her help. Dr. Thomas P. Martin and others in the Manuscripts Division of the Library of Congress have been most accommodating, and the photostat loan service of the library very helpful. For advice and encouragement I am particularly indebted to Dr. Herbert E. Bolton and to Dr. Joseph B. Lockey.

Special commendation is due the University of Oklahoma Press for courageously envisioning the series of documentary volumes on the Civilization of the American Indian. I would also thank Mr. Joseph A. Brandt and the staff of the Press for patient and expert assistance in transmuting my manuscript into this book.

J. W. C.

Los Angeles, September 1938.

No doubt there is precedent for a book's coming back into print twenty-one years after its first issue, but for me this is the first such experience and brings a tingle of pleasure. I thank, first of all, McGillivray and his correspondents for their vivid recording of the free-for-all contest for the Old Southwest in the years just after the American Revolution. I also thank Joseph A. Brandt for starting the series on the Civilization of the American Indian and carrying it through this the eighteenth volume and Savoie Lottinville for continuing and extending the series through the fiftieth volume, with many more undoubtedly to come. After all these years I am able to move the Black Warrior River westward and have it empty into the Tombigbee. Belatedly I also can record my gratitude to my wife, LaRee, who was of more help than any other person in the making of this book.

J. W. C.

Los Angeles, January 1959.

THE CAREER OF
ALEXANDER McGILLIVRAY

I

A NATIVE CREEK

"It is necessary for me to Inform you that
I am a Native of this Nation & of rank in it."
MᴄGɪʟʟɪᴠʀᴀʏ ᴛᴏ Mɪʀó, March 28, 1784.

THE London *Gentleman's Magazine* in August, 1793, carried an unusual
obituary notice. Its columns headed "Marriages and Deaths of Considerable Persons" were ordinarily reserved for the bluebloods of royalty
and nobility and for those most distinguished in politics, war, or wealth.
In this issue its mark of distinction was accorded a young Indian chief
who had died at far-away Pensacola in the Spanish province of West
Florida; a young half-breed, who in the tongue of his mother and his
people was called Hoboi-Hili-Miko, the Good Child King, and in the
language of his father and historians, Alexander McGillivray.

To the best of our knowledge no likeness of McGillivray exists.
Tradition, as Pickett was able to discover it eighty-five years ago,
described him as "tall, rather slender, and of a constitution by no means
robust." Several observers mention the gravity of his bearing and the
immobility of his expression, typical Indian traits, so it seemed to them.
He was noted for unbounded hospitality and for sparkling conversation
whenever his interest was aroused. "He is decent," said caustic Fisher
Ames, "and not very black." Long, tapering fingers, with which he
could write at prodigious speed, piercing eyes, and an abnormally
broad and high forehead are the other features that must suggest the
rest of the portrait.[1]

Many other items of personal information are no longer retrievable.
Several determined searches have failed to locate McGillivray's personal
papers. Presumably they no longer exist. A large fraction of his public
papers has also disappeared. Those which are extant convey a vivid
impression of McGillivray's achievements and of many of his individual
characteristics, but they are silent on a number of points concerning
which our curiosity is not idle.

Among the indisputable facts about McGillivray are several indicative
of the handicaps under which he labored. He was not endowed with all
the heroic attributes. His health was persistently bad. His letters are
interspersed with references to gout and rheumatism, splitting head-
aches, and confinement in bed for weeks on end. Once he wrote that
he was afraid that he would lose all his fingernails. On another occa-

---

1. Pickett, *History of Alabama*, p. 345. Ames is quoted in McMaster, *History
of the People of the United States*, I, 604.

sion he received from his friend the Governor at New Orleans a package of Olvenza's famous powder, a venereal specific. The incontestable fact that much of his ill health was traceable to social disease may deprive him of certain sympathy. Others will find it all the more to his credit that he achieved in spite of serious physical handicaps. He was often so weakened that he could not mount a horse, so stiffened by rheumatism that he could not grasp a quill, so racked by pain that he could not enter into conversation or exercise his full powers in the administration of tribal business.

In practically all Indian tribes, chiefs were chosen by some sort of merit system, though often in conjunction with what amounted to hereditary nomination of eligible candidates. Hence it followed, since military and religious power were the abilities considered most valuable, that few chiefs in aboriginal America could not boast at least one of these qualifications; for example, Joseph of the Nez Percés, Gerónimo of the Apaches, and Caupolicán of the Araucanians are well-known warrior chiefs, and Montezuma of the Aztecs was a typical priest-chief. But McGillivray possessed neither martial prowess nor supernatural power. The fact that the Creeks accepted him as head of their nation demonstrates at once the sagacity of the tribe and the remarkable qualities of McGillivray which led to such a departure from precedent.

Perhaps the best picture of McGillivray as a warrior is provided by his brother-in-law Louis Milfort, a French adventurer who spent about twenty years in the Creek Nation in close association with him. Milfort is always suspected of exaggerating or of downright falsifying, but one anecdote of his about McGillivray's slight penchant for warfare has at least the germ of truth in it. He told of a "small affair" with the Americans which McGillivray came out "to witness." To be *de rigueur* he laid aside his clothes and wore only war-paint. But when the fight started, he hid in the bushes and remained there until night when the combat was over. Then he rushed shivering onto the battlefield, despoiled one of the American dead, and wrapped himself in his cloak.

Milfort excused himself for telling such a story by saying that McGillivray had often "laughed with him about his terror and about the American's cloak," and he hastened to make amends with this handsome statement: "When one has so much administrative capacity and so many qualities of heart as had Alexander McGillivray, he does not need the military virtues to be a great man."[2]

Whether or not it was just in this wise, McGillivray made early discovery that he did not possess the military virtues. Having found himself out (and herein lies one of the secrets of his success) he seems

2. Milfort, *Mémoire ou coup d'oeil rapide*, pp. 134-35.

4

to have wasted no time or energy in trying to remake himself along more warlike lines. Actual military operations he left to others, such as Red Shoes, Mad Dog, or Milfort, while he concentrated upon affairs of state.

Most historians affirm that McGillivray's worst handicap was his mixed parentage. A single writer applauded the union of civilized and savage strains in McGillivray as "the most felicitous compound of the kind ever seen,"[3] but the general opinion is that this was a serious drawback. No apologist has denied that he came of a Scotch father and a French and Indian mother. There has been a tendency to attribute some of his shortcomings to a mestizo's inevitable emotional instability and psychic dualism.

Our language contains several words that may be applied to a person of mixed blood: half-breed, half-blood, half-caste, hybrid, mestizo, miscegenate, mongrel. Not one is complimentary. The implication is obvious. The tendency with regard to McGillivray has been, naturally enough, to commiserate him for the bad luck of his racial admixture. Yet the sociologists, to the best of my knowledge, have found no tangible proof that the offspring of mixed unions are physically or mentally inferior. Such persons, however, often encounter very serious social difficulties. Had McGillivray attempted to live in an Anglo-American community, it is altogether likely that he would have found his Indian blood and characteristics a handicap. He chose instead to live in the Creek Nation where a different set of mores functioned.

The Creeks seem to have entertained race prejudice against Negroes. Patterning after their white neighbors, they held Negro slaves, though comparatively few. But toward the whites, whether French, English, Spanish, or American, and toward other Indian groups they had a very complaisant attitude. For generations prior to the time of McGillivray outsiders had been entering the Creek country, and singly or in groups they were accepted in tribal society. Thus, for example, a large fraction of the Natchez had been assimilated shortly after the French broke up their towns on the Mississippi. The Apalachicola, Yuchi, Yamassee, and Oconee were other groups that were cordially received by the Creeks.[4]

From a very early date also, white blood had been filtering into the nation. Statistics are lacking. The precise percentage of Caucasian blood cannot be determined. Probably it was less than ten per cent,

3. Chappell, *Miscellanies of Georgia*, p. 28.
4. Swanton discussed the Creek incorporation of foreign elements in his *Early History of the Creek Indians and Their Neighbors, passim,* and especially pp. 421-56.

perhaps even less.[5] Yet a conspicuous feature of the documents which follow is the number of whites and part-whites resident among the Creeks: Burgess, "the Bully," the Cornells, Durand, the Galphins, Grizzard, Kinnard, McQueen, Milfort, Perryman, Sullivan, Walker, Weatherford; these names suggest the importance of this element. Nor is there anything to suggest that the Creeks discriminated against half-breeds. Reckoning descent in the female line, these Indians had a measure of indifference toward fathers that is a trifle difficult for a paternal people to understand.

Except in his relations with the white people outside the nation— and even there he was seldom the victim of condescension—McGillivray seems not to have suffered because of his racial make-up. In Creek society he was on the same footing as everyone else. Accepted as a normal person, he had full opportunity to live his life, an equal among his peers.

On the other hand McGillivray must have had a sense of frustration at having no better material to work with than that provided by the Creek Nation.[6] In his day the Creeks occupied the western part of the modern state of Georgia and the northern part of Alabama. For Indian neighbors they had the Seminoles on the southeast, the Choctaws and Chickasaws to the west, and the Cherokees on the north. Their land was fairly extensive, but Creek title to it was clouded by the whites' habit of divorcing ownership and sovereignty. A land map would properly show a block of Creek territory as large as a modern state. Political maps assigned the area to England up to 1783 and afterwards to Spain and the United States.

In the late eighteenth century the Creeks are estimated to have numbered about 5,000 gunmen. If anything, the figure is too large. Later figures are smaller and so are earlier ones. Even the least of the American states possessed greater man power. But in comparison with the northern tribes this was a large number; the Creeks in fact were as numerous as any Indian group east of the Mississippi, and perhaps as numerous as any north of Mexico. In military effectiveness, however, they were not to be compared with the Shawnees or the Wyandots, the Delawares or the Mohawks. Individually, the Creek warriors were

5. Swan set the white population at nearly 300, "a number sufficient to contaminate all the natives." He estimated that the Indians numbered between 5000 and 6000 gunmen ("Position and State of Manners and Arts in the Creek, or Muscogee Nation in 1791," in Schoolcraft, *Indian Tribes*, V, 263).

6. The best general descriptions of the Creeks are Swanton's *Early History*, and his "Social Organization and Social Usages of the Indians of the Creek Confederacy," and "Religious Beliefs and Medical Practices of the Creek Indians," *Bureau of American Ethnology, Forty-Second Annual Report*. Swan's description in Schoolcraft, *Indian Tribes*, V, 251-83, and Roosevelt's, in his *The Winning of the West*, I, 49-69, apply specifically to McGillivray's period.

6

redoubtable enough, but they were notoriously undisciplined. We have it on good authority, shortly after McGillivray's death, that not in the memory of the oldest inhabitant had half the nation "taken the war talk" at the same time.[7]

The Muskogean group, consisting of the Creeks and their immediate neighbors, is sometimes dignified by the title Confederation. Yet as an effective governmental unit it fell far short of the famous Six Nations of the Iroquois League, and still farther short of the Aztec and Inca Empires. Except briefly under the genius of McGillivray, this so-called Confederation had never functioned. In fact, rather than emphasizing the Confederation, a nearer approach to the truth would be to think of the Creek Nation as consisting of several score tribes, usually called towns, which were regarded as the largest natural units. The old Greek conception of confederacies as a sort of artificial superstructure on the natural units, the city-states, is a very close parallel.

In many other particulars, cultural development among the Creeks had stopped at a rather low level. They practiced agriculture, raising fair crops of maize, squashes, and pumpkins. From the whites on their borders they had acquired a mild interest in cattle raising. Yet these "civilized" pursuits were secondary to hunting. The hunt, of course, had a special significance because of the trade value of deerskins and other peltries. It also contributed the major portion of the food supply. A clue to its volume is to be found in the division of labor between the sexes. The men, according to several eighteenth century observers, rode about, stretched out at their ease, amused themselves with a pipe or a whistle, engaged in the ball play or in various dances, went on war parties, and hunted.

Squaws' work, on the other hand, included "cultivation of the soil and almost every other domestic drudgery." "The women are employed," Romans reported, "besides the cultivation of the earth, in dressing the victuals, preparing, scraping, braining, rubbing and smoaking the Roe skins, making macksens of them, spinning buffaloe wool, making salt, preparing cassine drink, drying the *chamaerops* and *passiflora*, making cold flour for traveling, gathering nuts and making their milk; likewise in making baskets, brooms, pots, bowls and other earthen and wooden vessels."[8]

Nevertheless, the Creeks were not entirely devoid of Southern chivalry. "You may depend upon my assertion," said another early visitor, "that there is no people any where who love their women

7. Hawkins, "A sketch of the Creek Country," *Georgia Historical Society Collections*, III, 70.
8. Romans, *A Concise Natural History of East and West Florida*, p. 93.

more than these Indians do, or men of better understanding in distinguishing the merits of the opposite sex, or more faithful in rendering suitable compensation. They are courteous and polite to the women. . . . . I never saw or heard of an instance of an Indian beating his wife or other female, or reproving them in anger or in harsh language. And the women make a suitable and grateful return; for they are discreet, modest, loving, faithful, and affectionate to their husbands."[9]

Two tribal customs made women especially influential. One was that the care and control of pre-adolescent children was in their hands. The other was that, although women had practically no place in religious or governmental ceremonies, descent was in the female line and so also was reckoned eligibility for office. Thus McGillivray was eligible for a chieftaincy at Otciapofa through the fact that his mother was a member of the Wind clan.

A great many features of Creek society can be reserved for subsequent description. Too much emphasis cannot be put, however, upon the degree to which Caucasian influences had permeated the life of these Indians. Through generations of contact with French traders from Mobile, and with British traders from the Carolinas and Georgia, they had learned to deck themselves out in glass beads and silver jewelry, in trade shirts and blankets. They rode about on horseback, and when they could afford it, with expensive saddles and bridles. The Malay word "tafia" (molasses rum), taught them by the Europeans, had become one of the favorite words in their vocabulary. Even more momentous was the substitution of steel knives and hatchets for the ancestral stone tomahawks, and of powder, ball, and flintlocks for the aboriginal bow and arrow. Thus the traders had risen from traffickers in luxuries to dealers in necessities.

These are the outlines of the environment into which McGillivray was born. It was a peculiar combination of the primitive and the civilized. The former predominated; yet it was perfectly feasible for a person of heterogeneous ancestry such as McGillivray's to feel and to be a native Creek.

9. Bartram, "Observations on the Creek and Cherokee Indians," *Transactions of the American Ethnological Society*, III, 31.

II

LACHLAN AND SEHOY

> "The shrewdness, the robust sense and crude force of the Scotch Highland Chieftan were blended in him with calm Indian subtlety and intensity."
> CHAPPELL, *Miscellanies of Georgia*, p. 28.

ALEXANDER'S father, Lachlan McGillivray, had been one of the later agents in making available to the Creeks the benefits of Old World civilization. As a youth he had migrated from Scotland, arriving at Charleston with the traditional one shilling in his pocket. The frontier naturally beckoned him. He fell in almost immediately with a group of fellow Scots in deerskin attire who were about to set out with a pack train for the Indian country. There his first venture in private trade was to barter his jackknife for pelts. With this capital and with the wages for his work, Lachlan bought trade goods on his own account, and persisted in the business to which chance opportunity had led him. Hard work and thrift and canniness in trade were then the sure road to success. By the time the American Revolution broke out, Lachlan had pyramided his shilling and jackknife into a very respectable fortune. He had liquid assets that enabled him to retire to Scotland, he had other wealth in the Creek Nation, and in addition there was $100,000 in real property which the patriots of Georgia confiscated. The date of Lachlan's migration to America is not precisely known. Evidence points, however, toward 1738, the same year that William Johnson left Ireland for the Iroquois country of western New York. The coincidence is appropriate, because the two men developed along parallel lines. Both became wealthy. Both came to live among the Indians, the one at Mount Johnson on the Mohawk, the other at Little Tallassie on the Coosa. Both earned the respect and confidence of the Indians. Both had Indian wives and half-breed children whom they proudly acknowledged. Both rendered signal service to Britain in the French and Indian War, Johnson at the head of the Mohawk forces at Crown Point, McGillivray in keeping the Creeks from going over to the French side. Johnson, to be sure, attained the greater fame. He was knighted in 1755. This honor was followed by appointment to the council of New York colony, and finally by designation as superintendent of the northern Indians. Sir William's fame has been further ensured through the publication by the state of New York of six fat volumes of his correspondence, and by the appearance of as many biographical studies. Lachlan's only approach to such glorification was when James Adair

9

strongly recommended him for the superintendency of the southern Indians and dedicated to him his *History of the American Indians*, which appeared in London in 1775.[10]

Lachlan McGillivray passed on several things to his son. First of all he gave him his name. This may seem a very obvious thing to have done. Yet in Anglo-American society, even in the colonial period, racial prejudice had great weight. Any man who was openly a squaw-man and who accepted his half-breed children lost a certain amount of caste. One wonders, for example, what remonstrances Lachlan's mixed marriage elicited from his ministerial and Calvinist cousin, the Reverend Farquhar McGillivray of Charleston.

The plantation at Little Tallassie was another tangible legacy from his father. This site, near the ruins of the old French fort Toulouse, became Lachlan's headquarters soon after he moved into the Creek Nation. As a trader he was, of course, heartily welcomed by the Indians. The red men as a race have been just as consistent in welcoming those who brought them the boon of trade as in resisting the farming folk who came to encroach upon their hunting grounds. Lachlan subsequently became a planter as well as a trader, but the Creeks did not object, because his agriculture seemed to be an afterthought, a whim that he indulged as a sideline to the fur trade. Little Tallassie was no Mount Vernon. It included the "Apple Grove" which Lachlan set out. There came to be a complement of Negro slaves, and its masters enjoyed many of the amenities of life as did other country gentlemen of the Old South. The Indian town of Otciapofa, however, was always hard by, and the plantation never entirely lived down its trading post past.

It would seem probable that so vital a father would pass on a good many of his qualities to his son. Yet hardly anything in Alexander's psychological make-up seems to be traceable to this source. Of his father's business instincts, for example, Alexander seems to have inherited hardly any. The hackneyed adage, shirtsleeves to shirtsleeves in three generations, was enacted on perfect schedule. Aleck, Junior was left where Lachlan had started, but without the shilling and the jackknife. Alexander was not especially profligate. He did not throw money away extravagantly. His economic failing was that he did not demand his full due in salaries and commissions and shares of profits. Nor did he exploit the money-making potentialities of his position and his connections. All of which may be to his credit; but it was not to his financial credit. And it does not stamp him as his father's son.

10. The basic reference for Lachlan's career is Pickett, *History of Alabama*, pp. 342-44.

10

Alexander's mother was the famous Sehoy Marchand. Her French name harked back to the early days of Fort Toulouse.[11] This outpost thrown into the Indian country four hundred miles upstream from Mobile had been established primarily for the control of the Creek trade. Yet unlike its contemporary outposts in the Mississippi Valley and west of the Great Lakes, it had at first a definitely military and missionary tinge. This deviation from the national pattern in favor of what was essentially the Spanish mission–presidio device is the more surprising since the leading figures in the Gulf Coast colony, Bienville and Cadillac, were men of experience in Canada. Explanation is to be found not so much in the close association of the Bourbon monarchs of France and Spain as in the propinquity of Spanish Florida.

That Toulouse began with soldiers and Jesuits instead of mere traders is a fact of considerable moment in the McGillivray genealogy. Thus was the stage set for the convergence of the French and Indian lines of his family tree. One of the first officers at the fort, a certain Captain Marchand, fell in love with a belle of Otciapofa and took her to wife. Sehoy was their daughter.

When Lachlan McGillivray reached the banks of the Coosa, Fort Toulouse was a crumbling ruin, and Captain Marchand was long since dead. His daughter Sehoy was blossoming into the full beauty of womanhood. Such descriptions of this maid as have come down to us are tantalizingly vague. One of the exasperations of historical study is that the annalists, while preserving the lifeless important, have let slip through their fingers the illuminating and personable trivia. We can chance it that Sehoy was brunette. How copper-hued is another matter. Sparkling, vivacious, bewitching are adjectives customarily bestowed upon her, but perhaps on no surer foundation than that her father was French.

For lack of a direct description, and on the principle of "like mother like daughter," we may insert a sketch of one of Sehoy's daughters, "a pretty girl, clad in a short silk petticoat, her chemise of fine linen clasped with silver, her ear-rings and bracelets of the same metal, and with bright-colored ribbons in her hair."[12] These words of Milfort's betray a truly Parisian interest in clothes, but Milfort fell in love with the girl, too, and made her his wife.

Sehoy had exerted much the same charm over Lachlan McGillivray. As to how they met, the nature of the courtship, and the particulars of the marriage ceremony, the records are distressingly blank. In all

11. On the early history of Fort Toulouse see Reynolds, *The Alabama-Tombigbee Basin in International Relations,* and Heinrich, *La Louisiana sous la compagnie des Indies.*
12. Milfort, *Mémoire,* p. 23.

probability there was an Indian wedding ceremony. Sehoy's family connections were so powerful that no struggling young trader would antagonize them by flouting tribal customs. A second strong probability is that the marriage did not occur during the first months of Lachlan's residence among the Creeks. At the outset he was too poor to have been able to finance the marriage "purchase" from Sehoy's clansmen and clanswomen.

It is often said that the Creeks took marriage and sex very lightly, that a succession of mates was a regular occurrence. The more important men had several wives at a time. Marriage was a simple proposition and divorce almost equally easy. On the other hand the exogamous groupings were strictly observed, and adultery was severely punished. If a man so much as passed to windward of a mourning widow, or stepped into water upstream from her, both parties were apt to have their ears lopped off.

There was an abbreviated marriage ceremony, called the *Toopsa Táwah*, which we hope in all sentimentality Lachlan did not employ. The Toopsa Táwah was, literally, a "make-haste-marriage." No one took such a marriage seriously or expected it to last long.

Proper courtship was by proxy. The man sent his talk, together with some presents, to the lady of his choice. If she looked with favor upon the proposal, the proxy asked the consent of her clanspeople: her maternal uncles and aunts and her brothers. Her father of course had no voice in the matter since he was not a member of her clan. Lachlan doubtless proposed in this fashion, employing some woman friend as his proxy since he had no clanswoman in the nation.

But he may have followed the more ancient and impressive formalities. If so, we may picture him going out and killing a bear and sending a panful of its oil to the beautiful Sehoy. Her acceptance of the oil would authorize him to help in the hoeing of her field of corn. Next he would plant her beans, and set the poles for them to climb. When the vines had entwined themselves about the poles, symbolic of the future union, the betrothal was considered complete.

The actual marriage ceremony was engagingly simple. Before the proper witnesses the groom broke an ear of corn and gave half to his bride, or they exchanged reeds which were kept as a sort of marriage certificate. It was customary, too, for the groom to give his bride a piece of venison, and for her to give him an ear of corn. An essential part of the ceremony was performed by the girl's uncle, who conducted the couple to the bed that had been prepared for them and said, "This is your bed. Lie in it." Except for dancing and feasting this was the entire ritual. For a month, however, the groom was not supposed

12

to have much to do with his new in-laws, or to be with his wife during the daytime.[13]

Such a marriage was binding—until the Green Corn Dance. Then, if either party was dissatisfied, the match could be called off. Neither Lachlan nor Sehoy exercised this option. By all reports they were a happy couple all the years of Lachlan's residence among the Creeks.

From the historical standpoint the culmination of Lachlan's and Sehoy's idyllic romance was in the birth of Alexander. This great event did not excite enough immediate attention to insure the recording of the day or month. There has even been gross miscalculation of the year, which was in actuality 1759, a date made glorious by the Anglo-Prussian triumph on the bloody field of Minden and by Wolfe's audacious victory over Montcalm on the Plains of Abraham. Pickett and various writers in his wake, hit upon 1746 as the year of Alexander's birth; another asserted 1740.[14] But notwithstanding this apparent neglect, Alexander was not dismissed as just another papoose, for during her pregnancy Sehoy had dreamed of paper and ink and quills, a forecast, it seemed, that her son was to be an extraordinary Creek.

III

EARLY TRAINING

> "No Wisdom or foresight can form any plan in the closet that can always suit to manage Indians, as nothing but a long experience & knowledge of them can direct them properly."
> McGILLIVRAY TO CARONDELET, November 15, 1792.

ACCORDING to tribal customs a father had little to do with the upbringing of his children, or more properly his wife's children. Lachlan may have taken a Scotch interest in his young son, but the meager evidence that exists indicates that Alexander in his childhood was almost entirely under his mother's supervision. Her oversight was probably supplemented by that of the *tawa*, or maternal uncle, who was the proper person to inject the masculine note into child training.

Child rearing with the Creeks was in large degree a matter of

13. Marriage customs are described in Swanton, "Social Organization," *loc. cit.*, pp. 368-84.
14. The only direct testimony is Pope's observation in 1791, "This Gentleman to Appearance is at least Five and Forty, tho' in Fact only Thirty-two Years of Age" (Pope, *A Tour*, p. 48). It is suggested that Pickett may have arrived at 1746 by misinterpreting this sentence of Pope's. Another improbability in Pickett's chronology is that it stretches McGillivray's schooling over sixteen years, his fourteenth to his thirtieth.

ensuring hardihood, strength, bravery, and other warlike qualities. Thus a baby boy was couched on a panther skin that he might acquire cunning, a prodigious spring, and a powerful sense of smell. Again, a medicine man anointed the mother's nipple with a preparation designed to make the child "hardy and brave, and an active ball player." Month-old babes were included in the general tribal ritual of the early morning cold bath, which not only aided the hardening process but also "purged away the impurities of the preceding day."

The standard form of punishment was to scratch the child's thighs with a thorn or the teeth of a gar. This punishment may have originated as a method to let out the evil that had brought about the wrongdoing. It was also supposed to serve these other useful purposes: to loosen the skin and give pliancy to the limbs, to familiarize the child with the sight of blood, and to make him indifferent to wounds.[15]

With Alexander these practices seem to have been ineffectual. Or it may be that Lachlan interfered and denied his son the possible benefits of this orthodox training. But it must be admitted that the Indians were becoming more and more lax in following the old ways. Adair commented on the "decline of dry-scratching." Witness also the Creek echo of a universal refrain: "Young people are not so orderly and obedient to the old people now as they used to be. . . . . When we tell them to do anything they seem to stop and think about it. Formerly they always went at once and did as they were told."[16]

The Creeks had no formalized education. They had no schools. Yet the opinion that children were allowed to grow up unrestrained, undisciplined, and untutored is largely due to the surprise of white visitors over the sparing of the rod. As a matter of fact these little savages were made aware of the inexorable thou-shalts and thou-shalt-nots of the society in which they were to live. They learned to use the tools which their race had found indispensable. What more should we ask of elementary education? Some of these lessons were brought home by the smarting of scratched thighs or by the blistering sarcasm of their elders. Others were implicit in the tribal store of myths and folk tales. Perhaps the largest increment of learning was through play in imitation of adult occupations: warfare, hunting, the ball game, etc. It was an outdoor school, a play school, a child-centered school, with the project method favored rather than content courses. Shall we say that little Alexander in the 1760's had the same educational advantages that are offered in the "progressive" schools of the 1930's?

15. See Swanton, "Social Organization," *loc. cit.*, pp. 363-67.
16. Adair, *The History of the American Indians*, p. 279; the old man's complaint is quoted from Hitchcock's notes in Swanton, "Social Organization," *loc. cit.*, p. 367.

Alexander's report cards are not on file. But if we may judge by his later record, he did not lead the class in archery, and while he may have been manager of the boy's ball team he doubtless was not its playing captain. Similar reasoning suggests that these were happy years, because a short time later when a choice offered, Alexander unhesitatingly returned to the scenes of his childhood.

In Alexander's fourteenth year, according to the traditional chronology, his father prevailed on Sehoy to permit her son's being sent off to school. Sometime in 1773, then, he left the nation for Charleston. It was the same year that a better known band of "Indians" descended upon a tea ship in Boston harbor.

Charleston was then three years past its centennial. It was the one "city" south of the Potomac, the metropolis of the lower South, and had a population of perhaps fifteen thousand. A materialist would stress its unpaved streets, foul and ill-smelling, its unsanitary neglect of sewage, its annual epidemics of smallpox. Reverend Jedidiah Morse in his *American Geography* (1789) came nearer catching the spirit of the place, "In no part of America," he wrote, "are the social blessings enjoyed more rationally and liberally than in Charleston. Unaffected hospitality, affability, ease in manners and address, and a disposition to make their guests welcome, easy and pleased with themselves, are characteristic of the respectable people of Charleston." Charleston was the logical place for young Alexander's schooling, the more so since his cousin, Reverend Farquhar McGillivray of the Presbyterian church, had agreed to be his tutor.

It is a temptation to dwell on the sociological readjustments that Alexander must have had to make. Going off to school is an experience to any youngster who has a home to leave. For Alexander it must have been a much sharper transition. He stepped from one plane of civilization to another. The actual distance was only a few hundred miles, but he left behind the language of his youth, the customs, conventions, and usages to which he was accustomed. His cousin's utmost kindness could not have eliminated all the bewildering confusion.

Greek and Latin, English history and literature are listed as the studies Alexander pursued. How assiduously is not known; his letters seem not to contain a single Latin phrase or a classical or literary allusion. But he did become a very skillful penman, perhaps with the assistance of some preliminary instruction from his father, and he attained a literary style that could not have been based exclusively upon Indian models of conversation and oratory. For a brief period he was at Savannah in the countinghouse of Samuel Elbert, subse-

15

quently a governor of Georgia. This work proving distasteful, study was resumed at Charleston.

Again it was interrupted, and this time permanently, by the Revolution. Lachlan McGillivray was an ardent loyalist. The Georgia patriots honored him by placing his name at the head of the proscription list, whereupon Lachlan and his son went home, the one to Scotland, the other to the land of the Creeks. Father and son corresponded as occasion offered, and there is mention of yearly presents, yet one suspects that Lachlan was not anxious to take his half-caste son with him to Scotland. On the Coosa, however, Alexander was most welcome. Because of his mother's position in the powerful Wind clan he was eligible to be a lesser chief, and this rank was promptly accorded him.

The British soon commissioned him colonel and made him one of their agents to maintain the loyalty of the Creeks. It was a congenial task, especially in view of his animosity toward the Americans who had proscribed his father and many intimate friends, and who had confiscated family property valued at more than $100,000. As colonel and Indian agent he was one of the chief factors in securing the British unfaltering support from the Creeks during the war.

His presence with Indian auxiliaries helped delay the fall of Pensacola in 1781.[17] The next year he arrived in the Chickasaw country just after Colbert had seized several Spaniards in reprisal for the punishment of the leaders in the Natchez rebellion. Colbert was hazy as to methods but not at all reticent. He talked very freely to his prisoners and boasted about his plans. McGillivray's first act was to advise Colbert to hold his tongue. Then he drew up a "Parole of Honour," whereby the prisoners were permitted to go to New Orleans on their pledge that the nine Natchez prisoners would be set free. He also penned a vigorous letter to the governor of Louisiana, stressing the humanity and consideration of Colbert's procedure, and protesting against "a matter that is prevalent in West Florida, particularly at Mobill, that is offering Great rewards to Indians for the Heads of particular Men in the Indian Country." In this affair he demonstrated more sagacity and incisiveness of mind than any of the other leaders.[18]

McGillivray's work and that of the Southeastern Indians was only incidental in the war, which was won and lost on more distant battlefields. He was merely one of many Creek chiefs, and his reputation purely local. The period of the Revolution, in fact, may be regarded as essentially an apprenticeship for the work that was to engage him

17. Described in Caughey, *Bernardo de Gálvez in Louisiana*, pp. 187-214.
18. *Ibid.*, pp. 215-42. The letter that McGillivray wrote for Colbert and a copy of the Parole of Honour, both dated May 15, 1782, are in AGI C 2359.

subsequently. The years to follow, from 1783 to his death ten years later, constituted his real career. This decade, spanning his late twenties and his early thirties, is the basis upon which he has been judged the most remarkable son of Alabama and an Indian statesman unsurpassed.

IV

A GLANCE AT TRIBAL HISTORY

> "For Indians will attach themselves to & Serve them best who Supply their Necessities."
>
> McGILLIVRAY TO O'NEILL, January 1, 1784.

McGILLIVRAY'S work will be best understood if displayed in relief against the background of Creek tribal history.

Except for purely ethnological material the first available information dates from the early sixteenth century, when Spanish conquistadores were feverishly exploring the mysteries of the American wonderland. Ponce de León sought his fountain of youth just south of Creek territory. Lucas Vásquez de Ayllón, who set out a few years later in search of Chicora and Giant King Datha, seems to have encountered only the Siouan Indians of the Carolina and Georgia coast. The Pánfilo de Narváez expedition of 1528, best known because it included that great wanderer and narrator Cabeza de Vaca, established first contact with Muskogean Indians. Narváez came to Apalachen in high hopes that it would prove another Mexico City. Twenty-five days later he left the squalid village, completely disillusioned.

De Soto in 1540 saw much more of the Creek country. And of all the places his men visited, from Carolina to Arkansas, the valley of the Coosa impressed them most favorably. They still remembered it two decades later when another leader proposed a colony on the Coosa, and many of them hastened to join the party. Some three hundred Spaniards resided with the friendly Indians there for a little more than a year in 1559-60, but when hurricane, famine, and mutiny played havoc with the main party stationed near Pensacola Bay, this settlement was withdrawn.[19]

Ten months later King Philip took stock of the series of Spanish

19. Brief accounts of these early expeditions are available in Lowery, *The Spanish Settlements Within the Present Limits of the United States;* Bolton, *The Spanish Borderlands,* chaps. i, iii, and v; and González Barcía, *Ensayo Cronológico para la Historia General de la Florida.* Hodge and Lewis offer examples of the original documentary materials in their *Spanish Explorers in the Southern United States*

17

failures in La Florida, then the name for the entire eastern part of North America. From Ponce, Ayllón, Narváez, on through De Soto, Cancer, De Luna, and Villefane, he could list half a dozen expeditions larger and better equipped than the one with which Cortés had conquered Mexico. This strength had been dissipated in Florida, yet no progress had been made toward establishing Spanish control. The king felt justified in ordering the project abandoned.

Almost immediately Philip changed his mind. French Huguenots under Ribaut and Laudonnière intruded. Spain could not brook a hotbed of heresy so near her American settlements or a potential pirate haven on the Florida Channel, and Philip sent his best naval officer to give battle for orthodoxy and the Silver Fleet. Menéndez struck down the despised Lutherans with such zealous fury that Parkman stigmatized him as a "pious cutthroat." This bloody purge, however, was effected just outside the Creek domain. It was a quarrel between the whites, and the Indians did not figure in it directly.

But it was with something more in mind than the mere expulsion of the French that Menéndez had brought ten ships and 2,646 persons to Florida and had invested $1,800,000 in the enterprise. He had come as *adelantado* of Florida. He brought missionaries, priests, artisans, colonists, and Negro slaves; he founded San Agustín and established a permanent Spanish colony at one of the natural gateways to the land of the Creeks. Previously the Spaniards had only made occasional *entradas* into Creek territory. After 1565 they were constant neighbors. [20]

For a round century the Spaniards of San Agustín were the only Caucasians in contact with the Creeks. English settlers, to be sure, arrived at Jamestown in 1607, but expansion from this small beginning was very gradual. Not until after the founding of Charleston in 1670 did the English reach out to the Creeks.

The coastal tribes meanwhile were being levied on by Spanish, English, and French raiders who came from the West Indies to gather slaves and sassafras. The Florida Spaniards also concentrated upon the coast proper. It is a period of Florida-Georgia history that for a long time was sadly neglected. Several recent publications, however, rescue this important chapter from oblivion. [21] In them one may read of Jesuit martyrs in Georgia, Carolina, and Virginia, of Franciscan labors, martyrdoms, and success. At first the Franciscans were few.

20. On Menéndez see Lowery, *Spanish Settlements*, Vol. II; Parkman, *Pioneers of France in the New World;* and Solís de Merás' contemporary memorial, published in English translation by Jeannette Connor under the title, *Pedro Menéndez de Avilés.*
21. See especially Bolton, *Arredondo's Historical Proof of Spain's Title to Georgia;* Johnson, *The Spanish Period of Georgia and South Carolina;* and Lanning, *The Spanish Missions of Georgia.*

A reinforcement of five friars in 1595 was offset by the losses sustained in the Yamassee Revolt of 1597, but the missions were restored and new ones added. By 1606 seven additional Franciscans were laboring in the Florida-Georgia field. In 1612 twenty-five more workers arrived, and throughout the century the Franciscan force was maintained at thirty, forty, or even fifty. Missions dotted the inland passage from San Agustín to Santa Elena (Port Royal) in Carolina. The Franciscans were the principal agents, too, in pushing out another Spanish salient toward the Creeks. By mid-century they had nine, and eventually fourteen, missions in operation in the Apalache district, which came to be an important shipping point for maize and beans, deerskins and wild turkeys.

Spanish settlements hugged the coast, but now and again the hinterland beckoned. Pardo ascended the Wateree in 1566. The next year Boyano crossed to the Coosa and Alabama, returning with tales of an abundance of diamonds. In 1595 Fathers Chozas and Velascola went inland eight days' ride to the Creek towns of Tama and Ocute on the Altamaha. To bolster the case for missionary expansion they revived Boyano's diamond tale. The Yamassee Revolt intervened, but in 1600 another expedition reached Tama. Rumors of whites, presumably English, in the back country stirred Governor Salinas to action in 1624. He sent a detachment on a 150-league tour of investigation, and followed it up with a second party. Pedro de Torres in 1628 penetrated 200 leagues inland. None of these parties encountered any whites. Nor did an expedition in 1661 which reached the Apalachicola towns.[22]

A century after the founding of San Agustín the Creeks were still entirely independent; Spain had not encroached upon their territory, and no other nationals had reached them. Some Old World influences were modifying their culture, especially through the avenue of the Apalache hide trade, yet these modifications were slight compared to those that were to arise during the succeeding hundred years.

The year 1670 may be designated as introducing a new period which was to be characterized by international rivalry for control of southeastern North America. The English occupied the Bahama Islands and founded Charleston in 1670, establishing thus two bases from which they could advance southward and westward. The French that same year "took possession of the West" in a picturesque ceremony at Sault Ste. Marie. Three years later Joliet and Marquette led the French vanguard over into the Mississippi Valley. LaSalle was not far behind, and in 1699 his compatriots arrived in force at Mobile Bay, whence

22. For further details see Bolton, *Arredondo, passim.*

their fur traders soon overran the Alabama-Tombigbee basin, the very heart of Creek land.[23]

On the Georgia coast Spanish missionaries and soldiers resisted doggedly, but step by step they were forced back by the Charleston slave raiders, fur traders, backwoodsmen, and planters, who were assisted from time to time by British regulars and naval forces. After 1732 Oglethorpe's Georgians were the spearhead of this advance. Spain retreated to the Altamaha, to the St. Marys, and finally to the St. Johns, but not until 1763 did she give up her claims to the Georgia coast.[24]

Due in part to the cordiality existing between Bourbon France and Bourbon Spain the Franco-Spanish rivalry on the Gulf Coast was less bitter than the Anglo-Spanish contest for Georgia. But even friends were not entirely to be trusted. Spain occupied Pensacola in 1698 to forestall the French, and she maintained the post to checkmate Mobile. In fur trade, however, the Spaniards were no match for the French, consequently the Creeks were times over more attached to Mobile than to Pensacola. In fact, except for the decade following the Yamassee Revolt in 1715, Spain's hold and influence upon the Creeks was practically negligible. So far as the coastal areas were concerned Spain was a staunch participant in the three-cornered struggle for empire in eastern North America, but back from the Atlantic and the Gulf, England and France were the real contestants.[25] Spain's century or more of priority in the area was no substitute for capacity to carry on fur trade.

Needless to say, the regional contest was merely one phase of the worldwide struggle of the three great colonial powers of the eighteenth century. Occasionally a local development had repercussions in Europe, as in the diplomatic controversies over Fort King George at the mouth of the Altamaha. More often, local issues were decided by the relative status of the empires as a whole. Thus at the close of the Seven Years' War, which had not produced any decisive results in the American Southeast, the English victories in India, at Quebec, on the continent at Minden, and at Havana resolved the hundred years' contest with Spain and France. The map of North America was redrawn. France was eliminated, Spain was deprived of Florida but put in possession of everything west of the Mississippi plus the island of New Orleans, and England was given the eastern half of the continent from the Gulf of Mexico to Hudson Bay.

For the Creeks the Treaty of Paris marked the end of an epoch,

23. On the English advance see Crane, *The Southern Frontier*. Reynolds gives an excellent description of the contest for control of the Creek country in *The Alabama-Tombigbee Basin*.
24. Bolton, *Arredondo*.
25. Reynolds, *The Alabama-Tombigbee Basin*.

an epoch in which the bow had given way to the gun, the canoe to pack animals, the earthenware bowl to the copper kettle, the stone knife to one of steel, and in which simple aboriginal tastes had been supplanted by a preference for European shirts and blankets, a penchant for glass beads, ribbons, and other foreign gewgaws, and a craving for hard liquor. French fur traders had been largely responsible. The French would be missed more than the Spaniards.

Fortunately for the Creeks, England recognized responsibility as well as opportunity in her newly acquired monopoly of eastern North America. The famous proclamation line of 1763, beyond which settlers were not to go "for the present," was primarily a device to protect the Indians. England appointed capable superintendents to handle Indian affairs, Johnson in the north and Adkins and Stuart in the south, and there was sufficient competition among her merchants to keep trade goods at reasonably low prices. No better proof is needed of England's good treatment than the loyalty of the Southeastern Indians to her throughout the Revolutionary War. The American patriots did not succeed in detaching any important Indian groups, nor did Spain a little later when she entered the war against England.

The outbreak of the Revolution ushered in a new period of international rivalry in the Southeast. Spain made the recovery of the Floridas her principal American war aim, overshadowed only by the desire to recapture Gibraltar. The brilliant campaigns of Bernardo de Gálvez won the Floridas and set the stage for Spanish efforts to extend control over the Indian country at least as far north as the Tennessee. The treaties terminating the war necessarily took into account these Spanish conquests on the lower Mississippi and in the Floridas, because they had made England's position east of the Mississippi untenable. England accordingly partitioned that vast area between Spain and the United States, with some measure of injustice shunting the lion's share toward the latter.[26]

Thus it happened that the Creeks in 1783 found themselves between a new pair of neighbors: in the Floridas and Louisiana the Spaniards, who had never satisfactorily supplied the trading needs of the Indians; in Carolina and Georgia, the Americans, whose trading capacity was unproved but whose land hunger was notorious. The Creeks faced a double predicament. England had abandoned her erstwhile allies without making any provision for the trade that was so essential to them. She had also signed away the Indian territory with no regard for tribal titles. With one or the other of their recent adversaries the

26. The Spanish campaigns are described in Caughey, *Bernardo de Gálvez in Louisiana*, pp. 149-214.

21

Creeks must arrange for a satisfactory trade and recognition of Creek sovereignty. In tribal history so serious a problem was unprecedented.

V

A BID FOR SPANISH PROTECTION

> "For the good of my Country I have Sacrificed my all & it is a duty incumbent on me in this Critical Situation to exert myself for their Interest. The protection of a great Monarch is to be preferrd to that of a distracted Republic."
>
> McGILLIVRAY TO MIRÓ, March 28, 1784.

SUCH was the ominous outlook for the Creeks when McGillivray took over the management of their affairs. They faced as grave a crisis as that which led John Fiske to characterize these same post-Revolutionary years as the Critical Period in United States history.

What McGillivray did for his people is best described in the correspondence comprising the documentary section of this study. It is fitting to emphasize, however, that although the problem of the Creeks can be stated very simply as a question of trade and recognition, its solution could come only through consideration of innumerable complicating factors. Besides the domestic questions within the Creek Nation there were those concerned with "foreign" affairs, including intertribal relations in the so-called Creek confederacy, some proposals of common action with the Indians north of the Ohio, the obviously important issues of relations with the Americans and the Spaniards, and also with English interests in the Bahama Islands, under Bowles in Florida, and perhaps in the Ohio Valley.

Several of these factors were compound. Of the United States, for example, at least these component parts had to be taken into consideration; the central government, Georgia, the Georgia frontiersmen, South Carolina, North Carolina, Virginia, Kentucky, Franklin, Cumberland, Tennessee, Natchez, and the land speculators. Conflicting interests within such a group were inevitable. It was a recurrent question which faction to favor.

Furthermore, these factors were dynamic, changing from year to year in the course of the decade. The Spanish policy while Miró was governor at New Orleans was not identical with Carondelet's subsequent interpretation. The United States government was one thing under the Articles of Confederation and something very different after the

22

adoption of the Constitution. Consequently, the attitude that was indicated toward some particular locality or official in 1785 might have to be modified in 1787, reversed in 1789, and reverted to in 1790. Inconsistency with regard to the particulars was often the only means of working consistently toward the ultimate goal. Not all the vacillation as to detail supports the verdict of superficial criticism that McGillivray was mercurial, moody, and vacillating, as well as faithless and unscrupulous. At least in part, the changes were inherent in the larger problem of the Creeks and were not mere psychological outbursts.

Even before England had completed the formalities of signing away her claims to the Creek country and its adjacent gulf and Atlantic coasts, McGillivray began to put out feelers to see if Spanish trade and support could be secured. There were several reasons why a Spanish connection seemed preferable to an American one; most of these reasons are brought out clearly in McGillivray's early letters to the governors of Pensacola and New Orleans. A personal reason had to do with the persecution of his father and many of his friends by the patriots in the states. Under the circumstances it was easier to turn to the other recent enemy, Spain, than to the Americans.

The restlessness of the American frontiersmen and their propensity for encroaching upon the land of the Indians was a most powerful argument against the United States. McGillivray had no confidence that the American government would be able to restrain these land-hungry backwoodsmen. Spain, on the other hand, might see that it was worth her while to assist the Creeks to preserve their lands from usurpation by these Americans. For Spain's possessions in America were similarly endangered, and her logical defense was to strengthen the Indian nations as buffer provinces against the expanding Americans.

McGillivray was also skeptical about the United States' enduring as a nation. Along with many others he had little confidence in the republican form of government and gave natural preference to the tested monarchical type. The United States, in addition, was "a distracted Republic," torn by violent dissension. "The whole Continent is in Confusion," he observed. "Before long I expect to hear that the three kings [of England, Spain, and France] must Settle the matter by dividing America between them."[27]

From the standpoint of convenience, Pensacola was the most eligible town through which to supply the Creek Nation. McGillivray had geography in mind when he asserted that for protector of the Creeks no other power was "so fitting as the Master of the Floridas."

Later, it developed that the Americans could supply better trade

27. Document 7, *infra*.

23

goods and on better terms than could Spain. But in 1783 there was no positive assurance that this would be the case. American manufactures were entirely inadequate, and there was no guaranty that England would continue to permit the United States to acquire by importation the necessary goods for supplying the Creeks.

But the decisive circumstance seems to have been an arrangement entered into with William Panton. When it appeared that the British were soon to evacuate St. Augustine, the one remaining channel for the Creek supply of English goods, McGillivray approached Panton to urge him to stay and to keep up the Indian trade. Panton agreed, but only on condition that McGillivray associate himself with the trading company and guarantee that it would be safeguarded.

The connection thus established was to prove momentous to both men. One immediate effect upon McGillivray was to deepen his prejudice against the Americans, for Panton had also suffered at the hands of the Georgian patriots and was most vindictive against them. His quaint outburst to Miró that the Americans could not bribe him, not even "Washington himself, had he the thirteen United States in his belly," was typical of his spirit. Panton, moreover, saw for himself a financial opportunity if the Creeks became partial to Spain, and he persuaded McGillivray to amend his request for a trade through Pensacola and Mobile and to specify the house of Panton.[28]

McGillivray visited Pensacola in September, 1783. To judge from Governor O'Neill's report of their conversation, he simply requested the establishment of a trade and tendered his services to enlist the friendship of the Creeks. Three months later, when he learned of the signing of the definitive treaty between England and Spain and of the retrocession of the Floridas to Spain, he renewed his petition for trade and protection. This time he made the request much more emphatic, supporting it by a statement of "reasons to Shew it would be good Policy in the crown of Spain" to grant the request. The principal argument set forth in his letter of January 1, 1784, and augmented and reiterated in others of January 3 and 7, February 5 and 8, March 26 and 28, and May 1,[29] was that Spain needed the allegiance of the Creeks as a barrier against the Americans, who, he said, were trying to win over the Indians, and who, he insinuated, were planning attacks on Pensacola and Mobile.

McGillivray's letters bore fruit. O'Neill and Miró were ordered, in pursuance of McGillivray's suggestion and their own recommenda-

28. For further information on Panton see note 25 in the documentary section of this volume. The quotation is from document 143, *infra.*
29. Documents 4-8 and 10-12, *infra.*

tion, to hold a meeting with the Creeks at Pensacola and with the other Southern tribes at Mobile. They looked upon McGillivray as the principal representative of the Creeks. His earlier letters had not made the claim in just that form. He signed himself merely "A Native and chief of the Creek Nation." He was not absolute dictator of the tribe, but since he carried on the tribe's correspondence and acted as its spokesman at the treaty, the impression was given that he was *the* chief and not merely *a* chief. Panton insinuates that he fostered this assumption on the part of the Spaniards, and that after the Spaniards came to regard him as such the Creeks followed suit.

There is no gainsaying that McGillivray's authority was still in the process of growth at the time of the congress. On the other hand, it must be observed that the English commission as colonel, which he had held for almost eight years previously, raised him above the level of the average chief, that he did not lay claim as yet to absolute power in the nation, and that the Creeks of their own volition designated him their spokesman and principal representative in the negotiation of the treaty.

In two particulars the treaty fell short of McGillivray's hopes. The Spaniards refused to guarantee the Creek territories in full, and agreed merely to protect the Creeks in so far as their lands fell within the Spanish limits. Secondly, they declined to install Panton in the Indian trade at Pensacola and Mobile. That privilege had already been promised the New Orleans firm of Mather and Strother. McGillivray later reported that he had been informed that Miró and Navarro had an interest in this firm and that it was futile for him to hold out for any other award of the trade. Panton was confirmed in his trading privileges at St. Marks of Apalache, which was all that McGillivray could obtain for him at this time.

The two-day meeting concluded on June 1 with the signing of the treaty and the tariff of prices for the Indian trade.[30] McGillivray was rewarded with an appointment as commissary for the Creeks at a salary of fifty dollars a month.

The outstanding feature of McGillivray's correspondence in the next year and a half was his efforts in behalf of Panton. He was incessant, in season and out, in recommending his friend. His arguments were particularly directed to convince the Spaniards that a good trade was requisite, that the only way to be sure of the valuable loyalty of the Creeks was by seeing that they were well supplied. The principal docu-

30. The essential parts of the treaty appear as document 13, *infra*. The tariff of prices is printed in Caughey, "Alexander McGillivray and the Creek Crisis, 1783-1784," *New Spain and the Anglo-American West*, I, 285-86.

ments of this period were by all odds the memorial of July 10, 1785, and its cover letter dated a fortnight later.[31] In these documents McGillivray expressed concern over the irregularity and uncertainty of the trade that Mather and Strother had been supposed to provide. To his plea for a better trade such as Panton could furnish, he joined a request that his Majesty "enter into no terms with the American States that may Strengthen their claims or that may tend to deprive us (the Creeks) of our Just inheritance."

Mather and Strother had experienced difficulties almost as great as those which befell their predecessor, Maxent, in trying to conduct an Indian trade from West Florida. Permission had been granted them to bring in two shiploads of English goods, one to Mobile, the other to Pensacola. Their credit sufficed only for one shipload, and Pensacola would have been left without any Indian goods except that Panton volunteered to meet the emergency by bringing goods from St. Augustine or the Bahamas. He edged into the Pensacola trade in this fashion, and through a series of "temporary" permits was enabled to monopolize its Indian trade and much of its domestic commerce until his death eighteen years later.

The Creeks were handicapped by uncertainties as to their trade but they were quite assiduously and quite deferentially courted by the Americans and by the Spaniards in these eighteen months following the Congress of Pensacola. McGillivray found that his lot was in happy contrast to that of the King of England. "The King, poor fellow," he wrote, "is not even equal to the President of [the American] Congress. I would rather remain governor of my savages than change places with him."[32]

Expressions began to appear in McGillivray's letters shortly after the Congress of Pensacola which indicate that his control over the Creeks was steadily on the increase. The one just quoted, "governor of my savages," is a case in point. The increased authority was natural enough, since McGillivray's diplomacy had reaped such benefits for his compatriots, and since no other Creek chief was fitted by education or native ability to carry on the work that he had begun.

31. Documents 24 and 25, *infra.*
32. Document 18, *infra.*

VI

AMERICAN OVERTURES REBUFFED

"I go down amongst these Americans who
are a set of crafty, cunning, republicans."
McGillivray to Miró, June 12, 1788.

IN ORDER to attend the Congress of Pensacola, McGillivray had declined a Georgian invitation to Augusta and Savannah. But though the Spaniards carried off first honors in the competition for the support of the Creeks, the Americans did not give up their hopes of persuading the Indians to shift sides.

The Congress of the United States acted in the spring of 1785, appointing five men, the first in a procession of Indian commissioners, to try to negotiate a peace and to cement it by a commercial treaty. Three of these men, Hawkins, Pickens, and Martin, actually undertook to treat with the Creeks. First and last there were a dozen United States commissioners who had dealings with McGillivray. A few of them were miscast as Indian commissioners, but almost without exception they were men who had already distinguished themselves or who were to go on and attain distinction in some public capacity. The majority had held commissions in the patriot army. Several were college trained; one was an alumnus of the College of New Jersey, another received the Master of Arts degree from Harvard, and a third was to be honored with the doctorate of laws by Brown and Dartmouth. There were United States senators, a former president of Congress, generals from the army, frontier leaders, and a man from Washington's own household. Yet in the correspondence that they exchanged with McGillivray the advantage lay all with the half-breed. It was he who wrote with most vigor, he who analyzed the issues with greatest clarity, he who determined the course of most of the negotiations, he who had his way in the diplomatic exchanges.

A partial explanation is that the Americans thought it necessary to write down to the Creek chief. They came to the business, apparently, with preconceived notions of what phraseology was appropriate for addressing redmen. Their letters were replete with salutations like "friends and brothers," and "trusty and beloved men," and with such phrases as "warriors of the thirteen great fires," or "the hatchet once lifted is not easily buried." Such expressions were harmless enough; they gave a picturesque touch to the American papers but the unfortunate aspect was that some of the American commissioners made only this artificial effort to sense the position of the Creeks and to under-

27

stand the nature of their problems. McGillivray's characterization of Daniel McMurphy, who was sent by the state of Georgia, would be only slightly hyperbolic if applied to several of the United States commissioners. "They had Sent up an Agent & for what purpose I know not without it was to play the fool, which he performd with Considerable Insolence."[33]

The experiences of the commissioners of 1785-86 indicate clearly the extent to which McGillivray was the factor preventing American success in these negotiations. The commissioners invited the Creeks to meet at Galphinton on the Ogeechee. In his reply,[34] McGillivray applauded the American desire to put matters "on an equitable footing" with the Indian nations but deplored the long delay about making this move. Meanwhile, he added, the Creeks, in view of Georgia's vengeful attitude, had sought and obtained the protection of Spain and the promise of a free trade through the Floridas; they had determined to use force against the encroaching Georgians, but in deference to the request of the commissioners he would call off the proposed attacks. After remarking that he "could wish that the people of Cumberland shewed an equal good disposition to do what is right," and mentioning their written acknowledgment that they had begun the hostilities, he concluded by censuring the commissioners, though most deferentially, for selecting a horse thief as their messenger. The combined result was to put the commissioners on the defensive, to pose to them a set of questions that they could not possibly answer with any éclat.

He saw to it also that only two chiefs and a handful of warriors went to Galphinton. The commissioners refused to enter into any treaty with such an inadequate delegation, representing only two towns, "instead of about one hundred." They talked with the Indians and gave them some presents, but made no treaty. The Georgians were less scrupulous, concluding the next day the treaty of Galphinton, the legality of which McGillivray and the Creek Nation as a whole would never admit.

At Seneca and Hopewell on the Keowee, however, these same commissioners were greeted by large delegations of Cherokees, Choctaws, and Chickasaws. These Indians accepted the presents which Congress had provided. They feasted on the rations issued to them, their capacity proving a source of great astonishment to the American agents. Their improvidence was so obvious that the commissioners felt impelled out of humanity to furnish additional clothing and provender to be doled out by the interpreter on the long journey back home. These were the

33. Document 47, *infra*.
34. McGillivray to Pickens, September 5, 1785, ASP IA, I, 17-18.

same Indians who had professed allegiance to Spain in the Mobile Congress in 1784. Now they had no scruples about making a like compact with the United States. The minutes of their parleys with the commissioners contain evidences of a certain canniness on the part of the Indian chiefs. Piomingo, for example, differentiated very sharply between the traders whom the Indians would always be glad to have come among them and the agricultural settlers whose encroachment upon the hunting lands did the Indians irreparable damage. The chiefs' astuteness, however, was that of untutored savages. They were at the mercy of the commissioners and the interpreters: McGillivray later insisted that the written treaties at Hopewell were one thing, and the Indians' understanding of them another.

Nevertheless, it was a typical Indian attitude, not only to be willing to receive presents from anyone who wanted to give them, but also to see nothing inconsistent in entering into two alliances that might prove conflicting. As Gané Houman phrased it: "I found the two talks just. Being a red man, poor, and not knowing how to do anything, I extend my arms from the south and to the north to receive the hands of both, waiting to see which will be the first to speak the truth."[35]

The American commissioners laid the blame for their failure at Galphinton squarely upon McGillivray. Commissioner Hawkins first suggested to McGillivray that, when he had the leisure and the opportunity, he might let him know the reasons why the Creeks were not better represented. Then he wrote more threateningly, "The Creeks alone seem blind to their own interest and still desirous of provoking new troubles."[36] McGillivray, meanwhile, after reporting the quarrel between the Georgians and the commissioners, admitted to O'Neill, "However the Americans all agree in this one point that it is my fault that they cant bring their Schemes to bear with the Indians, & on that account their attention is engaged in Contriving the manner in which they can bring about my assassination, & then they are Sure they will meet with no Interruption to Succeed in all their plans."[37]

The Spanish authorities praised McGillivray for the loyalty he had shown to the Treaty of Pensacola by his refusal to meet with the Americans. But when he took the next logical step in the expression of his loyalty, they were slightly taken aback. At a special meeting of the Creeks in March, 1786, the question of American aggressions was considered, and the chiefs decided to resort to arms to expel the invaders from the lands of the nation. McGillivray promptly reported this deter-

35. Palabra dicha en el Yazú, March 19, 1787, AHN E 3887.
36. Document 32, *infra*, and Hawkins to McGillivray, January 11, 1786, AGI C 2360.
37. Document 33, *infra*.

29

mination to the governors of St. Augustine, Pensacola, and New Orleans, and called for "the speedy Interposition" promised at Pensacola. This was interpreting the treaty rather loosely, since the war was defensive only on the theory that all land grants since the one to Georgia in 1773 were defective. Allowing that the Americans had encroached upon the land of the Indians, still Spain might have insisted upon being consulted before a war was started to expel them.

The governors, however, did not stand on formality. Zéspedes at St. Augustine praised "the moderation unexampled among Indians," which the Creeks had shown by their announced purpose of contenting themselves with driving off the encroachers. "We don't engage in general Hostilities with the whole American States," McGillivray had insisted. "When we free our Hunting Grounds Fronting the Georgians we Stop." Zéspedes pronounced the Creeks fully justified in repelling invasion by force of arms. Pending definite orders from his superiors, he promised that he would issue the customary amounts of powder and ball for "hunting," and larger quantities to those whom McGillivray accredited.[38]

O'Neill also began to furnish military stores at once, using some powder and ball that had not been distributed at the congress two years earlier. Miró, however, foresaw embarrassment if the United States learned that Spain was furnishing the Creeks arms and ammunition for use in the Oconee War. He advised O'Neill not to send any written promises to McGillivray. In the meantime, the normal issue of powder and ball "for hunting" continued.

In May, McGillivray visited Pensacola, and there he was prevailed upon, in spite of his "mortal fear" of travel by water, to go to New Orleans to see Miró. "Withal I was overcome," he said, "or rather in the literal meaning of the word they carried me on board ship, and after a longer voyage than usual for such a trip we landed at New Orleans, where the reception that was given me was enough to erase the memory of the bad voyage." Major Enrique White, an English-speaking Irishman attached to the fixed regiment at New Orleans, seems to have been his personal host. McGillivray mentions his "most obliging attentions" and "generous hospitality."[39]

A record of McGillivray's conversations with Miró has not come to light. The latter's letter of June 20 to O'Neill,[40] however, indicates very clearly that McGillivray had convinced him that Spain ought to support the Creeks. It authorized O'Neill to issue 5000 pounds of powder

38. McGillivray to Zéspedes, April 25, 1786, LC EF 114J9.
39. McGillivray to Howard, August 3, 1786, Spanish translation in AGI C 2352.
40. Document 41, *infra*.

and 10,000 pounds of ball, together with some guns, flints, and other military items. O'Neill was instructed to find some indirect method of getting the military supplies into the hands of the Creeks. He followed the suggestion that Panton might be the proper channel. Thus it happened that another link was forged in the chain whereby Panton's hold on the Indian trade was strengthened. The Indians received their presents from his warehouse; they did not always keep it clearly in mind that the presents were really from the Spanish authorities. McGillivray also profited, because the supplies were issued only upon his requisition. His "slips of paper" were not the least of the forces building up his authority.

While McGillivray was at Pensacola and New Orleans, a Georgian agent arrived in the nation. The Indians immediately dubbed him Yellow Hair, though he introduced himself as Daniel McMurphy. Yellow Hair was astonished at the importance of McGillivray among these Indians. He found, for example, that whereas trading licenses issued by Georgia were not at all esteemed, every trader had to have one from McGillivray. The Indians told him that they could not listen to his talk until McGillivray returned, but before that happened, Yellow Hair came to realize how unpopular Georgians were among the Creeks and left the nation abruptly.

Shortly after McGillivray's return, and before he had entirely recovered from a fever contracted on the journey home, a general meeting was held at Tuckebatches. It was the best attended of any meeting for some years past, and the chiefs were unanimously pro-Spanish. They drew up some very spirited resolutions to send to the Georgians, demanding that the latter withdraw "within the natural limits of the Ogeechee River" and threatening the use of force if the demand was not met. The generous Spanish support, for which McGillivray had arranged, was the principal reason for the unanimity of the Indians.

Georgia chose this unfavorable time to appoint a group of commissioners to try to negotiate a cession of the disputed lands along the Oconee. The seven commissioners, through their chairman, the distinguished John Habersham, invited the Creeks to a conference at Shoulderbone Creek on the Oconee on October 15, but under the circumstances it was quite useless. The Creeks had assurances of Spanish backing; they were not particularly interested in peace with Georgia and certainly not on the terms that the latter would propose. McGillivray answered with appropriate dignity that the Creeks had peace much at heart, but that evacuation of the lands usurped since the treaty of 1773 was an absolute prerequisite, and that ill health prevented his attending a conference until the ensuing spring.

His discipline over the Indians was not complete, as is illustrated by the fact that two chiefs, the Fat King and the Tame King, obstinately insisted upon attending the conference. Their experiences at Shoulderbone confirmed McGillivray's judgment, for the Georgians, irate that the Creeks would not make peace on their terms, seized these chiefs and their attendants in order to hold them as hostages to force the nation to capitulate. This action lent credence to various rumors to the effect that the Georgians had prepared a large-scale ambush, involving 1500 to 3000 armed men, with the intention of laying hold on all the important Creek leaders. Seizing these two chiefs profited the Georgians little. McGillivray's attitude was that these men had always professed particular friendship for the Americans and now might stay with them as long as they wanted. The Creeks would make no sacrifices "to obtain their enlargement."

Furthermore, the two chiefs after a time took umbrage at their imprisonment. "The Tame King," McGillivray reported, "for once in his life time behaved like a Man. When he found that he & people were to be detained he thunderd out a furious Talk & frightend the Georgians from their purpose of keeping them."[41] The Georgians released him, gave him some presents, and sent him home, but retained five Indians as hostages. Yellow Hair came up again with a talk, which McGillivray would not allow him to present to the chiefs; whereupon it is charged he offered four horseloads of goods to the Indian who would procure McGillivray's death. A truce for the winter was agreed upon, but McGillivray could report, "I had the Satisfaction to Make that Scoundrel McMurphy run off as hard as Coud for His life."[42]

In the spring another United States commissioner appeared, a certain James White, who was later to be the founder of Knoxville, Tennessee. He arrived just as the Creeks were convening at Coweta to decide what measures to take against Georgia. White was well received at the meeting—McGillivray was always much more ready to treat with a representative of the United States than with one from Georgia.

White quickly decided that the holding of the hostages was a great mistake, and he arranged for their release. He discovered that McGillivray had the enthusiastic support of practically all the Creeks. He received a very different impression than the one that had been imparted to him in Georgia about the legality or illegality of the treaties of Augusta, Galphinton, and Shoulderbone, by which title to the Oconee

41. Document 59, *infra.*
42. Document 65, *infra.*

lands was claimed. He also came to realize how vital a matter it was to the Indians to keep their hunting grounds. "Our lands are our life and breath," said the Hollowing King, "if we part with them, we part with our blood. We must fight for them."[43] This was particularly true for the Creeks because there was no vacant wildernesses behind them into which they could retreat.

White left the nation without having brought peace any nearer. His failure was principally because of the defectiveness of his information about the history of the Creek-Georgian dispute. He had heard only the Georgian side of the story, and when he proposed measures based on such premises, the Indians in rebuttal were able to demonstrate the fallacies of his program. It was a great handicap, however, that he reached the nation just after the Shoulderbone and Yellow Hair episodes. Nor could anyone have made much headway so long as the Spaniards were so generous in the supplying of arms and ammunition. White's visit at least served the purpose of carrying back to the seat of American government a more accurate description of the Creek Nation and of the issue with Georgia.

At the time of the meeting at Coweta in 1787, McGillivray was obviously in control of the nation. His rise to power had been, if not easy, at least the result of following a simple, consistent policy. He had cleaved to Spain and held away from the Americans; and thus far the Spaniards had done their part, they had made military supplies available generously and almost without question. McGillivray's consistent policy had produced another effect equally significant: it had entrenched the Creeks in a strong position; they were well set, it appeared, to prevail over their adversaries and to preserve their territory intact.

43. McGillivray to White, April 8, 1787, ASP IA, I, 18-19.

VII

THE TALLEYRAND OF ALABAMA

"We doubt if Alabama has ever produced,
or ever will produce, a man of greater ability. . . . . We have called him the Talleyrand
of Alabama."
                PICKETT, *History of Alabama*, pp. 414, 432.

IN THE ensuing three or four years the problems of the Creeks became much more complicated. McGillivray held his position as their principal chief, with only occasional and minor defections from his leadership, and the Creeks held their own successfully against their several Caucasian neighbors. Simple, consistent policy, however, had to give way to artful tactics such as are customarily attributed to diplomacy. These changes arose, not from mere whim on McGillivray's part, but from shifting realities in the environment of the Indians.

First and most serious was the tendency of the Spaniards to withdraw their support. Even before he learned the outcome of the meeting at Coweta, O'Neill raised the question to Miró if McGillivray was not becoming too powerful. Could Spain count on his loyalty? Was he not more strongly attached to the British (i.e., Panton's) trade? O'Neill's distrust increased. It became a regular refrain in his letters to Miró, who at first was inclined to dismiss the suggestion lightly and even ridiculed O'Neill for his insistent reiteration of concern. But later he too joined the critics.

Several rather inconsequential matters contributed to O'Neill's distrust. In the summer of 1787 McGillivray reported that a war party which he had sent out had succeeded in killing Davenport, Georgia's agent in the abortive attempt to extend its sway to the Mississippi by erecting Bourbon County in the Natchez district. Davenport's removal was a convenience to Spain and a service to the Spanish cause, yet O'Neill had some qualms about the manner in which this agent had been disposed of and some apprehension that the Americans might be provoked to still more vigorous aggressions. The testimony of Timothy Lane, a trader whom McGillivray had expelled from the nation, also indicated that high-handedness was increasing on the latter's part. McGillivray, in addition, was blamed for certain Alabama threats against the Spanish-protected settlers on the Tensaw and Tombigbee, though it appears that he and the Creeks were not responsible.

The enthusiasm with which the Creeks were waging war against the Georgians and the Cumberland settlers was a more valid cause for

34

Spanish uneasiness. With the Indians so manifestly on the aggressive, issuance of arms and ammunition was less logically justifiable as a measure to protect them against American invaders. Spain, furthermore, had no real interest in the aggrandizement of the Creeks; all she wanted was that they should hold their own against the Americans. Now that they were doing considerably more than that, it appeared that Spain had been unnecessarily generous and that economy was indicated.

Early in January, 1788, McGillivray learned from Miró that Spanish support was to be diminished. He immediately wrote to Zéspedes, whose interest had always seemed warmer. Mentioning the recent successes of the Creeks, "My Warriors are Victorious in every quarter over the americans, the people of Cumberland are drove over the Ohio river & the State of Georgia now lays at our Mercy," he expressed his astonishment and regret at Miró's action, remarked that the Creeks were engaged in a war not entirely their own, and requested a prompt answer from the captain general so that he would know what to say to the chiefs when they assembled in April.[44] Panton added his protest against the "miserable and wretched" policy of their "Western Masters," O'Neill and Miró.

Curtailment of military supplies did not occasion an immediate crisis, because Georgia and Cumberland had been partially paralyzed by the attacks just delivered. In Georgia, furthermore, a contention raged over whether Congress had any right to interfere in its conduct toward the Indians. But in view of the uncertain Spanish support, McGillivray returned equivocal answers to two emissaries from Cumberland and to Pickens and Mathews, who proposed a settlement of the Georgia issue. He promised the latter that hostilities would be suspended but insisted on evacuation of the Creek lands as a necessary preliminary to peace. Meanwhile, he appealed again to Miró and to Spain for renewed support and painted this lugubrious picture of the result of the Spanish desertion, "If it is the Royal Will that we must make peace at any rate even at the expence of the Sacrifice of all those lands which was the principal object of the War, in that Case we Shall Consider ourselves as a Ruined Nation."[45]

Succor came from an unexpected quarter. A young man arrived on the Florida Coast, announcing that he had been sent out from England by a charitable society which had heard of the distress of the Creeks and sent a present of powder and ball for their relief. McGillivray accepted without hesitation. Subsequently, when he was called to task

44. Document 78, *infra.*
45. Document 91, *infra.*

35

by the Spaniards for having broken faith with them, he insisted that there was nothing out of the way in an Indian accepting gifts from anyone who wanted to present them. This acceptance he further justified because of the dire straits of the nation and the uncertainty of the supply service from Pensacola. Governor O'Neill, in his impatience, was ready to credit two most improbable charges. The first was that when McGillivray and Panton met at Apalache after McLatchy's death, they determined to invite this assistance from the Bahama Islands. The second was that McGillivray planned to unite with this stranger and his few followers in making an attack upon Pensacola.

The real backers of the expedition were Lord Dunmore, better known as the last colonial governor of Virginia but at this time governor of the Bahama Islands, and a certain John Miller (whose name is sometimes spelled Millar) of the firm of Miller and Bonamy of Nassau.[46] Miller had a grudge against Spain for certain damages incurred during the investment of Nassau in 1782 and another grudge against Panton, Leslie and Company. Dunmore is described as a money-grabber who had been led to expect profits if Panton's trading monopoly could be invaded. Panton obviously would not have been party to a scheme directed at the ruin of his own business. McGillivray's correspondence gives the impression that he was innocent.

As their agent, Miller and Dunmore selected William Augustus Bowles,[47] a young adventurer who had plied the trades of soldier, painter, actor, and gambler. What particularly recommended him for this enterprise was that, after he had been drummed out of the loyalist garrison of Pensacola during the Revolution, he had gone off to live with the Lower Creeks and Seminoles. He knew the country and the Indian tongue and could promise that Miller's goods would be warmly received. The idea was to win the good will of the Indians by presents and then gradually to wean them away from Panton and the Spaniards.

McGillivray went to the Lower Towns to see this "stranger," and discovered to his surprise not a stranger but his old associate Bowles, whom he had known at Pensacola. McGillivray was ready to accept him as what he purported to be, but in spite of persistent questioning he could not elicit much information about Bowles's designs or backers. He was happy to hear, however, that Bowles planned to return to the Bahamas for additional Indian presents. Thus the matter rested, and McGillivray returned home.

46. For further information about Dunmore and Miller and Bonamy see note 157 in the documentary section of this study.
47. Note 130 in the documentary section contains additional facts about Bowles.

He found that his *bête noire*, Timothy Lane, had persuaded O'Neill that McGillivray was doubly culpable in the Bowles affair, and that the governor was deliberately trying to alienate the Indians against him. No sooner had he begun to feel a trifle easier about the American danger because of the arms and ammunition that Bowles supplied than he had a new problem to face, that of regaining the confidence of the Spaniards.

Gradually additional information came to light about Bowles and the purpose of his expedition. Colonel Brown, formerly the Indian superintendent in Florida for the English, wrote a long letter to Zéspedes, telling him all that he had been able to learn at Nassau. O'Neill took declarations from several traders, and investigators sent by Zéspedes to the Mosquito Coast discovered still other facts. But though it became clear that the project was directed especially against Panton and his trade, McGillivray was insistent that Bowles should not be harmed: "Having had some personal acquaintance with him when in Garrison at Pensacola last war, I cant treat him as a felon, but will give him wholsom advice & dismiss him."[48]

When Bowles got back to Florida in November, 1788, he brought a few horseloads of ammunition, a few small brass cannon, and just enough cloth to trade for food for the thirty-odd men of his expedition. The Indians were grievously disappointed that his bold promises of presents were so skimpily fulfilled. Not long after they landed, twenty-six of his men deserted and surrendered themselves to the Spanish commandant on the St. Johns. They said that they did so because they learned that Bowles planned to use them in an attack on one of Panton's stores. McGillivray suggested that the wet weather discouraged them. Bowles later asserted that his men were lazy and cowardly and that their story was fabricated to curry Spanish favor. At any rate, Bowles's party fell to pieces, McGillivray and the Indians turned against him, and early in 1789 he left the nation.

McGillivray was worse off for Bowles's coming. The small presents received were more than offset by the bitter suspicions that were aroused and by O'Neill's persistent efforts to undermine his authority over the Creeks. Nevertheless, the Indians still had confidence in their leader, as this remark of the Warrior King of Cussetah illustrates: "What does the Spaniards mean by all this Bustle and noise about our receiving presents from an Englishman. Did not the Governr. send a paper to the Holloing King that he would give no more ammunition to us. This Shows that the little he gave us was meant only to get us to draw the americans upon our Nation that we might fall an Easy

48. Document 107, *infra.*

Sacrifice to themselves. It now appears Plain that their Talks are now both alike and we are treated as no people."[49]

In the meantime, McGillivray had to carry on a correspondence with various American commissioners. A truce with the Cumberland people gave him a brief breathing spell on that frontier. Commissioners Pickens and Mathews were joined by a United States delegate, Richard Winn, but they got no further than to appoint a meeting for the spring of 1789. Fortunately for McGillivray, the American commissioners were merely marking time until the Constitution should be adopted, when the new government was expected to handle Indian affairs with a firmer grasp. Governor Thomas Pinckney of South Carolina, however, offered his services as mediator between the Creeks and the Georgians.[50] Mindful of the delicacy of his own stituation, McGillivray answered Pinckney with studied care. The letter, dated January 26, 1789,[51] was a thorough exposition of Georgia-Creek relations since 1783, with emphasis on the outrages committed by the Georgians. It closed with a forceful plea for the restoration of the usurped lands, on which fifteen hundred Creek families were dependent for their living.

The commissioners were prompt to notify McGillivray when the new government took effect. "We are now governed by a President who is like the old King over the great water," they wrote. "He Commands all the Warriors of the thirteen great fires." They expressed confidence that he would see that justice was done the Indians.[52] McGillivray, however, did not meet these commissioners in June. He excused himself by saying that the Lower Creeks, in view of recent hostilities, strongly advised that negotiations would be useless. A more potent factor probably was the receipt of a new promise of active support from Governor Miró. The letter reached him just as he was about to set off to attend the treaty.

A few days later Miró acted to terminate a bitter contention between his nephew and McGillivray. The young man, Vicente Folch, governor of Mobile, had incurred McGillivray's wrath on several occasions. The most recent had to do with a rumored attack on the Tombigbee settlers which Folch attributed to McGillivray and the latter testily denied. After vain efforts to reason with his nephew, Miró laid down the law. "It will be best for the service of the king that you never again write to Alexander McGillivray."[53] Except for the personal convictions

49. Document 112, *infra*.
50. November 6, 1788, copy in AGI C 202.
51. Printed in ASP IA, I, 19-20, but erroneously dated February 26. There is a copy in AGI C 202.
52. Pickens and Osborne to the Creeks, April 20, 1789, AGI C 182.
53. Document 127, *infra*.

of O'Neill and Folch, McGillivray was back again in the good graces of the Spaniards.

At New York in July, Washington, Knox, and Congress gave serious attention to the Creek problem. Knox prepared for the president a long analysis of the possible alternatives, of the probable expenses of a war to chastise the Creeks, and of the steps advisable to settle the issues amicably. Washington incorporated most of Knox's ideas in a message to Congress, which approved it, and on August 29, they were restated in the instructions to Lincoln, Griffin, and Humphreys, who were to proceed at once to Rock Landing on the Oconee, there to treat with the Creeks.

These were distinguished commissioners: Lincoln, the general who had received Cornwallis' sword and who had put down Shay's Rebellion; Griffin, the last president of Congress; Humphreys, a poet, a member of Washington's household, and secretary of legation for Franklin, Adams, and Jefferson at Paris and London. They came post haste to Savannah and hurried to the frontier where they arrived just in time for the meeting.

The sequel was farcical. There were the customary formalities, including the ceremony of the black drink. The proposed treaty was read, and McGillivray asked permission to discuss it with the Indian chiefs. He entered objections to the boundary proposed and to the assumption of sovereignty, but the commissioners would make no concessions. Lincoln and Griffin left the actual negotiations to Humphreys, by whom "the arts of flattery ambition and intimidation were exhausted in vain." McGillivray was insistent that the commissioners make concessions to the Creeks, and Humphreys as insistently refused. At length McGillivray put an end to the wrangling by decamping with his followers. He did not bother to excuse himself or to serve notice of his departure. A delegation headed by Pickens overtook him at the Oakmulgee, but since Pickens could not promise any better terms McGillivray remained obdurate in his purpose to go home.

The commissioners retraced their steps with what grace they could muster. Lincoln hurried on to New England without tarrying at New York to offer any explanation of the report of the expedition. That report most emphatically put the blame upon McGillivray. In many respects the commissioners were at fault. But again it should be noted that just as McGillivray was starting out for the conference he received a letter from Miró containing promises that Spanish support would be continued. This news, McGillivray stated, "decided me clearly to insist at the treaty upon stipulations that will assure us our rights and pretensions. . . . These reports made me (to use the Indian expression) stout in my heart and strong in my mouth."[54]

VIII

THE TREATY OF NEW YORK

> "A Treaty concluded on at N. York ratified with the signature of Washington and McGillivray would be the bond of Long peace and revered by Americans to a very distant period."
>
> MCGILLIVRAY TO PANTON, May 8, 1790.

EXCEPT for the importunate clamorings of the land speculators the winter of 1789-90 was uneventful. As a bid for the active support of her neighbors in her western pretensions, Georgia had made the now famous Yazoo grants. The speculators who held these grants approached various prominent individuals to seek to draw them in. Warren Hastings, for example, is supposed to have taken an interest. No one, however, was more assiduously courted than McGillivray. His name on the list of directors of a company would serve as a guaranty against Indian attacks and would do much to stimulate land sales. But he turned a deaf ear, protested when his name was used, and reminded these land speculators that the areas in question were claimed by Spain or possessed by the Indians.

This land speculation was indirectly responsible for the journey of Marinus Willett to the Creek Nation. He came as a special envoy from Washington with a letter from the former commissioner and then United States Senator Benjamin Hawkins. Hawkins mentioned the incredulity with which the report of Lincoln, Griffin, and Humphreys had been received, and his and some others' belief that the commissioners were really at fault. He introduced Willett as a gentleman of honor and urged McGillivray to accept his invitation to come to New York to settle a firm and favorable peace.

Willett has left a vivid description of his journey to the Creek Nation.[55] At Pickens' plantation on the Carolina frontier he was royally entertained. Here also he found a guide to conduct him through the Cherokee country. Nothing extraordinary happened at the Cherokee towns of Santee, Little Chote, or Hunktoweekee, but at Pine Log the

54. Document 136, *infra.*
55. Willett, *A Narrative of the Military Actions of Colonel Marinus Willett*, pp. 96-113.

40

colonel was introduced to the prominent chief Yellow Bird, and there he was honored spectator at a ball play, which he pronounced "novel and thrilling." With a new guide he crossed the Etowah in a canoe, swimming his horses, and by way of the Pumpkin Posh approached the first Creek town. Advised by a trader that McGillivray was at Okfuskee, Willett turned off in that direction and, at Graisson's house in the Hillabees, met the chief.

McGillivray impressed him very favorably, as a "man of an open, generous mind, with a good judgment, and a very tenacious memory." Willett delivered Hawkins' letter and Washington's message and conversed freely with McGillivray. He witnessed the ceremony of the black drink, attended a dance at the Fish Pond Town, and accompanied his host to Little Tallassie.

While waiting ten days for the circulation of notices to assemble the chiefs to hear his talk, Colonel Willett familiarized himself with the locality. He rode out to see the ruins of the French fort Toulouse and found very little of it left. The "Apple Grove," which was the plantation that Lachlan McGillivray had started, he described as "a most delightful and well improved place."

In company with McGillivray, Willett set out on May 12 for Oussitche where the council was to meet. They stopped the first night at Tuckebatches with the interpreter Cornell, the next night with old James McQueen, veteran of sixty years of Indian trade. Next to be encountered were the Hollowing King and Durouzeau, interpreter at Coweta, where Willett reported much drinking of taffia and a night of noise and carousal.

At Oussitche the next day Willett delivered his talk to the assembled chiefs. He promised that Washington wanted none of their land and would see that their proper claims were respected. He said that the president was anxious to afford them a most favorable trade, and he urged them to select a delegation to accompany McGillivray to "the great council-house" at New York where a treaty would be made "as strong as the hills and lasting as the rivers." An hour later Willett was recalled to the assembly to hear the Hollowing King, "a fine-looking man and great orator," reply for the nation.

"We are glad to see you," he said. "You have come a great way, and, as soon as we fixed our eyes upon you, we were made glad. We are poor, and have not the knowledge of the white people. We were invited to the treaty at the Rock Landing. We went there. Nothing was done. We were disappointed, and came back with sorrow. The road to your great council-house is long, and the weather is hot; but our beloved Chief shall go with you, and such others as we may appoint.

41

We will agree to all things which our beloved Chief shall do. We will count the time he is away, and, when he comes back, we shall be glad to see him with a treaty that shall be 'as strong as the hills and lasting as the rivers.' May you be preserved from every evil."[56]

The coming of so distinguished a man as Willett was itself an argument in favor of McGillivray's going to New York. Another consideration which Willett probably mentioned and which certainly was stressed at New York was that Spain and England seemed to be on the verge of war over the Nootka question. In such a war Panton's trade would almost certainly break down and Spain might find it impossible to get arms and ammunition to the Creeks, which would leave them in a most embarrassing predicament.

Willett chose rather to emphasize the Yazoo companies and the contest between the United States and Georgia for control of these western lands. To put it baldly, he represented that Washington was so anxious to perfect the title of the national government to these lands and to get in ahead of Georgia that he was willing to concede unusually favorable terms to the Creeks. There was diplomatic verbiage, to be sure. Washington was represented as motivated by "justice and humanity," and as the true friend of the Indian. McGillivray doubted Washington's pure magnanimity, and intimated in a letter to Leslie that he believed the president's real end was to restrain the malevolence of the northern and eastern states against the southern. He went to New York because he believed that the situation held promise of advantage for the Creeks. Ambition also entered the picture, not merely for the recovery of his Georgia property which Willett did not neglect to mention, but also for the glory involved. "A Treaty," he confided to Panton, "concluded on at N. York ratified with the signature of Washington and McGillivray would be the bond of Long peace and revered by Americans to a very distant period."[57]

When Panton and Miró heard of this American coup they were much alarmed. Miró had repeatedly urged McGillivray to conclude a peace with the Americans, but a treaty negotiated at New York, he feared, would be entirely in the American interest. Panton hurried over from the Chickasaw country to stop McGillivray, or at least to give him advice before he left, but his three hundred mile trip was useless, for McGillivray was already gone, leaving behind long letters to Panton, Miró, and Leslie, promising to be true to them, assuring that Spain could still keep her western possessions, and recommending that she appropriate fifteen or twenty thousand pesos annually to hold the

56. *Ibid.*
57. Document 139, *infra.*

42

Indians in line. Panton was of the opinion that McGillivray would not find his expectations fully realized at New York. "I wish I had seen him before he went," he wrote to Miró, "but I have nevertheless Confidence enough in his Steadiness to rely that he will reject any overture which may be made to him, that can be considered injurious to Spain or disgraceful to himself and friends."[58]

Willett, McGillivray, and their entourage formed a veritable pageant. Through the wilderness, past Stone Mountain, and Pickens' home at Seneca, they traveled, McGillivray and several others on horseback, twenty-six chiefs and warriors in three wagons, and Willett riding in a sulky. All along the way the delegation was greeted with great interest and McGillivray was fêted by the more prominent citizens. Particularly was this the case at Guildford Courthouse, North Carolina, at Richmond and Fredericksburg in Virginia, and at Philadelphia. From Elizabethtown Point they boarded a sloop for New York, where the newly organized Society of St. Tammany met them in full regalia and escorted them up Wall Street to Federal Hall where Congress was in session, then to the president's house, and finally to the City Tavern, where Governor Clinton and Secretary of War Knox were hosts at dinner.

Social diversions and McGillivray's illness prolonged the treaty negotiations until into August. McGillivray was Knox's guest much of the time; the chiefs camped about half a mile from town.

International interest in McGillivray was much in evidence. The Americans "chaperoned" him as closely as possible, but they could not prevent all contacts with Jaudenes and Viar, the Spanish charges d'affaires, with Carlos Howard, who was sent up from St. Augustine on "sick leave," and with England's representatives, Beckwith and Dalton. These agents accomplished little directly, but McGillivray was of the opinion that their presence, especially Howard's, inclined the Americans to grant the Creeks more favorable terms.

Negotiations were opened by informal conferences between McGillivray and Henry Knox. When all was ready to draw up the final treaty, Knox was given a regular appointment as commissioner, the Senate at the same time being asked to take note of the secret articles that were to be a part of the convention. The treaty was concluded on August 7, and the ceremonies of signing took place a week later.[59]

The actual treaty was something of a compromise. McGillivray said of it that it was not exactly what he wanted, but about as good a treaty

58. Document 143, *infra*.
59. For a description of the ceremony see document 147, *infra*. The treaty is printed in ASP IA, I, 81-82, and summarized in document 145, *infra*.

as could be gotten under the circumstances, which was almost exactly what Washington had said about the Constitution when the convention completed its labors.

McGillivray held out against an acknowledgment of American sovereignty except over the parts of the nation that were within the limits of the United States. The effect of this provision was to make the ultimate disposition of the Creeks depend upon the settlement of the disputed boundary between the United States and Spain. If all or part of the Creek territory should be found to lie north or east of the ultimate line, it would be under American protection; any part south or west of the line would be under Spanish protection as specified in the Treaty of Pensacola of 1784. The Spaniards subsequently criticized this article bitterly, but McGillivray insisted, and correctly, that it was not a breach of faith with Spain.

Similarly the boundary laid down between the Creeks and the citizens of the United States was not entirely satisfactory. McGillivray had to relinquish that part of the disputed area on which the Georgians had already settled. To move them out would have been practically impossible. On the other hand, Georgia did not get the boundary set as far west as she had claimed, and the Indians gained a valuable hunting area on the Altamaha. Financial compensation was included for the territorial claims that the Creeks surrendered. Knox strove hard to get an American trade authorized, but McGillivray was true to Panton and would only consent to an arrangement for an emergency trade in case an English war closed the existing channels. This item was put in a secret article. It was provided also that the question of trade might be brought up again after two years had elapsed.

The other provisions were of less significance, with the exception of the secret commission of McGillivray as a brigadier with a salary set at $1200 a year.

Leaving New York after the treaty, the Creek delegation sailed to the St. Marys, a novel experience for most of the party. They completed the journey home in easier stages than most of them wished; horses for the trip being obtained only with the greatest difficulty. After six weeks' overland trip, the three or four weeks in New York, and the long voyage, the impatience of the Indians can readily be understood. In spite of the most urgent invitations, McGillivray declined to turn aside to visit the governor of St. Augustine.

A young lieutenant, Caleb Swan, accompanied the Creeks home. He was sent as deputy Indian agent—as a spy, McGillivray thought at first. Swan remained in the Creek country until McGillivray left in the fall for Pensacola. Then, not wishing to stay on as the only

44

civilized person in the nation, he returned to the states, where he wrote up his observations on the Creeks, their country, their ceremonies, their manners and customs.[60] It is one of the best descriptions of Creek society in McGillivray's day.

The Treaty of New York set a precedent in American treaty-making. Frequently thereafter the United States followed the policy of bringing Indian chiefs to the seat of government, partly for the sake of impressing upon them the nation's size, wealth, population, and power.

But though it was "ratified with the signature of Washington and McGillivray," the treaty fell far short of the latter's prediction. The Georgians, naturally enough, fulminated against it as a betrayal of the state, an admission that Georgia had been in the wrong in the entire controversy with the Creeks, and a questionable exercise of the powers entrusted to the central government by the new Constitution. The Georgia Assembly adopted pointed resolutions containing criticisms both general and specific. In Congress, Representative James Jackson of Georgia bellowed forth a denunciation of the treaty, which, he said, had "spread alarm among the people of Georgia," had ceded away "three million acres of land guaranteed to Georgia by the Constitution," had disregarded the report of the three northern commissioners of 1789, and, worst of all, had contained secret articles. He charged that the government, instead of recognizing the rights of Georgia, had "given away her land, invited a savage of the Creek nation to the seat of Government, caressed him in a most extraordinary manner, and sent him home loaded with favors."[61]

The Spaniards and Panton set about immediately to nullify the treaty. Several months passed before they succeeded in getting a complete copy of the treaty as published. The secret articles were disclosed to them only piecemeal by McGillivray, and they never came into full knowledge of them. Some of the rumors current, however, went far beyond the actual secret articles. McGillivray's salary was reported at several times its actual figure, and he was said to have admitted unqualified American sovereignty and to have arranged a definite commercial treaty. He did swear allegiance to the United States. Working upon the Indians, Panton and the Spaniards did all that they could to arouse dissatisfaction. They insinuated that McGillivray had been too much influenced by a desire to recover his family property and by the flattery of the Americans. They also took McGillivray to task for the concessions he had made or was said to have made.

60. "Position and State of Manners and Arts in the Creek, or Muscogee Nation in 1791," in Schoolcraft, *Indian Tribes*, V, 251-83.
61. Quoted in McMaster, *History of the People of the United States*, I, 604.

His replies were adequate to the occasion; he justified his steps by citing Miró's repeated enjoinders to him to conclude a peace with the Americans and by citing his refusal to give up Panton's trade and the Spanish protection.

He summed matters up with his customary acumen when he wrote that the Georgians should have been satisfied with the substantial concessions made to them and should have thanked O'Neill and Miró, except for whose urgings he would not have made such sacrifices to "rebellious vagabonds." He mentioned the bitter criticisms that were being made of him and Knox and even of Washington. "I signed the death sentence of the Company of the Yazoo," he continued "and if our allies and western protectors do not help us greatly, I shall have to accept the title of Emperor of the West, which was offered me on my journey to New York, and which I then refused. On the contrary, I want some rest after so long drawn out a dispute with my neighbors."[62]

IX

UNTIMELY DEATH

> "In fact, if McGillivray's friendship is lost, so also will be that of the Talapuches, who are the chief barrier against the United States."
> MIRÓ TO APARICI, October 2, 1791.

IN THE following twelve or fifteen months McGillivray's influence reached its zenith. He was at the peak of his power; his neighbors treated him with greater deference than ever before, and his nation was enjoying the full fruits of the masterly diplomacy he had exercised in its behalf. Washington had recognized him as the head of his people, and the United States stood ready to guarantee and protect the Creek territory against encroachments by Georgia, Cumberland, or the land companies. On the American side, therefore, the outlook was practically ideal. His Spanish neighbors were less well pleased with the Treaty of New York; they felt a coolness that had not been in evidence in 1787. Nevertheless, when they sought to counteract the treaty it was by offering greater advantages to the Creeks, by granting larger emoluments to McGillivray, and by courting him more assiduously.

Two circumstances, however, militated against his peaceful enjoy-

62. McGillivray to Leslie, November 10, 1790, Spanish translation in AHN E 3889 bis.

46

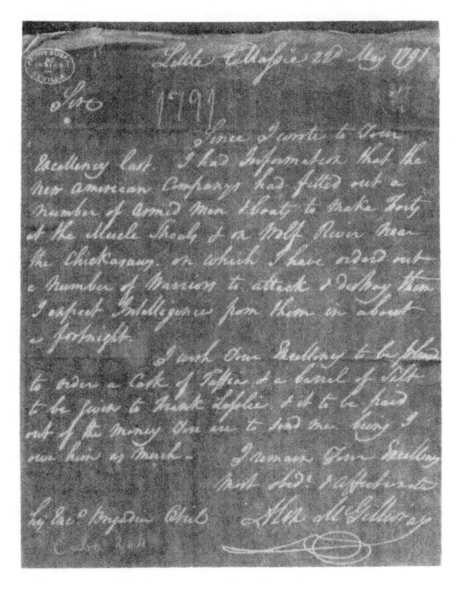

Facsimile of a letter from McGillivray to O'Neill,
May 22, 1791

ment of the results of his statecraft. Throughout the winter his health was very poor. All January he was confined to his fireside as the consequence of a scalded leg, following which his old enemies, rheumatism and fever, took him in charge. It was soon apparent, also, that underneath their surface cordiality the Spaniards were intriguing to undermine his authority over the Indians. They conducted what was virtually a whispering campaign against him and persuaded a substantial minority of the Indians that the Treaty of New York ought not to be put into full effect, and more particularly that the line dividing the Georgia settlements and the Creek hunting grounds should not be run.

This result, however, was not attained at once; in the meantime, McGillivray was the recipient of increased favors. In April, Miró announced that his salary was to be increased from $600 to $2000 a year, and later in the summer Lieutenant Heth arrived from New York with $2900 in gold, the balance of the first annual instalment that the United States had promised to McGillivray, the interpreters, six principal chiefs, and the nation. Though he expressed gratitude, McGillivray appears not to have been money-minded. When a slight dispute arose in the nation over the distribution of the American gold, he suggested to Knox that it would be better not to send anything for the nation in the future.

In June, McGillivray was host to another traveler, a Colonel John Pope, who was on his way back to Virginia after a tour of the Southwest. In the book that he subsequently published,[63] Pope not only sketched his swing through Kentucky, Natchez, New Orleans, and West Florida, and his contacts with such men as George Rogers Clark, Gayoso de Lemos, and O'Neill, but also gave an intimate description of McGillivray, his family, and his home. By him McGillivray sent a guinea to discharge a small account that he had forgotten at Richmond and a message to a fellow Scot who had entertained him on his way to New York.

The impression is also conveyed, both in the accounts of these visitors and by McGillivray's correspondence, that the spring and summer of 1791 were really the happiest days of his life. He was at home with his family, living in pastoral calm the idyllic life of a country gentleman of the older South. The affairs of state seemed to be settled; he could devote his energies to the management of his slaves and his stock and to the building of a new two-story log mansion with dormer windows.

In the autumn McGillivray's calm was rudely shattered by the return of the remarkable adventurer, William Augustus Bowles. After his expulsion from the nation in 1789, Bowles had gone to the Florida

63. *A Tour through the Southern and Western Territories* (Richmond 1792).

Keys. There he was lucky enough to find a wrecked schooner, the cargo of which he appropriated. He dressed his few Indian followers in elaborate uniforms found on the schooner and got passage to Nova Scotia on a fishing boat. At Halifax, Bowles gave proof of the plausibility of his address, by convincing the governor that he headed a delegation of Creek and Cherokee chiefs bound to London on business vital to the British Empire. At government expense he was sent to Quebec and thence to London, was granted an audience with the ministers and fêted by the public. Back at Nassau in the summer of 1791, Bowles gave out contradictory reports about what had happened in England and about what he expected to do next. He mentioned an alliance with England, an alliance with McGillivray, a determination to overthrow McGillivray, a plan to raid Georgia, and designs against Panton's trade. Even though Miller had lost almost two thousand pounds sterling in sponsoring his earlier efforts, Bowles was able to persuade him and Dunmore to support the new enterprise, another proof of his compelling personality.

Upon receipt of the news of Bowles's return, McGillivray went to the Lower Towns where he reported that Bowles, "aided & protected by Philatouchy & Perryman and their friends," was "making a great noise in the Chetaws, & has perfectly Confused & distracted the foolish & inconsiderate part of the Indians thereabout."[64] McGillivray wanted to seize Bowles, but refrained because of the shelter afforded the latter by his friends and his father-in-law Perryman. Indian custom forbade the use of violence in a friend's house or town. McGillivray went home without having seen Bowles, but convinced that, because of the very small stock of gifts that he had brought, his influence would not last long.

McGillivray expressed complete disapproval of Bowles. He called him a liar, a rascal, and a vagabond; he sent three warriors to dispatch him and proclaimed a reward of $300 for his head; yet he did not succeed in doing away with him. It may have been because he was not well enough to concentrate on the matter, for he was afflicted with rheumatism and fever almost constantly. It may have been because of lingering gratitude for the present Bowles had brought in 1788. More probably it was because McGillivray did not have power enough in the nation to run the risk of over-riding the small but militant faction that sided with the dashing "Captain Liar," as his foes called Bowles. At any rate McGillivray was, to borrow Panton's phrase, "strangely inactive" in the face of a most serious threat against his authority.

Bowles moved rapidly to solidify his position. He persuaded his

64. Document 162, *infra.*

48

supporters to recognize him as "Director of Affairs" of the Creek Nation. In their name he indited a memorial to Floridablanca and a letter to Governor O'Neill, announcing friendship for Spain, offering a Creek and Cherokee alliance, and demanding free navigation privileges for the commerce of the Indians. He charged that McGillivray was completely subservient to the United States.[65] His favor with the Indians rested in part upon criticism of McGillivray and the Treaty of New York and of Panton and the trade through the Floridas, but it rested more heavily upon the promises that he made of additional presents and trade goods that he expected from his supporters in England and the Bahamas.

Panton was inclined to dismiss these promises as most improbable of fulfilment. "I have no belief," he wrote to Miró, "that he is possessed of any authority from the Government of Britain, for what he does, nor am I of opinion that any Merchant of Common Sense, will trust a vagabond of that kind with their property in speculations so full of danger."[66] Nevertheless, the canny Scot recommended as an extra precaution that an armed boat be stationed at the mouth of the Ockalagany to intercept such a vessel if it were sent. He attributed the whole episode to the jealousy of Miller and Dunmore and to their fixed purpose of destroying his company. McGillivray also counted on Bowles's designs failing because of his inability to provide the presents that he had promised.

But Bowles had something else in mind, or else he was resourceful enough to shift to new tactics when his much-talked-of ship did not come. On January 16, 1792, he appeared at Panton's store at St. Marks of Apalache. The storekeeper and his few assistants admitted the first members of Bowles's party without suspecting that anything other than trade was intended. To their surprise they found that Bowles was taking over the store. He announced that he was acting by order of the authorities, presumably the British, and that the seizure of the store was to punish Panton for certain wrongs that he had done. Bowles kept some of Panton's employes at their tasks. There was the form, at least, of keeping account of the stores that were issued to the Indians, whites, and half-breeds of Bowles's party. The price list, however, was arbitrarily reduced, and quantities of goods were taken out without the bookkeeper's knowledge. There was no bloodshed, but so much loud talk and quarreling and carousing that Panton's men feared that their lives were in danger.

The Spanish garrison at St. Marks was inadequate for the recapture

65. Bowles to O'Neill, December 4, 1791, AGI C 2371.
66. Panton to Miró, December 11, 1791, AGI C 203.

of the store, but before McGillivray or Panton had time to take effective steps, Bowles had been eliminated by a strategem devised by Baron de Carondelet, the new governor at New Orleans. The Baron had already ordered Josef de Hevia to cruise, as Panton had suggested, to intercept Bowles's vessel. Now he was ordered to induce Bowles to come on board and to bring him to New Orleans for a conference with the new governor.

It is barely possible that Carondelet intended this as a genuine invitation, that the passport for Bowles was issued in good faith, and that only after the two had conferred at New Orleans did Carondelet recognize his guest as a menace by all means to be removed. More probably the trap was deliberately set. The bait, in any case, was an alleged answer from Conde de Floridablanca to Bowles's memorial for the Creek Nation.

Against the advice of most of his party, Bowles boarded Hevia's ship. He wrote letters of instruction to the chiefs and to the captain of the boat that he was expecting, and sailed for New Orleans. In retrospect it is easy to see that this step was a colossal blunder. Yet it was not utter stupidity on Bowles's part. He doubtless had good reason to believe that Carondelet was ready to recognize his authority over the Creeks and to conclude an alliance directed against the Americans. One must bear in mind, too, that he had a supposedly honorable safe-conduct, promising his return to the Indians within forty days.

Bowles did not come back. Carondelet listened to him and read his spirited letters at New Orleans and decided to send him to Spain. At this time and until his escape five years later Bowles was treated with a certain deference as a man who might prove very useful to Spain on her Florida frontier. He was a prisoner, none the less, shunted from New Orleans to Havana, to Madrid, and to the Philippine Islands, and started back toward Spain in 1797, when he managed to escape at Sierra Leone. He was again lionized in England and was assisted to return to the Creek Nation, where he set up the evanescent State of Muskogee and again alarmed Spain and the United States, but that goes beyond this story.

His faction was not entirely broken up by his arrest in 1792. Panton's store was soon evacuated and some of the white and half-breed leaders were taken into custody, notably a William Cunningham, who had taken the lead (had been forced to, he said) in the seizure of St. Marks. Many of the Indians held fast to the program he had outlined and greeted him with enthusiasm seven years later. Wellbanks assumed leadership of the group in 1792 and took charge of Bowles's papers. His one chance of success, however, was lost when the Spaniards managed to capture a vessel sent out by Miller and Dunmore early the following year.

Meanwhile, Bowles's absence operated automatically to return McGillivray much of the prestige that he had lost. McGillivray could not take credit for getting Bowles out of the way; on the other hand, he was not involved in the questionable methods that Carondelet had used to attain his ends. McGillivray also capitalized this intrusion of Bowles as an excuse justifying the failure of the Creeks to run the boundary as provided in the Treaty of New York. This issue was major from the fall of 1791 on. McGillivray had no real desire to see the line run, and in view of Spanish and Indian criticism of it he was anxious to find some means of postponing it indefinitely. The Bowles affair had its threatening aspects, but it did at least serve this purpose for McGillivray.

The summary action by which Bowles was removed was typical of Carondelet. His next step was against McGillivray. Carrying out a suggestion that had passed back and forth between the mestizo and Miró, he sent a Spanish agent to reside at Little Tallassie. The agent, Pedro Olivier, was French by birth and something of a linguist. Carondelet set him to work to get the Treaty of New York set aside, to spy upon McGillivray, and to seek to destroy his influence over the Creeks. All this Carondelet later confessed to McGillivray.

Olivier did not get far with his intrigue. At the meeting when he was introduced to the chiefs, he spoke against the Treaty of New York. McGillivray remarked, thereupon, that the new governor's attitude appeared to be very different from that of his predecessor, at whose request this treaty had been negotiated. He suggested, therefore, that he had better go to New Orleans to talk things over with Carondelet. The treaty of July 6, 1792, was the result of this conference. Article 1 bound the Creeks to expel all intruders on lands beyond the limits granted formerly to the British. Article 2 gave Spanish guaranty of these limits for the Creek Nation. Article 3 promised the Creeks "sufficient Supplys of Arms & ammunition," if the Americans refused to give up these lands. These were exactly what McGillivray had sought to obtain from Miró in the eighties. Granted them, they might have accomplished much in the way of restraining the American frontiersmen and strengthening the Indian barrier that was the first line of defense for Spanish America. The Indian barrier might conceivably have been made as potent in 1792, but other factors once favorable were no longer so. The American national government had been fortified by the adoption of the Constitution. The American settlements in Kentucky and Tennessee had grown apace, and these frontiersmen were considerably less interested in a Spanish connection than was the case earlier. Even the French Revolution must be mentioned as a factor reducing Spain's potential rôle in North American contests. Spain's prestige had also suffered because of the ignominious capitulation she had been forced to make in the Nootka controversy. Perhaps most important, McGillivray had not the same high enthusiasm for an uncompromising stand against the Americans that he had had in 1784 and 1787, before the Spanish support had wavered, before he had been accused as an accomplice of Bowles, and before the Americans had displayed the friendliness of the New York negotiations.

Carondelet's bellicose attitude went to further extremes. He took up another idea that McGillivray had favored in the eighties, namely, that of a general Indian confederacy. The four southern nations were persuaded to agree to articles of confederation at Natchez late in 1792, but fortunately Carondelet's entire program was not made effective. He wanted the Indians to demand that the United States and its citizens return to the boundaries of 1772, which anyone could see was quite impossible of realization. War was to be the alternative if the demand was not met. Carondelet, however, was mistaken in most of the policies that he sought to follow out in Louisiana. The fact that his program of guaranty of Spanish support and of Indian confederation was a failure in 1792 does not mean that McGillivray was guilty of equal folly in proposing the same steps five years earlier. A better deduction would be that McGillivray's coolness toward Carondelet's program indicated that he, at least, was aware of the realities.

Carondelet, it should be remarked, was showing an absolute disregard for Spain's traditional policy on this frontier, which had been to remain on the defensive. Upon him rests a good share of the blame for the Cumberland War that the Creeks carried on in 1792 and for the instances of renewed hostilities on the Georgia frontier. There was some color of American authorization of the Creek attacks on Cumberland and more particularly upon new groups of settlers who pushed out into the Indian territory. At New York, McGillivray had been given to understand that the national government would look with favor upon Creek resistance against the schemes of the land companies, and that Americans who encroached upon lands beyond the specified boundaries were interlopers and might be run off. But had Miró continued as governor at New Orleans, Cumberland would certainly have been spared much bloodshed.

At Mobile on his way home from the conference with the governor, McGillivray contracted a violent fever which did not leave him for a long time. He got back to Little Tallassie early in October, but was still not entirely recovered. "On my first Coming home," he wrote later, "I had so much to do that I coud not leave it soon & the Cursed Gout seizing me has laid me up these two months nearly. Every periodical attack grows more Severe & longer in Continuance. It now mounts from my feet to my knees, & am Still Confind to the fire side."[67] Yet throughout this letter to Panton and his next to Carondelet, dated January 15, 1793,[68] there is indication of his active control of Creek affairs. He mentioned the steps that he was taking to keep the breach open between the Indians and the Americans, outlined steps that should be taken to frustrate the designs of Dunmore and Miller, commented on Olivier's unpopularity among the Indians, and discussed the epidemic that had carried off most of the horses in the nation. What he wrote on these and other topics is proof of an active mind, even though his bodily strength was brought low.

These letters were his last. On February 16, 1793, Panton wrote from Pensacola, "It is with infinite Concern that I inform Your Excy. that Mr. McGillivray lies dangerously ill in my House of a Complication of disorders of Gout in the stomach attended with a perepneumony and he is so very bad as to leave scarcely any hope of his recovery."[69]

At eleven o'clock on the night of February 17 McGillivray died. Because he was not a Roman Catholic he was denied interment in the regular cemetery, but burial in Panton's garden was doubtless more in accord with what his wish would have been since death had overtaken him so far from his home and the apple orchard on the Coosa. Full Masonic honors expressed the tribute of his white friends; the savages who had accompanied him to Pensacola followed him to his grave, we are told, with "loud screams of real woe which they vented in their unaffected grief."[70]

67. Document 201, *infra.*
68. Document 203, *infra.*
69. Document 204, *infra.*
70. The quotation is from document 213, *infra;* for additional data on McGillivray's death see documents 205-8.

X

ROPE OF SAND

> "He was a consummate diplomat, a born
> leader, and perhaps the only man who could
> have used aright such a rope of sand, as was
> the Creek confederacy."
> ROOSEVELT, *The Winning of the West*, I, 67.

McGILLIVRAY'S death left at least three important posts vacant. Panton and the Spaniards needed an agent among the Creeks. The United States needed someone to represent American interests. Even more urgent was the Creek need for another leader with McGillivray's genius for diplomacy. The severe difficulty, or even impossibility of filling these vacancies is a measure of McGillivray's worth.

Panton considered his and Spain's necessity so urgent that he discussed the question at length in the very letter in which he announced McGillivray's death. He urged that Jack Kinnard and the Little Prince of the Broken Arrow be secured in the Spanish interest, though he frankly admitted that the latter was a "schoundrel." He thought that titles of Colonel and Major and salaries of $600 and $300 a year would "be their full price."

For the Upper Creeks he recommended merely a temporary appointment of Louis Milfort until McGillivray's son should come of age.[71] How unsatisfactorily this worked out is made clear by the complaint of the White Lieutenant, principal chief of the Upper Creek, "As for Millford & the man you sent last to us they are nobody & their hearts & tongues are not straight; there is now no beloved Man of yours amongst us."[72]

The plain fact is that Spain and Panton were never able to replace McGillivray satisfactorily. After a few years they gave up trying. By the Treaty of San Lorenzo (Pinckney's Treaty) Spain admitted that almost all the Creek territory was outside the limits of the Floridas. Consequently in 1798, when this treaty went into effect, Spanish search for a successor to McGillivray was definitely abandoned.

The Americans were similarly distraught in the spring of 1793, especially when it was rumored that Panton would probably succeed to McGillivray's influence over the Creeks. This belief apparently was based on reading too much into McGillivray's designation of Panton and Forbes as the executors of his personal estate. The Americans were

71. Document 207, *infra*.
72. Document 212, *infra*.

inclined to pin their faith on Kinnard and the White Lieutenant, neither of whom proved of much use.

But in 1796, with the arrival of Benjamin Hawkins as agent, American interests were competently served. This was the same Hawkins who had negotiated with McGillivray a decade earlier and who, as Senator from North Carolina, had pressed him to accept Washington's invitation to New York. Hawkins resided with the Creeks until after the War of 1812. He instructed them in farming and the simpler industries and persuaded them to have greater respect for law and order. An entirely different type from McGillivray, he was the next outstanding leader of the tribe.

In their own ranks the Creeks sought in vain for another McGillivray. There was no one in the nation who had his education, his broad background of understanding of the tribe's domestic and foreign problems, and his diplomatic finesse. After witnessing the incompetence of Milfort, Kinnard, and others, the Creeks ended by reposing their confidence in an outsider, Hawkins. In the main he was sympathetic, yet his first feeling of responsibility was inevitably toward the American interests.

The record of McGillivray's life as set forth in the foregoing pages leaves little uncertainty about his qualities, which also stand forth clearly in the documents from his pen that have been preserved.

Certain shortcomings are revealed. It bordered on duplicity for him to swear allegiance to the United States while he still professed loyalty to Spain and to accept concurrently Spanish and American salaries and English presents delivered by Bowles. There is some truth in the excuse he gave, that an Indian should not be expected to refuse any present offered to him. In addition, the services he was expected to render were largely consular in nature, and it is quite conceivable that all parties might get value received. But it was not proper for him, even in his time, place, and situation, to attempt to serve so many paymasters.

On the other hand, some of his supposed lapses from upright conduct were more apparent than real: for example, the opinion of one of his bitter enemies, which has gone echoing down the pages of history, "His importance & pecuniary emolument are the objects which will altogether influence his conduct."[73] The facts controvert this charge that he was a selfish, mercenary man.

Through eight of the ten years that Spain employed him as commissary his salary was only $50 a month, most of which was consumed

73. Humphreys to Washington, September 27, 1789, in Humphreys, *Life of David Humphreys*, II, 9-13.

in the expenses of his work, yet he never asked for more money, except to request that two interpreters be paid out of the royal treasury. Georgia, meanwhile, had the restoration of his family estate, valued at $100,000, to dangle before him as an inducement to desert Spain. He did not waver. At New York he might have demanded much more than the $1200 annual salary that was assigned him. The subsequent increases to $2000 and $3500 from Spain were unsolicited. A mercenary man would doubtless have made a deal with the land companies. Obviously he could have demanded that Panton pay him personally for the essential services rendered his firm. Instead, he asked favors only for the nation as a whole. It is significant that he died in approximately the same financial circumstances as when he entered into the first arrangements with Spain. He was perhaps worse off, for there is earlier mention of fifty or sixty negro slaves and many head of stock, whereas his children got very little from the estate.

McGillivray has also been roundly criticized for dissipating, for contracting a venereal disease, for practicing polygamy. There is no gainsaying that his indulgence in liquor contributed toward the decline of his health and it may have hastened his death. The other two assertions are also accurate. Yet any ethical judgment should take into consideration that heavy drinking was widely practiced and generally accepted in McGillivray's day, that the innocent as well as the culpable contract venereal disease, and that plural marriages evoked no frowns in the Creek Nation. We are hardly justified in asking that a man anticipate the moral standards of subsequent generations and conduct himself accordingly.

His skill in managing the affairs of his tribesmen and his adeptness in playing off their various adversaries against each other might possibly be minimized as mere cleverness, as things which McGillivray was able to do because of the accident of his family background and his special training. Underlying and irradiating this skill was a quality for which his contemporaries did him honor, namely his loyalty to the Creeks. Panton sometimes protested that his support of the trading company was lukewarm. Spanish officials charged that he wavered in his loyalty to the king. The Americans questioned to what extent they could rely on his continued good offices. No one had grounds for believing that he was not loyal to his people. Even O'Neill, whose opinion of McGillivray's scrupulousness was not the highest was ready to admit, "His efforts will always be directed toward the ends that he conceives to favor the Indians his tribesmen."[74]

From our vantage point of time we can see that the Creek cause

74. Document 62,*i nfra.*

56

was doomed to ultimate failure. The land-hungry Americans would not allow any Indian group of a few thousand warriors to retain an extensive hunting range of such manifest richness as theirs. Within a generation after McGillivray's death the Creeks were trodden down in the Jackson campaigns. They missed McGillivray's leadership; they had no powerful protector such as he had provided through the alliance with Spain. Soon, the remnant of the nation was forced to abandon its native country and move across the Mississippi.

Fate's heaviest blow against McGillivray's chance for enduring fame was struck a quarter-century after his death. Then it became manifest that he had been fighting against what was inevitable, that his efforts to preserve the Creek lands were doomed to ultimate futility. And of course, the world's heroes are the winners rather than those who fight for lost causes. The tragedy of McGillivray's career, poignant enough because of his untimely death, is intensified by the weakness, the incapacity, and the failure of those who should have carried on his work for the Creeks.

Distance does not always give perspective. Often it distorts and dims. In McGillivray's case the dismal failure of those who came after him tends to obscure the notable contribution that he made for the Creeks of his day. He found his people in 1783 abandoned and almost hopeless. He won for them territorial integrity and a favored position with their neighbors. As Roosevelt summed it up, his "consummate craft" and "masterly diplomacy" enabled the Creeks "for a generation to hold their own better than any other native race against the restless Americans."[75] To have done more would have required more than one lifetime.

Alexander McGillivray was a striking figure and with all his imperfections was cast in heroic mold. His contemporaries recognized him as a man of parts—head and shoulders above his countrymen and "the very soul of the Creek Nation." Even when he ventured out of the Indian country, as on the trip to New York, he still made a favorable impression. What he could have accomplished on a larger stage and with more substantial forces at his command is a tantalizing question. But it is beside the point, for he was definitely of the Creeks, and his talents peculiarly appropriate to their problems.

75. Roosevelt, *The Winning of the West*, I, 65.

McGILLIVRAY'S CORRESPONDENCE AND RELATED PAPERS

NOTE: Unless otherwise indicated, the documents that follow have been taken from the manuscript originals and were in English. Revision has been kept to the bare minimum which any writer might count on from his printer. The only liberties taken have been to supply an occasional capital letter to start a sentence or a period to close one, and these ordinarily where the longhand writer had used some other device such as spacing to indica.e sentence division. I have not presumed to improve upon spelling, punctuation, capitalization, or grammar. To polish the style would impute an education and an enslavement to convention that the characters of this drama did not enjoy.

In the translations I have striven for clarity and for faithfulness to the spirit and expression of the originals. The two, unfortunately, are sometimes mutually exclusive.

Parentheses are used only where they appeared in the manuscripts. Brackets enclose what I have supplied by way of explanation or correction, or to fill ellipses.

The following abbreviations have been employed:

AGI C Archivo General de Indias, Papeles de Cuba, Seville

AGI SD Archivo General de Indias, Audiencia de Santo Domingo, Seville

AGP H Archivo General y Público de la Nación, Historia, Mexico City

AHN E Archivo Histórico Nacional, Estado, Madrid

AN EI Archivo Nacional de Havana, Expedientes de Intendencia

ASP IA American State Papers, Indian Affairs

BL LC Bancroft Library, Louisiana Collection, Berkeley, California

LC EF Library of Congress, East Florida Papers, Washington, D. C.

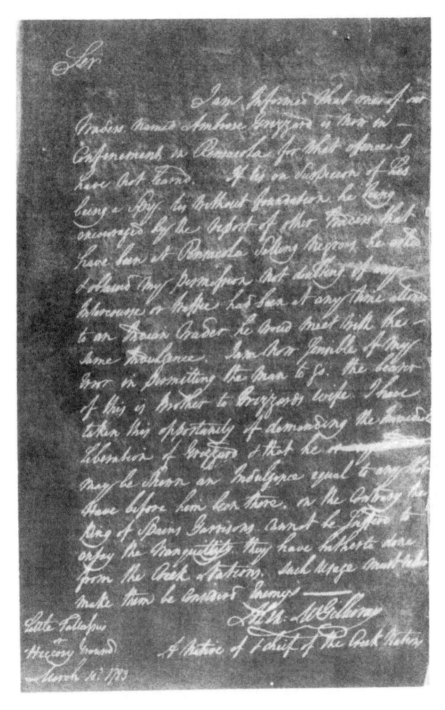

Facsimile of McGillivray's first letter to the Spaniards
(McGillivray to O'Neill, March 10, 1783)

SPANISH PROTECTION

1. *McGillivray to O'Neill,*[1] *March 10, 1783*

[AGI C 196]

SIR

I am Informed that one of our traders, named Ambrose Grizzard is now in Confinement in Pensacola, for what offense I have not learnd. If tis on Suspicion of his being a Spy, tis Without foundation, he being encouraged by the report of other traders that have been at Pensacola Selling Negroes, he askcd & obtaind my permission not doubting if any Intercourse or traffic had been at any time allowed to an Indian trader he woud meet with the same Indulgence. I am now Sensible of my error in permitting the Man to go: the bearer of this is Brother to Grizzards wife. I have taken this opportunity of demanding the Immediate Liberation of Grizzard & that he may be Shewn an Indulgence equal to any that Have before him been there, on the Contrary the King of Spains Garrisons, cannot be Sufferd to enjoy the tranquillity, they have hitherto done from the Creek Nations. Such usage must rather make them be Considerd Enemys.

ALEX: MCGILLIVRAY [*rubric*]
A Native of & cheif of the Creek Nations

LITTLE TALLASSIES[2] or HICCORY GROUND, March 10th, 1783.

The Honorable the Commandant of the King of Spains Garrison of Pensacola

1. Arturo O'Neill was the Spanish official in closest contact with McGillivray. Born in Dublin in 1736, O'Neill emigrated to Spain with his parents. In 1762 he served in military campaigns in Portugal and Algiers, and subsequently in Brazil. Under Bernardo de Gálvez he participated in the siege of Pensacola in 1781, becoming its governor in that year, in which office he continued until 1792, when he was made captain general of Campeche. When Napoleon invaded Spain, he emerged from retirement to hold an important command in the defense of Madrid.

2. Little Tallassie, or Otciapofa as the Creeks called it, was on the Coosa near its junction with the Tallapoosa to form the Alabama. During the French period Fort Toulouse had stood here; present-day Montgomery is not far from the site. This was McGillivray's headquarters where he spent most of his time, but he had a lesser plantation and another wife in the Tensaw district near Mobile. His home was a typical southern plantation, with mansion, apple orchard, cowpen, fifty or sixty Negro slaves, and overseers, but with the addition of an Indian village as an integral part of the ménage. White visitors were enthusiastic about the beauty and richness of the region and the comforts of civilization available. See Pope, *Tour*, pp. 46-51, and Swan, "Position and State of Manners and Arts in the Creek, or Muscogee Nation in 1791," in Schoolcraft, *Indian Tribes*, V, 251-83.

61

2. O'Neill to Ezpeleta,[3] October 19, 1783

[Spanish original in AGI C 36]

MY DEAR SIR:

About the middle of last month there arrived here Alexander Maguilberi, half-breed son of a Scotchman and an Indian woman of the Wind Clan, a sister of the Indian chief named Red Shoes, who, though formerly under our monarch, put to the sword the Spanish settlers on the Escambia River and in other habitations in this vicinity because of some differences existing at the time between the governor of this town and the Indians. The said Maguilberi, I am well informed, has more influence among the Creek Nations than any other person; therefore, and because he was educated at Charleston, the English named him commissary for the Upper Creek Nations. But when the English retired from the Florida Coast he was called to St. Augustine, his accounts adjusted and his salary paid, and the English bade him farewell, as he preferred to remain in his own land with the Indians, his wife, and his family. He has informed me that the English General MacArthur, who was in St. Augustine, urged him to hold the Indians in readiness to recommence the war, and that in case they were called anew to such activity it would be for the good of the Indians. At the same time Maguilberi assured me that he preferred peace, and to this end, accompanied by other Indian chiefs, he had come to solicit the establishment of a trade with them for the purchase of their deer-skins, offering his services to enlist the friendship of the different towns his neighbors. He as well as various other Indians friendly to us will refuse to gather at a congress offered them by the Americans in Augusta and Savannah.

He has a great number of cattle and negroes in his town on the Cositá, and a sister[4] married to an Indian half-breed named Duran, whose father was French, and they are actually on the road with a good herd of cattle and some forty slaves to settle on the Escambia River eighteen leagues from here.

In regard to the foregoing I must explain to you that it seems to me advisable to keep the friendship of Maguilberi and other creoles living in the nations and of such Englishmen as are married and have Indian children, since in what other fashion can we be assured of the trade and friendship of the Indians, who at present are strongly opposed to

3. Josef de Ezpeleta was acting captain general at Havana; after Gálvez' death he acceded to the full title and served until 1790. He had distinguished himself in the Florida campaigns of 1780-81, especially in the final advance upon Fort George. See Caughey, *Gálvez in Louisiana*, pp. 206-10.

4. Sophia; another sister, Jeannet, married Milfort.

the name of Americans. Of this situation I shall inform the provisional governor of New Orleans[5] and Colonel Gilberto Maxent.[6]

The Indian chief named Red Shoes, Maguilberi's uncle, has asked me for a medal and promises to protect all the Spanish subjects who are established on the Escambia. I would not have acceded except that without his consent they would be restrained from cultivating, because his town is nearer than those of the other chiefs of the nation.

May God keep you many years, Pensacola, October 19, 1783.

ARTURO O'NEILL [rubric]

Don Josef de Ezpeleta

3. McGillivray to O'Neill, December 5, 1783

[AGI C 196]

LITTLE TALLASSIE, December 5, 1783

SIR

Some time last Month one Jameeson came up here in Company with Gaines. He delivered me the enclosed letter, the Contents gave me some Surprise, which determined me to send it to Your Excellency, as Lisk has had the presumption to write in your Name of an affair, that I am well assured Your Excellency never Spoke of.

Lisk has likewise in his letter preferd Michael Walsh to be Commissary in this Country, but that I imagine to be like the rest. I must not forget to Inform you that Walsh on going to Pensacola the last time Stole a horse from my relation & the fear of Punishment has kept him from ever coming back, tho the horse is since recovered.

The Loyalists Corps at St. Augustine are disbanded & tis reported that above a hundred of them are coming this way & to Pensacola. For my part I dont wish for any of them as they can have no means of Supporting themselves here; we have disorderly people enough already among us.[7]

We have nothing new Stirring among us, but we shall how soon

5. Estevan Miró was Gálvez' right hand man in Louisiana during the American Revolution. He was sent to Havana in 1780 to persuade the captain general to support the campaigns against Mobile and Pensacola, and two years later he was assigned the important task of suppressing the Natchez rebellion. He became acting governor of Louisiana in Gálvez' absence and succeeded him in the office, which post he held until 1792. See Caughey, *Gálvez in Louisiana*, pp. 174, 233-42.

6. Maxent was to be informed because, through the influence of his son-in-law, Gálvez, he had been granted a monopoly of the Indian trade from Mobile and Pensacola. His venture did not succeed because the British intercepted his ships loaded with trade goods and the Spaniards arrested him on a charge of smuggling. See Whitaker, *Documents Relating to the Commercial Policy of Spain in the Floridas*, p. 225.

7. Swan's statement corroborates: "The whites living among the Indians (with very few exceptions), are the most abandoned wretches that can be found, perhaps, on this side of Botany Bay; there is scarcely a crime but some of them has been guilty of" (*op. cit.*, p. 282).

63

some Indians return that are with the americans, & some letters I expect from my friends in St. Augustine. About ten days ago, I received a letter from thence from a freind in London who mentions that a negotiation was going on with the Court of Spain for the Floridas. The letter was dated in 4th July last. However it be time must discover. Mean time beg leave to make you my best acknowledgements and the worthy Padre for the great Civilities you were pleased to Shew me when I was in Town, & have the honor to be with the greatest respect, Sir

Your Excellencys most obedient & most humble servant,

ALEX: MCGILLIVRAY [*rubric*]

Governor O.Neil

4. *McGillivray to O'Neill, January 1, 1784*
[AGI C 36][8]
LITTLE TALLASSIE, January 1, 1784

SIR

Having received Information a few days ago by letter from St. Augustine that the Definitive Treaty of Peace between their Brittanick & Most Catholic Majestys Was ratified and Signd on the 3d day of September last in Paris, I take the liberty to Congratulate Your Excellency on the happy event.

As the Floridas are Confirmd to the Crown of Spain by the Peace, I Solicit in behalf of the Creek Nations his Majestys most Gracious Protection for themselves and Country, as is by them claimd and now held in actual possession.[9]

If in the event of War Brittain has been Compell'd to withdraw its protection from us, She has no right to transfer us with their former possessions to any power whatever contrary to our Inclination and Interest.

We Certainly as a free Nation have a right to chuse our protector and on our Search what power is so fitting as the Master of the Floridas.

I shall offer Some reasons to Shew that it woud be good Policy in the crown of Spain to Grant us our desires.

8. Gayarré printed an English translation of a Spanish translation of the first half of this letter and summarized the rest. *History of Louisiana*, III, 157-60. Naturally he did not recover McGillivray's exact wording, and in a few places the sense was altered. Comparison of Gayarré's version with the letter of January 3 (document 5, *infra*) led Whitaker to conclude that there was "reason for thinking that this letter was written later in the year and antedated" (*North Carolina Historical Review*, V, 188). I see no reason to question the authenticity of the date.

9. O'Neill's reply contained an acceptance of McGillivray's offer and a promise of the king's protection. See document 9, *infra*. The court confirmed this action and directed that McGillivray be assured "the sovereign protection of his Majesty. . . as long as he merits it, without clashing directly with the United States" (Conde de Gálvez to Ezpeleta, May 22, 1784, AGI C 1418).

Since the General peace has been declared the American Congress has published a State of their Finances and an account of the heavy debt they have Contracted in Europe & at home in Carrying on the War (which I have now before me) estimated at Forty two Millions & upwards of Dollars, the Yearly Interest of Which is two Millions and near a half Dollars. The Court of France has made a Very pressing demand for the Interest Money. Congress in order to Comply with it to raise the Money they have laid on Taxes & Dutys on the thirteen States, which has been So Ill receivd that great Numbers of the Inhabitants are retired from their homes to avoid the taxes & are gone to seek new ones in the Wilderness & are chiefly directing their course to the Mississippi together with Numbers of disbanded Soldiers, who wish to possess themselves of a Great part of that River and mean to erect & establish what they Call a Western Independency out of the reach of the Authority of Congress. The Emigrations are so frequent that in a short time tis possible they Will attempt it, as their numbers will daily encrease & once they are Settled it will be a work of time and expence to crush them.

I can assure Your Excellency for a certainty that the South American States [*i.e.*, Georgia and the Carolinas] are exceding Jealous of the Countenance that is Shewn to the Indians at Pensacola & those States at this time are taking every measure in their power by Supplies of Goods and presents to fix this Nation in their Interests which if they are allowed to effect they Will Make the worst use of their Influence & will Cause the Indians from being freindly to Spain to become Very dangerous Neighbours. & will make use of them in all the designs they may form against Pensacola & Mobile or elsewhere. All this they declare openly.

I shall Say Something on what methods ought to be taken to frustrate the americans Schemes. One Principal Consideration Shoud be a plentifull Supply of Goods Shoud be carried to trade in the Nation on the footing that the English used to do, for Indians will attach themselves to & Serve them best who Supply their Necessities. There is a Stipulation made for that in the articles for delivering up East Florida to his Most Catholic Majesty, the Indian Trading Merchants remain and carry on their trade as usual but it is much more convenient for this upper Nation to have the trade from West Florida, for which purpose I have to pray for leave to be given me to be allowed to Bring a Quantity of Indian Goods from St. Augustine to Mobile from whence I coud Supply my People by Water Carriage preferable to pack Horses.

I had no desire to Carry on a trade but that I had engaged my Nation in the Cause of Loyalty & to Which they Stood Stedfast to

65

the last, I consider myself obligated to Support them for their fidelity.

I beg to offer to Your Excellencys Consideration what I have now written. If it shoud meet with approbation the Crown of Spain will Gain & Secure a powerfull barrier in these parts against the ambitious and encroaching Americans.

I likewise herewith beg leave to offer my Services as an Agent for Indian Affairs on the part of his Most Catholic Majesty, in which capacity I have Served his Brittanick Majesty for very near Eight years past.

Having full reliance in Your Excellencys best exertions in our behalf & wishing you every happiness, I have the honor to be Sir

Your Excellencys most obedt. & Humble servant,

ALEX: McGILLIVRAY [rubric]

A cheif of the Creek Nations

Governor O.Neil

5. *McGillivray to O'Neill, January 3, 1784*
[AGI C 197]
LITTLE TALLASSIE, January 3, 1784

SIR

By the bearer hereof Indian Munny I received the account Your Excellency was pleased to send me of the death of my relation old Red Shoes, for whose loss I am realy sorry, as he has been always a faithfull & a Couragious Leader, whenever I had occasion to employ him. I have often attempted to cure him of his fondness for Strong Waters but never coud. His other freinds blame Lucas & Allen as being in a great measure Instrumental to his loss by Stealing his horses. Was it not for that they say the old man woud have been on his return home. I am realy apprehensive that it will cost the life of one of the two whitemen that Stole the horses, as the brothers & Nephews of the deceased in Short the whole family are the crossest & most mischievous on the Tallapoussie River, & they are now all of them Shooting Deer & Bear between this & Pensacola.

Ever Since the Execution of Cor. Sullivan[10] the whole white people in this nation behave remarkably well & live with the Indians very Quietly. Public examples are sometimes necessary particularly in this Country, as executing one notorious offender, oftentimes saves the lives

10. In describing the struggle that arose over McGillivray's effort to place the warriors over the *micos*, or peace-time kings, Swan explains the execution of Colonel Sullivan. "The struggle became at last so serious, that the beloved chief McGillivray had one Sullivan and two others, partizans of the *micos*, put to death in the public squares. They were all three *white men* who had undertaken to lead the faction against him; but he finally crushed the insurgents, and effected his purposes" (*op. cit.*, p. 281).

of severals, as the Indians themselves in such cases observes no bounds.

I wish the Superintendent woud hold a general meeting, sometime in april next, that things be once Settled & then I shall know how to manage with Straglers, whether american or any others.

The Nation is now pretty well drained of Negroes. What few there is, dont answer the description, you wish.

As for Raw & drest deer Skins, I can purchase any Quantity whatever, if they woud turn to good account. If I knew the prices that Skins would fetch, I coud then be a better Judge, how to lay out money in them.

I wrote to your Excellency very fully by my Sister,[11] what I wrote concerning the Indian Trade, was on account that Messr. Panton Forbes & Co. Merchants in Augustine is by the treaty of Peace to remain & carry on the trade there & as I formerly mentiond they have petitioned the Spanish Ambassador in England for leave to establish a house either at Pensacola or Mobile for the purpose of Supplying the Trade in case it took place, those Gentlemen offerd me a part in it. They have hopes of Succeeding, & I am certain it will be good Policy to permit of such a measure by the Court of Spain, for reasons that I mentioned in the letter by my Sister.

As the american Independency is established by the general peace, I suppose your excellencys Court will Settle the boundary lines between them & the american States. If tis no Improper Question I would be glad [to] learn of Your Excellency the extent of Louisiana & the Floridas, as the americans talk largely of theirs.

A man of mine that I sent for some necessarys to Augustine was detaind there till a packet boat shoud arrive there from England, which was to sail from there 28' September last, from which she must have arrived some time ago, & of course expect my man up every day of which I shall write your Excellency by the first opportunity. A Spanish Garrison is expected to take possession of St. Augustine this month. Tis said an Irish Gentleman is to be Governor, but whose name I have forgot. Nothing more occurring I conclude with assuring you that I am

With respectful regard

Your Excellencys most obedient Servant

ALEX: McGILLIVRAY [rubric]

Governor ONeil

P. S. the bearer has executed his trust faithfully & he begs of me to recommend him to Your Excellencys bounty for 4 kegs Strong taffia,

11. Document 4, *supra*.

a good Carrot tobacco some ammunition & something to his wife and child.

A. McG.

6. *McGillivray to O'Neill, January 7, 1784*
[AGI C 197]
LITTLE TALLASSIE, January 7, 1784

SIR

The letters I enclosed to Your Excellency are from St. Augustine. Govr. Tonyn required them to be sent as Soon as they shoud come to hand, which I have now done by the bearer a nephew to the late Red Shoes, who goes in Search of the white men that Stole his Uncles horses. I desired him to wait upon & to receive Your Excellencys orders in what manner he is to proceed. If I did not tell him this there woud be bloodshed as that Family are Very Much Enraged.

1 did expect to have done Myself the pleasure to have waited on Your Excellency in the next month, but on receipt of letters from St. Augustine by Cornel I find that my presence is necessary there on affairs of consequence to myself as well as to others, which obliges me to begin to prepare for So long and disagreeable a Journey. If the letters I now send [require] any answer, Your Excellency Will be pleased to Send them to Me before this Month is Out. The Weather being Very foul & Severe I cant go off till then. In Setting off so early 1 do it with a view to be soon back for the Meeting that is to be heald With this Nation at Pensacola in the Spring.

I had forgot to Inform Your Excellency in My last letter of the Death of Capt. James Colbert[12] of the Chickesaw Nation who had been at St. Augustine, concerning demands that was made on him by the Governor of New Orleans for damages he did on the Mississippi: he got full powers to Clear up that Complaint, & on his Way to the Chickesaw Nation three days after he left my house his horse threw him down and Killd him before his Servant could assist him. . . . .

ALEX: McGILLIVRAY [*rubric*]

Governor O.Neil

12. Colbert had lived for forty years with the Chickasaws, had a rich lodging and about fifty-five Negroes, and several sons by Chickasaw women. According to Adair he spoke the Chickasaw language "with more propriety than the English" (*History of the American Indians*, p. 370). He had made a quixotic effort to get the release of the leaders in the Natchez uprising in 1781 by seizing Spanish travelers on the Mississippi, among whom was the wife of Governor Cruzat of St. Louis. The scheme failed, chiefly because Colbert relied on the pledged honor of his prisoners to return to captivity unless the Natchez leaders were released. The "full powers" that McGillivray mentions probably were statements that Colbert had been a regularly commissioned officer and that his actions were not mere brigandage. See Caughey, *Gálvez in Louisiana*, pp. 215-42.

7. *McGillivray to O'Neill, February 5, 1784*

[AGI C 197]

LITTLE TALLASSIE, February 5, 1784

SIR

At the request of a Gentleman lately from Georgia I now write to Your Excellency to Inform you that the american States Will on no Condition admit the return of the Loyalists to their estates, but on such terms as men of honor cant Submit to. One of those people a Cap Weekly, hearing that Your Excellency was Inclined to encourage & Shewd great favor to good men to Settle with Families in West Florida, he came to get a full Information of this matter from me. I took the liberty to mention to him what Your Excellency said to me concerning the Loyalists. He says that if Liberty of Conscience woud be allowed to them they coud be Contented & happy under the king of Spains Government, & that if your Excellency woud be pleased to write me that they woud be received & protected, & be allowed liberty of Conscience, that he will return & bring his family & a number of others—respectable men all who once possessed ample livings & are now reduced to very little on account of their Loyalty to their King, & men who have been accustomed to Industry, well Skilled in Farming, raising Stock or any thing in that way, which should soon put that province in a very flourishing Situation & of course become Valuable for its products & Supplys of every kind, whether for the Kings Garrison or shipping. They seem to prefer the lands on the Alabama for their purpose. Their Settling there woud be no hindrance to them Carrying their produce to Pensacola by land, as they have heard much of your Goodness & Humanity, they chuse to live under your patronage & protection, & as your Excellency has taken every measure to make your province a Valuable one I flatter myself that these familys will be accepted of to add to the making it a well cultivated one.[13]

I have Information given me that two men of the name of Tally & Ballard was seen passing thro the lower nation from Georgia to Pensacola with some negroes. Tis needfull to Inform you that these men are the most noted Villians that ever was, murdering fellows & great thieves. I hope Your Excellency will cause them & negroes to be seized; they must in all probability belong to some unfortunate person whom they have murdered, & Stolen the Negroes. They woud not Show themselves here as they knew that I woud seize them. A number of americans are disposed to leave their own government & their Taxes

13. These loyalists were obviously of a different stamp than those whose coming was discouraged in document 3, *supra*.

to Settle at Pensacola but I hope Your Excellency will not receive any of the rebellious crew.

The back Inhabitants of Georgia & Carolina are in arms, to oppose the Tax Collectors. The whole Continent is in Confusion. Before long I expect to hear that the three kings must Settle the matter by dividing America between them.

The Spanish Trader that carryd Goods to the Coolamie Town do not agree with those Indians. Ninne Wakitche & he has fallen out, upon which he made his complaint to me & says he has been ill used, & will not return again to the Coolamie Town, & remains at my house. Ninne Wakitche came here yesterday to excuse himself & says the Spaniard was frightened for Nothing, but I believe there has been reason for it. The Story that Ninne Wakitche tells is this, that some time ago, in a drunken bout a Coolamie Indian fought with a Couhuskie man & the latter some time after died, upon which the family of the deceased, according to the custom of Indians, was resolved to take a woman for Satisfaction, & as Ninne Wakitches daughter was next of Kin, She was seized to be Killed, & he to ransom his daughters life took some Goods & a Cask of powder from the Spaniard & for which he meant to pay, but doing his business without making use of the powder he returned it & says he will pay for the goods—all of which he begg'd of me to acquaint Your Excellency of in Writing. The Spaniard persists in that he has been ill used, & as he Speaks no Indian nor English & I no Spanish nor French we cant understand each other well so that I cant make out the particulars of his complaint. By desire Welch is gone to the Coolamie to look after the effects there.

I shall trouble your Excellency no further at this time but only request the favor of an answer to the proposal of the Loyalist familys, that they may prepare to move to West Florida. You may depend that they are people of good Characters.

Permit me to conclude with my hearty prayers for Your Excellencys prosperity & Happiness.

I am with respectfull Esteem, Sir

Your Excellencys most obedient Servant,

ALEX: MCGILLIVRAY [*rubric*]

Governor ONeil

8. *McGillivray to O'Neill, February 8, 1784*
[AGI C 197]

SIR   LITTLE TALLASSIE, February 8, 1784

I have the pleasure to acknowledge the receit of your much esteemed favor by Indian.

The assurance that your Excellency's pleased to make my Nation of Your Soverigns gracious protection fills me with Joy & on our part I can assure your Excellency that we shall endeavor by every measur in our power to Shew ourselves worthy of it.

It will afford us great Satisfaction to have a well Supported & regular Trad with our Friends which we hope will be the Case in time to Come. At present the Supplys that Come from Pensacola is not Sufficient for one Town. What I formerly wrote to Your Excellency proceeds from the Duty I owe to my Country to get them a well establishd Supply & that we might not be dependent on the Americans for a Trade.

I have a great Inclination to pay You a Visit at Pensacola, but at present I have another engagement, that is, as Soon as I am Informed that the peace was ratified & in Consequence, we had reason to believe that St. Augustine woud be soon evacuated by the British troops, I wrote to General MacArthur commanding that place that as we had drawn the resentment of the americans upon us for taking part with the British Nation in the War, we had a right to expect from our old friends the means of Defending ourselves if we Shoud be attacked by the americans, & I demanded that as they were going to leave St. Augustine, they would give us a large quantity of Military Stores. I am now going to St. Marks to prepare a place to receive it in. By the time I return expect to have from Your Excellency, Instructions to attend the Congress in May next. Permit me to assure your Excellency that it shall always be my Study to deserve your favors, Sir

Your Excellencys most humble and obedient Servant

ALEX: McGILLIVRAY [*rubric*]

P. S. The present Your Excellency was pleased to make me is a very acceptable one—the Winter being very Severe.

Governor ONeil

9. *O'Neill to Miró, February 17, 1784*

[Spanish original in AGI C 36]

MY DEAR SIR:

I enclose to you a copy of a letter I received last month,[14] the original of which I placed in the hands of Don Josef de Ezpeleta. I have replied to the said Magilbery accepting in the name of His Majesty the offer made by the Creek Nations, assuring them the protection of the King, and promising at the proper time to present to you and to Mr. Maxent his petition for permission to trade until the congress convenes. He is an Indian and Scotch mestizo. He has been commissary for the English

14. Document 4, *supra.*

among the Creek Nations, is a nephew of the Indian Red Shoes, and I understand has more influence than any other among the Indians. He has been here once and says that he will return to the congress. I hope the policy will be to keep him grateful.[15] Pensacola, February 17, 1784.

May our Lord keep you many years.

ARTURO O'NEILL [rubric]

Don Estevan Miró

10. *McGillivray to O'Neill, March 26, 1784*
[AGI C 197]

LITTLE TALLASSIE, March 26, 1784

SIR

I have the pleasure of receiving some letters from You, of January the 24th enclosing letters for Gov. Tonyn & Mr. McLatchy. The Indian said he was a long time Sick on the road that he coud not deliver them before.

I am last night returnd from St. Marks. When I was there Tom Miller brought some letters from Your Excellency ordering Mr. Mc-Latchy away from there. I can Inform you that the Store was Settled there by the desire of this Nation, as we were in great distress. The americans had no trade for us, they were poor, & the trade from Pensacola did not Suffice for one Village. Messr. Panton & Co. would not Consent to Settle a Store till I agreed for their Security to be concernd with them. Mr. McLatchy cannot remove without giving the Indians some reason for it, & if the real Cause was known everything woud be in Confusion, for if any attempt is made against it, the Indians in the Neighborhood will all take arms in his defence. So I hope nothing will be attempted that may make us disagree.[16]

15. Compare with the following description: "Alexo McGillibray, son of an Englishman and an Indian, ill rewarded by his nation, and by inclination a mortal enemy of the Americans, has established himself among the Talapuches or Creeks, from whom he is descended. The influence which he holds over them corresponds to the skill with which he manages them. . . . . Although the Creeks are reduced to seek asylum among the Spaniards under certain conditions, his expressions do not fail to make plain that in case they are not admitted they will of necessity claim the protection of America, which will not be denied. If it is indispensable to win over this nation by whatever expedients are practicable, then certainly the proposition ought to be extended to supply them lands in the possessions of his Majesty, in case that the determination of the boundaries excludes them, in order to prevent with the most scrupulous vigilance the establishment among them of an individual who would not be loyal to the government, and in order to separate them from the commerce and friendship of the Americans. . . ." (Navarro to José de Gálvez, April 16, 1784, AGI C 1375).

16. Charles McLatchy, Panton's storekeeper at St. Marks of Apalache, also protested to O'Neill, March 4, 1784, AGI C 196. See also Panton to O'Neill, May 1, 1784, *ibid.*

The enclosed is for Monsieur Maxent the Superintendant, as I do not know his address. I beg the favor of Your Excellency to direct it & Send it to him by the first opportunity, as I wish him to see it before the Congress. I have proposed to him to be Concerned with Messr. Panton Forbes & Co. as the only means to keep the americans from taking all the trade of this Nation. They have already Sent a great quantity of Goods among us. I dont deny them the liberty of trade till the Congress is over. Whatever we agree upon then I mean most firmly to Stand to it. It is my duty to do the best I can for my Country. If the Spanish Government dont answer our expectations, I Shall be Very Sorry that I shall be obliged to take the american offers, but I rest in hopes that all matters will be to our liking at the Congress, mean time permit me to assure Your Excellency that I am with the greatest truth

Your Excellencys most obedient & humble servant

ALEX: MCGILLIVRAY [rubric]

Orders is come from England to deliver up St. Augustine to the first Spanish officer that comes to it.

Governor ONeil

11. *McGillivray to Miró, March 28, 1784*

[AGI C 197]

LITTLE TALLASSIE, March 28, 1784

SIR

Some time before the General Peace, when there was a probability that America woud be declared Independent & East & West Florida ceded to the Crown of Spain, I applied in behalf of the Creek Nation to Governor ONeil at Pensacola & offer'd to put the Creek Nation under his Most Catholic Majestys Protection, as the americans pretend that we are in their Boundary. If the British Nation has been Compell'd to Withdraw its protection from us, She has no right to give up a Country she never coud call her own. Therefore as a free Nation we have an undoubted right to chuse what Protection we think proper. To which I had the Satisfaction of receiving a most favorable answer from Governor O'Neil, who likewise acquainted me with your Intention of holding a General Congress with the Indians at Pensacola in May next when these matters would be Settled.

Previous to the Congress I have to Inform you, that about a Year ago, at the desire of the Chiefs of this Country, I made a Proposal to some principal Merchants in St. Augustine to Settle a Store of Goods on any part of our Country they Judged most Convenient for Supplying this Nation with Goods, as the trade from Pensacola was very Scant & not sufficient for one Village, upon which a Store was Settled up the river St. Marks. Before the Merchants would consent & to give a Security to the Store I agreed to be concernd with them, as it is Situated in the Neighborhood of a Very Strong body of Indians. I was very lately Informed that this Store was ordered to be abandoned, a measure which if it was to be complyd with, woud very Soon reduce us to great distress, in the mean time We directed the Store to be kept up, & that One of the Gentlemen a Mr. Panton shoud come up here to go with me to meet you in Congress in May, that a Joint Concern may be agreed on & Settled for the Securing the whole Indian Trade of this Nation the Chickesaws & Choctaws. As these Gentlemen have an Extensive credit in London the trade will be advantageous at the Same [time] it will Secure to the King the attachment of a numerous & brave nation of Indians. This affair I beg leave earnestly to recommend to Your Consideration, for if this matter is not made up or Something like it, the Americans will very Shortly engross the Indian trade & of consequence gain the Indians to their Interest, & who will make the worst use of their influence. There are now three american traders in this nation with a Very large Supply of Goods. I cant deny them the liberty of trade during this uncertainty of affairs, as we are not Sure that we Shall enjoy a good trade from the Spanish Government.

It is necessary for me to Inform you that I am a Native of this Nation & of rank in it. At the commencement of the American Rebellion, I entered into the British Service & after a long Contest of faithfull Services we have at the Close been most Shamefully deserted as well as every other people that has relied on their honor & Fidelity.

For the good of my Country 1 have Sacrificed my all & it is a duty incumbent on me in this Critical Situation to exert myself for their Interest. The protection of a great Monarch is to be preferrd to that of a distracted Republic. If I am disappointed in my Expectations, I must as the last necessity embrace the american offers, however disagreeable it may be to my political opinions. I still hope that at our meeting every Matter will be agreeably Settled,

meantime I have the Honor to be

With great Respect, Sir

Your most Humble Servant

ALEX: McGILLIVRAY [*rubric*]

His Excellency Stephen Merot, Esqr.

74

12. *McGillivray to O'Neill, May 1, 1784*
[AGI C 197][17]

LITTLE TALLASSIE, May 1, 1784

SIR

I have the pleasure to acknowledge the receit of Your Excellencys letter by Mr. Antony Garcon, together with his Excellency Governor Merots very encourageing favor.

It is with the utmost Satisfaction that I received the Notification of the ensuing Congress to be held at Pensacola the 20th of this Month, when I hope in God that every thing will be Settled to our Satisfaction & from that time forward we will be no longer troubled with the American Talks. I held a General Meeting with all the Nation last Month, when I Sent to the Governor of Georgia a positive refusal to every thing they desired of us. This day notice is Sent to the greatest Chiefs in the Nation, that they prepare to Set off in ten days for Pensacola. I will endeavor to be in Town myself before the 20th with every Necessary Information.

I am Sir with much Respect
Your Excellencys obedient Servant
ALEX: MCGILLIVRAY [*rubric*]

Governor O.Neil

13. *Treaty of Pensacola, June 1, 1784*
[AGI C 2360][18]

Articles of Agreement, trade, and Peace stipulated & Granted by the Spanish Nation with the Creek Nations, in the Congress held with that View in the town of Pensacola, Metropolis of West Florida, the thirty-first day of May, and first of June 1784. . . . .[19]

ARTICLE 1. We the above mentioned Chiefs of the Creek nation, in our names, and in the name of the other Chiefs, Captains, Warriors, and other individuals of the Nation, of what ever quality, Sex, or Condition they may be, swear by the Supreme Almighty God, Creator of Heaven and Earth, to whom all things are subjected, to Keep and Maintain an Inviolable Peace and fidelity, with his Most Catholick Majesty his provinces, Subjects, and vassals. . . . .

ARTICLE 2. To correspond on the part of his Most Catholick Majesty to the Confidence merited by the worthy and honorable Chiefs of the

17. A similar letter was addressed to Miró, May 1, 1784, AGI C 197.
18. The original, 21 folios in parallel columns, Spanish and English, is in AGI C 2360. Several copies exist; that printed in ASP Foreign Affairs, I, 278-79, has a few minor errors.
19. The next paragraph enumerates the signatories and the chiefs whom McGillivray represented.

Creek and other Nations, who are on the land Conquered by the arms of his Majesty; We the above mentioned Stephen Miro Governor of the Province of Louisiana, Arthur O'Neill Governor of Pensacola in the Province of West Florida; and Martin Navarro Intendent General of the same, offer in the name of the King to procure for the Contracting Nation, a permanent and unalterable commerce, unless the inevitable event of a War Should impid the exact accomplishment of this offer, at the most equitable prices, for which purpose Tariffs shall be formed by the Consent of both parties assembled in the present Congress, upon which the mutual treaty shall be established, and which ought to be inviolably observed by the Individuals of both the Contracting Parties, with the utmost Scrupulous Exactness.[20]

ART. 3. In order more and more to encourage the Commerce, and agriculture, the Creek Nations will establish a General Peace with the Chickasaws, Chactaws, and other nations of the Continent. . . . .[21]

ART. 13. As the Generous mind of his Most Catholick Majesty is far from exacting lands from the Indians, to form settlements to the prejudice of the proprietor: from henceforward and from the perfect knowledge, We have of the paternal love he has for his beloved Nation, We offer in his royal name to secure and guarantee to them, those which they actually hold, according to the right by which they possess them, provided they are comprehended within the lines of the limits of his Majesty our Sovereign and to prove how different his way of thinking is far from that of his Britannick Majesty, and to render his royal Clemency more efficacious, if ever by War, or any other Event they should be dispossessed of their Lands, by the Enemies of his Crown, We Will grant them others, Equivalent, which may be vacant, where they may establish themselves without requiring any other recompense, than their Continual fidelity. . . . .

ESTEVAN MIRÓ [rubric and seal]   ALEX: McGILLIVRAY [rubric]
ARTURO O'NEILL [rubric]
MARTIN NAVARRO[22] [rubric and seal]

By order of their Excellencies,
ANDRÉS LÓPEZ DE ARMESTO [rubric]

20. The manuscript of the schedule of prices for trade goods drawn up by signers of this treaty on June 1, 1784, is in AGI C 2360; it is printed in Caughey, "Alexander McGillivray and the Creek Crisis, 1783-1784," *New Spain and the Anglo-American West*, I, 285-86.

21. Articles 4-12 specify that any stranger who urges an attack against Spain will be arrested and delivered to the governor of Pensacola; that no white person will be admitted to the Nation without a Spanish passport; that the practice of taking scalps will be renounced; that all white prisoners who are subjects of the United States will be delivered up; that no runaway Negroes will be admitted into the Nation; that horse and cattle stealing will be discouraged; that Spanish traders will be well treated, but that they must settle in the Indian towns; that the Creeks

14. [Miró] to McGillivray, June 7, 1784
[Draft in AGI C 2360]

Recognizing the particular merit and the services rendered by Alexander McGillivray in attaching to Spain the numerous tribes of Creek Indians, and confident of his well-known good disposition, zeal, and affection, with which to this day he has endeavored to preserve the friendship of his nation toward Spain, promoting by every possible means the honor, glory, and reciprocal interest of both nations, we have determined to appoint him, as by these presents we do appoint him, commissary of the Creek nation. He shall enjoy all the honors, exceptions and privileges attached to the office, and the salary which his Majesty, in whose name we are now authorized to act, accords him. Therefore we order the traders and individuals of the said Creek nation to recognize him as the commissary, obeying the orders which in the name of the captain general and the particular commandants of these provinces he shall give for the good of the service. In order to make the foregoing effective we issue these presents at Pensacola, the 7th of June, 1784.[23]

[Estevan Miró]

Alexander McGillivray

II

COMMENDATION OF PANTON

15. *McGillivray to* ——————[24]
[AGI C 36]

The protection that the Kings & Warriors of the Creek Nation Implored from his Most Catholic Majesty being happily Settled in General Congress at Pensacola, the Creek Nation & its dependencies will we hope be Considerd by the americans in that point of View,

---

will deliver the head of any Indian who kills a Spanish subject; and that any Spaniard who kills a Creek will be punished according to the law.

22. Martín Navarro was intendant of Louisiana, 1780-88. He is best known for numerous memorials, especially his *Reflexiones politicas* of September 24, 1780, and his and Miró's letter transmitting the first Wilkinson memorial. In 1790 he was banished from court, and serious charges seem to have been still outstanding against him at his death, *ca.* 1794.

23. This notice of appointment was supplemented on July 20, 1784, by a four-page letter of instructions from Governor Miró, copy in AGI C 2360.

24. Not signed, addressed or dated, but in McGillivray's hand and probably written shortly after the Congress of Pensacola.

& drop the pretended right of Sovereignty they Claim over our Country, the right they found on the Cession of Great Brittain is unjust, the Creek Nation being Allies & not Subjects to that Crown.

In order to Secure & firmly attach the Nations to the Crown of Spain, the first measure that ought to be adopted is by a Well regulated trade upon as reasonable terms as they can be furnished from any part of America, for which purpose it will be necessary to establish a house in Pensacola the Holders of which ought to be permitted to Import English Goods to which the Indians have ever been accustom'd & which it will be difficult to wean them from the use of, without much discontent & which woud be a pretext for the americans around them to Inflame their minds from motives of Jealousy. As by my advice the Indians were prevaild on to Come under the protection of the Crown of Spain, I expect the trade I ask for them will be permanent & as I have bound myself on their parts for the fulfillment of the Articles they have enter'd into, I may be looked upon as answerable to both parties which will of Consequence take up the best part of my time & will always be attended with a degree of anxiety & solicitude which arises from attempting to preserve & Negotiate the Affairs of an Indian Nation, for which reasons I beg to be permitted to Import Indian trading Goods from England to Pensacola for the purpose of Carrying on the trade with my Nation which I request Solely with the View of Serving my people their Safety & happiness being my only Consideration & in bringing all matters about, I have been actuated by principle relying Solely on the Honor & Faith of the Crown of Spain, & in preference to all the advantageous offers of the Americans which have been repeated to me.

16. *McGillivray to Panton*,[25] August 10, 1784
[Spanish translation in LC EF 116L9]
LITTLE TALLASSIE, 10 August 1784

MY DEAR SIR

25. William Panton, principal figure in Panton, Leslie and Company, with whom McGillivray concerted for carrying on the Indian trade. This British company had traded at St. Augustine and St. Marks during the English period. After the transfer to Spain it was permitted to continue temporarily. This permission was extended, and, largely through McGillivray's influence, the company was permitted to expand its monopoly to Pensacola (1785), Mobile (1789), the Cherokee country (1792), and Chickasaw Bluffs (1795). Except for Pinckney's Treaty, it seems likely that the company's trade would have been extended across the Mississippi. Even so, it engrossed the trade of the Southeastern Indians and much of the domestic commerce of the Floridas. Panton's influence upon McGillivray was great. A documentary study of the company is being prepared by Elizabeth Howard West for the Florida State Historical Society. For an excellent brief discussion see Marie Taylor Greenslade, "William Panton," *The Florida Historical Society Quarterly*, XIV, 107-29.

I received your favor by *Crook*, and I see with regret that you and Governor Onell have not understood each other well, a circumstance that has no advantage for us.

I spoke to two more of the Indian traders of going to St. Marks until the business relative to the establishment at Pensacola is finally adjusted.

The traders of the Chickasaw and *Choctaw* Nations will take the ammunition that I received at Pensacola and it is as much as they can do this year, since if they are told to return with tanned hides furs will not be gathered this fall, so that all the trade of this fall can be taken from Mr. MacLatchy.

The Indian traders circulate rumors here that MacLatchy is to [take] all their furs, unless they are damaged, for which reason the traders are very inactive; his long detention of them last winter at St. Marks made them somewhat dissatisfied. Altogether I hope for better news from Mr. MacLatchy, who should keep us here well informed relative to these affairs.

The other day I received a letter from Governor Miró and Navarro the Intendant General inviting me to come to New Orleans the last of September to treat of affairs of importance. The letter was written from Mobile, where they held a congress with the western Indians. I suspected when I was at Pensacola that it would be necessary to finish our negotiation with them (meaning Miró and Navarro) at New Orleans. Things being as they are, it will not be possible for me to see you at St. Marks at the time appointed.

(There follows a paragraph on the adjustment of his salary with Colonel Bron [Brown] which has nothing pertinent, and he closes his letter, signing himself the most obedient servant of Panton).[26]

ALEXANDER MACGILLRAY

17. *Memorial of Panton, Leslie, and Company to Zéspedes,*[27] *September 10, 1784.*[28]

[LC EF 116L9]

To His Excelly Don Vizte. Manuel de Zespedes, Brigadier General of His

26. Here, as throughout, brackets indicate something supplied by the editor and parentheses are carried over from the documents. In this instance, the last paragraph of McGillivray's letter was merely summarized by the Spanish clerk at St. Augustine.
27. Vizente Manuel de Zéspedes (sometimes referred to as Céspedes) was governor of East Florida, 1784-90. McGillivray promised repeatedly to go to St. Augustine to visit him but he never did. Zéspedes, however, was McGillivray's most consistent supporter among the Spanish officials.
28. In an earlier memorial, dated July 21, 1784, Panton had urged the advisability of a Pensacola store (Spanish translation, enclosed with Zéspedes to Conde de Gálvez, August 16, 1784, AGI SD 2543). Upon the recommendation of Conde

Majestys forces, Governor & Captain General of the City of St. Augustine, and province of E. Florida &c. &c. &c.

The Memorial of Panton, Leslie & Co.

MAY IT PLEASE YOUR EXCELLY:

By two Gentlemen just arrived overland from W. Florida, we have received letters from Alexr. McGillivray, principall of the Creek Nation of Indians, & Agent for His Most Catholic Majesty; intimating, that information had reachd the Indians & traders, of An Almost total Want of Good[s] at our Indian Stores, which Unless Speedily Supplied, will inevitably be Attended with dangerous Consequences; needless to Specify here, as they must be Sufficiently apparent to your Excelly. We further beg leave to mention to your Excelly, that it will be impossible for us to fulfill a promise made by our partner W. Panton lately, to His Excelly Don Arturo ONeil, Governor of Pensacola; to furnish a Small Supply of goods, for the Necessitys of the Indians in the Vicinity of that Government, from our Stores in this City; which on his return hither he found empty of Indian goods, ignorant at such a distance of time & place; that they had been taken off in his absence by the British Governor & Superintendent of Indians at St. Augustine, who had previously exhausted the Kings Stores. We therefore earnestly Sollicit Your Excellys. Attention to the Necessity of granting permission for the transportation of a part of the Indian goods we expect at N. Providence, to our trading house at Appalachie; & the remainder of them to this place, which will serve for a temporary Supply to the Indians, Untill a further one can be procured; & in this your Excelly. will perceive of how much importance it is, to Save time at this particular juncture, Not only for the reasons above alluded to, but also on Acct. of the approaching tempestuous Season: which May frustrate our Most faithfull & Zealous exertions in His Catholic Majestys Service, if the business Should be delayd till its arrivall. St. Augustine, E. Florida the 10th Septr. 1784

PANTON LESLIE & Co. [*rubric*]

18. *McGillivray to McLatchy, September 18, 1784*
[Spanish translation in LC EF 116L9]

SIR   LITTLE TALLASSIE, 18 September 1784

Yesterday I received letters from St. Augustine from Governor Zespedes and another from Mr. Panton, urging me to come at once to that place, which is absolutely impossible for me in my present cir-

---

de Gálvez the court approved the licensing of Panton to bring Indian trade goods to Pensacola from the Bahamas (Gálvez to José de Gálvez, May 6, 1785, AHN E 3898, and José de Gálvez to Gálvez, October 10, 1785, draft *ibid.*).

cumstances. One of my reasons is that a negotiation is pending between Governor Houston of Savannah and me. When Mr. Panton was here I wrote him a strong talk, which he has received. It was argued in the council, and was not a production of mine. Nevertheless, in his reply, he says to me that the matter of my talk is of such importance and magnitude that he will take the occasion very soon to submit it to the consideration of the legislature, which is certain to be convened this month. I have returned him an appropriate reply and have submitted to his future consideration that he recommend to them that they determine upon Indian affairs, if not upon the principles of equity and justice, at least upon those of sane politics, attending to the demands of the Indians, for only thus could there be honor and security for both parties. Enough of politics! The other reason that I have is having given my word to Governor Miro to be in New Orleans early in November to wait there briefly for the reply to the memorial sent to the court.[29]

I am greatly pleased to know that the goods have arrived at Providence. Mr. Panton wrote me that he was about to go there to get them. As our Creeks are by nature impatient, most of them, fearing frustration, wish to turn to the trader Clarke[30] on the Ogenche [Ogeechee] River (in Georgia), but as soon as goods are gathered at Pensacola, all the trade of the Upper Creeks will be concentrated there because it is so readily at hand. The establishment of the new house, if well conducted, cannot fail to be lucrative, and as the material is, so certainly will I be pleased to see your propositions for that which concerns my part.

The character which Governor O'Neill gives of Mr. Panton is that he seems to be a professing Calvinist, Scotch, and very pleasing to our people. I thank you greatly for the English papers. Old England finds herself split into factions which struggle for control, and the King, poor fellow, is not even equal to the President of Congress. I would rather remain governor of my savages than change places with him. I am, etc.,

ALEXANDER MACGILLIVRAY

Mr. Charles MacLatchy

29. Two days later, in a letter to John Leslie, McGillivray mentioned a third excuse. "I received a blow on the leg that has made it totally impossible for me to mount a horse. I got some remedies from Mr. Panton when he was here. They are used up and I find myself very little better" (Spanish translation in LC EF 114J9). On October 2 he presented the same excuses to Governor Zéspedes through the latter's secretary, Carlos Howard (*ibid.*).

30. Elijah Clarke was the Georgian most active in the Indian trade. A distinguished leader in the American Revolution, he accepted a French commission in the Gênet conspiracy in 1793. He subsequently endeavored to establish a "trans-Oconee state" in the territory of the Creeks, but was defeated in this effort by the Georgia authorities.

19. *McGillivray to McLatchy, October 4, 1784*
[Spanish translation in LC EF 116L9]

SIR

I wrote by conduct of Moniack, who, I suppose, has about reached you. I did not oppose his setting off, though I had not been advised that you were ready to receive him. I hope that your goods arrived in time to satisfy him; now that the time is fulfilled Francisco is setting off. All the traders of Clarke (the Georgian established on the Ogeechee River) were with me a few days ago asking permission to go down and back to adjust their accounts. I suspect that Clarke has arranged their accounts in such a manner as to enable them to make another journey. I saw no difficulty in granting their request, in view of Governor O'Neill's intimating to me a desire that I treat the American party suavely, and I granted them until next December to remove their property; after that time (I have given them notice of my intention) no one from there will be permitted to trade in this part of the nation.

It is not necessary to mention to you, who are so well acquainted with the nature of Indian trade, how necessary a copious supply of blankets and munitions is at this time. After what we have experienced on this point I do not doubt that future importations will be arranged to this end. The establishment of a house at Pensacola, notwithstanding the appearance of some inconveniences that may result, must be determined, for on mature reflection I consider that the advantages that will result from such a method (independent of the Indian trade) will counterbalance whatever risk you run in prosecuting it. I shall point out to you one good effect that it will have. Although many set out from these towns with the intention of carrying their furs to St. Marks of Apalache, when they arrive at the Lower Towns the agents of Clarke never fail (through making them run a gauntlet of malicious falsehoods) to make them take the left hand road to the place called Baird Bluff. All those whom I have seen prefer the idea of trading at Pensacola to anywhere else.

Since I have taken a share in the interests of your house, I am determined to work with interest and integrity. Consequently, I am going to communicate now a matter that until now was no more than conjectural, for which reason I have not related it to you before. Prior to the congress that we held with the Spaniards at Pensacola at the time when I proposed the alliance with this nation, I solicited permission to provide the Indians with a trade of British manufactures through any of the ports of the Spanish Floridas. I was answered by letter that in the congress all sorts of indulgences along this line would be granted us. Consequently, it was no secret in New Orleans that certain trading privileges were to be granted me. Therefore, at the time of the congress various propositions were made me by gentlemen (who had for a long time solicited the same without effect) to form a plan of trade on conditions very favorable to me. Among them was a certain Mr. Mather (formerly of the house of Morgan and Mather), who was recommended to me very warmly by Governor Miró and the intendant general. I alleged a previous commitment to your house. A Spanish official of distinction advised me not to refuse absolutely Mather's offer, for he could prejudice any other trading business, and intimating also very particular motives on which was founded the support that Mr. Mather had obtained; but even if I were to continue opposed it would not effect the project, and that they could not concede privileges except on the footing of the permit conceded to me and consequently I relented in some degree. As the conversation among the others was in French, I understood that they would include Mr. Mather as interested with me in the Indian trade. Governor Miró insisted that I should go to New Orleans in November to receive the stipulations of the court, and I gave my word to do so if I could conveniently. Thus we separated and had no more words on this subject until a few days later when I received a letter from Mr. Mather, in which he told me that he had sent the necessary authority to his correspondents in England to send out at once a ship with goods. I thought that his purpose was to establish himself at Mobile. This step was to attract most of the trade of the Choctaws and Chickasaws to that place, though I perceive that the Indian trade is not the sole object of that house. After I received that letter I decided to give you an account of it all for your guidance.[31]

Mr. Panton has written me that he will be with you shortly, wherefore this letter and my other by Moniack are submitted to his consideration as well as yours, and it would please me greatly to have a full reply on this subject. I wish that this affair which began so auspiciously was fully concluded. The concern that I show on this point, I assure you, does not spring entirely from motives of interest, my object is to assure for my poor, abandoned compatriots all the advantages that seem to me possible. From the slight conversation that I have had with Mr. Panton he seems to me too hesitant about risking his property with the Spaniards. I do not fear it; I recall the adage Nothing ventured, nothing gained. Moreover, in order to assure themselves of our alliance and attachment, they have bound themselves by treaty that the trade in question shall be permanent. I am etc.

ALEXANDER MACGILBRAY

Mr. Charles MacLatchy

31. A similar explanation of the transaction with Mather is contained in McGillivray to Leslie, September 20, 1784, LC EF 114J9.

20. *McGillivray to O'Neill, November 20, 1784*
[AGI C 197]

LITTLE TALLASSIE, November 20th, 1784

SIR

I have taken this opporty. to Acquaint Your Excellency that I have been detaind at home so long in expectation of receiving some dispatches from the American Governor of Georgia in answer to what I wrote him about our Lands on the Oconee river. The other day the tame King arrived from Augusta & I have the Satisfaction to Inform Your Excellency that the americans have given a very Satisfactory answer. The Governor & assembly have forbid the Settling of those lands in the Strongest Manner, so that the apprehensions I had that we Shoud be obliged to go to war with them to defend our lands is now at an end. But I must observe to Your Excellency that the americans are very uneasy that this Nation has enterd into an alliance with the Spanish Nation, & that they have granted leave to English Merchants to Supply this Nation with a trade from the Floridas, because such Measures have made the Indians Independent, & not beholden to the americans for trade, so that they cant have the Sway of the Indians but have lost it, by this Stroke of Policy in the King of Spains officers, who held the Congress with this nation in Pensacola. These are the true reasons that makes the americans pretend to be so moderate to us, tis out of their Jealousy to Spain, & I do not thank them for it. . . . .

21. *McGillivray to McLatchy, December 25, 1784*
[Spanish translation in LC EF 116L9]

LITTLE TALLASSIE, 25 December, 1784

SIR

D mg[32] and Moniack arrived here about ten days ago, the former almost dead, but he has regained his health. All the articles that you sent me came intact except the fancy goods of silver, and that which D. Mg. brought which was short in quantity. It is probable that Beeks has what is lacking. Nothing ever gave me so much satisfaction as your report of the safe arrival of the goods and that they were in good condition. The long detention of the people caused me great anxiety, and I am sure it was the same with you. Clarke as usual spread rumors that the ships had been wrecked, and these rumors did harm. The murmuring of the traders obliges me to mention to you that many articles, blankets, cloths, and shirts, are inferior in quality to those of Clarke's

32. Dan McGillivray, who frequently acted as a letter carrier. He may have been Alexander's brother, mentioned by Panton in document 207, *infra*, or more probably the nephew mentioned in Pope, *Tour*, p. 46.

and higher in price. I sincerely wish that attention should be given to these points. Since the goods of Apalache are sold to the Indians one or two marks dearer than those of Clarke's their murmuring and their complaints that they are not given justice are well founded. I assure you that my complaints spring from my anxiety for the credit of your house. The reason that your goods are so badly selected is because due attention is not paid to the orders which are sent to the manufacturers in England and because the articles are not inspected at the warehouses at the time of shipment.

Our friend Governor O'Neill has written me many times about the movements of Mr. Panton. I cannot refrain from observing to you that there seems to be on your part too great an appearance of lack of confidence and of distrust in your attempts to establish yourselves by virtue of the toleration conceded us. In all that I have seen thus far the Spaniards are well disposed to fulfill the agreement with us. In the memorial that I presented in the congress to open up the trade on their coasts, I explained in the best fashion that I could the wise policy of granting us such toleration, adding various instructions that their friendship without trade would be of very little value to us, and as they were informed of the conditions on which they could or could not conciliate and maintain our friendship, they had too much concern for the peace and well-being of the Floridas not to guard carefully against making us their enemies by denying us a toleration which was conceded to us in a most solemn fashion. This being the case, you may be sure that if they propose to break their promises I will then declare to them, as frankly as I have now to you, that they can not count on our friendship.

As to the business of Mather, I have received letters from him, telling me that I may have an equal share in his house provided that it is approved by the five partners. I do not doubt that the share will be admitted. The house will be established at Mobile in order to carry on more conveniently the trade with the Choctaw and Chickasaw Nations, for having discussed this point, we have found that that trade could not be handled from Apalache, the traders of these nations refusing to risk their pack horses in this country, and we have not been able to find another method to preserve that trade. The same arguments, more or less, offer against carrying on this trade through Pensacola. For these reasons and to prevent the Americans engrossing this trade, I accepted the partnership with Mr. Mather, to carry it on from Mobile, all the traders from these nations having given me their approval.

Clarke thought the place an excellent one and planned to possess

85

himself of that trade by establishing stores in the upper towns, but he will be dealt a blow by the arrival of the goods at Mobile next month. The house of Mather and Company is put on exactly the same footing as yours. Its permit is due to my actions with a view to placating the Indians; though he made many requests, Mather never gained such permission from the government until my concurrence. Furthermore, it was not actually for Mr. Mather or for myself that I consented; you know that one good turn deserves another. For at once to adjust the point with your house, and in order to give him with all openness my thoughts on the offer that Mr. Panton had made me so freely at the time of the establishment at Apalache, and in consideration of the inconveniences to which you were exposed to carry on that commerce, I admitted with pleasure what part (in the business) you had found convenient to assign me.[33]

I have no family which obliges me to accumulate possessions; for although I have some negroes and a few dependents, since I cannot use wealth in this country and expect never to leave it, all that I want is a decent living. Though I have accepted a commission from the Spaniards, I did not stipulate any salary, because I consider that the permit conceded me will repay whatever work their business causes me. They assured me, however, that the king would assign me a stipend and that I could count on it as soon as the court's reply arrived.

I have the satisfaction to inform you that my last talk to the American states produced the desired effect. They have declared it to be their invariable determination to remove all reasons for complaint and that no one, under any pretext whatever, will be permitted to settle on the lands in question, and they have promised to send me formal despatches on this particular next February. Clarke has written me that the principal heads contemplate restoring to me all my property and that of my father, located in the states, and that this business will be carried out in the present session of the Assembly, and he does not doubt that it will be approved unanimously for I have more friends among them than I had thought. This will be a capital thing for me, but if the offer comes accompanied by any conditions which could subject me to any imputation on the part of my friends, for tempting as the offer is and valuable as the properties are, as you know, without any hesitation I shall refuse them etc. etc.

A trader is now with me. It seems that some of Clarke's principal traders are discontented. If due respect is accorded the suggestions that

33. But Panton professed himself astonished and mortified at this action and announced his determination to force McGillivray to separate himself from one house or the other (Panton to John Leslie, March 21, 1785, LC EF 116L9).

I have made you about the trade goods, your house will feel the good effects and an increase of traders. I am &c.

ALEXANDER MACGILLIVRAY

Charles Mac-Latchy

22. McGillivray to Zéspedes, May 22, 1785[34]
[LC EF 114J9]

PENSACOLA 22d May 1785

SIR

I take the Liberty by this opportunity of making Your Excellency my Apology for not having done myself the honor of Waiting upon You long before this at St. Augustine; it has always been my earnest desire to do So but being Well acquainted with the turbulent & restless disposition of our American Neighbourhood & of Consequence I have been obliged to Watch their Motions with the most unremitting attention in order to Make some discoveries of their designs either against my people or the Kings territories. My being now at this place is owing to Something of these Matters which I judged it proper for the Kings Governors to know. A Short time ago I received Authentic Intelligence that some of the American States had appointed Commissioners to go & to ascertain the exact place where the 31st degree of North latitude woud Include on the Mississippi & elsewhere & that a body of 2500 men under two Generals were on the said River ready to take possession by force & establish themselves wherever the Commissioners shoud direct.[35]

The Inhabitants here before my Coming down were alarmd with a report that the Americans were coming against this place. I have

34. The first two paragraphs of this letter have been printed in the *American Historical Review* (XV, 74-75). Writing to Miró on May 16, McGillivray made similar apology for his failure to come to New Orleans. He transmitted the rumors of the American boundary commissioners and of the army on the Ohio, and expressed thanks for the assurance of Spanish support which would enable the Creeks "to make a powerfull Stand, against the Americans encroaching to the Southward beyond their own real boundarys." He continued: "I beg leave to offer you my earnest acknowledgement for the Suit of clothes you did me the honor to Send me & which I have received from the hands of Lt. Govr. Piernas & permit me to add Sir, that I hope the Conduct of my people upon every Occasion will continue to merit the attention & favors that the Kings Government has been pleased to bestow upon them & for my own part I hope my Actions will always Shew the Integrity of my Heart toward it" (AGI C 198).

35. In his letter to Miró on May 16 [see note 34, *supra*] McGillivray identified these generals as [John] Montgomery and [George Rogers] Clark. Congress appointed Clark and two others on April 18 to treat with the Northwest Indians, and in the fall he came to the Ohio with a small force and built blockhouses at the site of Cincinnati (James, *George Rogers Clark*, pp. 334-37). His actions are not a sufficient explanation of the reports that came to McGillivray, which seem rather to reflect the hopes of the Georgians with respect to their projected Bourbon County. See Burnett, "Papers relating to Bourbon County," *American Historical Review*, XV, 66-111, 297-353.

87

quieted their apprehensions on this Score by pointing out to them the Impracticability of such an attempt even if the Americans were really serious in such a design as not only the great distance by land but that they woud have to encounter with a powerfull Indian Nation thro whose country they woud be under a Necessity to March & that while those Indians continued to be on the good footing that they are now on with the Spanish Nation the Americans never woud attempt any thing of the kind.

This leads me to observe to Your Excellency that Mr. Pantons arrival here with the Supplys he has brought with him for the Indian Trade at this Juncture has been attended with the very best effects to his Majestys Interest with my people of the Creek Nations & the other Western ones, they consider it as a proof of the kings Sincere freindship toward them in Confirming the Articles respecting trade as agreed upon in general Congress held here in June last. I hope the king will in his goodness secure to us a permanency of trade & Support through the channel it has Commenced in.

At the Congress a House at Orleans [Mather and Strother] was recommended by the Governor to open & carry on our trade. We have been long in expectation of their Vessells arrival. None has as yet appeared nor can We now expect one, & if it had not been for the extraordinary exertions of Messrs. Panton Lesslie & company to throw in so ample & timely a Supply of Goods it woud have been attended with embarrassing Consequences, the Indians woud have begun to doubt of the Sincerity of the proceedings of the Congress that had [been] held between us & in the moment of Want & distress for Necessarys I'm not Certain but that the overtures of the americans woud have made some Impression upon them, as those people have been using all their Art & address to overturn & destroy the engagements enterd into by the Creeks & other Nations with the Crown of Spain & in particular they wish to gain my people over to their Interest, with the most liberal offers, which has been as Constantly rejected by us as being fully determined to Stand true & firm to our engagements with the Spanish Nation.

As to my own particular I have tis well known Sacrificed a Considerable property to these principles & to the great desire that I have to secure the Welfare of my people & if the Sound policy of keeping open the ports of the Floridas to the Indian Nations to receive their proper Supplys be Confirmd on a permanent footing the king will certainly Secure the attachment & affections of all the Indian Nations & who want only to be properly Supported to Cause them to be the most formidable Check to the ambitious Views of the americans upon

88

East & West Florida & over which Nations I retain a Considerable Influence as principal in the late general Confederacy of the Indian Nations in favor of the English Nation & whose attachment I am resolved to transfer over to his Most Catholic Majesty.

I beg leave to Mention to Your Excellency the propriety of Supporting the establishment of Apalachy, & that on St. Johns River, the former being evidently within the limits of your Government of East Florida, whatever may be advanced to the Contrary, beside as in that Neighbourhood a Considerable Number of Indians reside in many towns, who ought to be Supported equally with other parts of the Creek Nations.

Mr. Panton Informs me that the passports that Your Excellency was pleased to furnish him fully answerd all the good effects they were Intended for & enabled him to prosecute this so much desired business without difficulty, & as this business must be Conducted with vigour now tis set on foot, permit me to remark to Your Excellency, there is an absolute Necessity for his Majestys Governors to depart in some Measure from the Strict regulations that have been hitherto observd in the kings Colonies, a more liberal Intercourse will be Now Necessary. An establishment here to be well Supported will require as soon as any Needfull article is expended that it Shoud as Soon as possible be again procured to Accomplish which with effect bye trips with a Small Craft is unavoidable, & on these Indispensable occasions passports coud be given, as this House Strictly Speaking being a political affair, any Matters respecting extra Indulgences may with a good deal of propriety be deemd for the Kings Service.

I have to beg Your Excellencys pardon for troubling you with so long a letter but having an Idea that there woud be no impropriety in my offering you my opinions & advice on the foregoing Subject, as I had at the Congress in June last accepted a Commission for Superintending the Kings Indian Affairs for his Service, & this letter Your Excellency may Consider as official.

In Conclusion I beg leave to offer You my Warmest acknowledgements for the Steady attention You have been pleased to Shew for our concerns & I Sincerely hope Your generous Exertions will meet with the warmest approbation of Your Court, as the Steps Your Excellency has hitherto pursued has tended in the greatest Measure to promote the real Interest of Your Country in engageing the Confidence & affection of the Creek Indians, thereby Securing the ease & repose of Your Government, the good effects of which will be felt throughout the Whole.

I am with the Most respectfull Esteem, Sir

Your Excellencys Most obedt. Servant

ALEX: McGILLIVRAY [*rubric*]

His Excellency Governor De Zespedes

23. *McGillivray to O'Neill, July 6, 1785*
[AGI C 198]

LITTLE TALLASSIE, July 6th, 1785

SIR

It was with great pleasure that I heard of Your Excellency being safe arrived to your Government. I waited a long Time at Pensacola, expecting your arrival but finding myself to get unwell I left the place. Mr. Panton not coming to Pensacola before you left it, was rather unlucky for us, but I have that Confidence in Your Excellencys good disposition toward us that no material Inconvenience will proceed from his being so late in coming. It will be a great Satisfaction to me to hear that through Your Excellencys Interest with his Excellency Conde de Galvez,[36] that he has approved of everything you have been pleased to recommend in my behalf & my people. The Americans shew a great Inclination to persist in getting the Indian Lands from them, & the Americans have so many reports about their designs upon the Mississippi, I cant find out what they would be doing. The Algerines has made war upon them & have taken a great many of their vessels in the Levant & carried their crews into Slavery. I think they are well matcht, for the americans & the algerines are both alike & one is not better than the other. I wish you every happiness & remain with great esteem

Your Excellencys most obedt Servant

ALEX: McGILLIVRAY [*rubric*]

The bearer Mr. Scott requests Your Excellencys favor respecting a run away Negro of his in Town.

His Excellency. Gov. ONeil

24. *McGillivray for the Chiefs of the Creek, Chickasaw, and Cherokee Nations,*
July 10, 1785[37]

[Copy in AGI C 198]

WHEREAS We the Cheifs and Warriors of the Creek Chickesaw and

36. Bernardo de Gálvez, nephew of the famous minister of the Indies, José de Gálvez, had won a great reputation during the American Revolution. As governor of Louisiana he had rendered valuable assistance to the patriots. When Spain entered the war he was put in charge of operations in America and in three brilliant campaigns wrested West and East Florida from the British. By way of reward the king made him Conde de Gálvez and captain general of Cuba, Louisiana, and the Floridas, as well as governor of the latter. In 1784 he was in Spain, but retained these various titles and the salaries pertaining thereto. Later he was to become one of New Spain's most popular viceroys. See Caughey, *Gálvez in Louisiana.*
37. An index to the importance attached to this and the following document is

Cherokee Nations having received information that an Envoy has been appointed by his Most Catholic Majesty the King of Spain for the purpose of settling the boundarys of his territorys and those of the States of America, and as we have reason to Apprehend that the American Congress in those important matters will endeavour to avail themselves of the Late treaty of peace between them & the British Nation and that they will aim at getting his Majesty the King of Spain to confirm to them that Extensive Territory the Lines of which are drawn by the Said treaty and which includes the whole of our hunting Grounds to our Great injury and ruin—It behoves us therefore to object to, and We Cheifs and Warriors of the Creek Chickesaw and Cherokee Nations, do hereby in the most solemn manner protest against any title claim or demand the American Congress may set up for or against our lands, Settlements, and hunting Grounds in Consequence of the Said treaty of peace between the King of Great Brittain and the States of America declaring that as we were not partys, so we are determined to pay no attention to the Manner in which the British Negotiators has drawn out the Lines of the Lands in question Ceded to the States of America—it being a Notorious fact known to the Americans, known to every person who is in any ways conversant in, or acquainted with American affairs, that his Brittannick Majesty was never possessed either by session purchase or by right of Conquest of our Territorys and which the Said treaty gives away. On the contrary it is well known that from the first Settlement of the English colonys of Carolina and Georgia up to the date of the Said treaty no tittle has ever been or pretended to be made by his Brittanic Majesty to our lands except what was obtained by free Gift or by purchase for good and valuable Considerations.

We can urge in Evidence upon this occasion the Cessions of Lands made to the Carolinians and Georgians by us at different periods and one so late as June 1773 of the Lands lying on the bank of the River OGeechee for which we were paid a Sum not less than one hundred and twenty thousand pounds Stg. nor has any treaty been held by us Since that period for the purpose of granting any land to any people whatever nor did we the Nations of Creeks, Chickesaws and Cherokees do any act to forfeit our Independance and natural Rights to the Said

their wide circulation. Copies are extant in AGI C 37, 198, and 2352, in AHN E 3898, in BL LC, in AGP H 162, and in AN EI 598. A Spanish translation is printed in Serrano y Sanz, *España y los Indios Cherokis y Chactas*, pp. 21-23. In transmitting it to Gálvez on September 4, 1785, O'Neill observed: "Yet I expect these nations to embrace the trade that the Americans offer, and I expect that McGillbray, a native Talapuche, will follow willingly the resolution of the Indians his compatriots for greater profits, notwithstanding that at present they prefer our friendship and solicit its continuation" (AGI C 37).

King of Great Brittain that could invest him with the power of giving our property away unless fighting by the side of his soldiers in the day of battle and Spilling our best blood in the Service of his Nation can be deemed so.

The Americans altho' sensible of the Injustice done to us on this occasion in consequence of this pretended claim have divided our territorys into countys and Sate themselves down on our land, as if they were their own. Witness the Large Settlement called Cumberland and others on the Mississippi which with the Late attempts on the Occonnee Lands are all encroachments on our hunting Grounds.

We have repeatedly warned the States of Carolina and Georgia to desist from these Encroachments and to confine themselves within the Lands [granted] to Brittain in the Year 1773. To these remonstrances we have received friendly talks and replys it is true but while they are addressing us by the flattering appellations of Friends and Brothers they are Stripping us of our natural rights by depriving us of that inheritance which belonged to our ancestors and hath descended from them to us Since the beginning of time.

As His most Gracious Majesty was pleased to Express his favorable disposition toward all those Nations of Indians who implored his favor and protection and which we the Cheifs and Warriors of the Nations aforesaid did do in General Congress, held at Pensacola in June 1784 receiving at the same time his Gracious assurances of protection to us, our respective propertys and Hunting Grounds—Relying thereupon and having the greatest Confidence in the Good faith, humanity and Justice of His Most Gracious Majesty the King of Spain we trust that he will enter into no terms with the American States that may Strengthen their claims or that may tend to deprive us of our Just inheritance.

And we request that your Excellency will have the Goodness to forward this Memorial and representation so that it may reach the foot of his Majestys throne. Humbly entreating that He will be pleased to take the same into his Royal consideration and that he will give his Said Envoy at the Americans Congress such orders respecting the premises as he in his great wisdom and Goodness may think fitte.[38]

We conclude with the Sincerest assurances of our firmest attachment

38. Spain's envoy at New York from 1785 to 1789 was Diego de Gardoqui. A note on his career is to be found in Whitaker, *Documents*, pp. 233-34. Forwarding copies of these documents to him on October 27, 1785, Conde de Gálvez observed: "Since we have to obtain the separation of the Americans from our territory, it is necessary to have our friendship with the Indians assured and to take advantage of many occasions like the present to propitiate them" (AGI C 2352). Gardoqui's response was to ask for more definite instructions on the matter of the boundary, "an issue of moment to the Creeks" (Gardoqui to Floridablanca, May 13, 1786, AHN E 3893).

to Him and Gratitude for any favor His Most Gracious Majesty may procure us on this occasion.

Done at LITTLE TALLASSIE IN THE UPPER CREEK NATION

   This 10th July 1785

by order and in behalf of the Said Indian Nations

(Signed) ALEX: McGILLIVRAY

25. *McGillivray to O'Neill, July 24, 1785*
[AGI C 198]

PENSACOLA, 24th July 1785

SIR

Some little time ago Deputies from the Nations of Creeks Chickesaws & Cherokees, met in a general Convention at which I was present in the Upper Creeks & upon Consulting upon the present posture of Affairs they desired me to deliver their Sentiments in writing by Memorial and representation[39] to Your Excellency requesting the favor that you would be pleased to forward same with all Convenient Speed to your Court & which I have accordingly enclosed to Your Excellency as I was directed by the Above named Indian Nations.

These Nations are exceedingly well Satisfied at the arrival of the Supply of Indian Trading Goods brought by Mr. Panton for the Support of their Nations & they expect that the Trade thus begun will be established on the most permanent footing as was promised them in Congress. The Supply being now nearly expended, another Importation is become absolutely necessary.

The Americans ever Since the Congress of last year (which to them is a matter of much discontent) have been using every means in their power to Seduce these Nations from the engagements they have entered into with the Spanish Nation, particularly by offers of a Liberal Trade & which it is Certainly in their power to afford to the Indians, being at full liberty of Importing & exporting directly to & from London & their not being Subjected to heavy dutys & charges.

At present the recollection of past Injurys & the Strong Jealousy which Subsists among them lest they Should be deprived of their hunting Grounds (the greatest Injury an Indian can form an Idea of) affords a favorable opportunity of effecting a total Separation of those Nations from the Americans & of establishing an Interst Among them for the Spanish Nation which will not be easily dissolved, and which it is my most ardent wishes to accomplish. But if they are not allowed their usual Supplys from this place, necessity must compel them to accept the Friendship of the American States, through which Channel

39. Document 24, *supra.*

93

They will be Supplyd with all their accustomd necessarys to the exclusion of every power on the Continent. it is therefore my Opinion that it would be good policy to withdraw the duty which is at present laid upon this business especially the dutys on the exports of Skins & that measures be adopted to put the Indian Trade upon the easiest terms possible, agreeable to promises which has been made to them & which they respect.

Mr. Panton who has been long connected in this business & well Inclined to forward the Views of Government within his line & who is most Capable & able to furnish Goods equal to the Demand of the Indians, has been applyd to by me on the Subject of another Importation & I've requested of him to State to Your Excellency, the Terms & Conditions, on which he can with Safety continue to Import Goods for the Support of the Indian Nations in Alliance with his Majesty the King of Spain.

These matters being of great Importance I must earnestly entreat Your Excellency to recommend & cause to be established, what I have had the Honor, thus to represent to you in the foregoing Matters. I am With the Greatest respect Sir

Your Excellencys Most Obedt. Servant

ALEX: McGILLIVRAY [rubric]

His Excelly. Gov. O'Neil

26. *McGillivray to Miró, August 20, 1785*

[AGI C 198]

PENSACOLA, 20th August 1785

SIR

This Serves to acknowledge the receit of Your Excellencys most esteemd favor of 19 June. I beg Your Excellency to be assured that whenever any matters of Intelligence or Information That any way affects his Majestys Interest can be obtained by me I shall always make the earliest opportunity to transmit them to you to be warnd of every such matter.

The Reports of the Americans Desires & Intentions toward the Mississippi continued to gain ground,[40] & I believe with good Foundation, as they have been uncommonly Solicitous for a few months back in endeavouring to prevail upon the Creeks to meet them in Congress with a view of Settling all Differences & renewing treaties of Commerce

40. In a letter to Zéspedes on August 22, 1785, McGillivray reported that the Americans were moving in great numbers to the Mississippi and that they would "Certainly attempt to establish a New State in that Country at the risque of a war," but that to do so they would first have to win the Creeks over to them (LC EF 114J9).

& other matters which Invitations & offers we have constantly rejected & will continue to Refuse, these offers are made with Insidious views, as I well know from their present wicked disposition. They want to make use of the aid of the Indians to bad purposes. We rather rely on his Most Gracious Majestys assurancy to us in the late Congress, for a Support of trade & commerce, to be established on a permanent footing a representation for which purpose we have lately offerd to his Majesty to have the same Speedily effected.

Permit me to make my warmest Acknowledgements for that distinguishing mark of favor that his Most Gracious Majesty had been pleased to Shew to me & which Your Excellency has so obligingly notified to me. Praying that Yourself & the truly Amiable Madam Miro may enjoy many years of uninterrupted happiness & Felicity.

I have the Honor to be with the greatest Respect, Sir

Your Excellencys Most Obedient & Humble Servant

ALEX: McGILLIVRAY [rubric]

III

REJECTION OF AMERICAN OVERTURES

27. *Hawkins,*[41] *Pickens,*[42] *and Martin*[43] *to the Creeks, June 10, 1785*
[AGI C 121]

41. Benjamin Hawkins left the senior class at the College of New Jersey at the outbreak of the Revolution to join Washington's staff as French interpreter. He was a member of Congress, 1781-84 and 1786-87, and United States Senator from North Carolina, 1789-95. Then he became agent to the Creeks and general superintendent of the Indians south of the Ohio. For sixteen years he kept them at peace, instructed them in agriculture and animal husbandry, and earned for himself the name, "Beloved Man of the Four Nations." He was, in a way, successor to McGillivray in dominant influence over the Southeastern Indians. See his "Sketch of the Creek Country," Georgia Historical Society *Collections*, Vol. III (1848), and his letters, 1796-98, *ibid.*, Vol. IX (1916). See also document 32, *infra*.

42. Andrew Pickens was a pioneer on the South Carolina frontier. He fought with distinction in the Revolution, especially at Cowpens. Hopewell, his plantation on the Oconee, was the scene of treaties with the Chickasaws, Choctaws, and Cherokees in 1785 and 1786. McGillivray came to have an excellent opinion of him; see document 135, *infra*.

43. The biographical dictionaries seem to have overlooked Joseph Martin. One may turn, however, to Stephen B. Weeks, *General Joseph Martin and the War of the Revolution in the West*, and for a shorter sketch to S. C. Williams, *History of the Lost State of Franklin*, pp. 323-26. A veteran of the French and Indian War, of Dunmore's War, and of the Revolutionary War, Martin was also an experienced Indian negotiator, having been commissioned by Patrick Henry to deal with the Cherokees in 1777 and again in 1783 to treat with the Southern Indians. He took an active interest in the settlement of Powell's Valley and of the Great Bend of the Tennessee, but was one of the principal opponents of the state of Franklin.

CHARLESTON, 10 June 1785

To the Kings Headmen and Warriors of the Creeks.

FRIENDS & BROTHERS

The War being over the United States in Congress assembled have ordered their Swords to be Sheathed, and they have appointed five[44] of their trusty and beloved men to meet you the Kings headmen and Warriors of the Creek Nation to treet with you for the purpose of making peace with you and receiving you into their favor and protection and for removing between us all causes of future Contention & Quarrels.

FRIENDS

We are three of the trusty and beloved men and according to the power given us have appointed Galphinton on the River OGeechee to be the place where we will meet you—and the time of meeting will be the 24th day of Octr. next—we shall provide provisions and other things proper for your accomodation while you stay with us at the treaty and we hope you will be punctual in meeting us.

FRIENDS

The united States of America are a great and wise Nation they have a great many Warriors, and have Conquered all their Enemys, and are now desirous of peace with all the World. They remember you were once their friends and they intend to forget that you were their enemies in the Last War. But you must forget it also, and we will take you by the hand.

> BENJAMIN HAWKINS
> ANDREW PICKENS
> JOSEPH MARTIN

28. *Pickens to McGillivray, July 23, 1785*

[Copy in AGI C 121]

GREENWICH [SOUTH CAROLINA], 23rd July 1785

SIR

By Mr. John Brandon this will be delivered and informs you that the United States in Congress assembled have appointed five Commissioners to treat with the Creeks, Cherokees, Chactaws and Chickasaws & all other Indians within the [limits] of the United States of America for the purpose of making [peace] with them and receiving them into their favor and protection and removing as far as may be all causes of Contention and Quarrels.

44. Lachlan McIntosh, who was appointed after David Carroll declined, was not very active in the negotiation. William Perry, the fifth commissioner, did not participate.

96

A Majority of the Commissioners met at Charleston latter end of May last to consult on measures for Carrying the Intentions of Congress into Execution as soon as possible. We then proposed having the treaty early next fall, but as we wish to have an answer from Congress relative to some Matters we are not yet able to appoint the time of meeting the Indians—but would be much obliged to you to acquaint them that the time will not be longer put off than the Commissioners can possibly help, and am in hopes that at our meeting with the Indians every matter will be adjusted and Set upon an [agreeable] footing.[45]

. . . .Some mischief on Cumberland . . . . As it is well known that you have great influence in the Creek Nation it would be rendring great Service to put a Stop to these mischiefs. I am Sir

Your most Obedt. Servt.

ANDREW PICKENS

29. *McGillivray to O'Neill, September 14, 1785*
[AGI C 198]

LITTLE TALLASSIE, 14th September 1785

SIR

I have to Inform Your Excellency that I have received a Notification from Carolina, that the American Congress have appointed five Commissioners to meet Cheifs of these Nations for the purpose of Settling & fixing the Limits & boundary of the Lands between the Indians & the States of America. I have at divers times acquainted Your Excellency of the disputes between the Americans & the Indians on that account & that it might probably at one time or another create a War, & as we desire to do nothing rashly in any affair that may throw the blame on us & prejudice our cause in the Kings mind—Therefore have considered it best to agree to have this matter compleated & put out of all Contention & [I shall] be present at it myself, That Justice may be [done] to my Nation & if that is denied to us & [the Americans] will attempt to fix the Limits, where they please to our Injury, we then can with Justice take measures to do ourselves right & to require with propriety his Most Gracious Majestys Assistance & Support in defending our Just rights.

45. In his reply, dated September 5, 1785, ASP IA, I, 17-18, McGillivray congratulated the United States for proposing a treaty, upbraided it for delaying this action so long, reviewed the relations of the Creeks with Georgia, and explained why the Creeks had solicited the protection of Spain. "I have only to add," he concluded, "that we shall prepare ourselves to meet the commissioners of Congress, whenever we shall receive notice, in expectation that every matter of difference will be made up and settled, with that liberality and justice, worthy of the men who have so gloriously asserted the cause of liberty and independency, and that we shall in future consider them as brethren and defenders of the land."

In the prosecution of this Important affair I entreat of Your Excellency to believe that I am doing nothing Contrary to or prejudicial to the engagement, we are bound in with the Spanish Nation.[46] I find a Caution of this kind necessary as I have found that there are wretches base enough & ready at all Times & on every occasion to asperse my character & give all my actions a wrong turn to their Superiors. I am realy concerned to find that those reports make an Impression on the minds of those Gentlemen who has honord me with their patronage & Friendship.

I confess that I have faults but all that knows me, know that Deceit & Treason are not among them, therefore nothing can be more grating to a generous mind, than to have all its actions watched with Suspicion & Distrust.

It was from the result of my most deliberate Judgement that I engaged my Nation & all others that I had Influence with into a treaty of Alliance & Freindship with the Spanish Nation, because from our respective Situation we coud be of mutual advantage to each other & the Commercial priviledges, we Stipulated for in the Treaty, being the true foundation to establish & fix the Indians firm to the Kings Interest, & I again entreat Your Excellency to recommend that the Articles of the Treaty I Speak of [be] exactly complied with in order that the Indian Nations be kept Intirely Independent of every other [people] for trade of any kind, & its well known & experience teaches us every day that Commerce attaches one people to another.

I have only to add that Your Excellency may be assured that I shall give You the earliest Information how the Indians & the Americans have Settled the grand dispute in question about Lands, & any other Matters that comes to my knowledge in the course of this Negotiation.

I have the Honor to be with the Most Respectfull regard, Sir

Your Excellencys Most Obedt. Servant,

ALEX: McGILLIVRAY [rubric]

His Excelly. Gov. O.Neil

46. When O'Neill advised him not to treat with the Americans, McGillivray accepted the advice. He put in a request, however, for assurance of Spanish support if the Americans should start a war, and continued, "I have in consequence of the above declaration sent off the Lower towns to traverse the Country and wherever any Settlers are found on our Grounds to drive them within their own Boundary but to offer them no injury in their persons or property" (McGillivray to O'Neill, October 10, 1785, AGI C 198). In a subsequent letter he predicted that his property in the United States would be put up for sale because of his refusal to treat with the commissioners (McGillivray to O'Neill, October 26, 1785, *ibid.*). O'Neill forthwith urged that the Spanish court should "intercede and insist" that the United States leave the Creeks in peace without encroaching on their territory (O'Neill to Gálvez, October 31, 1785, AGI C 2352).

[AGI C 198]

LITTLE TALLASSIE, 8th November 1785.

SIR

When I did myself the pleasure of Writing last to your Excellency You had the letters & Talks that the American Commissioners Sent to us for the purpose of holding a Treaty with the Nations, & which we rejected as we have done all their former requisitions to the same purport.

I believe I can account for the reason why the Americans Seek to Conciliate the friendship of these Indians with so much Solicitude. The Brittish Nation has thought proper to alter the Boundary lines of Canada from that laid down in the Treaty of Peace, & have retained the Forts of De Troit, Niagara & all the other posts on the Lakes, & have lately Strengthend the Works & Reinforced the Garissons Whereby the Northern Nations of Indians are protected & meet with their Usual Support, & have renewed Hostilities against the Americans with great Vigour.

The Policy of your Government in Tolerating the Indian Trade in the manner it now is will not fail of having its effects in keeping up the formidable Indian Confederacy of the late War against the Americans & must always be [a] great check to the States, in preventing their ambitious designs of possessing themselves of all the Western Countrys.

As I have the Strongest desire to See the Americans kept within due bounds, so I have given my Opinion of the best way that can be accomplished & while these Nations Continue to receive the Same Support of Trade & encouragement, Through the Floridas as [the] English Nation afford the Northern Indians from Canada, the Indians will never Solicit the Freindship or the Alliance of the Americans.

I have been Informed that some Choctaw or Chickesaw Traders intend to apply for leave to Settle some land above Mobile as Inhabitants. At Same time I find out that if they obtain permission, they mean to Introduce into that Settlement a fugitive Banditti of Americans who have been banished from Natchez for Seditious practices, & other Vagabonds from Cumberland. To prevent the bad consequences that would arise from the establishment of those miscreants at that place I have to entreat of your Excellency, to advise the Commandant of Mobile not to give his Consent to any person from those Nations to Settle on any pretence Whatever. & Indeed there are Settlers enough already & no more ought to be received from no Country.[47]

47. McGillivray sent this same warning direct to Pedro Favrot, commandant of Mobile (November 7, 1785, AGI C 198).

I intend setting out for Mr. McLatchys in a few days, & from thence to S. Augustine if the Winter Shoud not prove wet & disagreeable & in the Spring shall do myself the pleasure of waiting upon You. Mean Time Remain with my best wishes for Your Excellencys health & happiness.

Your Excellencys Most Obedient & Obliged Servant

ALEX: MCGILLIVRAY [*rubric*]

31. *McGillivray to Panton, December 19, 1785*

[AGI C 198]

APALACHY, December 19, 1785.

DEAR SIR

I had wrote you before I left the Nation by D[aniel] McG[illivray.] I had Intended for Augustine but being desirous [of] learning the event of the Commissioners business with the Indians etc., & finding out that two american expresses had found means to Slip thro. the Nation from Natchez, & wishing to Intercept them on their return with Dispatches, I have postponed going to Augustine as I cant at this time afford to be absent 3 Months which is the least time it will require. I have the other day from here Wrote to Gov. De Zespedes Very fully Concerning our Most Material Occurences in the Nation, american talks &c &c &c.[48] However I Should have Strecht a point to have gone, but as the Gov. in his last to me expressed a desire that I woud be accompanied with Cheifs of Consideration officially the Famous Mad Dog &c. & these being gone to Kill Bear, I didnt think proper to go by myself, & as I Judge by the ensuing Spring our political Situation will be decided upon, We shall have leisure to prosecute other Matters.

Having been at this place but once Since Mr. McLatchys arrival & settlement, I took a Start here to See how he was, & Should have been perfectly Satisfied if I had found the Ship with the Goods had arrived, but that not being the Case we are all exceedingly mortified at the disappointment, great many traders being now in Waiting. We Imagine that as the Cap. Grant is a Stranger to the Coast & the Weather being Hazy some time that She must have passd this & proceeded for Your place. On this Supposition Mr. Dixon is Sent to look out in the Bays & if not finding her to proceed to Pensacola. If She Miscarrys as God forbid, the Nation is reduced to extreme Distress; however we hope for the best.

I remain with greatest Esteem Dear Sir

48. December 10, 1785, LC EF 114J9. Printed in part by Burnett, *American Historical Review*, XV, 348-49.

Yours truly,

ALEX: McGILLIVRAY [*rubric*]

William Panton Esq.

32. *Hawkins to McGillivray, January 8, 1786*
[AGI C 2360]

SENECA, January 8, 1786

SIR

Having an opportunity by our Choctaw Interpreter John Ritchlyieu to convey a letter to you, I am desirous of informing you of the progress the Commissioners appointed to treat with the Southern Indians have made in the execution of their Commission.

On the 24th of October we expected to have had the pleasure of seeing you at Galphinton, with a full representation from your nation, and the more so, as you had been apprized of the intentions of the United States in Congress assembled, which were founded on justice humanity and an attention to the rights of human nature. All nations as far as my memory serves have been governed by a different motive, an acquisition of territory without even giving the semblance of an equivalent for it. And latterly some of your neighbours pretend to doubt whether an Indian can have any rights at all but what are subservient to or dependent on the legislative will of the State claiming Jurisdiction over the lands they live and hunt on.

The Commissioners would not treat with the few of your nation who met them; 1 am since informed that the Agents of Georgia did treat with them, and obtained a cession of your claims to all the lands south of the Altamaha and East of a line to be run southwest from the Junction of Oakmulgée and Oconée till it shall strike St. Marys. They also obtained a confirmation of the treaty made at Augusta in 1783 explaining its extension to the South fork of the Oconée, thence down the same to the river, thence to the Alatamaha.[49]

We arrived here in november, and were met by nine hundred and eighteen of the Cherokees; and the 28th we entered into articles of a treaty with them; In which, we have secured them in the possession of the lands they live and hunt on—made the commission of and punishment for robbery, murder and other capital crimes equal with the citizens and Indians—rejected the Idea of retaliation as unjust and

49. The American commissioner had reported to Congress, on November 17, 1785: "We could not treat with so few of their nation, there being but two towns properly represented, instead of about one hundred" (ASP IA, I, 16). A copy of the treaty of Galphinton, concluded on November 12, 1785, between the Georgia commissioners and two Creek chiefs, the Tame King and the Fat King, is printed in *ibid.*, p. 17. On December 30, Hawkins and Pickens reiterated, "We did not think proper to enter into a treaty with the heads of these towns only" (*ibid.*, p. 49).

made a demand of satisfaction necessary in any violation of the treaty, and the final alternative a declaration of hostilities. We have taken them into the favour and protection of the United States; and the said States are to regulate the trade of the Indians and manage all their affairs for their benefit and comfort.

The Cherokee treaty was made the basis of the Choctaw, which we entered into the third instant. The Chickasaws arrived yesterday, and I expect a treaty will be concluded with them within the present week; we shall then return and report to Congress.[50]

When you have leisure and an opportunity offers, I wish you would let me know the reasons, why the representation of your Nation did not meet the Commissioners of Congress at Galphinton?[51] I wish to know also what progress the Creeks have made in agriculture and whether any in manufactures—what would be proper measures to introduce both, or either—whether your country is a proper one for the raising of fine horses, cattle and sheep and at what expense.

I expect I shall have the pleasure of visiting the Creek Nation in the Spring or next fall, not in a public character but as a private man, desirous of knowing how I can be usefull to your people and of gratifying my feeling of humanity towards them. Perhaps you may think me selfish in the close of my letter but you shall have reason to change your opinion: I shall remove from the Northward into Georgia this year and I mean to settle on the frontier of that State, as near your Nation as I can; and I must request the favour of you to choose for me a young damsel, out of one of your most reputable families, let her be handsome and agreeable, skilled in the customs of her own Country, and of a mind that will feel the station I shall support her in.

I am with respect, Sir

Your most obedient & humble servant,

BENJAMIN HAWKINS [rubric]

Alexander McGillivray, Esqr.

33. *McGillivray to O'Neill, February 10, 1786*

[AGI C 199]

LITTLE TALLASSIE, February 10, 1786

. . . .Your Excellency may recollect that I informd you in October last that the American Congress had appointed Commissioners to hold a Treaty with all the Southern Indians, but I have the Satisfaction

50. For a detailed account of the negotiation of these treaties see ASP IA, I, 37-41, and 49-50.

51. This request was elaborated and emphasized in Hawkins to McGillivray, January 11, 1786, AGI C 2360.

to Inform Your Excellency that there was not twenty Indians in the whole that went to OGeechee, & the few that did go went from motives of Curiosity & were not of any consequence except the Tame King; who is well known to be but a roving beggar, going wherever he thinks he can get presents.

However as far as I can find out the result of the Interview was this, that the Commissioners & Gov. of Georgia quarrelld & thereby rendered themselves Completely ridiculous, in the eyes of the Indians & parted all sides equally dissatisfied with each other.[52]

However the Americans all agree in this one point that it is my fault that they cant bring their Schemes to bear with the Indians, & on that account their attention is engaged in Contriving the manner in which they can bring about my assassination, & then they are Sure they will meet with no Interruption to Succeed in all their plans. I have Stood proof to their attempts to bribe my honesty & I hope I shall have the precaution not to expose my person to afford them the opportunity they so much wish for to assassinate me. However whenever occasion Shall offer I Shall not be backward to give them a Chance to effect their Malice in a more honorable way than they now aim at.

In examining the list of run away negroes. . . . I will preserve the Negro list & if chance Should direct any to these parts you may be assured of them. . . . .

34. McGillivray to O'Neill, March 8, 1786
[AGI C 199]

LITTLE TALLASSIE, March 8, 1786

SIR

I am favord with Your Excellencys letter by Weatherford,[53] but as I had done myself the pleasure to write Your Excellency about the Intelligence received from Philadelphia by an Indian which I hope you have received long Since, & which will explain the affair to you better than Cornels account.

We have been waiting a considerable time to hear the result of the Kings Envoys negotiation with the American Congress. In the mean time the Georgians are encroaching on our hunting Lands. I have repeatedly warned them of the ill consequences of such measures, &

52. Compare with Hawkins' account in document 32, *supra*, and with the reports of the American commissioners in ASP IA, I, 16, 49.

53. Charles Weatherford, a relative of McGillivray, was one of the pack horse men frequently utilized as a letter carrier to and from Pensacola. He was later arrested at Pensacola. McGillivray interceded for his release, but seems to have considered some punishment deserved (McGillivray to O'Neill, April 28, 1786, AGI C 199; and document 79, *infra*).

the dangers it might bring upon them, but they do not listen to it & Still persist in their encroachments. In Consequence I have Yesterday Sent Notice to all the cheifs of the Nation to assemble by the 24th of this month to deliberate & adopt such measures as our occasion call for. Altho I woud wish not to precipitate matters without the Concurrence of the Spanish Nations, Yet I hope they will consider that we have tryed every peaceable Method with the Americans without effect, & that they will act as friends & Guarantees to us in the Contest we are engaging in with the American State of Georgia.

We have no other occurrences worth relating to You, & beg to refer You to my last letters. After expressing a wish to hear from You on the Subject of this letter for your advice, I remain with the Greatest Esteem, Sir

Your Excellencys Most Obdt. Servant,

ALEX: McGILLIVRAY [*rubric*]

Gov. Arturo O'Neil

35. *McGillivray to O'Neill, March 28, 1786*
[AGI C 199]

LITTLE TALLASSIE, March 28, 1786

SIR

When I addressd Your Excellency last I then Informd You that I had Issued orders to all the Chiefs of this Nation to meet in Convention & which has been accomplishd. My Motives for assembling the Chiefs at this early Season was to deliberate upon the Conduct of the Americans toward this Nation (& our Western Neighbours the Chactoaws & Chickesaws) & in the discussion of these matters we observe with much concern that the americans are not at all disposed to Comply with our Just & peaceable remonstrances against their Usurping & settling our hunting Grounds. They Still persist in those oppressive measures, & which without a firm opposition on our parts must effect our destruction.

They have some Settlements & are Settling the oconee up to the Head, & are proceeding to the head of the Alabamoun River, that falls into the Bay of Mobile & from thence they are Stretching across to the Mississippi. Under such Circumstances we cannot be quiet Spectators. We the Chiefs of the Nation have come to a resolution in this last general meeting to take arms in our defence & repel those Invaders of our Lands, to drive them from their encroachments & fix them within their own proper limits.[54]

54. Writing to the Holloing King of the Cowetas on April 14, 1786, McGillivray announced that the "broken days" had been made and sent all over the nation,

This being absolutely a case of the last Necessity, we expect the speedy Interposition of our great Protector his Most Catholic Majesty, his royal word being pledged by his Officers in the Treaty of 1784 to Guarantee & defend our Territories to us.

It is needless to explain to Your Excellency what we have so frequently represented. Yet I Shall repeat to you the pretended Claims of the State of Georgia to the Lands in question,

Those people in the year of 1783 having by fair promises got two of our chiefs of the Second rank among them in Augusta, demanded of them a Cession of hunting Lands belonging to the Nation, which was refused, as knowing that they were not authorized to make any Such Grant. The Georgians finding they coud not prevail with the chiefs, they had recourse to Threats. The chiefs finding their lives in danger Consented, to amuse the americans till they effected their escape, & Since that time they get every Stragling Indian hunter to Sign an Instrument of writing, which they falsely call a Grant, made them by the Nation. This I assure, Your Excellency is the real foundation of the american Claims, as unjust as it is absurd, & which we have frequently represented to them in opposition to their pretensions.

Upon the Whole it will appear that the Nation has acted throughout this affair with a Moderation unexampled among Indians. They did not harshly fly to arms upon a discovery that the Georgians were encroaching upon their Lands, but Submitted a Memorial & humble petition through you to his most Gracious Majesty, the effects of which we have not yet heard of, but Still we have the firmest reliance that it will be productive of all the good we wish & expect from it. But matters approaching a crisis we think proper to Second it with this.

I have now only to observe to Your Excellency that in doing ourselves Justice, we dont engage in general Hostilities with the whole American States. When we free our Hunting Grounds Fronting the Georgians we Stop, & as a means to prevent further consequences we request of Your Excellency, if you can do it with propriety, to notify to the Georgians, that they must leave our Lands free, it being under the protection of his most Catholic Majesty.

When this is done we Shall then have leisure to turn our attention to the Lands we possess toward the Mississippi & toward which the americans are moving in numbers of families. That Quarter ought to be well lookd after, lest by giving time to them they form Considerable

designating April 23 as the day to set off against the Georgians (AGI C 37). The "broken days" was the customary and practical method of appointing a rendezvous. A bundle of sticks was sent, one to be broken each day.

establishments on lands they have no right to, & of Consequence may prove troublesome to remove.

Having a few days Since received a Talk & tokens of freindship from the Chactaw kings, we recommended to them to Consider the americans as Common enemies, to take care & not be duped by their promises—to the Chickesaws we Said the Same.

I have the Honor to be with great Regard Your Excellys. most obedient Servant.

ALEX: McGILLIVRAY [rubric]

Gov. Arturo O'Neil

36. *McGillivray to Miró, May 1, 1786*[55]

[AGI C 2352]

LITTLE TALLASSIE, May 1, 1786

SIR

I have taken this opportunity to write to Your Excellency to give You an account of Indian Occurrences Since the time l had the pleasure of writing to you last.

Ever Since the Congress of Pensacola in 1784 we have observed with much discontent the rapid encroachments made upon our Lands, by the Americans in every quarter that we possess, but particularly by the inhabitants of Georgia, who had encroached greatly to our Prejudice on our best hunting Grounds on the Oconee river & all its waters. In Justification of their encroachments they pretend to a claim of a cession as being made to them by some part of the Nation in the Year 1783, in which year the Americans had Invited the chiefs of the Nation in General to meet them in Congress in Augusta, in order to make a Peace with them. But the chiefs not having a Confidence in them & aware of American treachery only two chiefs of the Second rank & a few followers went to Augusta, to meet the American Governor & council & when instead of treating of a Peace, they demanded a grant of the land of the Oconee to which the chiefs objected as not being authorized by the Nation to consent to any Such demand, the Americans not being Satisfied with this answer the justness of which they well knew, they proceeded to threaten the Chiefs with Instant Death, unless that they complied. It was in vain that they declared that their consent to the Grant of Lands demanded would not be binding on the Nation & that cessions were made only in general Convention an act of the whole Nation who are Joint Proprietors in Common. The Americans kept the chiefs & their followers Surrounded by armd men for five

<hr>

55. McGillivray sent similar despatches to Zéspedes on April 25, LC EF 114J9, and to O'Neill on May 12, AGI C 2352.

days untill they consented to all that was demanded in order to Save themselves from the threatend destruction.

Upon the Nations first receiving notice of this ungenerous transaction, perfidious as it was base, the whole Warriors would have directly attackd the Americans of Georgia but it having been recommended to us by the Kings Governors in Congress to use no violent means in Settling our differences with those people, I accordingly restrained my Warriors from every act of hostility while there was any hope of our obtaining Justice any other way. I then represented to the Governor & Legislature of Georgia the wrongs they were doing to us in encroaching upon & taking our Lands without our Consent or without anything like an equivalent for them & desired them to desist from measures that must soon Involve them in all the Miserys & Horrors of a Savage War. This & Several other representations made in the course of the last two years have had no effect in procuring from them a redress of the Injurys complained of. However in the month of September last, we received notification from three persons, who Signed themselves Benjamin Hawkins, Andrew Pickens, Joseph Martin, three of five Commissioners appointed by the American Congress to treat with the Indian Nations & to Settle all differences & remove all causes for quarrel & contention between the Indians & Americans. They then Invited the chiefs of the Nations to meet them in Congress in the month of October following to be held at Galphinton on OGeechee river. I willing to shew our disposition & Inclination to terminate our disputes in an Amicable Manner with the States, it happened that I could not attend myself, Yet I deputed two chiefs from the upper Towns & two more from the Lower Towns of those I could confide in to execute their Trust & with Instruction to protest in the warmest manner against the encroachments that had been made, to Insist upon all Settlers to be removed & to ascertain & draw a boundary line or rather to explain the old one between us & the English, & which only would be a means to prevent future quarrels between us. However in this desireable affair we were disappointed owing to the disgust conceived by the Commissioners against the Georgians for the wrong measures that the latter were pursuing, & whom without Speaking to the Indian deputys retired from the place of Conference, & the Governor of that State being left to finish the treaty. He so far from Satisfying us respecting our Lands that he even asked for more & Insisted upon a boundary line that plainly proved their Intention to wrest more than one half of our most valuable lands from us.[56] Affairs being thus circumstanced determined me to Call for a General Convention of the whole Nation to deliberate on this

56. Compare with the account in document 32, and note 49, *supra*.

Subject & to adopt Such measures as the Critical posture of our affairs now required. Accordingly the Chiefs of the Following Towns, (being those that always decide on National affairs of Importance) assembled at the Tuckebatchey Town, the Second of April last, the great chief called the Mad Dog presiding in the Council, the chiefs of the Abecootchee, Natchez, Coosaws, Upper Eufauly, Waccokoy, Weokey, Hillabee, OKchoy, Okfuskee, Kyalejie, Great Eufauly, Toushatchie, Ottassie, Cluewally, Tallassies, Coosadas, these of the Upper Nation. Numerous Villages not attending. Of the Lower Nation these principal Towns, the chiefs of the Cowetas, Cussitas, Thlaycatska, Chiaha, Oussitches, Nitchetas, & numerous Villages not attending & who are ruled by the above Towns.

I then opend to the assembly of the Chiefs, the business for which I had called them together, that it was now become highly necessary from the Conduct of the Georgians, to deliberate Seriously on what Steps to take respecting those people, that the transactions of the last Congress fully discovered that under the mark of Friendship they were Contriving our Ruin. That our frequent applications for Justice had been treated with Contempt, & of course the only alternative that was left us, War with arms in our hands to force them abandon their unjust usurpations, & to Set Limits to their ambitious Views on our Country. 1 likewise reminded the Chiefs that we had obtain the protection & patronage of a Great & Powerful King, who in any contest we enter into with our & his Enemies in asserting our rights, will afford us means of Defence & his great Captains in Congress had promised in his name that we Should be Supported in the possession of Lands that our Fathers have owned & possessed, ever Since the first rising of the Sun & the Flowing of the Waters, & which has always been acknowledged as Such & Confirmd to us & Secured in the quiet enjoyment of by our former Protectors the British Nation, when they were Sovereigns of North America, & that we acquit the Congress of any designs against us & believe that the State of Georgia do act in these matters in opposition to the recommendations of that body, Tho to keep up some Shew of form that State has been deceiving Congress to Countenance their proceedings by alledging that we had made a voluntary Cession & Grant to them of the Lands in Question, than which assertion nothing can be more false, & to Support their pretensions, they have recourse to the Shameful transaction of the year 83, when they extorted a consent of two chiefs as before related, & to other forgeries of the like nature which they pretend to have obtain on other occasions, all which forgeries we can prove as tis well known that a proper representation of our Nation never met the Americans in Congress to negotiate any treatys or Compacts whatever. Without such representation no business is ever done by Indian Nations neither do we now Consider ourselves at Liberty to grant any Lands to any People whatever, without the Concurrence of our Most Gracious Protector the King of Spain.

Upon the whole after the most mature deliberation on the foregoing matters, my opinion was for directly adopting the most decided measures in defence of & for the preservation of so great a part of our Lands that altho we have the greatest reliance on the Interposition of our great protector in our behalf, Yet the Artfull Americans might protract the conclusion of these affairs untill they had by fraud & violence possessed themselves of our lands. To prevent future evil being the general policy of all Nations, it was our duty to check the Americans in time before they got too Strong for us to contest with them.

The advice I had thus given to the Chiefs, they unanimously resolved to adopt. I then Issued orders & Instructions needfull for the occasion & directed them to Collect a Sufficient Number of Warriors & to Set out without loss of time & to traverse all that part of the Country in dispute & whenever they found any American Settlers to drive them off & to destroy all the buildings on it but in their progress to conduct themselves with moderation & to shed no blood on no pretence but where Self defence made it absolutely necessary. Neither were they to cross over or within the acknowledged Limits of the States.

The Cheifs then proceeded to execute their Instructions and Parties of Warriors Set out in every direction to whereever the Americans were Settled, & where they were forming new establishments. The Oconee Lands were the first visited & cleard of the Settlers. Other parties went on the Cherokee river to a place called the Muscle Shoals where we were informed the Americans were forming a New Settlement but the Indians found at that place only a few working utensils & some preparations for buildings & which they destroyed.

Cumberland being an old establishment & the Inhabitants numerous the party that went against it could not drive them Intirely off but the Indians forced them to retire & take Shelter in their Strong Holds when they ravaged & destroyed the plantations & out places which has much Interrupted their cultivation for this Year. Operations of this Nature must in Time cause them to abandon that encroachment.

I have much Satisfaction in finding the Indians conducting themselves in the manner I had recommended to them. The Americans of Georgia were removed without Injury to their persons, & but a few were killed at Cumberland which was unavoidable as those people bear extreme hatred & rancour to Indians, & the latter from a Sense of the many Injurys they had Sustained from the Inhabitants there caused them to exceed their orders in Satisfying their revenge.

I have now to represent to Your Excellency upon this Occasion that as we are well acquainted with the revengefull disposition of the Americans, they probably will consider the measures we have adopted in asserting our rights against fraud & violence, as a declaration of war (which is not yet our Intention & which is evident from our not pushing the affair to the extent we might have done) & from motives of resentment, they may attempt to take Revenge. & I have farther to represent that encouraged with the hope & expectation of a certain Support, determin'd us to the measures as above related, & Judging the Interest of our great protector concern'd with our own for the reasons I have Stated. I have to earnestly request of your Excellency to afford us a present Supply of Ammunition & through any channel it may be most convenient about Fifty Barrels Powder & Ball in proportion, That we may be prepared & found in respectable posture of defence, Whenever occasion shall require that we must repel force with force.

From the experience we have already had of the Humane & benevolent disposition of our Great Protector the King, toward us in so many proofs of his generous mind, & for which we entertain Sentiments of the most Sincere Gratitude, We cannot but rely with the most perfect Confidence that in Your Excellencys compliance with our requisition for means of defence but he will approve of your conduct in this case. . . . .

ALEX: McGILLIVRAY [rubric]

Gov. Estevan Miró

37. *A Gentleman of Augusta, Georgia, to Another at Charleston, May 16, 1786*
[Spanish translation in AHN E 3887]

Realizing that you would appreciate reliable information about the state of affairs between the Georgians and the Creek Indians, I relate to you the principal occurrences that I have been able to gather. On my arrival here the day before yesterday I found the people in general and likewise the government in a state of such profound indifference concerning the Indians as to make me confident that nothing important would happen. I had a long talk with the governor, who was inclined to belittle the matter and showed (like all others here) very little respect for the Indians. I knew then that two settlers on the Oconee River, one in Washington County and the other in Green, had been killed, and that one of the bodies was found with all the sure signs of war according to the cruel custom of the Indians. I knew that several of the old traders had been driven back and that Colonel Clarke had marched (although without orders) to protect the frontier with 150 men. Nevertheless, the

110

opinion still prevailed that the Indians would not carry their excesses very far or cross the Oconee River in large force.

A certain Toole, an old trader, had come from the Creek nation some three weeks ago in company with an Indian partial to us. Having been with the colonel, he told me that when he left the nation he had heard nothing of hostilities being contemplated, but that he was certain that the Spaniards were inciting the Indians to take up arms. He reported that they had named MacGillivray lieutenant-colonel in the service of Spain, had sent the Indians arms and ammunition, and had given them positive assurance of help. The said Toole set out yesterday to return to the nation, bearing a friendly talk, but from what can be learned his trip was stopped yesterday afternoon. No hope of reconciliation remains.

It is clear beyond peradventure of doubt that for a long time the Georgians have being provoking the Indians and that they have long desired a pretext for seizing the hatchet. Three weeks ago a trivial incident gave them their chance. Since the settlements have been extended up to and even beyond the Oconee River, many Indians remain among the whites and live with them on the most peaceful terms. One of these became enamored of a girl, daughter of a white man in whose house he was employed, and asked her for a wife. The man consented, on condition that he should receive one hundred deer skins, part of which the Creek gave him. Before this singular transaction was completed, a brother of the girl returned home, and not being of the same mind as his father, he soundly thrashed the Indian. Whereupon, all the Indians left the place immediately, and a little later a party of them returned and burned the man's house, which was on their land. There was no bloodshed until ten days ago, when the killings mentioned above took place on this side of the river. I learned later that the reason the Indians did not cross the river before was because of high water, but the present fall has made the crossing easy.

Yesterday I dined with Governor Telfair, and in the afternoon a messenger from Clarke arrived with very bad news. Clarke wrote that he had been directed to the Oconee where he found the Indians (accompanied by many whites) in such large force (about 300) that he was obliged to fall back and to send a request to Washington County for a reinforcement, which set out for him two days ago. He added that three parties of Indians had crossed the river. One went toward the Broad River, another went toward the Little Ogeechee, and the third was directed toward Williamson's Pastures. It crossed the river much higher up at the plantation of a certain Altries, whom they killed with all his family. Another messenger arrived from Williamson's Pastures,

111

some 65 miles from Augusta, with the news that this party of Indians had been seen there last Thursday. The general opinion was that they intended to loot Augusta since among them there were several fugitives from Georgia who knew the country well.

ZÉSPEDES [rubric]

38. Zéspedes to McGillivray, May 22, 1786
[Spanish copy in AHN E 3887]

ST. AUGUSTINE, FLORIDA, May 22, 1786

MY DEAR SIR:

Your letter of the 25th of last month[57] proves your zeal for the service of the king and your attachment to the crown and confirms the high opinion that I have formed both of your patriotic spirit and of the unusual talent with which the Almighty has endowed you[58] that you might further the interests of the Indians and defend them against the usurpations of an ambitious greed. To prevent the spilling of blood has always been the most invariable maxim of all sane morality and a universal law. The only exceptions admissable arise from the attempt of one individual upon the life of another or from the just repulse of a direct invasion or the violent appropriation of property whether by an individual or by the forces of an empire or republic.

The Creek nation, according to what you say, is in this last predicament. You have displayed moderation, as you express it, without example among the Indians of your acquaintance. You have petitioned against the flagrant injustice of the state of Georgia's taking possession and occupying a territory which, it appears, has always been the unquestioned property of your nation. Consequently, you are acting not only legally but also meritoriously in the determination you have indicated to me that the Creek Indians shall take up arms and by force of arms shall compel their neighbors to be just. No less worthy of admiration and praise is the resolution you express that, once the

57. LC EF 114J9. Document 36, *supra*, expresses the same ideas.

58. Writing to Gardoqui, two days later, Zéspedes gave this description of McGillivray: "He is yet a young man. Although he had a liberal education, he preferred the rude and simple ways of the tribesmen of his Indian mother instead of the cultivated and brilliant society of the compatriots of his father, a British merchant, who at his death left him heir to considerable possessions in Georgia. These possessions were confiscated because the mestizo like almost all the Creek Indians, followed the royalist faction. When peace was made, the Georgians, moved by the influence that Alexander exerted over these Indian nations through his cultivated talent, offered to restore his property. But opposed to republicanism, he rejected their propositions and lent his ear to the proposals of the governor of Louisiana, with the consequence that he has been for two years in the pay of our sovereign with the charge of guarding the royal interests among the Indians" (AHN E 3887). The reference to Lachlan's death is in error.

invaders are obliged to retire from the usurped lands into their own limits, there you will stop.

You express concern that the United States may consider the forces sent by the Creek nation to put an end to the usurpations of the Georgians the beginning of general hostilities. I am inclined to trust that Congress, in its justice and wisdom, instead of approving such extortions will use its influence (authority, I believe, it has none) to prevent in time the bad consequences that might result, first to Georgia, and later to the general American confederation.[59]

In any event, my friendship for the Indians, which is due as much to my own inclination as to my obedience to the will of my sovereign, moves me to communicate at once to my superior what you have related to me, asking at the same time specific instructions for my guidance. I doubt not that the magnanimity and the well known inclination of my royal master to protect and raise up the oppressed, especially his friends such as the Indians, will result in his royal powerful mediation being brought to bear to gain for the Indian nations the justice that they deserve. I am persuaded that the United States, mindful of the benefits and protection with which they were favored through the generosity of the king in the day of their great trouble, will hesitate to take measures that not only might make them fall from his esteemed friendship but could provoke his royal wrath.

Until I learn the sovereign will, which possibly will be known in New Orleans and Pensacola sooner than here, you may rest assured that I will continue attentively giving powder and balls and other presents (there are few guns, though I took care that a sufficient number were sent me)[60] to the Indians as formerly for their hunting, and an even larger quantity of ammunition to whoever gives me a letter from you for the purpose.

I learn with regret that the present circumstances will not permit you to leave the nation to give me the pleasure of seeing you. I had various points to discuss with you, in particular to get your opinion (I hope to have it in writing on the first occasion) as to the best way for me to deal with the Indians (without antagonizing them), because they repeat their visits to this place three, four, and even five times a year, and each time it seems to them that they ought to be given presents. Such a grave abuse calls for a remedy, but I wish it to be as

59. On June 30, 1786, Gardoqui wrote to O'Neill that the United States was not in position to start a war because of the depleted state of its treasury, nor could it restrain the "multitude of emigrants" who were moving off toward the Spanish frontier (AGI C 104A).

60. On May 24, 1786, Zéspedes made urgent request to Ezpeleta for more arms and ammunition. He stated that there had been issued to the Indians 4524 pounds of powder, 9176 of balls, and 7994 flints (AGI C 1395).

suave as possible and most suitable to the Indian character.[61] I remain, with great appreciation and with true desire to serve you, your affectionate and most sincere servant,

VIZENTE MANUEL DE ZÉSPEDES

Señor Don Alexandro Mac-Gillivray.

39. *Talk that Zéspedes the Governor of Florida had with Yntipaya Masla, principal warrior of the Lower Creek Indians, called Toclatoche, on the ten articles that were proposed and the answers that he gave to each one of them in order. May 29, 1786*

[Spanish copy in AHN E 3887]

Article 1

I come as a friend to give you the hand and to talk with you in the name of the several towns (fifteen in number) that comprise the Lower Creek nation, which are about a third part of the entire Creek nation, and the closest to the Georgians.

Reply

You have come and you are welcome. I am glad to see you, because my sovereign, the great king of Spain, has ordered me to love all the Indians like brothers.

Article 2

I saw you, O Governor, a few days after your arrival in this land, at the time of the last conference with the English. They told me then that the great king of Spain was already in possession of this land, and that they were leaving. They advised me to take you by the hand, telling me that in the Spaniards the Indians would find brothers and friends as formerly in the English. We have come today to see if it is true, and I find that they have talked to me as such a brother and friend, and I am glad of it.

Reply

It is certain that the Indians will not find any difference between the Spanish and English treatment. Since they expelled the English, the Spaniards have been consistent in assisting the Indians and in giving them ammunition and guns for their hunting, furnishing them

61. "I would tell them also," wrote McGillivray in reply, "that there could be no doubt that it must be very inconvenient to you to bring repeated replacements of goods, and that your country does not produce them. By reducing the gifts little by little for those who come frequently to a keg of taffia and a little tobacco and salt, they will come unconsciously to desist from their present practice. In the coming of a chief the nature [of the question] is changed" (McGillivray to Howard, August 3, 1786, Spanish translation in AGI C 2352).

at the same time stores of goods for conduct of the fur trade. Now again I give you the hand of a friend and brother.

Article 3

The Georgians, when they were English, had their frontier separated fifteen days' journey from our towns. Since then they have so encroached upon and usurped our land that at present they are distant from us only two days' march, not leaving us land enough for our hunting.

Reply

I greatly regret the usurpations that you mention of the Georgians, but I cannot believe that the chiefs and wise men of Georgia tolerate such unjust procedure. The aggressors are without doubt youths and vagabonds who have settled on your lands without the authorization or knowledge of the government of Georgia and the officers of America.

Article 4

We have resolved to avail ourselves of force of arms to drive them off our lands by vigorous action. Once they are evicted and put within their own limits, there we shall stop.

Reply

It is lawful to repel by force of arms any invader or usurper of foreign extraction when good offices have not served. The moderation, with which the Creeks have determined to desist when they have expelled the usurpers, is worthy of praise.

Article 5

It is true that we were the first to shed the blood of the invaders. We wish to know if the great king will allow them to take our lands without giving us anything in return, and if he will give us powder, balls, guns, knives, and hatchets.

Reply

I have always said that I consider it lawful to repel an unjust invasion by force of arms. The great king my master is at peace with the Americans and will not break that peace without just cause, but as a father and friend of the Indians he will not fail to interpose effectively his powerful mediation in their favor with Congress. I shall transmit this information to him, and until he signifies to me his will, rest assured that I will give to the Indians, as I have done, arms, ammunition, and other presents as customary for their hunting.

Article 6

The Americans told us that the Spaniards had joined with the French

115

and English to expel us by force from our lands, and to make us slaves, together with our women and children.

Reply

No good American could have conceived such a falsehood. It is notorious that the king of Spain, father and friend of the Indians, has enough land, for he has so much that the sun always shines on some part of it.

Article 7

Alick (the mestizo Alexander) is the greatest man among the Upper Creeks. I come to learn if the Spaniards will give us at St. Augustine the same supplies that they give at Pensacola to the Upper Creeks, and at Mobile to the Choctaws and Chickasaws.

Reply

The Spaniards are friends of Alick and of all the Indians in general. The Spaniards of Mobile, Pensacola, New Orleans, and St. Augustine are all children of the same father, the great sovereign of Spain, by whose order and by their own inclinations they are friendly toward all the Indians and will help them in any just deed.

Article 8

I see already that you talk to us as a true friend and that you do not speak as a false brother; I hear now that you have involved yourself in this affair, be the consequence what it may, and I am content.

Reply

The great king of Spain will never forsake his true friends. He will speak to the Americans with a powerful voice in your favor, and until the results are known the Spaniards and the Indians will live as brothers.

Article 9

The talk that I have just heard satisfies me, and therefore I ask that you give it to me written in English, for there is in my nation, one who will explain it to the assembled chiefs and warriors, and I want them to credit what I shall tell them. Hearing me they will be happy.

Reply

I shall have this talk put in writing as you ask, so that you can explain it to the chiefs of your nations, to whom I wish all well-being, and to you a happy return home.

Article 10

I have drunk aguardiente that you have given to other Indians.

116

I have smoked with them tobacco that they got here, blowing the smoke very high in the air in order that the great king of Spain might see it.

Reply

To you also I will give aguardiente and tobacco, so that you may be happy with your people at home, to which place I again wish you a happy journey.

St. Augustine, Florida, May 29, 1786.

ZÉSPEDES [rubric]

40. *Zéspedes to McGillivray, June 16, 1786*
[Spanish copy in AHN E 3887]
St. Augustine, Florida, June 16, 1786.

My dear Sir:

I have had positive news that some Indians, just after the beginning of hostilities against the state of Georgia, scalped alive a girl, the daughter of a certain Mr. Karns, one of the British settlers who remained in this province, established on the south bank of the St. Marys River. The middle of this river constitutes the dividing line between this province and Georgia. I have forwarded to the court these settlers' petition to be accepted as the king's subjects. Until the king reveals his royal will concerning this petition I have thought it wise to send you this letter by messenger so that you can make known to the chiefs, warriors, and all the Creek people that all persons, of whatever nation they may be, living on the south bank of the St. Marys are under the protection of his Majesty and therefore ought to be considered as friends and brothers of the Indians. Your sagacity and humanity doubtless will move you of your own free will to take the steps most effective and most prompt to explain to your tribesmen the distinction that they must make between those with whom they are in perfect peace and friendship and those against whom they wage war. I shall await impatiently for your reply by the bearer, whom I shall reward on his return, and I trust that you will be able to send me thus whatever message seems to you in order. I remain, with true respect, your most affectionate and loyal servant.

Vicente Manuel de Zéspedes

Señor Don Alexandro MacGillivray

41. *Miró to O'Neill, June 20, 1786*
[Spanish draft in AGI C 4]

Alexander McGillebray asks for a supply of five thousand pounds of powder and balls in proportion for the needs of his nation. He would be satisfied now to receive half, while necessity does not demand the remainder.

This matter should be handled with the greatest circumspection; therefore I hope that you will prudently find means to deliver these supplies with the fewest possible persons knowing about it. If you know someone in whom you have absolute confidence, I would think it a good method to deposit this ammunition in his warehouse, so that in all events they might seem to have been bought by McGillebray. I recommend the further arrangement that the Indians should come to get them at different times, as from week to week, with only two horses each time, in order that they would appear to have been purchased by different tribes. They should be careful always to take them out at night or at an hour when there probably would be no one in the neighborhood to notice it. Nevertheless if you, through your familiarity with that place and its circumstances, find some other method that you consider more opportune, put it into practice. McGillebray's receipt will serve as clearance for the storekeeper.

May God spare thee many years—

ESTEVAN MIRÓ

P. S. If you do not have enough balls of 28 caliber, I will send them to you and likewise a replacement of the powder if the corresponding quantity is not left there.
Don Arturo O'Neill.

IV

TUCKEBATCHES

42. *McMurphy*[62] *to O'Neill, July 11, 1786*
[Copy in AGI C 37]
LOWER CREEK NATION, July 11, 1786
MAY IT PLEASE YOUR EXCELLENCY—The Honorable the Assembly of the State of Georgia has appointed me their agent to reside in the Creek Nation to preserve peace with their Friends the Creek Indians & to see that each Trader had a Lycence from the Govr. of the State of Georgia & for to deliver Talks to the said Indians & receive their

62. In the nation Daniel McMurphy assailed McGillivray just as vigorously as in this letter he criticized the Spanish policy. He tried to bring about the assassination of McGillivray, but when the Spaniards and McGillivray sought to apprehend him, he fled to Georgia. The Indians called him Yellow Hair. See documents 44, 46, 47, and 49, *infra.*

answers & put a Stop to persons passing & repassing thro' Said Nation without proper passports from the Government they Came from & if any Should attempt to pass without Such to Send him or them Back to whence they came from.

But upon my arrival here I called the principle Indians together & also the Traders requiring them to Show their Lycences When I found they had not any from the State of Georgia, but had a Lycence from Alexr. McGillivray. The Said Traders to be Subject to him & no other & to observe the regulations given by former Superintendents.

I was surprised to See Such Lycences as I am well assured the Upper & Lower Creek Nations are within the State of Georgia as far as the Junction of the Chatahochie & flint River.

Your Excellency will See by the inclosed paper how far Mr. McGillivray has infringed on the Territory of the State against Law & Government in Consequence of Which order the Mad Dog of the Tuckabatchees sent his Brother & 14 other Indians from his Town Who were to be joined by all the other Indians but none of the Lower Towns would go with them on the Contrary they had a White Wing sent after them but they being on Horseback could not be come up with. The Said Indians Killed a Young man & burned John Galphin's House & would have done much more damage had the whole turned out. They had orders to drive all White people before them over Ogeeche river & take all their property & burn their Houses & rob two Stores that had a great many Indian Goods one on the river Altamaha & the other on the Okonnie River also about one hundred Indians from the Hillibies & Calichies went down upon the upper Settlement & killed four men & one Woman & brought of a Great Number of Horses. I have demanded Satisfaction for the outrage done but I am informed that the Mad Dog & Joseph Cornell who Came up Lately from Pensacla, say that Your Excelly told them not to Listen to any Talk they heard untill Mr. McGillivray came up with a Spanish beloved man & if I was in a Hurry back the Mad Dog had an answer in Writing to give me to Carry down & if I wanted the Head men to go down to mark the Line there was no occasion as the Line was marked already & if the Georgians would Still incroach on the Land between Ogeechie & the Ockonnie river for the Indians to drive them off & take their property & that You would give them Powder & Bullets to defend themselves & had given Seven Loads amunition to the Tuckabatchy Indians & if any of the other towns Wanted a Supply of Powder for them to get a paper from Mr. McGillivray.[63]

63. These "papers from Mr. McGillivray" were a fundamental factor in the latter's dominance over the Indians. His authority to issue requisitions upon the

119

Can it be possible the Indians could get Such encouragement in time of Peace! For to be encouraged to break their Last Treaty & in the End to have them drove of their Lands—But I am of opinion that Your Excellency has not given any Such Talk to them but it is given out by persons who were dissatisfied that they Could not get their Ends when the British were at War with the Americans.

I have Had a Meeting of the Lower towns & they are for Peace & also of the upper Towns only thirteen met & say they will not hear any Talks but those for Peace & agree to take all White people by the Hand & have a Trade with all who Chuse to Come to their Land.

The Kings & beloved men of the Lower Towns required me to Write Your Excelly if You have given any Such Talks & if so how they will Support their Women & Children in Case of War which they expect except Satisfaction is given agreable to the Many Solemn Treatys they have had with the Americans & they Say that they will Expect Trade from Georgia as usuall as Soon as every thing is made up & they also wish to Know What is the reason that Talks are given out in private so that the Whole Nation Cannot hear the right & expect that any Talks that come from their friends the Spaniards will be given out in publick so that all may Hear them & they think the King of Spain has not given any Such Talks as Alexr. Mcy. brings up to them but when the Bearer returns they Expect to hear the right Talk & as they Hear there is to be a great Talk in the upper Towns soon when they will hear all that their Freinds has to Say to them & will give their full answer.

I have also to inform Your Excellency that Mr. McGillivray it is Said is in Company with Mr. Panton & has ordered all the Traders that had Goods from Georgia not to pay their Debts but carry their Skins either to Pensacola, or St. Marks.

I am of opinion that every power that has any Connection to Indians ought to use their Greatest influence for to reform the Savage Mode of Killing & Scalping Christians rather than give them the least Encouragement & this affair has been the most Cruel attempt ever I heard of but it Seems as Providence Interfered & turned their Hearts to see, that what they were told to do, was Wrong & I flatter myself if proper measures were adopted they might be brought so far under Controul that we would have no more of their Cruelties—but it will be impossible untill the White people in their Land is brought under the proper Subordination. These Hints I have Taken the Boldness to Lay before Your

Spaniards for powder and ball, blankets and cloth, brass kettles, tobacco and taffia established his ascendancy. For sample requisitions see documents 45 and 53, *infra*.

Excely. & I shall be happy to Have Your approbation. I am your Excys Most

Hmble Servant,

DAL. McMurphy

Governor O'Neill

43. *McGillivray to O'Neill, July 29, 1786*
[AGI C 199]
LITTLE TALLASSIE, July 29th, 1786

SIR

On My arrival here I found the enclosed letter for Your Excellency from Govr. de Zespedes.

I am only returned a few days, & was taken with the Fever on the road, & tis just leaving me, & am very weak.

I can give Your Excellency very little Information as yet, but Shall have a General Meeting in a few days, after which I Shall write you.

The Indian Ninne Wakitche has heard that you want to see him & he is Im told preparing with a good party to visit you.

The chiefs that I will Send down for ammunition, will generally expect some few present & Indeed, some expence at some times cannot with propriety be well avoided as it will have very good effects. Being very unwell, I beg leave to Conclude with assuring you that I am always with respectfull regard Your Excellencys

most obedt. servt.

ALEX: McGillivray [*rubric*]

Gov. Arturo O'Neil

44. *Reports from Augusta, Georgia, August 1 and 15, 1786*[64]
[Spanish translation in AHN E 3887]

Under date of August 1 it is reported from Augusta, Georgia, that since the incident on the Oconee River between the Indians and the Georgians, which was as bad on one side as on the other, a chain of small forts has been constructed on that river. They are seventeen in number, each defended by thirty men of the militia of Wilkes, Green, Washington, Franklin, Richmond, and Burke Counties.

Colonel MacMurphy, who returned just three days ago from the Indian towns, and who was ordered by the Spanish agent to depart, says that these towns contain 4000 men, of whom only 800 are inclined toward peace, that MacGillivray (who is the Spanish agent) had gone to Pensacola, and that until he returned nothing could happen, that they had received from the Spaniards 300 quintals of powder, and that

64. Remitted by Zéspedes under date of September 22.

they expect a greater quantity. In addition the Indians say that, as they are more numerous, it is their prerogative to make the first proposals. They ask that the American settlers retire from their territory as far as the old dividing line.

On the other hand, the people here clamor for war to force the Creeks to the other side of Flint River. They have already gotten arms and ammunition and they will ask larger quantities still from Virginia. For this end the legislature is at present occupied in taking the appropriate measures.

Under date of the fifteenth of the same month news also comes from Augusta that the legislature of the state of Georgia has suspended its meetings until the month of January next. The state has been divided into three districts, namely the lower, middle, and upper. The command of each has been given to a brigadier general, that of the upper to General Twiggs, that of the middle to General Clarke, and that of the lower to General Jackson. The legislature also passed a law for the better regulation of the militia, directing that when it is called out no brigadier shall draw his salary unless he is at the head of one thousand men. It likewise provides that whoever is not present when called to assemble shall be fined fifteen pounds sterling unless he has provided an able substitute in his place. While in the field all shall be subject to the military penal law of the confederation.

New commissioners are named with discretionary powers, who are to be escorted immediately by 1500 men to the frontier of the Creek Nation, there to call the Indians together and demand from them the perpetrators of the murders committed last spring. The commissioners are also to insist that they send hostages as security for their future good conduct and pay due reparations for the costs that the state has had, or will have in the future, to defend itself against invasion and to punish the Indians' perfidy. In case the commissioners do not receive ample satisfaction on these points, they must surrender their powers to the military and retire. To meet the costs of this martial force the legislature determined to issue, as soon as possible, 500,000 pounds sterling in stamped bills, which must be accepted as legal payment of any debts, contracted or to be contracted. To fund this issue of bills the legislature hypothecated 70,000 square (miles of land).[65] It is also said that a commissioner is appointed to treat with the Choctaws and form an alliance with that nation against the Creeks, and that Governor Serveir[66] has

65. On the problem of financing the Indian war, see Handley to Winn, Mathews, and Pickens, August 14, 1788, ASP IA, I, 28-29.

66. John Sevier was an Indian fighter and a Revolutionary hero, better known on the frontier as Nolichucky Jack. He was the dominant figure in the Watauga Association, was chosen governor of the proposed state of Franklin, and later

offered his aid with a thousand men to operate against the Upper Towns.

45. *McGillivray to Panton, August 3, 1786*
[AGI C 199]

TUCKEBATCHES, August 3d, 1786

DEAR SIR

The Meeting is over & the Chiefs are Come to Very Spirited Resolutions. The Talks I will Send in a few days when I have Strength, at present I'm quite exhausted with fatigue.

I must trouble you respecting the ammunition as it is delivered from you; the bearer is the Holloing King of the Cowetas who is to get 10 horse loads or 500 lbs. powder 500 Ball, for his Town & dependencies, the other is Second Man of the Oussitches & chief, 200 lbs powder 400 Ball & Flints in proportion. Cornels Son[67] Sets out in a few days & these people wait.

Dear Sir Yours &c.

ALEX: McGILLIVRAY [*rubric*]

William Panton

I shall direct others to the Governor, I do not know certainly how to manage this affair.

46. *Talk of Part of the Creek Indians to the Georgia Legislature, August 3, 1786*
[Spanish translation in AHN E 3887]

To his lordship the governor and to the other beloved men of the state of Georgia.

FRIENDS AND BROTHERS:

Early in the summer there came among us a man named Yellow Hair (Mr. MacMurphy), who told us that you sent him on important business. He asked for a council of the chiefs to tell it to. We then told him, the Tame King, and the Fat King that the persons whom we had placed at the head of our councils were absent from the nation, and consequently we could not assemble to deliberate on public business. If he could wait, however, until it was possible for us to assemble, a reply would be given. This he offered to do.

The persons for whom we waited having arrived, notice was sent to all the chiefs of the upper, middle, and lower towns to meet in

---

became the first governor of Tennessee. To this post he was five times reelected, besides holding other high offices at the bestowal of the Tennessee electorate. His principal biographers are J. R. Gilmore (1887) and F. M. Turner (1910). See also S. C. Williams, *Lost State of Franklin.*

67. George's son, Alexander, who was mentioned as a possible successor to McGillivray after the latter's death in 1793. See document 209, *infra.*

general council at the town of Tuckebatches in order to hear your talk. In the meantime your messenger departed for Augusta, and as a result, we did not hear your talk. Nevertheless, we tarried to hear it from the Tame King and the Fat King, which was the same as if we had heard it from Yellow Hair. We believe that you are guilty of bad conduct pertaining to the lands of which we have spoken often enough. Brothers, do not allow yourselves to be further deceived by these men; they have no authority to cede lands. Yellow Hair would have known this if he had waited until now and had met with the council.

We have sent you several talks concerning the behavior of your people who have encroached upon the hunting grounds, asking that you make them retire. You have never sent us any reply. We do not treat you thus when you send us talks. Never were we scorned in such fashion by the English, Spaniards, or French. We insist now in this assembly that you send us an answer promptly, indicating your intention to satisfy us respecting our lands, or indicating whether you are of a mind to satisfy us or not. We warn you again to keep your people within the natural limits of the Ogeechee River, for we are resolved not to permit your people to enjoy the usurpations that they have made on our land.

The Indian chiefs order Alexander MacGillibray to send the aforesaid to those indicated in the salutation of this talk.

TUCKEBATCHES, August 3, 1786

P. S. An answer is expected by the end of next September. If you do not send an answer, we must then infer that you do not intend to give us satisfaction, and we shall govern ourselves accordingly.

47. McGillivray to Zéspedes, August 3, 1786
[LC EF 114J9]
TUCKEBATCHES 3d August 1786

SIR

I have to acknowledge the receit of two of Your Excellencys letters,[68] the first enclosing one for Governor ONeil which he has received ere this, & Your last Containing an Account of the Melancholy fate of the poor girl, Concerning which matter I have Spoken very fully to the Lower Town Cheifs who are now here, as well as all the Cheifs of the Nation, met together for the purpose of deliberating on the State of Affairs.

It is a Matter of the Most Sincere Satisfaction to myself in particular, & a Subject of the most general heartfelt Joy to all my people in general, that I had the giving at this time Your Excellencys assurances of Continuing Your Support to them in every emergency. For so Generous &

68. Documents 38 and 40, *supra.*

Magnanimous a declaration in our favor I cannot refrain from testifying my warmest Gratitude & acknowledgments in the name of all my people—

When I was at New Orleans I obtain a present Supply of five thousand pounds Weight of Gun powder with a proportion of Lead or Balls & Flints, with which I Supply the people in this part of the Nation. I have to request the favor of Your Excellency to furnish the Chihaw & Oussitches that live on Flint River as being nearer to you, with about Six Hundred pounds Weight powder & Ball in proportion. The bearer is principal of the Ousitches and will receive their proportion of three hundred weight powder or Six horse loads. Viz. 50 lb powder in a bag & 100 lb Ball is a horse load. If the Chihaws have not as yet received any the Leader at War called Folotouiche, whom Your Excellency gave the Written Talk to, Can receive for that people, there are No other that I need recommend, as for the Semanolies I have but little Acquaintance with the present leaders, the former ones whom I knew are dead. But they are known to Mr. Lesslie, whose Judgement in these Matters I much Confide in. I instruct the people that gets the Ammunition that they are Not to Squander it Idly away, but to be careful & reserve it for meeting the Hostile attacks of any people that may attempt them.

When my freind Mr. Lesslie Went from here he left me very Ill with the Fever, of which I have not yet Intirely recoverd, it has brought me very low & am not very able to go through the Fatigue of the Meeting on hand. Our Occurences are much the same as when Mr. Lesslie was here, & who will Inform you of them. I have not been able to learn how the Americans Considers our late Conduct to them respecting our Lands, they had Sent up an Agent & for what purpose I know not without it was to play the fool, which he performd with Considerable Insolence & then took a French leave of the Nation. If any thing of moment shoud occur, I Shall not fail to give Your Excellency due Information mean time wishing you great Happiness, I remain with the most respectful esteem Sir

Your Excellencys Most obligd Servt.

ALEX: McGILLIVRAY [*rubric*]

His Excellency General De Zespedes, Governor &
Commanding in Chief East Florida St. Augustine

48. *O'Neill to Sonora, August 10, 1786*
[Spanish original in AHN E 3887]

MOST EXCELLENT SIR:

MY DEAR SIR: His Excellency Señor Conde de Gálvez has ordered me to write directly and expeditiously to Señor Don Diego de Gardoqui

125

(chargé d'affairs with the United States of North America) so that he may be promptly informed of any developments in connection with the settlements that the Americans intend to establish on the frontier that runs between them and the Creek Indian nations. Under date of April 19 and May 20 I have informed him of the resolution of the Indian nations to drive the new American settlers from their lands and to oppose vigorously all attempts of that nature that may be made by the states of Georgia and South Carolina.

As I reported last April, various bands of the Upper Creeks and Cherokees patrolled their frontiers, expelled the Americans settled on the banks of the Oconee River and the Altamaha, and forced these emigrants to return precipitately to Georgia. They dealt similarly with the Carolinians who had settled on the Cherokee or Hoghego River at the place called commonly in English Mossel Cholls [Muscle Shoals] or Chake Thlocko.

Another band went to attack the settlements of Cumberland near the Ohio. Here the Indians lost ten killed and the Americans a few more, in addition to some buildings burned and some cattle stolen. Then an agent of the state of Georgia came to the nations offering peace, but insisting that the Indians give satisfaction and cede the lands of the Oconee River, at least the better part of them. Only three towns, Tallassie, Ochitas, and Chovacla, favored such a peace; the rest of the Upper and Middle Towns opposed; the Lower Creeks for the time being remained neutral.

Several chiefs and principal warriors have come here, one after another, asking advice and soliciting the protection of our monarch in the war that they intend to wage against the Americans in defense of their lands. To resolve better in common accord the principal Indians of the three nations are now assembled at the town of Toquibachi, with our commissary Alexander McGilbray participating as the half-breed that he is and as the chief of one of their towns. The result will be, I think, that they will order the agent of Georgia out of the nations, with a warning to the Americans to remain strictly in their own limits, and in no fashion to push out towards the Mississippi because the lands from that river to the banks of the Ohio belong to the Creeks and Cherokees, who are determined to hold them at whatever cost. So great is their confidence in our nation that they have proposed that we build forts at various places within their nations for the defense of them and of our frontiers.

As soon as I learn what they determine in their assembly, I shall do myself the honor of communicating it to your Excellency, as I take the liberty of doing on this occasion, in order that you will know what

I have communicated to Señor Don Diego de Gardoqui and so that you may be able to place this information at the disposition of his Excellency the viceroy.

I have informed Señor de Gardoqui to what extent I can influence these nations to actions that will be convenient in his negotiations with the United States, and it is natural that the conduct of these Indians will be governed largely by the recommendations that he sends me.

I am at your Excellency's esteemed orders, and pray our Lord to spare your Excellency many years. Pensacola, August 10, 1786, etc.,

ARTURO O'NEILL [rubric]

Most Excellent Señor Marqués de Sonora.

49. *McGillivray to O'Neill, August 12, 1786*
[AGI C 199]

SIR   LITTLE TALLASSIE, August 12, 1786

I did myself the pleasure of writing to Your Excellency Soon after my arrival here, enclosing You letters from Governor De Zespedes. I have acquainted you that though I was very unwell I had Issued out a Summons to the Cheifs of the Upper, Middle, & Lower Creeks to meet me in General Convention at the Tuckebatches Town, for the purpose of receiving McMurphy, & to deliberate on the propositions that the State of Georgia meant to offer to us by him. & altho he heard of my arrival & calling the chiefs together while he was at the Cussitahs, he abruptly left the Nation. The only reasons I can assign for such extraordinary behaviour on McMurphys part is that during my absence he had repeatedly attempted to get a meeting of the chiefs & in which he faild, & what few he had any discourse with proved adverse to all my [sic, his] views, & was once on the point of being drove out of the Okfuskee Square, & on general he met with a cold reception from all but the Fat King & Tame King, & their efforts in forwarding his views proved of not the least Service to him. From all which he plainly Saw that his great freinds from Their bad conduct had lost their Influence with Their Countrymen & that it woud be folly in him to meet the Cheifs in Convention. He therefore retired with a budget of Falsehoods to report to his Masters that Sent him.

The meeting that we had on the 3d Inst. at the Tuckebatches was the fullest one we have had these many years past. The lower cheifs brought with them a Talk wrote in English from Governor De Zespedes. He Speaks to the Chiefs in the Same manner as Your Excellency does & promises them a Support of Ammunition etc. from his Government. Such assurances from you both has much encouraged all the Nation to give up no one point to the Americans, & what little ammunition

127

is already come up, has had the best effects, as from a prospect of being Supported, they are more unanimous than I ever knew them. After agreeing upon a Talk to be Sent to the Georgians, which was demanding a full & explicit answer to our former representations, respecting the encroachments of their people upon our Lands, & to let us know whether they mean to Satisfy the Nation, in denouncing every Idea of encroachment or if they mean to endeavour to Support by Force, pretentions founded on fraud & violence & that we Shall await their Answer till the first of October next, & if none at that time, we Shall adopt Such measures as the Case may require.

The Cumberland people are begging hard for a peace. They Intend to Send in two of their leading men to know what terms it may be obtained upon.

We have reports that the Georgians are Collecting their people to attack us. I think it highly necessary that we Shoud be in a Situation to meet their Force if ever they Attempt us.

From Governor Miro's promises to me, I must Suppose that the Ammunition he agreed to furnish to us is arrived before now at Pensacola & if it Shoud not I hope Your Excellency will furnish all the Cheifs of the different Towns that are now going down to receive for their people & as many arms etc as can be got.

The Cowetas in coming up to the meeting told me that they met two Cussetah Indians who told them that McMurphy has Sent them with letters to Your Excellency & that you had Sent answers back by them. I Shoud be Glad to know upon what Subject he has presumed to address you upon respecting Indian affairs, that I may be able to regulate my Conduct accordingly when he comes back as he told the Cussetahs he would return from Augusta in twenty five days, which time is nearly expired.

The Fever has reduced me very low & it has been Succeeded by a breaking out over my body. I'm Apprehensive that I Shall lose all my finger Nails & tis with much difficulty, that I can take the pen in my hand to write. I have furnishd the Cheifs with tickets for their ammunition & arms as far as can be got. I request of Your Excellency to make Some little present to the people that I Send on this occasion, as the most of them wont visit you again for a long Time to come & more especially as Govr. De Zespedes is very liberal to cheifs on Such occasions. If any thing Material Shoud occur Soon I will give you the Speediest Information. Mean Time I remain

With most respectfull Esteem

Your Excellencys Most Obdt. Servant

Governor O'Neil   ALEX: McGILLIVRAY [*rubric*]

128

V

SHOULDERBONE AND COWETA

50. *The Georgia Commissioners to McGillivray, August 15, 1786*
[LC EF 116L9]

AUGUSTA, 15th August 1786

SIR,

The General Assembly of this State having been pleased to appoint us Commissioners to hold a Conference and Treaty with the Nation of Creek Indians, we have this day transmitted a Talk to their Kings, Head Men, and Warriours, and invited them to a meeting to be held on the upper Trading Path, near the mouth of Shoulder bone Creek, on the Oconee river, the 15th October next. Having no doubt of your disposition to prevent, if possible, the further effusion of human blood, and being sensible at the same time of your influence with that people, we do not hesitate to request that it may be exerted in this instance, in endeavoring to prevail on them to accede to our proposal; and that you also will meet us on this momentous business, being persuaded that your presence will be highly beneficial to both parties.

The object of our appointment is, to endeavor to remove all causes of discontent, and bring matters to an amicable adjustment, so that a permanent peace may be established between us.

We have heard that the Indians have some complaints respecting encroachments on their hunting grounds. If they have such, they certainly ought to have made them known to our Government, as such proceedings are strictly forbidden and punishable by our Laws. At the proposed meeting, this and every other matter can be fully explained.

The late Acts of Hostility have induced the Supreme Authority to order matters in such a manner, that in the event of Peace or War the State will be prepared; but as they prefer the former, so the latter will only be the effect of necessity; a necessity that may be prevented by our mutual efforts.

We are told that a report has been handed to you, of an intention on the part of this Government to procure your death by unmanly and infamous means. We hope, however, that you do not harbour a suspicion, that an enlightened People could authorize or even meditate an Act so incompatible with the feelings of generous Minds.

We shall expect and have to request, that we may be favored with as early an answer as possible to this Letter; and will only observe, that the Man who is instrumental in bringing the business to an amicable issue, will be intitled to and receive the grateful thanks and rewards of this Country

We have the honor to be, Sir,

Your most obedient Servants,

JOHN HABERSHAM,[69] *Chairman*

J. CLEMENTS

J. M.NEIL

JOHN KING

JAS. POWELL

F. ONEAL

JARED IRWIN

Alexander McGillivray, esquire

51. *McGillivray to Habersham, September 18, 1786*

[Spanish translation in AHN E 3887]

LITTLE TALLASSIE, September 18, 1786

MY DEAR SIRS:

I received your letter of August 15 by which you made known to me your appointment in the capacity of commissioners for the assembly of your state to deal with my nation and to try to remove all the causes of dissatisfaction among the Indians.

I can do no less than express my surprise at seeing the ignorance that you display concerning the dissatisfaction of the nation over the usurpation of our hunting grounds by individuals of that state. We have represented it to your governors as the greatest harm that could be done us, and even as recently as last July through Mr. James McGillevray, but your government has never taken the least notice of our representations to make amends for the offense.

The acts of hostility of last spring, to which you allude, were in consequence of your not having given attention to our complaints and of our having discovered a determined intention on your part to take from us the best of our lands. Then I as a native chief, vitally interested in the welfare of my country, gave my opinion that no time should be lost in resisting such iniquitous measures by the only effective means that we could employ.

We sent a band of warriors to drive out all the settlers that they might find on the lands in question. My instructions to those charged with

69. John Habersham is less famous than his brother Joseph. Active in the preliminaries of the Revolution, he held the rank of major in the First Georgia Continental Regiment, was a member of the Continental Congress in 1785-86, and collector of customs at Savannah, 1789-99.

the execution of this business were to be careful to avoid shedding the blood of any of these people. Those who have been killed suffered because of their folly.

Peace is equally the desire of our hearts and yours, and like you we are equally prepared to retaliate in kind for any attack that may be made upon our lands and families. If we have not received satisfaction for the injuries of which we complain due to failure of your assembly to know them, we demand again that your government remove the cause of our dissatisfaction by recalling from the Oconee lands all the individuals settled there, renouncing all idea of pretension to the disputed lands, and by restraining the settlers within the boundaries established and agreed upon in the year 1773, when Georgia belonged to the British government.

With respect to your invitation that we come to meet with the commissioners, we decline to do so until we see the sincerity of your proposals fully verified and proved in the way we desire.[70] Then we shall find no difficulty about joining in conference with you in order to agree on the regulations that may seem necessary for our mutual security and good peaceful conduct towards each other. I have the honor to be, Sirs, your most obedient servant,

ALEXANDER MCGILLEVRAY

Sirs, John Habersham, Esquire—President of the honorable committee of Indian commissioners of the state of Georgia.

52. *A Gentleman of Augusta, Georgia, to Another at Charleston, September 26, 1786*

[Spanish translation in AHN E 3887]

September 26, 1786.

I have space only to inform you that Mr. MacGilivray has ordered that all the white people retire by the first of October next from the lands that the Indians reclaim. He does not want to deal with the Georgians, because, he says, they have violated all treaties, but he will treat with Congress at the place it may designate. Fifteen hundred militiamen are chosen and should have started off the twenty-fourth of this month. The other militiamen of Georgia are divided into three parts and have orders to be ready to set out at any time. If the Indians do not find it convenient to deal with the commissioners—for we begin to suspect some trick—we shall believe that the Indians are incited by the persons for whom MacGillivray has a fondness. Who they are

70. Two days earlier McGillivray had declined to come to a meeting because his condition made it impossible for him to travel (McGillivray to Habersham, September 16, 1786; Spanish translation in AHN E 3887. See also Durouzeaux to Habersham, September 23, 1786, *ibid.*).

you know full well, and at your cost. The first detachment will be under the orders of General Twigs. In case all the militia sets out, Governor Elbert[71] (who according to reports is called Field Marshall) will be the commander in chief.

53. *McGillivray to O'Neill, October 4, 1786*
[AGI C 199]
LITTLE TALLASSIE, 4 October, 1786

SIR

This will be handed to Your Excellency by Some Okfuskee Warriors, whom I have Sent for ammunition. Please order them 450 ps. powder & 900 d Ball. 500 Gun Flints. 1 box paint to look warlike.

I beg leave to Inform Your Excellency that the okfuskee Town is among the largest & most repectable & of great Influence among the rest. I have at a good deal of Pains fixd them in our Interest, & it is of the utmost Consequence to keep them so.

It was my desire to Conduct Indian Affairs with Economy, & when I had the purse of the English Nation open to me in managing their affairs, I used to Study to do it with as little expence as possible. Yet some cases require one to give a little extraordinary. I consider it necessary in this case. I have therefore to request of Your Excellency to Send by the return of these warriors four Kegs Taffia for the White Lieutenant cheif of okfuskee, & a bag Sugar. If none in Store, if you woud be pleased to desire Mr. Henrique to furnish the Sugar & I'll pay him for it. I had likewise promised that the hire of the horses to pack up the ammunition Shoud be allowed at one keg Taffia each horse, which I request of Your Excellency to grant, as I woud not wish that these people Shoud Say that I deceived them &c. If any Spare arms Some is wanted & I shall write you a particular account of all our occurrences in a few days by Daniel McG. who is here Sick. Mean Time I remain with the greatest respect,

Your Excellencys most obed. Servant,

ALEX: McGILLIVRAY [*rubric*]

Governor O'Neil

54. *McGillivray to O'Neill, October 8, 1786*
[AGI C 199]
LITTLE TALLASSIE, October 8, 1786

SIR

I have had the pleasure of receiving several letters from You, &

71. Former Governor Samuel Elbert, in whose counting house McGillivray had once been a clerk (Stephens, *History of Georgia*, II, 430).

which have been unanswerd on my part owing to my Ill State of Health.

Your Excellency no doubt is desirious to learn our Occurrences since my arrival from Your place.

I had formerly advised You of McMurphys retreat from this Nation upon my coming home. He has not returned yet tho he told the Indians he would soon come up.

The enclosed are Copys of letters I received last month from the Georgia Commission & my answer to them. By their letter Your Excellency will observe that they had an Intention to attack us. Their not attempting it I am informd is owing to their not being ready as soon as they expected, that they had to Send to the Settlers over the Mountains, to embody & march into our Country on that quarter, while the Georgians were to march from their Country direct here but their delays & finding that we were in a State of defence, they have deferrd for another time their projected Invasion of us.[72] Notwithstanding their fair talks, I shall be upon my Guard & not trust them too far. Your Excellency has likewise heard that messengers from Cumberland have been here. Upon my arrival here in July last there was a Cherokee half breed here from thence, but as He was not much noticed, another man an Inhabitant of Cumberland came last month, solliciting a peace with us, upon any Terms & conditions most agreeable to ourselves, & declared their determination to give us full Satisfaction respecting hunting Grounds & are willing to be restricted to the boundary we Shall allot for them. I Shoud have answerd them as I did the Georgians without Calling the Chiefs to assemble, but the clamoror of the Tame King & Fat King who deemd the propositions reasonable, & to quiet the alarms of the people, Whom I have kept all together & under arms, this past Summer, that they have not hunted for their families, Whereby they were Somewhat distressed. I consented to a truce till next April, that the Indians might hunt this ensuing winter in safety, & in the Spring I agreed to consider of such terms as woud be Convenient & Satisfactory for our Interest. & another point I had in view for declining the Treaty now was that before next April Your Excellency woud certainly receive advices from Your Court respecting the final Settlement of the Limits between Spain & Congress from the knowledge of which we coud regulate our Conduct toward those people.

The foregoing is an exact account of all our transactions with the Americans, which I hope will be approved of by Your Excellency.

72. Compare with document 52, *supra*.

Considering the present Situation of our Affairs. & if any political measure of mine does not meet Your Idea, I Shall always be happy to receive advice from Your Excellency whose knowledge & abilities to Judge what is for our Good are so very far Superior to mine, & if any thing is wrong I hope you will consider it as an error & not a designd thing done. Your Excellency already knows my history. You likewise know that the Americans have greatly Injured me & my dearest friends, & all this is further aggravated by their open attempts to ruin my Country. Under these Circumstances & Supposing me to possess the most ordinary feelings, it cant be Suspected that I entertain a wish favorable to the Americans or to their Interests.

The Indians are mostly returnd with their quotas of Ammunition for which I Sincerely Thank Your Excellency. Tho I am Sorry to learn that Some of the Tallapousses Squanderd what they got, Yet the rest of the Towns have not done so. The Holloing King of Coweta is Satisfied, he is a brave good chief & his Towns are determind enemies to the Americans. The Okfuskee have been late in going for their ammtn. Yet I hope they will get Some as they lay most open to an attack from an enemy.

Moniac tells me of the bad behaviour of Some of the pack horse men that have been down lately. I am now taking Steps to have them Secured but I fear they have run off to the Cherokees, but l Shall certainly take Measures to prevent the like in future. My being so long confind by Sickness has Tempted those fellows to Commit Such actions, expecting to escape before their detection. Conclude wishing you to enjoy all Your desires & am with respectfull esteem,

Your Excellencys Most Obed't Servant

ALEX: McGILLIVRAY [rubric]

Governor Arturo O'Neil

I have just received Information that one Davenport[73] an American Commissioner that was chased from Natchez & ever since been lurking in the Choctaw & Chickesaw Nations has wrote in here to a trader, asking leave to pass through this country to return home, as he has received letters of recall owing to the limits having been Settled between Monsr. Gardoqui & Congress, & that the Natchez falls within the Spanish limits. He mentions no more, but I expect Your Excellency will soon receive accounts of the whole affair, when I shall be glad to hear it from you.

73. William Davenport was Georgia's principal agent in the Bourbon County affair; see Burnett, *op. cit.* McGillivray called him "a meddling, troublesome fellow," and subsequently had him killed, for which the Spaniards called him to task, but he was no more repentant than in the case of Colonel Sullivan; see document 5, *supra.*

55. *McGillivray to O'Neill, October 30, 1786*
[AGI C 199]
LITTLE TALLASSIE, October 30, 1786

SIR

Since I wrote to Your Excellency last, we had Intelligence from Several places that the Americans were Collecting men from every quarter to form an army to attack this Nation, which reports are confirmd by the Charles Town News papers, & by a letter from the American Agent in the Cherokees to Mr. McDonald formerly British Commissary to that Nation.

The Greater part of the Indians are gone to hunt for their families after having waited at home all Summer watching the motions of the Georgians, however Ive desired that they be all Sent for back as Soon as possible meantime have Scouts out on the Frontier. Some have returnd & Say that the Americans are fortifying a large Camp there, So that by this time they must be on their march toward this country. If they Shoud approach at this Juncture, our people nearly all out a hunting, I expect to have a parcel villages destroyed etc.

From the present posture of affairs with us, Your Excellency will See the necessity that obliged us to make a truce with the Cumberland & over Mountain people, otherwise at this time we Shoud have run the risk to have been attackd on two quarters at once & probably have had our Country over run & totally destroyed. Whereas now we have apprehension from one quarter. We Shall do our best to baffle the attempt of that people.

The Americans report that the boundary or Limits are Settled with Spain. I hope Monsr. Gardoqui did not neglect our representations, which had been Sent to him as the Americans do not Seem to take any Notice of them I expect Your Excellency will have it in Your power to Inform me of all these Matters, very Soon. Such is our present Situation. As other Matters occur I will Inform You of them. I remain with respect & esteem.

Your Excellencys Most Obedt. Servant,

ALEX: McGILLIVRAY [*rubric*]

Governor Arturo O'Neil

56. *McGillivray to Favrot, November 8, 1786*
[BL LC]
LITTLE TALLASSIE, 8 Novemr. 1786

SIR

I take this Opportunity by Reuben Dyer to apologize for my long Silence which has been principally owing to Severe & long Sickness, together with a want of any authentic Information to Communicate to you.

During the Course of the past Summer & till lately we have been threatened with an attack from the americans, & my time has been much taken up in preparing, that in the event of war or peace we might be ready.

The americans likewise, have twice Invited us to a Conference, pretending that they desire an amicable Adjustment, of our differences in preference to War, but having reason to distrust the Sincerity of their professions, I have declind all proposals tending to a personal Interview.

In the Course of my extensive Correspondency I have been fortunate enough to obtain Certain Information of their treacherous designs. It was their Intention had we agreed to meet them in treaty to have Seizd upon a number of principal chiefs, to enforce a Compliance of their unjust demands, & at once to extinguish their fears of an Indian war.

This plan they have executed in part. The chiefs of the Tallassie & Cussitahs Towns & their dependencies have been always freindly to the american Interest & when the rest of the chiefs refused to treat, these chiefs obstinately persisted to go & See their Freinds, the americans, & yesterday a Messenger from the Coweta brought me Information that some Cussitah & Pallachocolla Indians had arrived & gave account that the whole party that went down was Confind in forts & that all the chiefs six in Number, were carried off from their people to Philadelphia, as the americans told them on their first arrival that they must go to the white Town to Confer with their great Council, & these that are come up say that they made their escape at Night from a fort, where the rest remain. I am in daily expectation of hearing farther of this perfidious business.[74]

Please to accept Sir of my most Gratefull acknowledgements for the Civilities you was pleased to honor me with & I wish you with Madame Favrot (to whom I beg to accept my Compliments) many years of the greatest happiness, I remain Sir

Your Most Obdt. Servant,

ALEX: McGILLIVRAY [rubric]

Hon. Cap. Favrot

57. *Linder to Favrot, November 13, 1786*
[French copy in BL LC]

SIR:

74. A like report was sent to O'Neill on November 9, 1786, AGI C 199.

I have the honor of warning you that I have been informed by one Skreb Darbin that he has met at the fork of the road which goes to Pensacola and which is about four leagues from my house, Mr. Jacob Magnaque, father-in-law of Mr. Alexander McGuillivray, Commissary of the Talapuche Nation, who told him that the Americans had caused about 400 Talapuche men, women, and children to come under the pretext of holding a congress at Skalop Creek, about forty leagues from the nearest Talapuche village in the middle of the woods. When this group of savages arrived at the said place, the Americans had about 3000 armed men in ambush who surrounded them and made them all prisoners. They released one to carry a talk to the Talapuche Nation to say to their chiefs that they must submit to the demands that had been made of them previously, which are: first, to give them the lands which they had demanded of them; second, to surrender all the property which they have taken during the war with England, because they had absolutely no reason to mix in the war of the white people; third, they demanded satisfaction for all the murders that they committed on their citizens last summer; and in case of refusal of these three demands they were ready to declare war on them and invade the nation to secure justice by the force of arms.

This news has alarmed the whole nation. More than a hundred persons, most of whom are traders, are ready to leave in order to come into this government and into that of Pensacola. These demands are a result of the refusal of the Talapuches to other demands made upon them last May, the principal of which was to surrender into their hands Jacob Magnaque, Alexander McGuillivray, commissary of the nation, Joseph Cornel, and Richard Belly. These four are white. Furthermore, they ask for Mad Dog, king and chief of the whole nation, and three other principal chiefs whose names I do not know. The Talapuches, in the approaching danger which threatens them, have gathered all their cattle and horses, which they are driving into the government of Pensacola, and Mr. Alexander McGillivray is already on his way to return to his place, which is about eight leagues from here, and where he is to arrive in about a week.[75] I relate all this news to you because I think it deserves some consideration. I am with deepest respect, Sir

75. Zéspedes sent a similar report to Sonora, December 24, 1786. "It is patent that the Georgians tried to turn the Indians against the mestizo Alexander Mac-Gilliv'ay, and that in some measure they have accomplished their intention. . . . . There arrived here recently from the Indian nation a Spaniard, somewhat versed in the language, who assured me that he knows MacGillivray personally, and that he and other whites had retired to Pensacola, more than a month ago, with their slaves, cattle, and goods" (AHN E 3887).

Your most humble and most obedient servant,

J. LINDER

TENSA, November 13th, 1786
To Mr. Favrot

58. *McGillivray to Zéspedes, November 15, 1786*
[LC EF 114J9]
LITTLE TALLASSIE, 15 November 1786

SIR

No doubt Your Excellency has been long in expectation of learning from me the occurrences of the Nation in person. I beg leave by this Conveyance to offer you my reasons why it has hitherto been rather Impracticable & Inconvenient.

In my last letters to Your Excellency You was Informd of the hostile disposition of the Americans toward us, when they found that we have uniformly rejected & declined accepting their offers toward Concluding a peace on the Conditions they demanded, & more especially for the partiallity we discover on all occasions for our treaty of peace, Freindship & Alliance which we had Concluded with Spain.

Very early in the past Spring, I found that the Georgians were Solliciting the aid & assistance of the other States to attack this Nation, & at that period of time we were not well prepard to meet & resist an attack. I concluded to go to Pensacola & represent Our apprehensions to his Excy. Governor ONeil & endeavour to obtain a Sufficient Supply of ammunition & arms but on my Conferring with him, I found a Jaunt to New Orleans to Visit Govr. Miro essentially necessary for the Completion of my business, which I had the Satisfaction of Completing in part, & with Governor ONeils assistance we are in a respectable posture of defence. I returnd from Orleans with my friend Mr. Lesslie, who has I expect Informd Your Excellency of the State of Indisposition I was in when he left this place to return home, & which has been Succeeded by other disagreeable Illnesses until this time.

In September last I received a letter of Invitation to meet Certain Commissioners of the State of Georgia in Congress to treat of peace & an amicable adjustment of all our differences, propositions so fair in appearance we Judgd merited some Consideration. Yet knowing that good order & a due obedience to the Laws were not fully establishd in that State among the upper Inhabitants, who were extremely desirious to avenge themselves for past Injuries upon us, I deemd it prudent to obtain all the Information I coud upon this Subject before we Shoud agree to meet them. The result of my enquiries provd that the Upper Georgians had formd a plan to attend the proposed Con-

138

ferinces with all the Force that they coud raise, & to Seize upon & detain as hostages a Number of our Chiefs, at once to obtain their ends, & to extinguish their fears of an Indian War. All this had been lately Confirmd by Some ChasTown papers that Mr. McLatchy had Sent me, & fully explaind the Whole of their ungenerous, Cowardly & treacherous Intentions, & which is only worthy of those that are the Sweepings of the Continent.

We cannot boast of being perfectly clean ourselves, there are a few of Note as the Tallassie King & Fat King of Cussitahs, & a few others that have been long in the American Interest, forwarding their Views against this Country, on which account I lament that our Customs, (unlike those of Civilized people) Wont permit us to treat as traitors by giving them the usual punishment. However those chiefs & their dependents Contrary to all our opinions, went to Visit their freinds agreeable to their Invitation, & finding no Others came, the americans Conformable to their Concerted plan Seizd upon the principals that went to them & Some of No Note escaped & has brought up the accounts. Those chiefs so detaind having by their bad Conduct forfeited every pretension to Consideration & attention from the rest of the chiefs, their detention gives no Concern to us & their friends are Welcome to keep them as long as they chuse. We Shall not relax upon that account nor make any Sacrifices to obtain their enlargement.

Such is the present State affairs with us at present.[76] Any farther occurrences of Consequence Your Excellency Shall always be apprised of as early as possible. If I have not wrote as often as you expect, it has been owing to the want of material Informations, & as opportunitys from here are not frequent, I wish not to incur unnecessary expence by employing expresses upon trifling occasions, but I have done it in this Instance, as I conceive the Importance of the Subject will Justify it at this time.

I entreat Your Excellency to be persuaded that it is Not a Want of Inclination in me that I have so long delayd doing myself the honor of Satisfying the desire you have for my seeing you at St. Augustine. Tis known only to those in the Management of Indian affairs, the Watchfull & unremitted attention it requires to keep them in some degree of order, & in a State for to be prepared against the attack so long meditated against us by the americans. I even cant absent myself one Month, but everything is in disorder, & untill some pacification is Settled with Georgia it will be Impracticable for me to leave the Nation, & that can only take place when by our firmness we weary them into

76. But compare with the rumored panic in the Creek Nation as described in document 57, *supra*.

more moderate dispositions. Conclude assuring Your Excellency it will always afford me great Satisfaction to hear of Your good health & happiness, & expect that pleasure when Convenient. I remain with most Gratefull acknowledgments for the many & essential acts of Freindship, that you have Shewn & done for my Nation.

Your Excellencys most obliged & obedient Servant

ALEX: McGILLIVRAY [rubric]

his Excellency Governor De Zespedes

59. *McGillivray to O'Neill, December 3, 1786*
[AGI C 199]

LITTLE TALLASSIE, December 3, 1786

SIR

I have received your much esteemd favor of 20 Nov. for which please accept my thanks. In my last letters to Your Excellency, you woud have Seen that we were threatend hard by the americans, & they had actually raisd all the force that they were able & had proceeded as far as the Oconee, to proceed against the Nation. They however soon learnd that we had notice of them & that we were preparing to Set out to meet them. They then Concluded that they coud act with more Safety by Seizing & detaining their good friends the Tame king & Neah Mico (fat king of Cussitah) & which the americans Judged would be a good Security against a war with us, but the Tame King for once in his life time behaved like a Man. When he found that he & people were to be detaind he thunderd out a furious Talk & frightend the Georgians from their purpose of keeping them, & made them some presents & bid them go home. The Americans & the Indians parted from each other at Oconee & each returned home.

Soon after the Indians returnd back McMurphy & Young Galphin came up with a Talk for the Nation but I would not let the chiefs meet McMurphy to hear what he had to say as he is of an Infamous Character. Galphin came to me by desire to request a truce for this winter, as we might agree to terms in the Spring. I told him that we never Wantonly attackd the Georgians, but always in defence of our rights, & that it was their place to Satisfy us, & that the Indians Shoud go a hunting to provide for their familys & if the Georgians did not come to terms in the Spring when the Indians will be all at home, that they must look to it whether we have peace or war.[77]

The cold weather now Setting in has recoverd me a good deal better.

77. O'Neill informed Zéspedes of the substance of this letter on December 29, 1786, AHN E 3887.

I expect to have the Satisfaction soon to make my respects to Your Excellency in person.

Leslie has requested me to write concerning his affair with Weatherford. I think Your Excellency woud not Judge wrong if you made Weatherfords property answerable for poor Leslies debt. Circumstances are Strong, but may be not Sufficient in Law, however he ought to pay.[78]

I remain with the most sincere respect, Your Excellencys most obedient servant,

ALEX: McGILLIVRAY [rubric]

His Excellency Governor O'Neil

60. *McGillivray to Zéspedes, January 5, 1787*

[LC EF 114J9]

SIR   LITTLE TALLASSIE, 5 January 1787

I did myself the pleasure of writing to Your Excellency in the latter end of November last by a chief of the Oussitches Town, which I hope was safely handed to you. By that letter Your Excellency woud See that at that time we had reason to expect an attack from the Americans. We were informd by an Indian from Oconee River that the Georgians were in force there for that Intention & that they had detaind as hostages chiefs of the Cussitah & Tallassees who had gone to meet them in Conference, against the wishes of the Nation. Directly on receiving this Information we recalled our hunters from the Woods & began to take Measures to put ourselves in the best State possible to Meet with effect the threatend attack, & Just as we were ready to take the Feild, the chiefs whom we heard had been detaind all arrived safe & brought accounts that the American Army had dispersd & were returnd to their homes, but if I coud have had my Wish I had rather that they had advanced toward us & had afforded us a chance by a decisive action to have terminated the vexatious disputes so long Subsisting between us & is Still kept up as it originated with them, & by disbanding their forces at Oconee after the great expence & trouble they had put themselves to Convinces me that they choose rather to Carry on a War of Words than to trust to the more manly decision of Arms, but they will find themselves Mistaken, they will find that we are not to be bullied into their Measures so easily as they may flatter themselves with. They have lately held out more pacific Language[79]

78. In a letter to O'Neill, dated January 6, 1787, McGillivray characterized Weatherford and several others as "notorious offenders" and recommended that they be made to "Suffer the Rigour of the Law" (AGI C 200).

79. But the next day McGillivray wrote to O'Neill: "Daniel McMurphy has come into this Country. . . . to instigate the Indians to murder Six principle Traders & even to attempt the assassination of myself with five other chiefs" (AGI C 200).

than they have hitherto done, they have Invited us to meet them in Conference in May Next. This with other Matters shall be deliberated upon in the Grand Convention which I propose to hold in April Next, first in the Lower Nation & one in the Upper. The result of such deliberations I will take care particularly to Inform Your Excellency of in due time.

It is with Infinite Satisfaction I have learnd from Mr. Panton that Your unwearied application to Your Court in favor of the English house of Panton Lesslie & Co. has at last prevailed & that they have received the Royal Sanction for remaining at St. Augustine to Supply the Creek Nations with Brittish Goods. That House having been lately deprived of their Trade to the Chactaw & Chickesaw Nations by order of Governor Miro, in Consequence Mr. Panton has Signified to me his Intention of retiring from Pensacola, as he Confides in Your passports to protect his Commerce to & from St. Marks, Appalachy, a place Convenient & Central to our Nation, & if well Supplyd with Goods will render a Continuation of their expensive establishment at Pensacola no longer Necessary, especially now that their trade is limited to our Nation the Creeks. Permit me to recommend this matter to Your Excellencys most serious Consideration & that you will Communicate an answer as soon as possible.

for the Many Services done to our Nation by the Gentlemen of that Company & more especially at the Conclusion of the late Peace, they at the request of our Nation, when we were at a loss, generously resolved to Continue their Support to us under many Inconveniences so that whatever is Interesting to them is an object of no small Concern to us.

I have particularly to offer you my Sincerest Thanks for your humane & liberal Conduct toward all ranks of my Nation, Which when Contrasted with their treatment in other parts, places Your Excellencys Conduct in the most favorable point of View. You Sir by your generous & freindly treatment of those people who for ages have been the Inveterate enemies of the Spanish Nation, have now through Your Excellencys good Conduct made the Spanish Name be equally revered with their most antient esteemd freinds & Allys. Go on Sir as you have begun and assure yourself of the faithfull attachment of my people & the Sincere respect & esteem of Sir

Your Excellencys Most Obedt. Servt.

ALEX: McGILLIVRAY [rubric]

His Excellency General De Zespedes
Governor & Commander in Cheif East Florida, St. Augustine

142

61. *Zéspedes to McGillivray, February 3, 1787*

[Spanish translation in AHN E 3887]

MY DEAR SIR:

I received your letter of November 15 last[80] on the 2d of this month here in camp. Consequently your messenger will have to wait in St. Augustine until he receives this.

By direct reports, as also through the American gazettes, I have already been informed of the congress held at Shoulder Bone Creek on the Oconee River and of the resultant treaty. But since the articles that are supposed to have been included seem to indicate a mode of thinking on the part of the Indian chiefs quite different from that set forth in your previous letters to me and also in your letter to the president of the committee of Georgian commissioners published in the Savannah and Charleston gazettes, I was very anxious to hear from you directly the true state of affairs.

Also, by your letter of November 15 it seems that you yourself have not been perfectly informed about the treaty of Shoulder Bone. Consequently, I shall suspend the formation of any judgment until you write to me again, which I hope you will do as soon as you receive this. I shall be the more anxious to hear from you because rumors are circulating here that you and other whites have been compelled to leave the Indian nation. In the meantime I shall communicate the contents of your letter to the court. I do not doubt that his Majesty will adopt officially such measures as in his wisdom seem most conducive toward restoring the rights and well-being of the Indians under his royal protection, without prejudice to the good harmony that exists at present between Spain and the United States of America. According to the general understanding the United States neither approved nor helped the violent acts which you in your letter blame particularly upon the upper inhabitants of Georgia.

Your answer is still lacking to the letter in which I sent word that Tolintoneche had received the presents that you requested for him. In it I also enclosed a gazette.

The reasons you advance for not coming here are quite adequate. Come when you wish, you will always be welcome. Rest assured of my friendly interest in the prosperity of your nation in general and particularly in the recovery of your health.

May God spare you many years. Amelia Island, February 3, 1787, etc.

VIZENTE MANUEL DE ZÉSPEDES

Mr. Alexander Mac-Gillevray.

80. Document 58, *supra.*

62. O'Neill to Sonora, February 20, 1787

[Spanish original in AHN E 3887]

MOST EXCELLENT SIR:

. . . .By this opportunity I must submit to your Excellency that it appears to me indispensable, if we are to retain the friendship of these Indian nations, that the king appoint three commissaries who shall not carry on any trade with the Indians, but be established in the Chickasaw, Chocataw, and Lower Creek Nations to observe and gain full knowledge of what those nations deal with frequently in their meetings and to counteract the influence of the American emissaries and agents.

The commissary Alexander McGilbray was employed during the last war by the British and up to the present has been an open enemy of the Americans. He has been most useful thus far in gaining for us the friendship of the Creeks. But one must not lose sight of the fact that he lives at an extremity of the nations, where as a mestizo he is chief of a town, and one must consider that his efforts will always be directed toward the ends that he conceives to favor the Indians his tribesmen, who, as he says, consider themselves brothers and allies of Spain only. . . . .

ARTURO O'NEILL [*rubric*]

Most Excellent Señor Marqués de Sonora

63. McGillivray to O'Neill, March 4, 1787

[AGI C 200]

LITTLE TALLASSIE, 4 March, 1787

SIR

Upon my arrival here James Keeff, a trader deliverd me Your Excellencys letter of 3d decemb. last, which sayd he was orderd to deliver into my hands himself.

It being only last night that I arrived I have not as Yet Seen any person from abroad to Inform me Concerning McMurphy & other americans, except that I understand that a person is lately arrived in the Lower Towns at the Cussitahs from Georgia & he is orderd to endeavor to get Some body to Murder me privately as they expect that next Spring I Shall order all the americans that remain on the Oconee off or order them to be killd & are apprehensive of a war. However this Shall not deter me from going to the lower Towns next month to hold a meeting at Cowetas, & every american I find in the lower Towns Shall either be drove away or put to Death for Cowardly Murdering Villains as they are.[81]

81. Although he agreed that McMurphy should be eliminated, Miró urged a more humanitarian method. He also hoped that the Indians could be dissuaded from taking scalps (Miró to O'Neill, March 12, 1787, AHN E 3887).

As there have been Several Towns of late that used to be friends to the Georgians have Shewn a disposition to Join the rest of the Nation, I am of Opinion that they Shoud be encouraged & when I See their chiefs & Speak to them & find them Sincere it will be Necessary to furnish them with ammunition as the rest have received, for as we have begun a dispute with the Georgians about Lands we must now go through with.it, & a Spirited exertion of our force in the Spring, if it Shoud be necessary, will Im of opinion efectually Crush their hopes of possessing our Country. About Six hundred weight more of powder woud Just Compleat our wants for those Towns that I did not give any to last Summer.

I shall be glad to learn from Your Excellency if I can depend upon receiving that quantity if I Shoud Send, as if I was to Send chiefs & they not to get any woud be attended with a bad Consequence to our Cause.

The Tallassie & Okfuskee Indians have made an attack upon Cumberland in my absence & have brought in Scalps & horses, as likewise the Shawnees or Savnahs.[82] This is rather unexpected as the Tallasses have been always great freinds with the americans. Any more news that may occur I will not fail to Communicate the Same mean time remain with great Esteem & regard,

Your Excellencys obed. Servant,

ALEX: McGILLIVRAY [rubric]

Governor Arturo O'Neil

64. Miró to O'Neill, March 24, 1787

[Spanish original in AGI C 4]

Under date of the first of this month you informed me of Alexander McGillivray's resolution to attack the Americans this spring. He has shown you the need of a good number of guns for this purpose, and he hopes that they will be furnished.[83]

The protection that his nation has solicited and obtained from his Majesty requires that you and I advise McGillivray and the other chiefs what action would serve them best. Therefore it seems to me that they ought not to make another attack while the United States does not harm them. If they exasperate the Georgians with new hostilities all the states will make common cause. I think the Creeks would

82. Governor Caswell of North Carolina wrote to McGillivray on February 24, 1787, in conciliatory vein. He announced the defensive garrisoning of Cumberland, but disclaimed any hostile intentions (State Records of North Carolina, XX, 619-20).
83. See also O'Neill to Miró, March 8, 1787, stressing the necessity of Creek preparedness against an American attack (AHN E 3887).

not be able to resist them, as McGillivray himself solemnly predicted in the letter he wrote you on October 3 last. In it he said, "Your Excellency will see the necessity that obliged us to make peace with the inhabitants of Cumberland. Otherwise we should have run the danger of being attacked by two parties at once and probably we should have had our land overrun and totally destroyed."

If he realizes that Cumberland with Georgia would destroy them, how much more should he fear if the general congress were to take part, as it must in this war.

Last year they committed hostilities, though justified ones, without first asking the approval of this government. Fear that the Georgians would come to take revenge moved them to ask our aid under the condition that they remain on the defensive. On this assumption the most excellent Señor Conde de Gálvez gave them aid with all possible precaution not to compromise ourselves with the United States. Yet I do not believe that we can avoid it if we furnish them a larger number of guns as McGillevray asks. Therefore I do not consider it prudent to provide them. It would better suit the king's service under the present circumstances to induce them to remain at peace until they see the outcome of the boundary dispute, for if it does force us to make common cause against the usurpations of the United States, then the Talapuches, enabling us to support them openly, will be more capable of doing themselves justice.

You see already that this affair is not of the sort that should be entrusted to the pen. Therefore it would be wise for you to summon McGillevray to a conference or that you send a trustworthy and discreet agent to carry the message orally.

Nevertheless, as a gift to the different chiefs and bands you may distribute one hundred guns, on condition that they are not to make any attack this year. But if the American army forms to invade their lands, I authorize you without tarrying for my approval to give them the ammunition and military stores that they need under the same precautions as last year.[84]

May God spare you many years, New Orleans, March 24, 1787, etc.,

ESTEVAN MIRÓ [rubric]

Most Excellent Señor Arturo O'Neill.

84. A like report was sent to Sonora, AHN E 3887. On July 31 Valdés communicated royal approval: "The king has seen fit to approve your actions and that you did not accede entirely to McGillivray's request. And it is his royal will that you continue advising McGillivray and the other chiefs of these Indians not to attack the Americans but to remain on the defensive, for if they are invaded you will support them as is appropriate" (*ibid.*).

65. *McGillivray to O'Neill, April 4, 1787*

[AGI C 202]

LITTLE TALLASSIE, 4 April, 1787

SIR

The Bearer hereof named Cooseah informs me that Some White Ground or Conhatke Indians had killd Some of Doctor Ruby's Cattle of which Your Excellency Spoke to him about; I have been so much engaged of Late that I had no time to Enquire into it but Shall the first meeting which will be next month.

I had already informd Your Excellency that I entended to go this Spring & hold a General assembly of all the middle & Lower Creeks & Seminoles & the last Week I Sent a Messenger to Notify to the Chiefs of those parts to assemble themselves as Soon as Convenient for I woud be down among them to give them my Talks.

My Messenger returned here Yesterday & I received a notification from a Coll. White[85] that He was a Commissioner appointed by Congress & that He was just Come from Philadelphia to hold a conference with this nation to make peace & that He would be in the Lower Towns very Soon to meet me.[86]

I mean to Sett out for the Cowettas in four days & if Colo. White is in those parts on my arrival there I will on my return inform Your Excellency of whatever passes between us if we see each other. I had the Satisfaction to Make that Scoundrel McMurphy run off as hard as Coud for His life.

I can assure Your Excellency for a Certainty that a General Indian War rages from the Lakes of Canada thro' all the American Outsettlements to Cumberland, Some of which are Effectually broke up. Mr. Hutchins Surveyor I doubt has come but bad Speed in his appointments to Survey Lands on Ohio River. Some of His assistants are Killed by the Indians as they took some plans & drafts among other papers which they did not bring home but gave to Some Cherokee Traders.

I have been unwell Some time past. I am Sorry to inform Your

85. Although James White bungled this enterprise, he is notable as the founder of Knoxville, Tennessee, whose site was assigned him by North Carolina as payment for his service in the Revolution. Its subdivision and sale made him wealthy. He commanded its defense against the Cherokees in 1793 and was state senator in 1796-97.

86. Introducing himself to McGillivray by a letter dated April 4, 1787, White stated that the territory of Georgia seemed to him "amply extensive," and that, the Georgian government could not want "to disperse its subjects still more widely while there is so much internal room for cultivation" (ASP IA, I, 21-22). Replying on April 8, McGillivray reviewed the history of Creek relations with Georgia, and stated that he counted on White to remove the principal barrier to peace, by securing to the Creeks their hunting grounds. In the course of this letter he asserted, "I aspire to the honest ambition of meriting the appellation of the preserver of my country" (*ibid.*, pp. 18-19).

147

Excellency of the sudden Death of my Interpreter Moniac who dyed of a dry Belly Ache. I feel his Loss. He was a Just & faithfull man in his place. I Shall never have Such another again. Wishing You Health & prosperity I remain

Your Excellencys Most affectionate Servt.

ALEX: McGILLIVRAY [rubric]

Gov. Arturo O'Neill

66. McGillivray to Zéspedes, April 10, 1787

[LC EF 114J9]

COWETAS LOWER TOWN 10 April 1787

SIR

I have Just time to Inform Your Excellency that I have held a Meeting at Oussitche, when a Commissioner from the American Congress was present, & he is not yet gone his name is James White & being rather busy I Shall dispatch the Younger Perrymont in a few days with a full Account of the result of our Conferences,[87] which I imagine will not be altogether so Satisfactory as I coud wish in any event I Shall treat with this American Negotiator without Concedeing in any points that my be prejudicial to us under a firm Persuasion that we will be properly Supported by Your Government in Maintaining our rights against the Americans.

The bearers did not get their Complement of powder & Ball last fall, he has a ticket from some officer of yours. Being of opinion We Shall Soon want some, for I find we must drive the Georgians from our lands, as they are not disposed to do us Justice, the attacks of last Spring has not answered as well as we expected, as those people have again returned to the Oconee & over it. 150 lb powder for these people they have a Memorandum in Spanish.

Wishing Your Excellency every happiness I remain With most respectfull Esteem

Your Most Obedt. Servant

ALEX: McGILLIVRAY [rubric]

His Excellency General De Zespedes
Governor East Florida

87. The letter, written on April 15, closely resembles document 67, *infra*. McGillivray also stated: "It is true that the Georgians in November last in a Conference held at Oconee made a hard push to get their freinds among the Indians to effect my destruction with Several other Chiefs & Some traders, in order to remove every obstacle in their way to accomplish their favorite Schemes of depriving of the Nation of a great part of its possessions, but the greatest & most violent of their partisans have not dared to avow Such a design in this Country, Nor has my Influence & authority Suffered the least diminishment in Consequence of the American Talks" (LC EF 114J9).

[AGI C 202]

LITTLE TALLASSIE, 18 April, 1787

SIR

In my last letter to Your Excellency I acquainted You of my intending Soon for the Lower Towns of this Nation to Call a meeting of all the Chiefs of that part of the Country. Upon my arrival at the Cowetas I found that a person had arrived at an Indian Village, who announced himself to me by the name of James White & a Commissioner appointed by Congress to treat with this Nation. Upon our Meeting I had some Conversation with him on the Subject of his Commission, & we did not agree in our opinions, he wanted to obtain a Confirmation of the disputed Lands to Georgia.[88] I told him that when I heard he was Sent by Congress to our Country, we expected that he was come with full powers to do our Nation Justice & remove all Causes of our discontents & Complaints, but I found that we were deceived in our expectations, & he might as well have not Come into our Nation. However as he had Come Just in the time of My Meeting, he was welcome to deliver any Talk he chose in public to the chiefs of the Lower Nation then assembled & he would hear from their mouths their Sentiments respecting our dispute with Georgia, & then upon his return back he coud Satisfy both Congress & the Georgians of the true disposition of the Nation concerning these matters, & then it woud be found that all my proceedings had been directed by the general voice of the Whole Nation, & for which the Georgians had endeavourd to bribe Indians & employd white men to Murder me. McMurphy by orders had offerd four horse loads of Goods to any Indian that woud procure my death, upon a discovery of which he run away, for fear of the chastizement his Villainy deservd.

When the chiefs were all assembled in the Square of the Oussitche Town we repaird thither, & Mr. White the Commissioner gave a Talk from Congress, which was expressed in freindly terms. In his Talk he mentiond that the great kings over the Sea was contriving Schemes to Subdue america & the Indians, therefore they Shoud both Join in defence of the Country, an Idea that Seemd to please the chiefs, that the americans were afraid of some power.[89]

88. But White's report to Knox indicates that he did not consider Georgia's claims valid (ASP IA, I, 20-21). A committee of the Georgia legislature, furthermore, censured White for "too sudden interferences with treaties of the State," and blamed him for the reopening of the Oconee War (*ibid.*, pp. 23-24).

89. White's version of his speech is printed (*ibid.*, pp. 22-23). His urging that the Creeks and Americans make common cause "against a power that intends to subjugate them" was taken by Miró as the basis for urging redoubled efforts to retain the loyalty of the Creeks to Spain (Miró to Sonora, June 1, 1787, AHN E 3887).

After a chief was appointed Speaker for the rest, which was Yaholla Mico of Coweta,[90] an answer was given, from all the Lower Creeks to the Commissioner, & told him that I had been appointed their first chief to manage all affairs Concerning of the Nation, & that the Georgians had Insolently disregarded all my representations to them respecting our Lands, that being averse to the Shedding of the blood of the Americans, every peaceable Mode was tryd without effect, & when entreatys coud not prevail the Nation had been Compelld to have recourse to arms to maintain its Just Rights—& that they now expected Justice from Congress, & to prevent all bad Consequences they must directly take Steps to remove the Cause of our Complaints.

The chiefs likewise observd that when the Georgians had made the demand of the lives of certain men of us, they took & detaind five principal men of the Cowetas & Cussetas as hostages, to Instigate their relations in the Nation to perpetrate the Murders of those people, which hostages the Nation Now required of the Georgians to deliver up & if not Soon Complyd with they woud make a Severe retalliation. This was the Reply & answer of the Lower Creeks Chiefs to Commissioner White. I request of Your Excellency to be pleased to Send a Copy of this to Governor Miro being unable to write much at present.[91]

A few days before I got to the Cowetas Town a Messenger had been dispatchd[92] from the lower Towns to Augusta demanding the release of those Indians that were there detaind, & as I find them people much disposed to retalliate, I desired them remain quiet the time out in which they expected the arrival of those hostages (which was thirty days) & after that, if those people did not return, they were at liberty to attack the Georgians & make reprisals, & advised them to make prisoners of double the Number of Indians that were detained at Augusta for an exchange.

I had wrote to Your Excellency for an additional Supply of ammunition, there being Several Towns that got none, as the Wackakay, Puckentallahassie & two other Villages in the upper Creeks & at this last

90. According to White's report, the Hallowing King spoke very eloquently, predicting that Congress and the Indians could, no doubt, adjust matters amicably, "but there was a third party (Georgia) who had no mind to do justice" (ASP IA, I, 22-23; see also White to Knox, May 24, 1787, *ibid.*, pp. 20-21).

91. McGillivray does not mention a remarkable proposition which White quotes him as making: "I will now put it to the test whether they [the Georgians] or myself entertain the most generous sentiments of respect for Congress. If that honorable body can form a government to the southward of the Altamaha, I will be the first to take the oath of allegiance thereto; and in return to the Georgians, for yielding to the United States that claim, I will obtain a regular and peaceable grant of the lands on the Oconee" (ASP IA, I, 22-23). These were approximately the terms of the subsequent treaty of New York.

92. By White; see his explanation in the letter to Knox, May 24, 1787, *ibid.*, pp. 20-21.

150

Meeting in the Lower Towns I had the Satisfaction to find the whole Nation Now Unanimous, the Cussitahs & Tallasses &a. assisted at the Convention & declared themselves openly. Such an event makes the further Supply asked for absolutely Necessary. The Cowetas &a. I am Certain by this time has attackd the Georgians on account of the hostages & beside the war that is Carrying on against Cumberland & those Places cause Some expenditure of ammunition. I wish to know if I may Send for it. The Indian Ninne Wakitche came from You as he says, when I was in the Lower Nation, he reported to me that Your Excellency told him that you were preparing to be in a readiness 'to evacuate Pensacola to the French who were Soon expected there, & that you did no further business with this Nation but desired that we Shoud take the Matter into Consideration & to Send if we wanted any more means &a. The News papers give an account that an exchange was likely to take place with France. I shall be glad to hear of this from You in Your next letter, whether tis so or not. Meantime I remain with most Sincere regard & esteem Your Excellencys

Most obedt. Servant

ALEX: McGILLIVRAY [rubric]

his Excellency Governor ONeil

68. *McLatchy to John Leslie, May 14, 1787*
[Spanish translation in AHN E 3887]

CABANNY, May 14, 1787

DEAR SIR:

They have had a famous meeting as the Chehawes between the Indians and the Georgians. A certain Mr. White, who came as superintendent, met with the major part of the Indians from all the towns.

Sehaky, or king of the Checowetas, made a speech. He said that he was happy to attend a general congress, since he would know those who were of the same way of thinking. He was happy to see the men who had ceded the lands to the Georgians seated in their places. He told them to rise and say clearly whether they had in fact ceded the lands, and in case they had done so that they show by what authority or right they had ceded that which was not theirs.

These chiefs did not endeavour to say a word, but sat immobile like sentenced criminals. Doctor White urged them to speak, but they did not wish to answer anything, to the great confusion of White and of the others who came with him and to the great satisfaction of MacGillivray and the traders. White returned immediately to Georgia, and I suppose that shortly they will assemble their vagabonds for another expedition.[93]

I suppose that Mr. MacGillivray will have written to his Excellency the governor, giving him a full account of everything. I got my information from the chiefs and traders who came here just after having attended the meeting. I have many other things to relate, but I must leave the rest for another occasion. I am

Yours sincerely,

CHARLES MCLATCHY

Mr. John Leslie, Esq.

69. *O'Neill to Miró, May 21, 1787*
[Spanish original in AGI C 37]

To avoid the inconvenience of informing Alexander McGilbray in writing of the 600 pounds of powder and the 100 guns that you warn me are needed now as a gift to the Indians, I am ordering that Antonio Garzon go quickly to Little Tallassie where McGilbray resides to tell him about it verbally.[94] I have arranged for him to go to other Indian towns in order that by some dissembling pretext he can better find out about the treaty of the Indians and McGilbray with Colonel White, who represented the United States of America. I fear that there will result from these conferences some agreement not conducive to the best service of our monarch, for I am certain that the Americans hope to turn McGilbray away from our interests. Recently and at present, it

93. Hostilities broke out very soon. On June 14, the Hallowing King of the Cowetas and the Fat King of the Cussitahs complained to Governor Mathews that, though it was the Oakgees of the Upper Creeks who had gone to war, the Georgians retaliated by killing a larger number of the Lower Creeks (ASP IA, I, 32). Mathews put the blame on McGillivray and recommended that the Lower Creeks exact satisfaction from the Upper (*ibid.*, pp. 32-33). The Fat King denied that McGillivray was at fault and demanded of Mathews "immediate satisfaction, life for life, an equal number for twelve of our people destroyed by you" (*ibid.*, p. 33). "When I think of this insolent demand," Mathews exploded, "I feel my blood run warm in my veins, and a just impulse to chastise them for their insolence and perfidy" (*ibid.*, p. 31; see also document 70 and note 97, *infra*).

94. A step proposed by O'Neill to Miró, April 27, 1787, AHN E 3887. Replying on May 4, Miró approved the sending of Garcon. He was to urge McGillivray to make peace upon the basis of the Oconee boundary and that American trade should not be admitted. Spanish support was promised, provided the Creeks remained on the defensive (see document 64, *supra*), and to that end Miró promised to send O'Neill an additional 500 stand of guns. Garcon's instructions were not to be put in writing; for one reason, because he did not know how to read (Miró to O'Neill, May 4, 1787, AHN E 3887). To McGillivray on May 9, Miró wrote: "I wish you could make up matters with our Neighbours the Americans in such a manner as that you live in quiet & that your Nation continuing under the Protection of his Majesty should persevere in refusing to have any Intercourse with them as agreed between us in Congress" (AGI C 200). All these precautions were belated, for the meeting had taken place on April 10.

seems to me, he has found it convenient to endeavor to restrain the Americans. I conceive, however, that, notwithstanding the port already established on the Apalachee coast with permission for those Indians to trade as they please, it is not best that McGilbray become such an authority in the nation that he could bring about the entire independence of the Indians. I am sure that should he succeed in this matter he would prove more loyal to the British trade than to the Spaniards, and given more time that he would consider himself chief of the Indian nations and independent, even though he has cooperated effectively to drive out the Americans.[95]

May God spare your Excellency many years, Pensacola, May 21, 1787.

ARTURO O'NEILL [rubric]

VI

WAR ON CUMBERLAND AND GEORGIA

70. *McGillivray to O'Neill, June 20, 1787*
[AGI C 200]
LITTLE TALLASSIE, 20 June, 1787

SIR

I have to Inform Your Excellency that we have had a great Meeting with the Chiefs of the Northern Nations, the Chiefs of the Iroquois, Hurons, Mohocks, Wyandots, Oneidas, & Shawnese.[96] They are Sent from the northern Confederacy, Consisting of Twenty five Nations, that Inhabit about the Lakes, River Ohio, Wabash & other parts of the Western Country of North America. I have concluded Matters with them to Serve the Kings Interest, to the wishes & desires of Don Gardoque. These Northerns tell me that they have routed & dispersed many partys of Surveyors from the Ohio & Western Country, & we have agreed Jointly to attack the Americans in every place wherever they Shall pass over their own proper Limits, nor never to grant them Lands, nor Suffer Surveyors to roam about the Country. They are now gone back but another deputation is to arrive here in November next, to let us know how affairs come on to the Northward.

95. See O'Neill to Miró, April 27, 1787, AHN E 3887; also notes 84 and 94, *supra*, and Miró to Sonora, June 1, 1787, AHN E 3887.
96. A detailed account of this meeting, together with comments on the earlier meeting with White, is to be found in a letter from McGillivray to a correspondent in the Bahama Islands, June 30, 1787, Spanish translation in AHN E 3901.

I had wrote to Your Excellency Some Time ago requesting another addition to our Ammunition. We have at least eight Hundred warriors who have received none, to which You made me no answer. The particular Situation of our affairs make a Repitition of Such a Request absolutely necessary. I had Informed Your Excellency in a former letter that the Tallasses & Cussitahs & other of Georgians Indian freinds, were come over to our Interest, that they ought to have ammunition. Yesterday an Express arrived from the Cussitahs Informing me that the Georgians have barbarously murderd Six of their men, without any cause whatever & Shockingly mangled the dead Carcasses by Scalping & cutting to pieces. The Indians were killed hunting for the Americans among their habitations. I have been at great pains to Inculcate Ideas & Sentiments of humanity in the minds of the Indians, but from such proceedings of the Americans, my good Intentions are frustrated.

Last Summer they killed two of our people, which I bore with, but this last Stroke & Insult offerd to us by those people deserves the Severest Chastizement, which they Shall Certainly receive in due time.[97]

There is another matter which gives me some uneasiness which is owing to Timothy Lane,[98] a trader who for his many crimes I punished in Suspending him from trading, as an example to others it being the mildest punishment I coud Inflict. I gave Him many necessarys & left him all his horses & other effects. He has been lately at Pensacola, & Reports to Indians & others many things, that he Says Your Excellency Shoud Say about me, tending to make people act desobediently, & undervalue me in the minds of the Indians. For my own part I give no credit to it, knowing the Considerable Share of regard Your Excellency was always pleased to Shew me, & I mean no flattery when I declare ever Since I knew You I had an affection for Your Excellency equal to the brother of my own Father & if Lane is not Silent in future

97. Writing on November 15, 1787, Mathews gave this picture of casualties in the Indian War since August 9: "Our frontiers have been the scene of blood and ravages; they have killed thirty-one of our citizens, wounded twenty, and taken four prisoners; they have burnt the court house and town of Greensburgh, in the county of Greene, and a number of other houses in different parts of the country" (ASP IA, I, 23). On November 6, he had recited the woes of the Georgians in a letter to Zéspedes and requested the latter to see that the Creeks were not supplied arms and ammunition (AHN E 3887). Zéspedes replied on December 10 that he "sympathized perfectly," that the cruelties of the savages would "stir sentiments of horror in any civilized breast," and especially among the Spaniards who had witnessed such atrocities during the Revolution, that he had tried to persuade the Indians not to take scalps, and that he would be careful not to give them more ammunition than was necessary for their hunting (ibid.).

98. The feud between McGillivray and Lane became increasingly serious, and since O'Neill sheltered Lane as a Spanish citizen, he also was involved. For a time it kept McGillivray away from Pensacola. See document 101, infra.

considerations for my authority must oblige me to take other more harsh Steps to Silence him effectually.

As I conceive it to be necessary for Your Excellency to be duly Informd of our public occurrences I Sometimes employ an Indian for the trifle of two kegs Taffia, for his trouble. Neither Shall I give any Indian in future any papers of a trifling nature.

I entreat Your Excellency to order the bearer two kegs of Taffia. I have desired him to return directly that I may know what to do as Soon as possible.

Wishing Your Excellency great prosperity I remain
With respectful esteem
Your Excellencys most obedt. Servt.

ALEX: McGILLIVRAY [*rubric*]

Governor Arturo O'Neill

71. *McGillivray to O'Neill, July 10, 1787*
[AGI C 200]
LITTLE TALLASSIE, 10 July, 1787

SIR

I take this opportunity of Informing of Your Excellency that five days ago I received the Second Notice that the americans of Cumberland had attackd & killed the most of the French traders that used to trade upon the Cherokee River, together with Some of our Indians & Cherokees are likewise killed. In Consequence of this affair I have Sent off between five & Six hundred warriors under approved leaders to go & ravage the Settlement of Cumberland & destroy their houses & plantations.

All the different Towns are now getting Ready to Celebrate their yearly New Fires,[99] directly after that we mean to give the Georgians a hearty Chastisement for the barbarous Murder that they Committed on the Cussitahs & Some Cowetas Indians of which I have already Informd Your Excellency of.

The bearer is Mico of the Weokes Town he goes to buy some Necessarys. He is a brother of the great chief that we used to Call the Big Fellow, & is Never been down to You Since the great Congress three years ago. I request Your Excellency to take some Notice of him.

I had Sent down to the Lower Towns to have Lieut. Verduca favorably received with his detachment at St. Marks & expect to hear Soon that he is arrived there.

Antony Garcon is gone to the Lower Towns about Cattle, I believe

99. For a description of the "new fires" ceremony or busk see Swanton, *Social Organization. . . . of the Creek Confederacy*, pp. 546-614.

155

he has had pretty good Success in buying about here.[100] Any farther News of Consequence that May occur I Shall take care to Inform Your Excellency. Mean time remain with most affectionate regard

Your Excellencys Most obedt. Servt.

ALEX: McGILLIVRAY [rubric]

his Excellency Governor O.Neil

72. *O'Neill to Sonora, July 11, 1787*

[Spanish original in AHN E 3887]

MOST EXCELLENT SIR:

The full understanding that I have acquired of the Indian nations, particularly the Creek or Talapuche, and the great advantages that I think will accrue to the crown, assuring it hereafter the friendship of these Indians, and proceeding thereafter to civilize them entirely, reducing them shortly to loyal subjects of his Majesty, move me to take the liberty of explaining to your Excellency what seems to me would be convenient. Meanwhile they would serve usefully as a vanguard for the protection of the Mississippi and these other dominions of our king, which the insatiable and turbulent ambition of the Americans menaces. I ask your Excellency to pardon this intrusion if it does not merit your attention.[101]

These Indians comprise several tribes or families of distinct names, such as the Tiger, the Wind, the Bear, the Wolf, etc., generally opposed to the Americans, motivated by their haughty treatment, which has roused most of the Indians to abhor them.

To keep them grateful and to preserve their friendship the royal treasury has the constant expense of presents, without in this fashion securing their permanent affection for us, but tending rather to place principal emphasis upon the gifts. Not to weary your attention I omit further reflections as to the object which I have the honor to present in brief terms for its usefulness in the better service of his Majesty. Action to put the plan into operation will be more effective than a multitude of arguments. In brief, it is to enlist six or more companies of

100. McGillivray seems to have had no inkling of the secret purpose of Garcon's visit. See O'Neill to Miró, April 27, 1787, AHN E 3887, and note 94, *supra*.

101. Compare with Gardoqui's suggestion that control of the Creeks in the Spanish interest would be expedited if the nation could be persuaded to "organize itself with some civilization, appropriating to the individuals definite tracts of land" (Gardoqui to Floridablanca, June 25, 1789, AHN E 3893. See also Knox to Washington, July 5, 1789, ASP IA, I, 52-54). Knox called for a "noble, liberal, and disinterested administration of Indian affairs." He advocated civilization rather than extermination of the Indians. His "conciliatory system" comprised presents of sheep and other animals, instruction in tilling the soil, conferring of silver medals and gorgets, provision of missionaries, and introduction of a "love for exclusive property."

156

one hundred Indians of the most distinguished warriors of the most valiant tribes, with a great chief and four lesser chiefs for each; rewarding each man annually with a blanket, a pair of leggings of ordinary cloth, a loincloth of the same, a hat, a shirt of ordinary linen, two pounds of powder, four pounds of balls,[102] two flints, one half ounce of vermillion, eight bits worth of aguardiente of sugar cane, 365 pounds of rice, and eight ounces of tobacco, the product of this country. To each chief should be given a double quantity of the goods listed for each man, except the rice, of which the quantity indicated would suffice.

The cost of the things listed for each man would amount under good management and at the prices now current, to twenty-seven hard silver pesos annually.

I should not fail to inform your Excellency how docile these nations are, swayed generally by what the Europeans or whites advise, letting themselves be governed entirely by those who have lived with some European women of the English nation.[103] And the mestizo sons of these are most inclined toward the whites. There is need that a good missionary should come promptly to make all the necessary arrangements to bring about marriages between the persons of these nations and some of our Europeans already distinguished for excessive fondness for the Indian women, and these equally enamored of the whites. Through these alliances in due course I think that in a short time the most fertile lands from the head of the Escambia River to the Tensaw River and all those on that side to within sixteen leagues of this town would be immediately cultivated by friendly Indians and mestizos, where those who have just finished their exile here would go to settle, as also all those Indians married to white women, and not merely those enlisted in the said companies.

All these nations are armed with good carbines and muskets, and their principal warriors now numbering seven thousand want for their better defense against enemy cavalry some halberds with light heads, arms which please them greatly and for which they have asked me many times.[104]

102. "Valas de Freta" which may indicate the caliber.
103. ". . . .algunas Europeas de Nacion Ynglesa." I would question the gender, but the idea recurs toward the end of the paragraph: "como tambien todos los Indios, Casados con blancas." The Southeastern Indians had absorbed a great deal of Caucasian blood by this time. Most of it came from white men, but white women were sometimes captured (see document 182, *infra*) or voluntarily married Indians (see document 37, *supra*). Almost without exception, however, the mestizo leaders had Caucasian patronyms: McGillivray, Colbert, Durand, Galphin, Kelley, Cornell, etc.
104. O'Neill's plan of enlisting Indian warriors closely resembles the one which Knox unfolded later. See ASP IA, I, 249-50.

May God keep you many years. Pensacola, July 11, 1787.
Most Excellent Sir

ARTURO O'NEILL [rubric]

Most Excellent Señor Marqués de Sonora

73. *McGillivray to O'Neill, July 12, 1787*
[AGI C 200]
LITTLE TALLASSIE, 12th July 1787

SIR

I have received Your Excellencys two letters by Keeff. The Uchees are a Set of Notorious thieves, & always were so, & theres a party that almost lives down about Your Settlements: old Mark Nose is a great Villain, but the people of LeCoste is mistaken, because Mark Nose has been at home these two months past & more. It was only a Short time Since, I orderd him to be punishd for a horse, the which he deliverd & promising good behaviour in future he was forgiven.

The bearer is Your former friend Red Shoes Nephew, Who being a good resolute Man I have directed to try & find out if possible those lurking thieves down there, that Such practices may be put a Stop to. An alabama chief & Some Coosadas I am informd, were the last offenders in killing Cattle Near to Town, but they were detected as I'm informed & had the meat taken from them, people of those Towns will no doubt be properly noticed if ever any more goes to Pensacola.

I wish that Weatherford had been better Secured, & have reason to believe that they are harboured about Tensaw or Tombegbe river, there are as Some bad people as him on Tensaw & the other place. I thank Your Excellency for Your Caution if ever Weatherford Shews himself within ten Miles of my house, he will be Servd as he Justly deserves.

I had wrote to Your Excellency that I had Sent to the Lower Towns to get a favorable reception to the detachment that intended for St. Marks. I again repeat to Your Excellency my assurances of exerting my Influence to give Satisfaction if in my power to the wishes & desires of the principal officers of Government. I remain very affectionately Your Excellencys Most obedient

ALEX: MCGILLIVRAY [rubric]

his Excellency Governor ONeil

74. *McGillivray to O'Neill, July 25, 1787*
[AGI C 200]
LITTLE TALLASSIE, 25 July, 1787

DEAR SIR

Having wrote very fully to Your Excellency at Several times lately, this Serves chiefly to Inform you that a party of Coosadas has returnd from reconnoitreing about the Chickesaw Nation, where we heard that the americans were building a fort. The Indian Leader reports that within four leagues of the Chickesaws, he found a party of americans at work upon buildings & that he attackd them, & dispersd them & Killed seven of them, & took near Seventy New Rifle Guns, & brought in a German boy a prisoner, who Speaks good English. He tells me that the american Agent Davenport was killed & an officer from Cumberland named Allen. This will be a warning to them chaps how they go about building forts. I think the Coosada leader deserves great Credit for the Spirit & Gallantry he Shewd upon this occasion, having only a handfull of men he attackd a Superior enemy & defeated them with the loss of one man, & even marchd with the trophys of his victory through the chickesaws nation, & who were all Davenports freinds. The fall of this man will alter american affairs in those Nations, for he was a meddling, troublesome fellow among Indians. The warriors that Marchd against Cumberland are not Yet returnd, but expect them every day. Before we attackd the Georgians, we have demanded Satisfaction & we wait for their answer & am Just Informed that it is arrived at the Cowetas, where Im going in a few days, when I Shall know what to do. Mr. Bruin deliverd me Your Excellencys letter a few days Since. The times are Not Suitable for his travelling as Yet, he proposes to Wait a little longer. Mean time Shall make his Stay as agreeable as possible to him.

Durant Stands in need of Your Excellencys good offices to recover his Negro at Mobile. Mr. Favrot didn't do him Justice, he was very partial in his Government. Durant has a likely Young Negro Man & who is of No Service to him but Steals horses from every one, & an Indian Wench his wife. Now he owes a great deal of Money, & Mrs. Durant dont desire to part with them. Yet We advised Durant to get Your leave to Sell them to clear his other Negroes, whatever his wife may Say against the Contrary.[105] I remain

Your Excellencys Most obedt. Servant

ALEX: MCGILLIVRAY [*rubric*]

his Excellency Colonel O.Neal, Governor Pensacola

I have not wrote to Governor Miro a long time, please forward his letter.

105. Durand's wife, against whom McGillivray here sided so emphatically, was his sister Sophia.

[Duplicate in LC EF 114J9]

PENSACOLA 4th Octr. 1787

SIR

I had done myself the pleasure of writing to Your Excellency in August last in which I gave you a full State of our occurrences.

About the middle of last Month a Considerable body of my people returned from an attack upon Cumberland which place was abandoned by the Inhabitants upon the approach of my Warriors who destroyed the principal part of the Standing Crop of Corn &c. together with the best buildings in the Settlement.

I had likewise informed Your Excellency that Eleven of the Cussitah Indians had been Murdered by the Georgians; the Indians have taken Satisfaction for that affair.

Mr. Folch the Commandant of Mobille wrote me a letter by Way of the Choctaw Nation, the Stile of which in my opinion amounts to a dissaprobation of Davenports affair which I believe he wrote at the instigation of some Traders in those Nations who are Secret favourers of the Americans & are alarmed for their own Safety.

With respect to Davenports affair, there was sufficient Cause for it; I had repeatedly received good information of the intrigues he was Carrying on in the Chickesaw & Chactaw Nations & he had actually gained a great influence over the minds of those people & was nearly on the point of efecting his scheme of establishing the American interest with them & the Speeches that he made in the Yassou Congress[106] last Spring convinced me that it was become absolutely necessary to dispose of him.

However he has left an able Successor in a Capt Bouchier to Compleat the plans he had in view who I am told has taken his stand with a party of Americans at the Chickesaw Bluffs, & I had some intention of driving him off, but shall now defer the attempt untill I learn your Excellencys Sentiments on these Matters.

I came to this place to look after the additional Supply of Ammunition I requested of Your Excellency & shall receive it from Govr. ONeill. Requisitions of this Sort will be frequent on our part while the present Contest between us & the americans exists & arms begin now to be wanted by my people.

We have information that the late inhabitants of Cumberland are retreated to the frontier of No. Carolina & Virginia & are Collected on Holsteins River & conclude from the reports from that Country,

106. There is a description of this meeting, dated March 19, 1787, in AHN E 3887.

that they intend to leave their familys in a place of Security & then with what assistance they Can obtain from the old States they mean to return in force in order to erect Forts along the Cherokee River at all the Crossing places to Serve as a Barrier to Cover their settlement of Cumberland & when this is accomplished they will bring their familys to their former dwellings.

Now upon this occasion I judge it very important to our Interests that I should Clearly understand Your Excellency's Sentiments, that we may have a line to Conduct ourselves by in future.[107] Your Excellency will I am sure believe me when I declare that it is the Wish of my Heart to Sieze every occasion in my power to manifest my desire to promote the Kings Interest & Service, it was from those motives that davenport fell, & that after repeated & obstinate attacks the Settlement at Cumberland is at length dispersed & it was to promote these Ends that I finally Settled the Grand Indian Confederacy of the Northern & Southern Nations, in order to Keep the Americans from Settling themselves on the Western Side of the Ohio River, a measure that I have ever understood to be extremely interesting to the Spanish Nation & agreeable to Your Excellencys Views; but while I am exerting myself in this Manner it is requisite that I should understand whether these measures meet with Your Excellency's approbation or not, & if they do I must rely upon Your Excellency's Countenance, together with a full & ample support of Arms & Ammunition, which is necessary to give effect to our Exertions on the Waters of the Mississippi & to Contend with Vigour for our Oconnee Lands with Georgia without this I may hurt that Interest which I desire to promote & endanger the Safety of my own people.

Amongst the reasons which I have for pressing the foregoing matters to Your Excellency's Consideration one is that I have received a letter from Govr. Caswell of No. Carolina expressing a desire to bring about a peace between my people & Cumberland & it's not impossible but that the Georgians may be brought to accede to more moderate terms than they have hitherto insisted upon.

I had observed with satisfaction that a Correspondence had been opened with Mr Panton respecting his Conducting the Chickesaw & Chactaw Trade:[108] a prospect which afforded great Hopes that by such a measure those Nations would have been satisfied in their Trade, & their murmurings & discontents would have Ceased; but on Coming to town I was Sorry to find that plan altogether dropped.

107. Miró replied on October 16 that he was referring the question to the captain general at Havana, English copy in LC EF 114J9.
108. See Panton to Miró and Navarro, February 15, 1787, Spanish translation in AGI C 177; and same to same, May 9, 1787, AGI C 200.

A Short time before I left the Nation a talk was sent by us to the Chickesaws & Chactaws which they will not dare refuse to accede to; But however those people may be intimidated by the Grand Confederacy of the Nations, yet, while they have any reason to be discontented with their Trade, it will always be in the power of any American Emissary to blow it to a flame & to dissagreable Consequences.

I hope I shall not stand in need of any apology to Your Excellency for the freedom with which I represent Matters of Such Consequence to You for they are the Words of Truth & Sincerity. And I should think myself Culpable if I was to deceive You by Glossing over affairs of Such Moment.

Wishing that You may enjoy uninterrupted happiness & prosperity, I Remain with sincere esteem

Your Excellency's most obedt. Servant

ALEX: McGILLIVRAY [*rubric*]

His Excellency Govr. Colo. Miro

76. *McGillivray to Zéspedes, October 6, 1787*
[LC EF 114J9]

PENSACOLA 6 October 1787

. . . . With respect to Davenport, this man appeard under the Character of Commissioner of the State of Georgia upon the Mississippi, to demand as he declared the Surrender of the District & Fort of Natchez from the Spanish Government by Virtue of the late treaty of peace, & actually made a demand of the Surrender from the Commandant of that Fort. Davenport however growing Suspicious of receiving the punishment his presumption deservd, he retreated precipitately into the Chactaw Nation, & there assumed the character & had Since acted as American Superintendent for that & the Chickesaw Nation, & he made the latter his place of residence, & by his dextrous management of the discontent of those Indians, who were extremely dissatisfied with the bad footing on which their trade was placed he became an object of great anxiety & embarrassment to these Western Governments of whom I eased them[109] as is Mentiond in Gov Miros letter.

The Supply of Ammunition which I received of the Governor of Louisiana, the delivery of it was accompanied with some degree of backwardness & Caution & from another Circumstance that occurred I thought Necessary to address him as enclosed. I am given to understand by a freind in office, that this present Supply was given to me upon the Condition of not using it against the Americans. This how-

109. That is, he had Davenport killed. See the letter to Miró, document 75, *supra.*

162

ever Governor ONeil, who sees the Impropriety of such an ill timed reserve, has not thought proper to Insist upon, but this Conduct on the part of Governor Miro appears Strange & after what has happend I am realy at a loss to Account for.

If it is realy the wishes of Government that I shoud be at peace with the Americans at the expense of every Sacrifice, surely they shoud speak a plain language & which I ought Clearly to Understand. But I still flatter myself that Governor Miro in the present Instance may be under the Influence of an Impolitic delicacy & that it cannot be the Intention of Government at this time, after having encouraged me to resist the encroaching disposition of the Americans, to withdraw its Support, when by persevering I have so fair a prospect of terminating the dispute in a way proffitable to the Kings Interest & to that of My Nation.

If there is Such an Intention, it is most probable that it has come to your knowledge, & as I have always experienced from Your Excellency the utmost Candour I cannot but rely on you for Information & advice on this Occasion.

I feel most Sincere regret that the same Consideration still exist which has hitherto prevented me from doing myself the honor of Visiting so great a freind of my Country as Your Excellency has Invariably provd Yourself ever since You Came into the Government of East Florida.

Wishing that You may enjoy a long & prosperous life I remain, With most respectfull esteem & regard Sir

Your Excellencys Most Obedient Servant

ALEX: McGILLIVRAY [rubric]

his Excellency Governor General De Zespedes
C. C. E. F.

77. *McGillivray to O'Neill, November 20, 1787*
[AGI C 200]

ST. MARKS, 20 November 1787

SIR

Upon my arrival at my plantation at Little River after leaving Pensacola I found one [of] my people there from the Nation, Who gave me Some Information respecting the Indians operations this fall against the Americans, & having but little paper I wrote an account of it to Mr. Panton who left the Towns before he received it, but Suppose that Mr. Forbes has received it, & has Shewn it to Your Excellency. At Same Time came to my hands a petition from the American Chiefs of Franklin County, a copy of which is enclosed in my letter from little river.

From Various paragraphs in the American Newspapers & this petition, we may reasonably Conclude that the American Lads have been pretty well drubbd[110] notwithstanding that Clark & other American officers, Insert falsified reports in the news about the different actions that have been fought on both Sides. Clark was certainly Completely defeated by the Ottassie Captain & Ninne Waketche, who fell, & So much as regards the Indians clothes & blankets is partly true, was lost in Shifting their ground, to prevent the Americans from taking too great an advantage from their Numbers. As numbers of the Cowetas & Cussitahs are now out, & who will no doubt compleat the Just retalliation upon the Georgians I intend that no farther attack Shall be made this winter upon the Americans, but Shall Content myself with watching their Motions & to act as Necessity requires.

I am Just arrived here, to look after matters, hearing a Short time ago of Mr. McLatchys death & not expecting that Mr. Panton would be here so soon. We are Satisfied with Capt. Bertucats management, in preserving good order here after that Melancholy event tho I have not yet Seen Capt. Bertucat, Tho I mean it tomorrow.

I learn from Mr. Panton, that the Commandant here had Informd him that he was not to permit our Vessels to bring our Goods here from Providence or any port. This matter I cannot but Consider as amounting to a prohibition & distress of our trade, of which I have right to Complain. Your Excellency will be pleased to recollect that it was upon Condition that the Commandant who was to be placed at the fort was no ways or by no means to Interrupt or Interfere with our Concerns & trade which was carried on here for my peoples Support, & no dutys or Imposition or restrictions were to be laid on our Imports & exports here, & my being fully persuaded, that the Government woud not have any the least pretensions of this Nature, I consented & used my Influence & Authority among the chiefs of the Semanolies to receive the Garrison upon freindly terms. Upon the whole our trade from Pensacola is already too much burdend, to carry on the trade so as to make it an object worth the pursuit of the House now carrying it on. I entreat Your Excellency to represent this matter to those whom it Concerns to know, that our post of St. Marks at Apalachy be as free as before the Commandant & Garrison arrived there, or else descontents may arise among my people on account of an encrease in price of their goods, & myself blamed for it. I wish Your Excellency the greatest prosperity & good health & remain with true Esteem

110. See the description of the losses at Cumberland in the report of Bledsoe and Robertson to Governor Johnston, January 4, 1788, *State Records of North Carolina*, XXI, 437-38. For the Georgia frontier see the "Extract of a Letter from a Gentleman in Georgia to his Friend in this City," in the *Daily Advertiser*, New York, November 12, 1787, copy in AGI C 200.

Your Excellencys Most obedient Servant,

ALEX: McGILLIVRAY [*rubric*]

78. *McGillivray to Z̆éspedes, January 5, 1788*
[LC EF 114J9]

APALACHY 5 January 1788

SIR

The enclosed Copy of a letter that I had wrote to Governor Miro[111] was forwarded here to Mr. McLatchy to be Sent to Your Excellency & its not being done I impute to his long Illness. On my comeing here & finding the letter still here I deferd sending off untill the arrival of Mr. Pantons Vessel from Pensacola by which I expected an answer from Governor Miro a Copy of the English translation is likewise enclosed.[112]

Your Excellency will perceive by the answer that it holds out no encouragement to me to persevere in my present line of Conduct toward the americans.

Our operations of the last Six months have provd very favorable to us. My Warriors are Victorious in every quarter over the americans, the people of Cumberland are drove over the Ohio river & the State of Georgia now lays at our Mercy. Affairs being in this favorable train, when there is so good a prospect of Compelling the americans to relinquish all Idea of Encroachments, by following up the blows lately given to those turbulent people with Vigour, & which cannot be effected without a farther aid of ammunition, & what has been already afforded to us may appear great, but it has not been in a proportion of one pound & a half a man, & which is generally expended in every excursion, as besides what is Spent in fighting an Indian has to Subsist himself upon game when on an expedition. Governor Miros apparent reluctance in Supplying us farther was the occasion of my writing the enclosed letter to him, & as he mentions that he waits the orders of his Excellency the Captain General of the Havannah &c, being very anxious to know his determination respecting these matters, I request of Your Excellency to lay a State of our affairs together with a Copy of the enclosed letter to Govr. Miro before his Excellency the Captain General & if possible that I may obtain an answer in all the Month of March next, that I may know how to regulate myself in the annual assembly of the Chiefs which will be in April next.

It is always extremely disagreeable to me to make Complaint, but in this Instance in Common Justice to my people I cannot refrain from

111. Document 75, *supra.*
112. Miró to McGillivray, October 16, 1787, copy in LC EF 114J9.

it. I find myself disappointed by the Western Government,[113] which assured me that the establishing a post here woud no way be the least detrimental to the Commerce we have enjoyd here for some years past.

Relying upon these promises & at their request I used my Influence with the Semanolies & others to afford any detachment of Spanish Soldiers that might arrive at St. Marks a freindly reception & Suffer them to establish themselves without Molestation, which agreeable to my orders was accomplishd. Soon after this a Vessel arrived from Providence with our Usual Supplies of Necessarys. To my astonishment I found that Capt. Bertucat the Commandant had it in his Instructions to Seize & detain all such Vessels. Their Motives for such measures I cannot penetrate, if this Measure is not done away & if such orders is ever executed by a Commanding officer here, it will have the most dangerous effect among the Semanolies, & may spread thro the Whole, & may give me much trouble to lay the ferment.

Upon the Whole tis a pitifull Policy to Cramp & embarrass our little Commerce as much as they do, for so much as we are burdend with Certainly cannot be an object or add much to the treasures of so great a king. Yet my people feel them much particularly now being engaged in a war not altogether *our own* they cannot devote much time to killing Game so cant afford to bear heavy burdens on their trade.

I have been several times at Fort St. Mark, & admire at the works that the Commandant Bertucat has compleated in so short a time. He appears to me to be a very fitting officer for the post, the Indians hereabouts are getting fond of him, & Yet We Just heard that this deserving officer has received orders of recal because he differd with a worthless drunken Guarde Magazin.

Perryman tells me that he got a letter from Your Excellency for me & which he has Sent up to my house.[114] I Shall have a pleasure in receiving it as I have not had a letter from you a long time. I shall take the first opporty. to write you on getting home. Mean time I remain
with most respectfull Esteem
Your Excellencys Most obt. Servt.
ALEX: McGILLIVRAY [*rubric*]

his Excellency Governor General de Zespedes

79. *McGillivray to Miró, January 10, 1788*
[AGI C 201]
LITTLE TALLASSIE 10 January 1788

SIR

---

113. Panton also protested sharply against the "miserable and wretched" policy of Miró (Panton to Zéspedes, January 8, 1788, LC EF 116L9).
114. Zéspedes to McGillivray, October 22, 1787, copy in AGI C 1395.

I have received the letter that Your Excellency did me the favor to Write to me of 16 October last.[115]

It woud have been Very Satisfactory to me if I coud have had a full answer to the Matters Contain in my letter to Your Excellency, but as You promise to Communicate the Sentiments of the Captain General when you hear from him, I am content to Wait, expecting them, In the hope that he will decide for giving us an ample Supply of the means to enable us to Compleat fully what we have hitherto so Successfully Conducted. My warriors are Victorious over the Americans in every quarter, in the Course of the present Winter, they have given the Georgians repeated defeats, & there is not a Single building now Standing on the Contested lands. I have before acquainted Your Excellency that we had drove the Inhabitants of Cumberland over the Ohio River, which you may depend on as a Fact.[116]

It had been my Intention in Consideration of the distresses of Weatherfords wife & children to have requested of Your Excellency the release of that Man that he might return back to his family, but a report prevailing that he had made his escape from Confinement, I deferd for a time, but as I find that report to be without foundation & Weatherford lately has applyd to Pensacola for Necessarys, I now resume my desire to have him returnd to Pensacola or Mobile that he may come to his family, his effects having made Satisfaction for the damages he had Committed, & probably the punishment he has received will make a favorable alteration in his manners & disposition.

I had Visited the post at St. Marks Commanded by Capt. Bertucat & found him well establishd as to Situation & much liked by the Neighbouring Indians, which last Circumstance is very Essential to a Commandant of such a post. I find that he is removed from his Command at the Instigation of a Commissary of the Kings Stores who disagreed with him. Many Indian chiefs wishd that he had remaind. I wish You great happiness & remain

Your Excellencys most obedt. Servant

ALEX: McGILLIVRAY [*rubric*]

his Excellency Governor Miro

115. Copy in LC EF 114J9.
116. In a letter to Zéspedes on January 28, 1788, LC EF 116L9, Leslie quoted Panton as writing: "The Success of the Creek Indians, over the boasters of Georgia, has exceeded their Most Sanguine hopes, & will Convince people, they are Braver Men, than Some are willing to Allow. The Seminolies since I have been here, have agreed to join the rest of their Country, & the Mickasuckie people are now in Georgia; in fact the Nation is Unanimous."

VII

WAVERING SPANISH SUPPORT

80. *McGillivray to O'Neill, March 1, 1788*
[AGI C 201]

LITTLE TALLASSIE 1 March 1788

DEAR SIR

I am favord with Your Excellencys letters of 28t December last & the 25t January enclosing at Same time a Copy of a letter from the Commandant of Mobile[117] to his Excellency Governor Miro, in which I am chargd with putting the Inhabitants of that Country in alarm of Hostile apprehensions.

Conscious of my Innocense I cant forbear to Vindicate myself from so Injurious a charge. These alibamons that did the damage Complaind of by Mr. Folck to abraham Walker dont live in the Nation, but they are Settled down the river near to Durants, & were always very troublesome to the English Government formerly robbing the Settlers, & they pretend to be the Masters of Mobile River. These people were not at the Pensacola Treaty in 84 but met Governor Miro at Mobile, therefore the disorders of these alibamons Cant be imputed to us, they living always down the river & never attending our publick meetings, & are a people Insignificant in Numbers or Consequence. So being out of our reach they Commit disorders on the river.

When the said man Walker Complaind to me he estimated his loss at a womans Saddle one rifle gun & about thirty Carrots Tobacco, which I Now find is swelld to five hundred Dollars, whereas he was never worth one hundred in his life. However that is not the Case, every body that knows me knows that I coud take no pleasure to distress such a poor wretch as Walker or any one else without a good Cause.

Nor Sir will I deny that I have thrown out menaces against those Settlers of the Tansaw, because 1 have found them ungratefull & are americans in their hearts. They with the Tombegbie Settlers are Very desirious of being Joind with the americans, of which I gave Notice to Your Government long ago. There is one Walton Come from Cum-

117. Vicente Folch y Juan, a nephew of Miró, fought in Morocco in 1774, in Algiers in 1775, and at Gibraltar in 1780. He was stationed at Mobile from 1781 on, and was governor of Pensacola, 1795-1811. He and McGillivray disagreed violently (see especially documents 125, 127, and 129, *infra*). Subsequently he had a bitter dispute with Intendant Morelos.

168

berland & Georgia who is now making plans of all that Country & Sending to Georgia. The Chactaws had agreed to grant Davenport & the americans twenty five miles square of Country on the Yasou River & one Capt. Woods is Now gone for Goods from Congress to Conclude the bargain, & Ben James & other Traders is to Join the americans in it, besides getting a large tract on the Tombegbie. All this I have got from the best authority, my Situation gives me opportunitys to find out these matters which Your Government Cannot obtain, but through me.

I now again repeat what I have formerly done, that unless proper Steps are taken a Croud of americans will be Introduced by those people, within Spanish limits, of this no Notice has been taken, but that shall not prevent me from acting on this occasion as Necessity shall require, & before that I will be an Silent Spectator of such doings I woud drive altogether from those Settlements. Govr. Zespedes has done the same in East Florida, such people being troublesome under any Government. These being my confirmd Sentiments respecting those Settlers, I Shall again return to the Subject of Folcks letter. When I left Pensacola last was in October last as well as I can recollect. I then went out to my plantation, where this man Walker came to me with his Complaint, & told me that Bailey & Randal had overtook & spoke to the alibamons party, & they declared that they had not seen me for above a twelve months before, so coud get no orders from me but that they had warnd Walker the Winter before to leave their land & he had not done it by which they forced him away. Baileys Motive for his false report was in hopes to Create a difference, as he had fallen under my displeasure for his former roguery & bad behaviour, & for which I Shall not fail to give him the first opportunity, the Chastisement due for such Conduct.

As to the Next charge respecting those people that live on my Uncles lands, it is as false as the rest for I am not to learn that those possessions with all that was Brittish was Ceded to Spain. Consequently neither he nor I Coud have any Claim but through favor of the King, & which if I had asked for the favor might have been granted to me as soon as any other, & my uncle I am Sorry to observe I have reason to believe is no longer in this World.

The foregoing is what I have to offer in my Justification from that Calumny that has been thrown upon me, of which please to transmit a full Copy of to his Excellency Governor Miro,[118] & Shall now leave

118. Miró had already expressed his doubts as to the correctness of Folch's charges against McGillivray (Miró to Folch, November 23, 1787, draft in AGI C 56).

169

the Subject with observing, that Mr. Folck woud do better to Consider well the truth of such rash assertions before he offers them to his Superiors.

I have had good grounds for not Cultivating his Correspondence before this, & now I Shall have less Inclination.

Your Excellencys attention to the relations of the deceased Ninne Wakitchy was very proper. Indian Chiefs will by that have a well grounded Confidence to obtain the kings bounty by exerting themselves to merit it.

I have received a Notification from General Pickens of South Carolina Informing me that the american Congress had appointed Commissioners to treat with us about peace, the Georgians being Now reduced to Extremity & great distress will now tis likely agree to Such terms as will Secure us in all our Claims to our Lands thereby putting an end to war of Cruelties & devastation, shocking to humane feelings, & but which they themselves first wantonly provoked.

My sister Durant is now here & seems Very much concernd about her Negroes that Doct. Ruby has got, but she Confesses Your Excellencys goodness in Standing her freind so long, & doubts not but You will be pleased to Continue Your goodness, till she can redeem them. She thinks Ruby takes advantages of her. I coud help her a little if Your Excellency woud take some beeff cattle & allow a reasonable price for the king, Concerning which I will be glad to hear from You. Mean time remain with the most respectfull Esteem & regard

Your Excellencys most obedt. Servant

ALEX: McGILLIVRAY [rubric]

His Excellency Governor O.Neill

Those alibamons I am just told is a going to Mobile to make up Matters with the Commandant for robbery of Walker.

81. *McGillivray to O'Neill, March 12, 1788*

[AGI C 201]

LITTLE TALLASSIE, 12 March, 1788

SIR

The bearer is a Tuckebatche Indian who desires me to Inform Your Excellency that this winter five Spaniards in a boat, met with these Indians at the mouth of Yellow Water over Pensacola bay, & the Spaniards fell upon the four Indians & Robbd them of three Guns three kettles about twenty Skins, & some ammunition, for which they entreat of your Excellency some Compensation. The Spaniards seizd the Indians Canoe & made some attempts to kill the Indians, who not resisting further than to Save themselves, these being our best Indians. I hope Your Excellency will consider their case.

I have lately heard that five Spaniards in a boat Came to Chactaw hatchie near the Bullys & a few Indians tryd to take them, but the Spaniards drew their knives & wounded the Indians & escaped. This Shews that the Indians are so well disposed to the Spaniards that they woud not kill them in their own defence. I am with most respectful esteem

Your Excellencys most obedient Servant,

ALEX: McGILLIVRAY [rubric]

82. *McGillivray to Miró, March 15, 1788*

[AGI C 2361]

LITTLE TALLASSIE, 15 March 1788

SIR

. . . .After the most mature Consideration I found that a protracted war with the americans was attended with its inconveniences, determined me to Seize the occasion of the massacre of the Cussitahs to exert more Vigour & enterprise than I had hitherto done, to bring to a period one way or the other this long Contest. Agreeable to this decission I pushd the Georgians hard all the last fall & winter, which in the event has effected the purposes I wishd to bring about. I am informd by General Pickens from South Carolina that the American Congress has come to resolves to endeavor to terminate our differences by treaty; & had recommended to Georgia to appoint a Commissioner to act Jointly with one from Congress.[119] . . .as the assembly of Georgia are agreed to Nominate one I expect to receive an official Notification from those people, the Georgians being now fully convinced of our Superiority in the Field, will no longer persist in the Folly of encourageing a Scheme of encroachment, in their back Woods Inhabitants, which has been the Source of great Calimity & distress to those people,[120] & for my part It is perfectly agreeable to my principles to have it in my

119. Georgia had sent James Seagrove to St. Augustine with a demand that Zéspedes cease supplying arms and ammunition to the Indians (Mathews to Zéspedes, November 6, 1787, AHN E 3887). Zéspedes answered "that the part the Spaniards were taking in the war was one of humanity and Christianity." To his court Zéspedes reported that Seagrove's real object seemed to be to inquire into the official standing of Panton, Leslie and Company (Zéspedes to Valdés, January 10, 1788, *ibid.*). Antonio Valdés had succeeded José de Gálvez, Marqués de Sonora, as Minister of the Indies.

120. A "Gentleman of Georgia," whose letter was printed in the *Daily Advertiser,* New York, November 12, 1787, had blamed the war on "the impossibility of controlling the crimes and passions of Indians, or of the rude and unmanageable inhabitants of a frontier" (Copy in AGI C 200).

power to put an end to a barbarous war, upon an equitable & honorable basis.

I have to request the favor of Your Excellency to take into Your Consideration the claim of my Sister Durant to a Negro fellow named Billy now in Orleans, & passes as free owing to a Certificate given to him by Capt. Favrot late commandant of Mobile. This Negro please Your Excellency, was Sometime hired to Padre Veler at Pensacola & from him eloped to Mobile. When Governor ONeil upon Durants application, gave him an order to the Commandant to deliver his Negro to durant but instead of which he gives the Negro a pass & connived at his escape to Orleans. This Negro I advised Durant as being in debt to Mr. Joyce at Mobile to Sell making no doubt but he or Mr. Mather woud easily recover him at Orleans, but these Gentlemen say that they have not got hold of the Negro owing to the pass he has got. The Negro was taken from the americans during the War, of course he is the property of Durant, for which I entreat for & expect Your Excellencys Justice. They are a poor family & have no other way at present to pay their debts but by the Sale of Negroes, & this fellow has no pretention to his freedom but from the pique of Mons. Favrot. This Gentleman likewise differd with me on the Suggestions of that Banditti at Tensaw & for no good reason, as I had always treated him with marks of attention & respect Suitable to the rank of a Spanish officer. I have advised to Mr. Joyce to apply to Your Excellency through Mr. Mather on the affair of the Negro.[121]

I remain with respectfull esteem
    Your Excellencys most obedient Servt.
                    ALEX: McGILLIVRAY [rubric]

83. *McGillivray to O'Neill, March 28, 1788*
                    [AGI C 201]
                    LITTLE TALLASSIE 28 March 1788

SIR

I have the pleasure to receive Your Excellencys letter by Antonio Garson, & I Shall directly proceed to execute Your Excellencys Instructions in the manner which you desire.

The quarter you point out in your letter has been an object of my attention for these eight months past & we have four partys now in Scouting about the River Cherokee & its main branch the Tenessee.

121. Miró answered on May 16, 1788, "I differed till this moment to give you an answer upon the Mrs. Durand Negroe, because I charged Mr. Joyce to inquire about him & now I have the pleasure to acquaint you, that in consequence of Mrs. Durands power of Attorney the said Joyce has settled this matter, giving the freedom to this Negroe by the price of two hundred hard dollars, this arrangement has been very satisfactory to me" (AGI C 2361).

One party of this Town has arrived & Inform me that they fell in with a party of americans between Cumberland River & Ohio, Whom they attackd & bested killing Six & taking their baggage & horses, among the papers found with them I learn that they belong to a larger party of Surveyors, Surveying all that Country by order of Congress. The whole apparatus was taken by the Indians. This party that was routed was headed by Capt. Nash who is killed among the rest.

There is a report at present prevailing here that there has been a Severe action on Cherokee River, between our people & the Americans.[122] It is not Yet Confirmd. There are three flying partys of twenty Indians out & who are not under fighting orders, & I Shall Send out two more.

It gives me great Satisfaction to learn from Your Excellency that Mr. Pantons Commercial affairs are recommended to his Majestys attention, & I make no doubt but his Royal & gracious disposition will Incline him to extend his Royal favor to that Concern agreeable to our wishes. The ambitious designs of the Republican States regarding territorys has forced us into hostile measures to check them & preserve our general hunting lands, & I do entreat of Your Excellency to believe that while the Indians are obliged to maintain so Various a war, they can have but little time to Collect Skins & peltry to purchase Necessarys for their familys, therefore Indian trade shoud be placed on as free & liberal terms as possible, & at least on as easy terms as other Nations are agreed to Supply us on.

I have already Informd Your Excellency that the events of war were so much in our favour that Congress had come to resolutions to Compel the Southern States to agree & accede to generous & liberal terms of Peace & the distress & Calamity that the Georgians are now plunged in render Peace absolutely necessary to them. Commissioners have been already appointed by Congress for that purpose. They have like-wise advised the Georgians to appoint some on their part to act in Conjunction, but that distracted people I imagine are taken up in vain debates upon the right of Congress to Interfere in their affairs, So that every day that they lose will add a month of distress to them. Besides these matters my private letters Inform me that they are fully resolvd to make us more offers of a free Commerce thro their ports & every Advantage in every affair that we Shall desire thinking no Sacrifice almost is too great to purchase a peace from us. North Carolina too is likewise very pressing to have peace & have twice offerd to Sub-scribe to very favorable Conditions, to all which I have not hitherto

122. In another letter of the same date, carried by the chief warrior of the Chu-wallys, McGillivray identified the Tuckebatches as the participants (AGI C 201).

made any open reply, but as I now find these States are to Negotiate under the Sanction & Authority of Congress I am induced to listen to their proposals concerning agreeing to a general Peace.

Some of the most distinguishd chiefs of the Lower Towns were here a few days ago, to know my Intentions of these affairs. I have not let them know fully what I intend but desired them all to assemble in Next month, when I Shoud go down & decide either on Peace or War & to be in readiness to make a Campaign this Spring if terms of Peace was not Concluded.

Agreeable to Your Excellencys desires I will See You in Pensacola before I give the american Commissioners a Meeting, but as My private affairs now Stand I will Sustain much Inconvenience if I leave this before ten days, having lost poor Moniac I have now No one to look after affairs in my absence. I have therefore sent back Garcon with an assurance that I will follow him in ten days.

Mr. Folch Certainly deservd Censure for his Conduct toward me, it is my Inclination to Cultivate a good Understanding with him in his public station, as a Commandant, & he ought by no Means to listen to any Suggestions on which to ground Complaints to his Superiors to my prejudice rashly & unadvisedly. Such Conduct will always meet with my resentment. However I am Satisfied with the Steps that his Excy. Governor Miro took in advising him to more Caution in regard to these Matters.

Having detaind Garcon here four days in trying to get ready to go with but finding I cannot, Now dismiss him back knowing that Your Excellency can but ill spare him at this time. I remain with most respectfull Esteem

Your Excellencys most obedt. Servant

ALEX: McGILLIVRAY [*rubric*]

Excellency Governor ONeil

84. *Pickens and Mathews to McGillivray, March 29, 1788*
[Copy in AGI C 121]

FORT CHARLOTTE, 29 March 1788

MEN & WARRIORS

In Consequence of Some disputes that had unluckily arisen between You and our Sister State of Georgia, The United States in Congress assembled did in the Course of last Year Send as their Agent their beloved man Doctor White to Your Country to learn from Your own Mouths the Grounds of Complaint & the reasons for Your Hostile proceedings: He was favorably received by You & it was thought from what passed between You and him upon his representation to Congress, every thing would have returned to a friendly footing, he having obtained Your promise that no Depredations Should be Committed on any of the Citizens of these States. From Some unhappy fatality or Gross Casualty & in express violation of that promise two of our people were killed & others plundered of their property before it was possible for Congress to have received or taken any resolution upon Doctor White's representation.

However being Still anxious to bring about a general peace upon a Strong and permanent footing they have thought proper to appoint an Agent and to recommend the appointment of a Commissioner from each of the different States of North Carolina, S. Carolina, & Georgia, that Should You meet their Ideas & Wishes for peace they might receive a deputation of Your headmen & Warriors at a certain time & place in order to talk over and discuss every Complaint or Cause of uneasiness on either Side that may possibly have arisen or led to those outrages and to prevent the further Shedding of innocent Blood.

In Consequence of this recommendation Georgia and South Carolina have thought proper to make Choice of us—the Agent & Commissioner from North Carolina are not yet Come forward but as it is our Wish to forward & promote so good a Work and as soon as possible to heal those Wounds, We have thought proper to Send to You to See if your minds are now disposed for peace.

We Can Say for our own part that we have the Stronger desire to fulfill the wishes of Congress, which are, to give peace and Stability to all the Citizens of the union upon just, reasonable and equitable principles, and to every nation or people who feel a Wish to be their friends. Were not facts So recent it might appear like boasting to Say, they feel a power at all times to do themselves Justice Should the voice of Equity & reason not prevail.

Should You be disposed to join this friendly interposition You will See the Great impropriety of treating with Arms in hand. We shall acquiesce in & in the most pointed terms insist upon as a first principle that every hostile procedure Should instantly Cease.

We Send this Talk by our Friend Mr. Whitfield and, who, possessing our full Confidence, have Committed a Great deal to his prudence. He is known to many in Your Country & we hope you will freely rely upon whatever he may Say to You. Hopeing to meet You at a future day in a friendly manner We Conclude & wait Your answer.[123]

ANDREW PICKENS
GEORGE MATHEWS

123. This letter was received early in June; document 90, *infra*, is the answer.

To *Alexander McGillivray, Esqr.* & the rest of the Headmen & Warriors of the Creek Nation.

85. *McGillivray to O'Neill, April 15, 1788*
[AGI C 201]
LITTLE TALLASSIE 15 April 1788

SIR

I have received Your Excellencys letters from Garcon by which I observe his Majestys Minister has Instructed the Governors of Luisiana & Florida to use their endeavours to dispose us the Creeks to agree to terms of accommodation with the United States of America & particularly the State of Georgia. I Shall accordingly pay due attention to the Notification Now given to me & more especially as I find that his Majesty has graciously Caused it to be Signified to the American Congress that it is his pleasure that our Territorys shall not be encroachd upon nor Usurp'd by the Georgians. I will most Cheerfully Consent to Conclude a peace upon this basis, with the United States, as we have possessd no other motives for Hostillities with them but on account of their Violence & Injustice in seizing not a few miles of Country, but an extent of several hundred miles, & it is to be regretted that Congress had not long ago Interposed their authority with Georgia to effect an amicable Settlement of our differences by which the effusion of so much bloodshed woud have been prevented on both Sides.

I informd Your Excellency in my last letter of my having seen some resolves of the Congress in the Georgia news papers, recommending to them to terminate our disputes by treaty under the mediation of Congress, they appointing a Superintendent & Georgia to Nominate a Commissioner for that purpose, the knowledge of which gave me reason to expect soon some overtures Concerning a treaty from Georgia, but I have not received any as Yet, & can account for the delay only in this manner, that the Georgians being a distracted divided people & are Spending themselves in vain debates on the right of Congress to Interfere in regulating their Conduct toward the Indian Nations. It is a favorite plan of theirs to seize upon our Territorys & it is a Measure that they will not easily be Induced to secede from, & if Congress decides in our favour, those Upper Georgians will refuse to Comply & Insult the Commissioner as they did last Year.

In the mean Time I will desist from farther Acts of hostillity & wait untill the Middle of Next Month, & if then they Continue Silent it will be a Clear proof that they have no Intention to adopt the recommendation of Congress to terminate our disputes by treaty, in which case there will be a Necessity on our part to Continue the same hostile measures

176

as hitherto to Compel them to be Just, as I do not Conceive it to be the Sense of the Ministers Instructions that I have received that we Shoud at any rate agree to terms of Peace by which we Shall Sacrifice that for which we have been so long Contesting & arduously Strugling for.

In any event Sir You shall hear farther from me on the foregoing Subjects before I pursue any farther measures of a hostile Nature, tho I am in expectation that the distresses & clamours of all the higher˙ ranks of people in Georgia will operate so as to force the lower & turbulent orders to agree to equitable terms of Peace.

I feel perfect Satisfaction in having it in my power to assure My Nation from Authority that they may repose a firm reliance on our great Protector the King that he will exert his powerfull Influence with the americans in such a manner as we shall be secured in our Native & Just rights. I remain with great regard, Sir

Your Excellencys Most Obedt. Servant

ALEX: MCGILLIVRAY [*rubric*]

his Excellency Governor ONeil

86. *O'Neill to McGillivray, April 21, 1788*
[Copy in AGI C 205]

PENSACOLA, 21 April 1788

SIR

Governor Miro has directed me the Copys of two letters from His Excellency Antonio Valdez Minister of the Indian Department, in answer to Colo. Miro's representation of the 24th March last year. My Sovereign approves of all the Governor has transacted heretofore, regarding the Creek Indians, but also not having given you the arms to make war on any of the United States of America; whereas his Excellency Count Florida Blanco, Minister of State, by Royal orders has prevented [*sic,* directed] our Envoy Mr. James Gardoque in North america to officiate so as the Indians may not be molested; as his Majesty cannot fail in showing them the protection he offered: at same-time he requires by all means to dissuade the Indians from further hostile proceedings against the United States.

Goverr. Miro will be happy to hear of the conclusion of peace: and I also pray you will contribute to it, whilst I hope no farther transgressions will ensue; which otherwise could not be looked on with indifference.

These orders were forwarded me by Governor Miro last November; yet the Vessel in which they were, was overset, and sunk on the passage from Orleans. A few days ago I had the Duplicates, which I loose no

177

time to inform you of. My last was to acquaint you of ye Folks of Franklin, these and some other restless people on the Westward, consider themselves quite independent of Congress; and are only flattered through their own whimsical ideas. Mr. Antonio Garzon will deliver you this; and receive your commands.

I am with greatest esteem, Sir
Your etc.,

ARTHUR O'NEILL [*rubric*]

87. *McGillivray to O'Neill, April 25, 1788*
[AGI C 201]
LITTLE TALLASSIE, 25 April, 1788

SIR

I have to Inform Your Excellency that Since the departure of Garcon with my letters to you there has arrived here two deputys from Cumberland with some propositions toward the bringing about a Peace between this Nation & the Cumberland people. They represent that they are reduced to extreme distress by the excursions of our warriors, & to obtain our peace & freindship that they are willing to Submit themselves to any Conditions that I Shall Judge to Impose on them: & thinking no doubt it woud be a greater Inducement to me to favor them they told me that they woud become Subjects to the King & that Cumberland & Kentucké were determined to free themselves from a dependence on Congress, as that body coud not or woud not protect their persons & property nor encourage their Commerce, So that where there was No protection no Submission was due.[124] The New State of Franklin is broke up, the land being divided one part being within the limit of North Carolina & the other adjudged to the Cherokee Indians from whom it has been usurpd, & that Kentucké meant to form a connexion with the Brittish of Canada to whom they were Contiguous.

These deputys wishd to know my Ideas on this matter of their proposal, but it being a Subject that Involved Important political questions, I kept my own opinion close from them.

The chiefs & delegates of Cumberland are Colonels Robertson, Bledsoe, Ewing & two others. They Sent in proofs of the purchase of the County of Cumberland more than forty Years ago by a Virginia Company from the Northern & Cherokee Indians. My answer to them

124. See document 4, *supra*, for an earlier comment on the separatist tendencies in the Kentucky-Tennessee country. Robertson and the Cumberland settlers had other reasons, of course, for thinking about a connection with Spain, but surcease from Creek attacks was not the least. Roosevelt characterized McGillivray's answer, written on December 1, 1788, as cautious and noncommittal (*op. cit.*, III, 138).

was that when I held my first grand Convention these matters Shoud be discussd & in the mean time all hostilities Shoud Cease on our parts, when we agreed upon Conditions a full peace Shoud take place.

I remain with great regard & esteem

Your Excellencys most obedt. Servt.

ALEX: McGILLIVRAY [*rubric*]

88. *Folch to McGillivray, May 23, 1788*

[Copy in AGI C 52]

MOBILE, 23 May 1788

SIR

Joshua Barber, the Br. will hand you this, his friend in Orleans recommended him to Governor Miro, who consequently sent him to me in order to procure him a safe Conveyance to his home, for which he is ready to pay every expence that may offer, tho you May see by Governor Miro's passport that his Intention was to go immediately thro' the Chactaw or Chicasaw Nation, Notwithstanding I proposed it to him, as the most secure road, to take that Way, not in the least doubting but that you will do honour to Governor Miro's Passport & be kind enough to get him a guide either for Cumberland or Cantuckey (just as you think proper) to whom, on his arrival, he will give an Order on Mr. Joice for the Expences. I am exceedingly happy to have this Opportunity of Writing to you, & explaining my candid Sentiments.[125]

When I came, I was desirous to cultivate a Correspondence & friendship with you for two Reasons, the one, for having heard Governor Miró speak so frequently & so much in your favour, & the other on acct. of our being Neighbours, but am sorry to find that my desire has been hitherto frustrated, which I can attribute to Nothing else but the bad interpretation of a letter I wrote you, & the affair of Walker. Please, Sir, to believe me that tho the Alibamons said, you gave the Orders to do what they did, yet I coud not be persuaded it was true, nor coud I give the least Credit to it. It's true, I wrote Governor Miró about it, just as they informed me but my View in that was that he might write you to chastise them for their Misdemeanor & availing themselves of your Name on Such a protest, as it was out of my power to do it. These were my Motives, I assure you, for Which I expect your Pique against me will subside, & that for the future you will look upon me as a person that has Your Interest at heart & shall be happy to

125. As a matter of fact Folch had just been chided for his repugnance toward writing to McGillivray (Miró to Folch, May 2, 1788, AGI C 56).

see you in Mobile when ever you think it Convenient which will afford infinite pleasure to your most obet. & very humbe. Servt.

FOLCH

89. *O'Neill to Miró, June 4, 1788*

[Spanish copy in AGI C 1394]

Since a year ago, and especially lately when some break with England is feared, I have noticed the disinclination of the trader William Panton and the commissary Alexander McGillevray to concur willingly or even to obey orders for the government of our sovereign. . . . .

As concerns Alexander McGillevray, he considers himself independent of our government, though employed by it by virtue of the monthly honorarium of fifty dollars that he receives. I understand that he proceeds with almost complete arbitrariness. . . . .

It is very certain that these two individuals have been until now very useful; the one by having sustained trade, though to his own profit, and the other by having helped to gain for us the friendship of various Indians of his nation. Yet it should be understood that this was principally due to their bitter opposition to the Americans, which is born of their love for the British nation. I do not know of a single bond of affection whereby these individuals are bound to the Spanish government.

Therefore, I leave it to your penetration to adopt with your well-known prudence the most convenient means for a permanent trade with these Indians, arranging that they be supplied as soon as possible by persons who take pride in being loyal vassals of the king, so that in whatever contingency or breach that may arise with England they cannot acquire notices of the poor defenses of this province and very easily disturb us. . . . .

90. *McGillivray to Pickens and Mathews, June 4, 1788*

[Copy in AGI C 201]

LITTLE TALLASSIE 4th June 1788

GENTLEMEN

Your talk or letter addressed to me & the rest of the Chiefs of the Creek Nation dated at Fort Charlotte 29th March last[126] was handed to me by Mr. Geo. Whitfield whom You Commissioned for that purpose. That Gentleman likewise favored me with a Sight of a printed paper Containing Sundry Resolutions of a Comitte of Congress to whom was referred a report of the Secretary at War and Sundry Reports

---

126. Document 84, *supra*.

180

relating to Indian affairs in the Southern Department and also a motion of the delegates from the State of Georgia.

No act however has been produced which authorises me to believe that Congress has adopted those resolutions. Yet as Mr. Whitfield has assured me that he has every Reason to believe that they have received the spirit of that Honorble. Body, and as I firmly believe him to be a Man of Veracity, and as You have desired us to pay implicit belief to whatever he tells us; We are inclined to give the Circumstance our entire Credit altho it woud have been more Satisfactory had the act of Congress accompanied the other papers.

For these reasons relying on the Honour of Congress & your Candour in the desire expressed of accommodating the differences existing between us and the State of Georgia, on account of their unjust incroachments on our hunting Grounds, & for putting an End to the War which has in Consequence Commenced, & to Show to the World that our dispositions are now what they at all times have been before, inclined to peace on just and Equitable Grounds, we have acquiesced in Your desire to Suspend hostillitys which will Cease on our part as Soon as the parties which I have kept out on the frontiers of Georgia to watch their motions are Called in, which I have ordered to take place immediately. Having so far Conceded to the disposition of Congress and Your request I Shall immediately expect to see a Requisition from You to the people of Georgia to retire from the oconee Lands to Within the Limits prescribed to that State when it was a British province & to abide the result of the friendly negotiation You propose to open, for it Can never be expected that our Warriours and Chiefs can go down with Confidence or to meet You on Such unequal terms, that while our hands are tied up they are left in possession of any part of their usurpation which was the Sole Cause of the Warr.

The two men you mention to have been killed last Summer by our people was Satisfaction for two of ours killed by the Georgians before the Conference took place with Doctor White. It was what I foresaw and what I mentioned to that Gentleman might happen, & altho I promised my endeavours to prevent it, no blame ought to be ascribed to the Nation in General from the Circumstance for the injured family had Slipt away from the upper towns before my Return from the Conference, & who however Contented themselves with bare Satisfaction for the injury they had Sustained; & how far the Georgians are justifiable for the barbarous manner in which they put to Death, not the party who had taken Satisfaction nor any who were at Enmity with them but thirteen Indians of the Cussitahs a town who had been in their Interest during the late Warr, whom they found hunting Game in the

181

neighbourhood of the Settlements, & who even pointed out the Rout of the Indians who had killed the two men to the Georgian Scout, is a Circumstance which I leave to You Gentlemen & to the World to admire or Condemn.

I observe the threat held out by Congress & by You, and likewise that the force of the union may be Called out to punish us if we do not Submit to Such terms as they think Just and reasonable. On this occasion I will only observe, that, if it were a thing possible for men to divest themselves entirely of all prejudice, which will hang about the best and most upright when they Come to Judge on matters in which they are interested, or if our dispute with the Georgians was a matter which no part of the union had any Concern, there are few tribunals to whom I would Sooner Submit our Cause than 1 would to that Honorable Body, but as neither of these Can be the Case and as there may be points on which we Shall differ, before the other States draw the Sword against a people who have given no Cause of Quarrel with them, they ought to recollect that the opinion of one Nation in their Concerns with another about matters of Equity, Justice & Right, does not all times hit the General Sense of Mankind, and they ought to be well assured that they have this on their Side before they attempt the extirpation of the first inhabitants of this Country, a Contest wc. may be very doubtfull & which had better be avoided by not Seeking to deprive us of Lands which have been ours from the beginning of time, the possession of which is absolutely necessary to our Subsistence.

I am led to these observations by remarking the recommendation of the Committee of Congress to Georgia & North Carolina to make liberal Cessions of Lands to Congress but as I have been taught to entertain the highest opinion of that Body I hope that the Committee had not in their View the lands which the Georgians are attempting to Wrest from us, for that would be leading to reflections directly opposite to the Equitable & pacific disposition they otherwise possess.

As the Superintendent & Commissioner from North Carolina must ere this be Come forward to S. Carolina, I hope to be favored with a Speedy answer, & by adopting the measures I have recommended all obstacles towards an Effectual peace will be removed and if you are equally well disposed with us towards a reconciliation the meeting You require for that purpose may be in Septr. next, when perhaps we may discover that our respective Territorys are Sufficient to Contain their proprietors, & that there is no necessity for trespassing on the property of one another.

If it is agreeable to You all Gentlemen I prefer General Pickens place near Seneca for the place to hold the Conference to any place out of my own Country. I refer You to Mr. Whitfields information for other matters in this Country & I have the Honour to be Gentlemen, Your most obedt. Servt.

ALEXR. McGILLIVRAY

Hnble. Genl. Pickins & Matthews, Commissioners &c. &c.

91. *McGillivray to Miró, June 12, 1788*

[AGI C 177]

LITTLE TALLASSIE, 12 June 1788

SIR

I have the Satisfaction of acknowledging the receit of Your Excellencys letter of 16t April last, which I received after my return home from a Conference which Governor ONeil had Invited me to, at which time he Informd me that it was the kings pleasure that my Nation shoud make peace with the United States of america. He likewise read some paragraphs of a letter which Your Excellency wrote him concerning these matters as well as some part of the Ministers Instructions to Don Gardoqui, to represent to the American Congress in our behalf by the Royal orders. As this is matter of great Importance to us, I requested a Copy of a translation of the above letters which I couldn't obtain. I must Still entreat the favor of You to furnish me with them, that I may have time to Consider of them at leisure & see how far the Royal Intention goes, for notwithstanding that Governor O'Neil read them to me yet my memory being generally much charged with Various affairs, I cant exactly remember them.

If it is the Royal Will that we must make peace at any rate even at the expence of the Sacrifice of all those lands which was the principal object of the War, in that Case we Shall Consider ourselves as a Ruined Nation, to Shift for ourselves, If on the Contrary, the King has declared his resolution to protect us in those Lands & the other parts of our Territory in that Case it is Necessary that I Shoud be furnishd with an official paper concerning it, that I might tell my Countrymen & Confidently avow to them the Important favour & in the most publick manner declare & acknowledge the Royal Protection in the treaty of peace which we may Conclude with the americans. There is not I conceive any Impropriety in this requisition, if the matter has been declared to Congress. Nor is there any danger of our making any Improper use of such Notification.

I consider myself & Nation in general highly obliged to the Goodness of his Majesty for approving of Your Conduct in Supplying us when we stood in Need of assistance first with the five thousand wt. Gun powder & afterwards with some additional Supplys as our Necessitys

183

required, which Certainly has helped us Considerably in defending our Country from the Unjust attempts of the americans to wrest our Country from us.

On the 12t of last Month George Whitefield Esq. an american from South Carolina arrived here, who deliverd a letter from General Pickens & General Mathews (late Governor) two Commissioners of Georgia, who Informd me that another Commissioner from North Carolina & an agent from Congress was Shortly expected to Join them in order to Settle all disputes & enter into treatys of freindship & alliances with the Southern Nations. Their letter after making an allowance for the boasting & Cracking Natural to the americans was Well enough.

Whitefield also showd me a printed paper which contains the opinion of a Committee of Congress who were appointed to consider of Indian affairs & who recommended Sundry resolutions for the Consideration of Congress & he assured me that these resolutions were all adopted & would be made the ground or basis on which the Intended treaty was to be found. That you may see them in full I shall enclose a duplicate of it to you. I also transmit you a Copy of my letter in answer to the Commissioners that you may see exactly the State on which the Negotiation at present rests.

I woud have given these Commissioners an earlier meeting than September next for the purpose of closing the war, but for the receit of your letter of 16: April which required the explanations that I have asked as well as advice from you before I go down amongst these Americans who are a sett of crafty, cunning, republicans, who will endeavor to avail themselves of every circumstance in which I cannot speak or act with decission.[127]

In regard to what you say about commercial matters, I will only observe that the States have for some past discoverd a presing anxiety to recover the trade of these Nations which the absurd & blind policy of the Georgians in what regards Indian affairs had so foolishly lost to them, & they may attempt to rectify it at this treaty. On this Subject I will only say that if the terms which Mr. Panton has proposed to the Court (a Copy of which he has Shewn me) are acceded to there will be no necesity for my people to desire another market, because in that case he will furnish Goods as cheap as the Georgians can. On the contrary if his commerce is burdened & embarrased tis to be feard that he will leave off a traffic which has much hurt him—in Such an event

127. After making a similar request to Zéspedes on June 10, McGillivray added that he also wanted to avail himself of Zéspedes' advice about the commissioners' letter and his answer (LC EF 114J9).

I am ignorant of what arrangements you have made to Supply his place.

I beg you to believe me that on Subject of trade most of the chiefs understand perfectly their Interest & can manage them as I please in political cases, but on matters of the above nature they are perpetually teizing me in comparing the former State of trade & now. This the Americans know well & have always endeavord to avail themselves of by promising always as easy trade & such a one as they used to have formerly from Georgia, which the Indians believe to be in their power.[128]

In regard to the small difference I had with your nephew Mr. Folch I have the pleasure to Inform you that he has lately wrote me an explanatory letter[129] which is Satisfactory, & according to a saying of my country the Talk is now Strait betwixt us & I shall be glad to cultivate his Friendship.

You will please observe that the Alabamans of themselves cannot pretend to describe limits. It must be done by a requisition from yourself to the Creek Nation—& they in asembly will direct it to be done by proper persons.

I remain with regard Sir

Your Excellencys Most Obedt. Serv.

ALEX: McGILLIVRAY [rubric]

VIII

ACCUSATIONS OF DISLOYALTY

92. *McGillivray to O'Neill, June 22, 1788*
[AGI C 201]

SIR

The Bearer is Red Shoes brother one of my Uncles he requests of Your Excellency to be pleased to give him a Gun his own being Broke & a large brass kettle. & he likewise says that he has had no Taffia a long time past & begs Your Excellency to give him some to buy a horse for himself, & he further says that the americans took his clothes in the battle he fought with General Clark in Georgia & he is in need of a great Coat &c. & as Your Excellency is his great friend he hopes You will assist him in his distress.

128. In his letter to Zéspedes, *ut supra*, McGillivray stated: "The affair that embarrasses me most is the knowledge of the Strong desire that the Americans have to Conclude a Commercial treaty with us as well as one of Peace."
129. Document 88, *supra*.

I was going to the Lower Towns Concerning some reports there of a Strangers arrival.[130] I have been laid up with pains in my feet & a fever but am now getting the better of them. I remain Dear Sir

Your Excellencys most obedient Servant

ALEX: McGILLIVRAY [rubric]

his Excellency Govr. O Neil

22d June 1788

93. *Miró to O'Neill, July 8, 1788*

[Spanish copy in AGI C 177]

No. 9. confidential.

I have received two of your letters, both dated last June 22d.[131] In the first you enclosed the letter written to me by Alexander McGillivray, with the three papers mentioned in it, to which the accompanying letter[132] is a reply. It goes open so that you may be informed of the way in which this affair was handled for your guidance in cases that may arise.

In the second you tell me of the new pretensions which William Panton made to the court through our ambassador at London, a copy of which he has sent to me.

I must say to you that I am greatly embarrassed by the continual distrust that you express on every occasion when you mention these individuals, and always merely with the assertion that they have the British heart [*el Corazon Britanico*], without citing an instance in which by conversation, letter, or in other fashion they have given cause for

130. The stranger, it was to develop, was William Augustus Bowles. This is the initial reference to him in the McGillivray correspondence, but Zéspedes had an earlier report of "Englishmen from Providence" coming unlawfully to the Florida Coast, and on April 30, he sent a detachment under Lieutenants O'Hara and O'Donovan to find and arrest such persons (Zéspedes to Ezpeleta, April 25, 1788, AGI C 1395). Bowles had enrolled in a Maryland Royalist regiment during the Revolution but was dismissed from the service at Pensacola and went to live with the Lower Creeks and Seminoles. Chapters VIII, IX, and XIV of this study contain much information about his activities from 1788 to 1792. His subsequent career does not concern us directly. The Spaniards held him prisoner at Madrid and Manila. On his way back to Spain in 1797 he managed to escape, got renewed support in England, returned to Florida, and once more plagued the Spaniards and the Americans in their efforts to control the southeastern Indians. Captured again, in 1803, he languished in Morro Castle at Havana until his death three years later. A good biography or a documentary study of Bowles would be highly significant as well as entertaining.

131. O'Neill had written, "Neither McGillivray's nor Panton's statement is satisfactory to me. In view of the passion that these persons profess for Great Britain, I doubt not that in whatever rupture we may have with that nation they will seek to damage us and to disaffect the Creek Indians, who at present are so attached to us. I think that after deliberate reflection on all this, you will find it convenient to take measures to reduce the power of these two over the life of these nations, for all the success of these individuals with the Indians is derived from the favors and the toleration of their trade which his Majesty has granted them" (AGI C 177). Compare with O'Neill's earlier expression of distrust, document 89, *supra*.

132. Document 94, *infra*.

fear. Continually you propose to me steps to destroy McGillivray's influence with the Indians.

Once more I repeat that you embarrass me; so much so that I confess candidly that I do not find orders to give in this affair, and I can only refer you to the letter I wrote you under date of the 18th of last month.[133] But no doubt you have not desisted from conceiving these plans, and I do not know why you do not show me the means whereby they could be carried out, since they seem to you so important an object.

Nevertheless, I shall send to the court and to the captain general copies of all that you have written on this matter and of my replies, so that if means are found whereby another can carry on this trade, Panton will be ordered to retire. Meanwhile, as you say that it is necessary to dissemble with them and that it is convenient to permit him to bring for the Indian trade a quantity of blankets, shirts, and linen that he has at Providence, I authorize you to give him the proper passport for the rest of the cargo brought from London last year by the frigate the "Mary" [la Maira] by virtue of the last license granted him and because Panton informs me that he needs these goods to be able to continue supplying the Indians until his Majesty acts on the application he has made through the most excellent Señor Marqués del Campo, his ambassador at London.

May God, etc. New Orleans, July 8, 1788.

ESTEVAN MIRÓ

Señor Don Arturo O'Neill.

94. *Miró to McGillivray, July 8, 1788*

[Spanish copy in AGI C 177]

. . . .You also request an explanation of the circumstances under which his Majesty wants you to make peace with the United States, and you wish to know if royal protection will be extended to save your territory for you.

I have not the least doubt that the commissioners named by the Congress and those of Georgia and South Carolina are authorized to arrange the boundaries, for this is the basis on which peace must be established. Nor do I doubt that they will act justly, returning to your respected nation the usurpations that the Georgians have made. Therefore, no explanation is needed of the royal order of his Majesty, for it is clear that so long as they fail to keep their promise, wishing to retain the usurped lands, it will disturb you excessively. Consequently, you must

133. "As to that which refers to Alexander McGillivray," Miró had written, "it does not seem to me that he has given reason for distrust. . . . nor do I find it easy to end his influence over the Indians" (AGI C 177; see also document 95, *infra*).

show the copy of the royal order declaring yourself and all your nation under the protection of his Majesty, reading to them at the same time the articles of the Congress of Pensacola of 1784 which establish this protection under the condition, approved by the nation, that you do not admit trade other than that of Spain. . . . .

On the matter of trade you speak to me with all clarity, assuring me that you are not the lord and master of the chiefs, because they know their interests too well, and that they continually make comparison of the present trade with that which they had in the period of British domination. From this it is inferred clearly that William Panton has changed the prices of the tariff, because, since in the Congress of Pensacola this was made according and conforming to the previous one and approved by you and by all the chiefs who met there, there could be no comparisons since nothing has been changed. . . . .[134]

I can do no less than observe to you that if, in the treaty of peace with the United States, you deviate in the least from the stipulations of the said Congress of Pensacola, thereafter it will appear that you and your nation do not seek the protection of Spain, except for the object of providing yourselves, by means of the trade that I have procured, with the assistance needed to make a good peace with the Americans, and after that to abandon us. This reflection I trust will lead you to keep your word that you and the chiefs would refrain from making any commercial treaty. And if William Panton goes away, on his own account or by order of his Majesty, rest assured that another trader will not be lacking who will satisfy your nation.

I still have the greatest confidence that you will not have me diminish in the least the good opinion that I have formed of your gratitude, talent, and inclination toward Spain, as I have reported to the court, attaining by your constancy the glory of knowing how to manage your nation, and inspiring sentiments of justice and probity.

May God etc.,

95. *Miró to O'Neill, July 12, 1788*
[Spanish draft in AGI C 5]

MOST ESTEEMED FRIEND AND MASTER:

Although I am not sure that I shall rightly conjecture the wishes of the court in the reply that I give to McGillivray, I have made up my mind upon it. It is the first action that I have taken independent of the captain general, though I was authorized by royal order of June 13th

134. Concerning Panton's application for exemption from duties, Miró reminded McGillivray that the import duties did not yield enough to pay for the gifts to the Creeks, and so "what use is it to Spain to protect the Creek Nation?"

of last year to act in all cases in which there was not time to receive his orders, with the provision that I must solicit the approval of the court and report the action to the captain general for his information.

You will see that in the translation of the royal order I have omitted those words which, at the same time that they might serve as evidence to the Americans proving that we had furnished arms to be used against them, would make McGillivray realize that he doubtless would be given whatever he asked, and that I would instruct you to arrange with him on this understanding.

I greatly regret that you have developed such a great distrust of McGillivray, for I do not see any reason for it in all his behaviour. I forgot to say to you in reply to yours of June 4th that if Panton and McGillevray were charged with having said to the Indians that it was their powder and balls that they furnished, they would then reply that they did it to conceal from the Americans that the government gave them, in order that the Indians should make war, which was the reason that induced us to get Panton to distribute them.[135]

I suggest to the latter that he ask in place of exemption from duties the privilege of bringing one-fourth of the value of each cargo that comes for the trade in whatever goods he desires, and I say this because there has already been a decision against him on this point, which has been disregarded, and thus it would absolutely not be permitted him hereafter, because I would stake my reputation and my position on it, of which you will give him notice, telling him also that if he obtains said permission it would be easy to forward whatever goods he might bring of this sort to this capital, because once the duty is paid there, I shall have authority over it, since they do not leave the provinces under my command.

I very much wish that we might come out well in the treaty of peace of the Talapuches and Americans, since they boast unduly that all these nations covet their trade, expressing themselves in the printed paper that Whitfield sent to McGillevray, as if we had never supplied them. The Choctaws and Chickasaws I am sure will not admit them. On your part, try to gain for us the same success with the Talapuches, writing to McGillivray what seems best, and at the same time have an express carry mine.

I hope you are favored with good health, whose benefit my wife and I enjoy, and transmitting her most affectionate expressions,

I remain, etc.,

135. The same sentiment had been voiced in Miró to O'Neill, June 18, 1788, copy in AGI C 177.

96. *McGillivray to O'Neill, July 14, 1788*

[AGI C 217]

LITTLE TALLASSIE, 14 July 1788

SIR

I Sent to Your Excellency by Mr. Panton some open letters of mine to Governor Miró, by which you woud see that the american Congress had recommended the State of Georgia to treat with our Nation for a peace, the Commissioners that were appointed to treat with us having in Strong language Insisted upon a truce on our parts till the Meeting Shoud take place. Knowing that it was the kings desire that my Nation Shoud agree to terms of peace with the americans, I advised the chiefs to assent to the truce, that was required of us by the Commissioners, & to which we had Strictly adherd & I am Sorry to Inform Your Excellency that the americans of Georgia have discoverd No Such equal peaceable disposition, for when our people unsuspicious of any harm & relying upon the faith of the truce, were hunting game for their familys, Scouting partys of the Georgians have fallen upon the hunting Camps & have killed some & wounded others & taken their horses & provisions, & tis only two days ago that accounts have come in that some more Indians are Killed. Such Conduct plainly Shews that the Georgians are determined not to agree to terms of Peace. Ive thought proper to acquaint Your Excellency of these matters & altho I know that the Ministers Instructions are that we Shall get no more arms or ammunitions from the King, Yet we Cannot tamely Suffer such outrages to pass unnoticed, & there is a prospect the the War will be kindled afresh with as great fury as ever, in the prosecution of which we must have recourse to every means that shall offer to us a Chance of defending ourselves, being resolved to run the risk of perishing to a Man before we will put up with Such Insults.[136]

An attack of the Rheumatism in my feet confining me to bed has prevented me from Informing of Your Excellency before this time of these matters.

I remain with sincere regard

Your Excellencys Most obedient Servt.

ALEX: MCGILLIVRAY [*rubric*]

136. A more elaborate statement of these ideas is contained in a letter to Zéspedes, August 8, 1788, LC EF 114J9. Miró, however, counseled moderation. He advised McGillivray to ask redress of damages from the American authorities before launching any attack (Miró to McGillivray, August 16, 1788, draft in AGI C 2360).

97. *Miró to Ezpeleta, July 28, 1788*

[Spanish original in AGI C 1394]

After the mail closed, I received today the confidential papers that accompanied the report of the commandant of Pensacola. I enclose to you under No. 1 the letter that he wrote me previously dated June 10th.[137] By all these and by the translations Nos. 3 and 5 you will see that a boat arrived in the Savannah River (which I believe we call the Mosquitos and others call Indian River)[138] proceeding from Providence with goods for the Indians. The conduct of Alexander McGillivray, as the notice indicates, is strange and incriminating, and it is the first act that rouses suspicion against him.[139] Nevertheless it seems to me necessary, in the absence of confirmation, and convenient in all respects in the present situation, to dissemble until we see how he behaves in the assembly for making peace with the United States of America.

I do not believe that the British government has promoted this affair, or that it is certain that they are building a fort, as the trader O'Keefe asserts, or even that it is the pretended war against America and Spain. I am persuaded that it is merely a mercantile expedition, perhaps made at the request of McGillivray,[140] because he saw that on our part we were hoping to diminish his munitions at the same time when he proposed to attack the Georgians with great fervor, and when he believed that they would not come to seek peace. . . . . .

98. *McGillivray to O'Neill, August 12, 1788*

[AGI C 201]

LITTLE TALLASSIE, 12 August 1788

SIR

I received Your Excellencys esteemd favor by Juan Garcon[141] four days ago, but as I had no paper to write till young Moniac came home with his pack horses, I coud not write an answer till this day, & the weather being very rainy he Im afraid cant go off this day or two.

137. See also O'Neill's warning to the commandant at Apalache that McGillivray and Panton with help from the Bahama Islands were planning an attack upon Pensacola or Apalache (O'Neill to Vegas, June 26, 1788, AGI C 38).
138. Variously called the Ys, the Indian, the Mosquito, but not the Savannah River.
139. That is, the first to arouse Miró's suspicion. O'Neill had distrusted for some months past; see especially documents 89, 93, and 95, *supra.*
140. Thomas Miller declared upon oath, on August 11, 1788, that McGillivray had told him that he and Panton had formulated the project of getting aid from the Governor of Providence (AGI C 38). O'Neill also took the declarations of Enrique Smell (August 6), Carlos Hal, Juan Jones, Juan Linder, and Archivaldo Sion (August 12) (all in AGI C 38; see also O'Neill to Ezpeleta, August 15, 1788, *ibid.*).
141. Son of Antonio Garcon, the interpreter.

The letters from his Exc. Gov. Miró[142] Contain a full explanation of what I wanted to know, respecting how we were to treat with the americans, & I have no doubt but the Intimations of so great a king will have a proper effect on the minds of the American Congress, to Induce them to endeavor to do us Justice, but as experience has Shewn that the Authority of that Body does not Influence the whole States, so in the present case it is likely that the Interference of Congress to Settle the disputes between Georgia & us will not be attended to & have the good effects we expected to derive from that measure. . . . .

As a more certain proof of my Suspicions I shall observe to Your Exc. that the Commissioners letters to us Contain'd Some threats & it is publickly said among the americans that if I dont agree to their terms, they will make it a general quarrel & they have reports that we are to have no more support from the King of Spain. This will encourage them to provoke us to fresh hostilitys. . . . .[143]

I have no fears of danger from the No. West Country, having made peace with them as Ive been obliged to do, & the Governor of Franklin (at the head of a deperate Banditti) whose name is Sevier is now in rebellion to Congress. He has Sent me word that he wants much to come to me with his desperados but I give him no encouragement, tho he might do me Service against his Country.

No doubt but Your Excellency has heard much talk from Indians & others about a Strange man, Coming in the Nation. I have Seen him & he was a Captain in a Loyalist Corps in the last war. He certainly has brought in a good supply of arms & ammunition from a Society of certain charitible people, but he keeps a great Secrecy (& the Indians & others have made a great many Idle conjectures about him & the affair).[144] The Supply I have made no Scruple to accept of, in these uncertain times. If the americans as I believe do prosecute any ill designs against us, I Shall Certainly resist them, while I have one single bullet left. My acceptance of this I hope will not cause or be the occasion of any Suspicions in Your Excellencys mind, that we harbour any

142. Document 93, *supra.*
143. McGillivray had just received the commissioners' letter dated July 16 (copies in ASP IA, I, 29, and AGI C 201), in which they stated that they had no authority to require the Georgians to retire from the Oconee lands, but that they had asked the governor of Georgia "to issue a proclamation that no further trespasses be committed." He answered them on August 16, expressing his "surprise and concern" that they were not authorized to give the Creeks full redress. He reiterated that removal of the Georgians from the disputed lands was "an indispensable preliminary," without which the chiefs would not consent to treat (AGI C 201; a copy dated August 12 is in ASP IA, I, 29). This statement led Commissioner Winn to observe to Knox, "It evidently appears by his last, if we are to expect peace with these Indians, it must be on his own terms" (October 14, *ibid.,* p. 28).
144. See Panton to Miró, August 5, 1788, AGI C 2361, in which he quotes a correspondent in thē Bahama Islands.

Secret bad intentions against the Interest & welfare of the Spanish Dominions the rulers of which have shewn so much attention to us in every time of distress & want. If I had been Secure from apprehensions of present danger from the americans I Shoud not have accepted of any Gift that might have been in any way the means to create the least anxiety in your & our other freinds minds, but I entreat of You to believe me that I am Steadfast in my principles & mean nothing else than to keep & promote the attachment of my people Steady to Spain. . . . .

99. *McGillivray to Miró, August 12, 1788*

[AGI C 2361]

LITTLE TALLASSIE, 12 August 1788

SIR

. . . .& it now appears (I have my Information from reputable Authority in Carolina & Georgia) that tired out with our obstinate resistance & the expence & length of the dispute, & to accomplish their ends more effectually, the Georgians have lately made a Cession of their Western Territory to Congress,[145] which in truth is none at all as their real limits on that Side comes out only Sixty English miles west of the Town of Augusta. But if they absurdly ground their Western claims on the article of the late peace between Great Brittain & them, why then the Cession which they have made to Congress is great indeed! as it Includes our Nation & to the Natchez on the Mississippi. By this measure they meant to obtain the Sanction of Congress to engage the whole Union in the quarrel. Setting aside the other part of the imaginary claim, our hunting lands only toward the East of our Towns Compute nearly three hundred English miles in depth & near double in length, & which is an object, that I dare say will Stagger the boasted Virtue of the Congress. In Short to Speak out my Sentiments at once, I am of opinion that they will not Compel the Georgians to restore our lands & if we take Strong Measures to obtain Justice, the force of the Union will be employd to reduce us to accept of their own terms of peace, which if they are permitted to effect they must have ourselves into the bargain.

I do not therefore hesitate to pronounce that the measure which the Governmt. adopted to Withhold from us the Royal Support to Induce us to treat with the americans is premature. A moments reflection woud have foreseen the ill Consequence of Compelling a Naked unarmd people to treat with a designing & incensd Implacable enemy.

145. A mistaken rumor; Georgia did not actually cede her western claims to the Union until 1798 and 1801.

Such a mode of Interference Shoud have been reservd for the last, if it Shoud have been found that we woud not accede to Just & equitable terms of Peace.

My Suspicions are partly Confirmd by Seeing in an american paper "if the Creeks do not agree to terms of Peace the Whole Union will take the matter up. They are no longer supported by a *Certain power*."

However, notwithstanding my Suspicions Yet if we Shoud meet the Commissioners to treat of Peace I Shall endeavor to give Your Excellency Satisfaction on the points to which you recommend my attention.

I hope that Mr. Panton will Succeed in his application to be placed on the footing which he desires. He has been many years Concernd in the Commerce of this Nation & is generally known & much respected by the Indians, besides his long experience & ability gives him the power to carry the greater part of the trade to where he wishes, & I am myself attachd to him from a Sense of benefits I have to his freindship during the late war. For these reasons I hope that Your Excellency will not Judge of me that I give myself unnecessary trouble about him, & in any event I have no doubt but care will be taken that our people will Continue to be Supplied.

I readily allow of the axiom that "in all Political Compacts the parties intend always to derive advantages" but it is expected likewise that they will be reciprocal, but I can see none that we obtain, even in the article of Presents as we pay for them in an encreased price of the necessary clothing for our familys.[146] The Custom of Presents has been long ago established by all people who form any Connexions with Indian Nations. As for the extra Support which has been given or may be in future, it is answerd by an observation that the Interests & the Repose of the Kings Provinces are deeply Involvd in the Security of our Establishment as an Independent Nation.

When the Post of St. Marks was Surrenderd to the English by the peace of 1763 they soon [after] rather restord it to its proper owners the Indians & when a Spanish Garrison was admitted to it, our trade there was expected to be free as it was our own unoccupied port. Even were it otherwise it ought to be so to lighten in some Measure the Weight of the burdens on our trade, for exclusive of Your dutys there are more than equal to them imposed in England beside a heavy Insurance in & out on a dangerous Coast. All matters being Considerd our Merchants do not make Idle Complaints on their Commerce as it Now Stands & which we ultimately feel.

I have a Certain Circumstance to Inform Your Excellency of as I will always be candid & open to You. Last Month there landed a Gentle-

146. A reference to document 94, *supra;* see note 134, *supra.*

man for such he was, near a Semonolie Village, & came to me at the Lower Town where I was, making my annual tour among these Chiefs. He told me that a Certain Society having known our distresses thro the channel of News papers had purchased for & Sent to me by him a quantity of arms & ammunition for our releif. As he kept great reserve I couldn't find out from whom it came but Circumstanced as we are I did not think myself warranted to refuse them knowing that however affairs may go against us in being not able to obtain a Good peace Speedy & Vigorous enterprise must mark our operations, & that you do not furnish me with Means of defence untill You have orders from Court, & before which could happen an enterprising enemy might overrun our Country. However let not this Circumstance make any anxiety in Your Mind regarding my good Intentions.[147] I Take Your admonitions to that end in a freindly way. In the event of either war or peace with the americans, we Shall Stand firmly by Your Side. Be assured that I will make no Stipulations with the americans upon no occasion that are dissagreeable to or may have a hurtfull tendency to the Interests of the king, who certainly Shoud likewise have Such considerations for us, but in the latter end it might have been better. I am always Your Excellencys faithfull freind & obedt. Servant,

ALEX: McGILLIVRAY [rubric]

paper is very Scarce.

100. *McGillivray to Miró, August 20, 1788*
[AGI C 2361]
LITTLE TALLASSIE 20 August 1788

SIR

. . . .This is the Second time that I have had occasion to Complain of being Insulted by unjust Suspicious Imputations,[148] which are as disgracefull to my Character as hurtfull to my feelings, & since no professions that I make of attachment & Integrity can secure my honor from such attacks nor ensure Confidence, I must request of Your Excellency to Accept of my determined resignation of a Commission

147. Miró did question McGillivray's intentions; he was now ready to conclude that Bowles' coming was by the chief's invitation. Yet he did not believe that England had sent the expedition to Mosquito River, nor did he think it possible that the Creeks would attack Pensacola (Miró to Ezpeleta, August 16, 1788, AGI C 1394). One month later Miró concluded that McGillivray's act was "reprehensible but excusable," and that the arrival of Bowles' vessel was *not* managed by Panton and McGillivray (Miró to Ezpeleta, September 16, 1788, *ibid.*). And on October 20 he observed, "The persistence of O'Neill's fears of being attacked is worthy of admiration, after what Alexander McGillevray has written" (Miró to Ezpeleta, October 1788, *ibid.*). The captain general signified his approval of what Miró had done and advised that care should be exercised not to displease or disaffect McGillivray (Ezpeleta to Miró, October 24, 1788, AHN E 3887).

148. Explanation is to be found in documents 101, 103, and 104, *infra.*

which can be only regarded by me as a blank paper. At the same time I Shall assure you that the same principle of Policy which dictated to me the propriety of forming a political Compact with Your Nation still Influences my mind, & as you have never given me occasion to be an enemy, So I Shall continue my best endeavour to preserve & maintain a good understanding between my people & the Subjects of the king, equally as if I was Still an officer of his. . . . .

ALEX: McGILLIVRAY [rubric]

101. *McGillivray to O'Neill, August 22, 1788*
[AGI C 201]
LITTLE TALLASSIE, 22 August 1788

SIR

It is with extreme Concern that I take up my pen to address Your Excellency. Some frightend white men my Servants have arrived here & some Indians that are Come from Pensacola have thrown all this part of the Nation into great alarm & apprehensions, concerning Some reports that have been carryd to Your Excellency by that Villain Timy. Lane & Straggling Indians, that I have formd a design commence hostility against Pensacola & all the Spanish Floridas. It gives me great Concern that Such an Idle & ridiculous report should dwell for a moment in Your Excellencys Mind. I hope God in his mercy has not Intirely deprived my Nation & myself of our Senses, that we might provoke our certain ruin by so fatal a measure as to Create & Seek a Cause of difference with You at this time.

Your Excellency Certainly has a better opinion both of my heart & understanding, than to Suppose me Capable of a breach of my honor which I thank God has never yet been questiond either in publick or private life.

The whole Matter has arose from a Small Supply of arms & ammunition, which Some Generous Society has furnishd us with against the americans & if it had been offerd to me with any View of encourageing any Matter of a hostile Nature to the dominion of Spain I woud have turnd the present against the breast of the proposer of Such a base measure.

I write this to Your Excellency to remove every mark of Suspicion from Your generous mind, & not from any unmanly & fearfull disposition, as the World knows that I have a Spirit & resolution to execute whatever my heart conceives & am never ashamd to avow a just action.

I enclose to Your Excellency the Copy of a letter & my answer to it that I received from the american Commission just four days after

196

Juan Garcon went away from here, by which you will see that they refuse to give up their usurpations so that there is likelyhood that our war with the americans will continue, as I do not believe it is the King's desire that we Shall make peace with giving up our Country & ourselves to the americans, & I am resolved to Save my Country from them or to perish with the whole Nation.

I was just on the point of Setting off to go & see You but Your Excellency Cant Conceive the Confusion that is now among us by reason of Lanes & the Indians reports, our pack horses are all afraid to go to Pensacola & the Indians are all in a bustle which is encreased by that Villian the Tame King & his faction. So that to prevent bad Consequences I have despatched expresses to the Lower Towns & the Wild Indians to Settle their minds & I am now obligd to Call a Meeting directly to Satisfy the people that Your Excellency has no Intentions to distress the trade of the Nation. I wish Your Excellency had put Lane in Confinement, & had Sent for me before all this Stir had rose up. He has made the most daring attempt I ever knew, to make us enemies to each other who are the best freinds—for which he Shall. . . . .

I assure You upon my honor that the Tensaw people are Innocent of any Crime against Government, all that I know of them is that Ive been told that Some of them wishd to join the Indians against the americans for the Sake of plunder. I therefore entreat of Your Excellency to let every thing return into its old channel of Confidence & harmony, & by no means to prevent the traders from bringing the usual Supplys for the Nation.

I write this in great agitation of mind. I remain with great affection & regard,

Your Excellencys most obedt. Servt.

ALEX: McGILLIVRAY [rubric]

102. *O'Neill to Miró, August 22, 1788*
[Spanish copy in AGI C 1394]

Juan Garzon, son of the Talapuche interpreter, whom I sent to deliver your despatch in the town Little Tallassie to the commissary of those Indians Alexander McGillivray, returned here two days ago. He handed me the enclosed for you from McGillivray, and with it I send you a copy of a letter that McGillivray at the same time wrote to me.[149] From them you will see that his and Panton's behaviour is exactly what I foresaw and suspected, and it is as much as an unfortunate mestizo and a hide merchant could have the audacity to do. Although I am sensitive about it I shall dissemble with them (it appears

149. Documents 98 and 99, *supra*.

convenient for the present, until superior authority will prove what may be more convenient), for otherwise it would bring to a standstill the trade with the Indians, who would seek trade with the Americans and separate themselves from our friendship, in which it is likely they would be advised by those now interested in the trade here of the house of Panton and McGillivray.

The said Juan Garzon tells me that McGillivray kept him five days in the nation, excusing himself from replying earlier for lack of paper, and that in the meantime Garzon went to some neighboring towns where the Indians told him that after they harvested the crop they would go to receive the present that the English sent them. Some of the Indians told him that as soon as the troops or at least armed Englishmen arrived, who would come with a present in two boats to the coast of East Florida, they would make war on the Americans. But other Indians said to him that upon the arrival of these Englishmen with four small cannon they would unite with all the whites of the Tensaw to take Pensacola. He adds that the Indian chief of the town of Fosache was one of those who reported this latter.

Three days ago the trader Timothy Lain arrived here from the Creek Nations. He is the same who previously came to tell me of the English vessel on the coast or Mosquito River. He tells me that Alexander McGillivray was taking or gathering horses to bring back the present of the English, and that certain of the Indians who were with the English official Bowles or Bolans had returned, because they heard of the departure of some troops from St. Augustine to intercept the present, and that many Indians complain because the Spaniards intercepted this present. He says also that a rumor had been spread among the Indians (he believes by Alexander McGillivray) that the Spaniards and Americans have made an alliance and are now in accord, but that the one hundred Englishmen who disembarked at Mosquito River would come and unite with various traders and inhabitants of Tensaw to come against Pensacola. At the time of Lain's departure from the nation McGillivray was expecting an express to inform him definitely whether or not the troops from St. Augustine had seized the English vessel and the present. . . . .

103. *McGillivray to O'Neill, August 29, 1788*
[AGI C 201]

LITTLE TALLASSIE, 29 August 1788

SIR

I have received your Excellencys letter of 22d Inst. Some days before I received it hearing bad rumours which threw us all into alarm upper

198

& Lower Creeks. I Sent Weatherford express to you concerning the same.[150] Your Excellency as a Governor as well as a Military officer knows how much it is necessary for a proper Subordination to be kept up, & having a bad Sett to manage I am under a Necessity to give Lane a reprimand publicly for an example to the rest.

I am always happy to Comply with Your Excellencys desires, & nothing but Necessity to keep up an orderly behaviour obliges me to do so to Lane. I beg of Your Excellency to believe me that I have always Shewn great lenity to this man even when it was proved that he engaged to Sacrifice my life to the americans. Not Content with that he has now attempted a daring Crime to Create War & bloodshed between Your people & ours. This is too much & calls for some check.

I have Shewn to Your Excellency that the Congress regardless of the Royal Interference in our behalf has refused us Justice. In this Case I hope we Shall be Sustain'd, for You may be assured as there is a God & Saints in heaven, that if the americans gets the upper hand in the terms of peace of us that they will use our force directly against the kings territory, & be drawn into all their quarrels & to Support their ambitious Schemes—Concerning this I have wrote to Governor Miro —if my advice is Neglected I can have no blame. Negotiations ought now to be Set aside & the means given to us to Carry our point by force of arms. I am glad to hear from Your Excellency that all the late rumours occasiond by Lane is past away, & our Intercourse will be as free as usual. Conclude with assuring Your Excellency of the truest affection & esteem

Your most obedt. Servt.

ALEX: MCGILLIVRAY [rubric]

104. *McGillivray to Miró, September 20, 1788*
[AGI C 2361]
LITTLE TALLASSIE, 20 September 1788

SIR

I have received Your Excellencys letter by Mr. Nolan,[151] who is now Indisposed, but as soon as he recovers, I Shall agreeable to Your Request forward him in the Safest & surest Manner to Cumberland.

150. O'Neill's letter to Miró on the same date, document 102, *supra*, gives an idea of what he wrote to McGillivray. Weatherford carried documents 100 and 101, *supra*.
151. Philip Nolan is better known than some of his more significant contemporaries because Nathan Hale unwittingly appropriated his name for *The Man Without a Country*. Hale sought to redress the damages by writing a paper on "The Real Philip Nolan." Nolan's chief exploits related to horse-trading ventures in Texas in the nineties. The usual account is that he first came to New Orleans in 1790 as a protege of Wilkinson's; this document and the following indicate that he was there two years earlier.

The best rout for him woud have been from Mobile to the Chickasaws, as the Cherokees & other Nations are at war with the americans. This rout is dangerous, & he must now go by the Chickasaws.

Three days ago I received a letter from the american commiss. who say that they are under the Necessity of prolonging the time of the Treaty untill next spring. Among other reasons for so doing, they say that "the necessary despatches not coming in time, without which the Supplys for putting the Treaty into execution upon a liberal footing woud be Intirely Insufficient, next the change of Government taking place since & the probability of our receiving Instructions very shortly under the auspices of the New Congress whose fiat in this as well as in every other Case for the general welfare we presume will be more permanent than that of the expiring one."[152] They next assure that all hostillitys against us will Cease in Georgia, but that is more than they can answer for as at the time that a truce of arms was operating with us those people kept up hostillity in Molesting our hunters in the woods, & now Since the truce was proclaimd by the Government of Georgia, a Coweta Indian brought me a written paper that he found on a tree more than half ways to the Nation, wherein was expressd that we are not to expect a Peace till they had a full Satisfaction of all their desires, with some promises to myself if I woud agree to them. Thus we find that the Georgians will Counteract the Intentions of Congress. I have Sent the paper to the Commissioners. It is signed by a James Alexander who killed the Cussitaws & brought on the war of last winter.[153]

My answer to the Commissioners letters was to this offer that I shoud agree to prolong the time of treaty untill next spring, but for the truce of arms, that woud depend upon the Conduct of the Georgians, for I woud not bind myself & Nation to Suffer Neither Insult & outrage but that I woud act from Circumstances.[154]

A friend Informs me by letter that the Governor of the State of Georgia, Summond the assembly to meet in August at the request of the Commissioners to assist in the Negotiations for peace, when not

152. Governor Handley, in suggesting this excuse, had predicted that it would be sufficient, "particularly to Mr. McGillivray, who is a sensible, intelligent man." Georgia's financial distress and the governor's inability to persuade the legislature to convene, though equally important reasons, were not mentioned to McGillivray (ASP IA, I, 28-29).

153. In a letter to Panton, also dated September 20, McGillivray calls this document "a wretched, dirty and scandalous scrawl." "The chap that signs," he continued, "is Colonel Alexander, who murdered the Cussetas. He and Clarke sway Upper Georgia" (Pickett, History of Alabama, pp. 385-88), quoting from papers filed in the District Court of Louisiana).

154. McGillivray to Winn, Pickens, and Mathews, September 15, 1788, ASP IA, I, 30.

one half woud assemble & the Speaker of the house upon being wrote to upon the Subject by the Governor returnd a Verbal answer Saying that he had more Important business of his own private Concerns on hand to attend the house & that his time was too precious to waste in writing letters to his honor the Governor. From the foregoing account Your Excellency will plainly see that little is to be expected in the way of Negotiation, while a few leading men such as Colonel Alexander, Clark, &c sway the upper part of Georgia. The State of North Carolina, while Congress is holding out assurances of good will to the Cherokees, that State is in arms & burning the Villages of the Indians & destroying them. Pitying the great distress of the Cherokees, I Sent a Considerable party of my upper Warriors to their assistance & a runner has lately brought me the pleasing Intelligence that they had encountered the americans in the Cherokee Country & had defeated them killing a good Number, upon which the Americans had retreated altogether from that Country for the present.

It is with much Satisfaction that I find that the apparition of dangers & attacks has vanished from Governor ONeils mind & that Confidence & harmony is again restord, & the Intercourse for our traders is uninterrupted, all which had been well nigh lost through the Governors precipitation.

Your Excellency will always find me Steady to my first professions always expecting that good faith will be mutually preservd.

I remain with respectful regard & esteem,

Your Excellencys obedient Servt.

ALEX: McGILLIVRAY [rubric]

P. S. It may appear Strange to Your Excellency that the Georgians notwithstanding their distresses Shoud be so obstinate as not to agree to Just terms of Peace. The reason is that Just as we were on the point to humble them Compleatly, our Support of arms & ammunition given by the royal bounty was Suddenly Stopt from us, & we were unable to exert the Vigour & enterprise necessary to finish the war. Without it an Indian cannot afford to purchase ammunition for war beside providing necessarys for his family. Of course their Mode of war is very Irregular, Carried on by Starts & feeble. I Shall only add that You [encouraged] the origin of our war with the States, Succour & aid was promised us to enable us to defend our rights, a non performance of that engagement on Your part will be Considerd by the Cheifs as that You have releasd yourselves from it. You expect that we Shoud make no treatys with the States without Your Concurrence, this must be Mutual, you Should not take any measures of that kind in which our dearest Interests are so deeply Involvd without our Consent. We are the Most Competent Judges of the exigencys of our affairs & accordingly make the necessary requisitions to you Concerning them, which according to every Idea of good faith ought to be Complyd with by You. We have other resources in View, in case of need, but it is a point of honor with me to be Steady & keep engagements untill released from them by the other contracting party.

A. McGillivray

IX

RENEWAL OF SPANISH SUPPORT

105. *Zéspedes to McGillivray, October 8, 1788*
[Spanish copy in AHN E 3887]
St. Augustine, Florida, October 8, 1788

My dear Sir:

By the tenor of your letter of last August 8th,[155] I gather that you are not so warmly inclined toward making peace with the Georgians as you indicated in your previous letter of June 10th, in consequence of having been notified shortly earlier that this was the desire of the king. I assure you that this desire sprang from the pure paternal interest that the king takes in the welfare of the Indians. When you are at peace with Georgia, when the limits of your territory are determined and the commerce of your people established on a firm and liberal basis with Spain, then and only then will you be able to enjoy that repose, which, as you say in your letter of March 8th, you eagerly covet but have only been able to contemplate in the abstract. Take care that you do not lose that repose, already in your grasp, by giving ear to the tales of insidious knaves. I give you this warning, for I am informed on the most reliable authority that that villain Bowles (of whom Captain Howard wrote to you at my order last month) is a complete liar, and what he says in the Indian Nation of having been in England and of having been sent by that government with offers of help for you and your people is an infamous lie.

The man never was in England; he is not and never was a captain in the Fifty-fourth Regiment. The highest rank he ever had was that of ensign in the last war in the Provincial Loyalist Regiment of Maryland. His purpose is to gather a band of vagabonds at [New] Providence of

155. LC EF 114J9.

fortunes as desperate as his own, and with these, taking advantage of the war between the Creek Nation and Georgia, to steal negroes and horses, and to rouse the Spanish government against your friends Panton, Leslie and Company to the ruin of their house. Furthermore, it is not from this company that I have my information, but from a much more reliable authority.[156] It is certain that that constant friend of the Indians, Colonel Brown, is so fully convinced of the villainous designs of Bowles and his backers that he has stoutly refused to receive a call from the two Indians who accompanied Bowles to Providence. Your own experience and penetration will have made you see that Bowles is an ignorant man. He is of such rank, that he is no more than the foolish instrument of veritable scoundrels, though placed in high employ at Providence. Be assured that, although Bowles' backers[157] have distinguished positions, they are at the same time so far in debt that they lack the means to help, due to their bad projects. As Bowles must occasionally ship to Providence the wealth that he is able to steal, there is no doubt that his career will be ended shortly. Likewise, when you return to the nation, and make him prisoner and conduct him and his followers under sufficient guard to Pensacola or to this place, you will do a service to your own country, an honor likewise, and a deed of friendliness to your friends Panton and Leslie.[158] Once this is arranged, you will be free to pass on to other matters. You have seen already that I am a man of integrity and truth; as such I assure you

156. Colonel Thomas Brown, the last English superintendent of the Southern Indians, had been extended certain courtesies by Zéspedes at the time of his retiring from Florida. Partly out of gratitude, Brown sent Zéspedes in 1788 a very circumstantial account of Bowles' activities and supporters in the islands (AGI C 1395). Zéspedes described Brown as "a man of honor and truth, not hostile, in fact friendly toward Spain," and indicated that his influence among the Indians was still great (Zéspedes to Valdés, October 11, 1788, AHN E 3887). Zéspedes also had information from John Leslie, October 3, 1788 (LC EF 116L9), enclosing a letter from John Hambly, September 28, 1788 (ibid.).
157. Principal among these were John Miller, a merchant, and Lord Dunmore the governor. Miller, whose name in some of the documents is spelled Millar, was senior partner of the Providence firm of Miller and Bonamy. He was a determined foe of Panton, Leslie and Company. John Murray, fourth Earl of Dunmore, the famous Governor Dunmore of New York, 1770-76, and of Virginia, 1772-76, known also in connection with Dunmore's War, was a member of the House of Lords, 1776-87, and governor of the Bahama Islands, 1787-96. Brown pronounced him "as poor in money as in brains," and said, "no gentleman can deal with him without staining his reputation" (Brown to Zéspedes, —— —, 1788, AGI C 1395).
158. To Valdés on October 18, 1788, Zéspedes wrote that "Bowles must have enchanted the Georgian leaders and brought them under his influence for the purpose of ruining the house of Panton and Leslie" (AHN E 3887). Writing to the governor of Georgia on October 10, Zéspedes skipped over any possible advantages to Georgia from Bowles' activities and indicated the latter's purposes as: (1) to prevent peace between Georgia and the Creeks, and (2) to help the Indians rob Georgian settlements. He asked Handley to do what he could to frustrate this "bad plot," which he characterized as "actually piracy" (ibid.). Handley replied on November 25, "This man Bowles has stayed some time in this state, and he is well known in it, as a vile, infamous character" (AGI C 1395).

that all that I have related is true. If you adopt pacific measures toward Georgia, as I wish, remember what I told you in my last letter, to wit, that a treaty of peace in no way implies one of commerce.

All your own interests, as likewise those of your countrymen, require that you give preference to Spain, which has the power and the will to benefit the Indians as her own sons and certainly will never try to harm them or covet their lands. The apology that you make me for not coming to see me is most just. Come when you wish, you will always find on my part a hearty welcome, under the certainty that I am with true appreciation and great affection, your most attentive servant, who kisses your hand, etc.

VIZENTE MANUEL DE ZÉSFEDES

Señor Don Alexander McGillivray.

106. *O'Neill to Miró, October 28, 1788*
[Spanish copy in AGI C 1394]

According to the last reports that I have had from two traders, the one a private person and the other serving the Creek Nation from this place, the horses, that Alexander McGillivray sent to Mosquito River to bring to the nation the munitions that Captain Bowels brought to that place in two or three little vessels, have not yet returned to the nation. It is said that one of them was wrecked and foundered at the mouth of that river, although the Indians generally believe that the Spaniards of St. Augustine seized it. According to rumor, the rest of the cargo was burned by the Spaniards, except a quantity of salt piled up on the river bank. Some say the other vessels have unloaded, and others that they returned to Providence, to which place Bowels followed in a canoe, having given assurance upon his departure that he would return shortly with other shiploads of goods and munitions, which he promised by the 15th of this month. Meanwhile the horses must wait in the vicinity of Mosquitoes.

This same report is most common among the Creek Indians and the traders of that nation. The only difference is whether Bowels will return to Mosquito River, or St. Marys or some other place on the coast.

Now I am reliably informed that this expedition is made by British traders and that Alexander McGillevray is concerned and with the idea of protecting it, for he has frankly admitted so before different persons, two of whom have told me so, warning me that at the most Bowels will be delayed until the Christmas season, and that McGillevray's intention and that of the said merchants is to establish themselves on our coast, which he says is as much theirs as the lands of the Indians, who consequently may grant them to those who are their friends and desire to settle among them. He has the effrontery to say that although a boat has been lost his friends and partisans will send it, though thirty be lost, and that no one will prevent his receiving it. In his conversation he has made threats, saying that if the Spaniards of St. Augustine have sunk one of the boats that came from Providence to Mosquitoes, so much the better, for on this ground he would have something to fight us about. . . . .

Within twenty days one of McGillevray's confidants will be here, who, resenting past insults, has promised to inform me secretly what is going on now.[159] If this works out, this individual is the one most to the purpose of cutting short the sinister intentions of McGillevray and his associates, who, you may rest assured, and as I have no doubt, practice the greatest falsehood. I shall be obliged if you will report this in like terms to the captain general.[160]

May God preserve you many years, etc.

107. *McGillivray to Leslie, November 20, 1788*
[LC EF 114J9]
LITTLE TALLASSIE 20 November 1788

DEAR SIR

I have received your freindly talk by an Indian from Ned Forrester. Soon after the rogue was detected in Stealing a brydle from a trader in my yard Shame of which caused him I suppose to run clear off without waiting for letters to carry back. This being the hunting Season it is not easy to get an Indian to go. I'm trying to procure one if I give 80 chalks. I am obliged to you & your freinds for the early Information which you give me as a Caution against Bowles. It is true he gave me great hopes of Succour & aid, beside many other fine things which wore rather an Improbable face. I questiond him a good deal about who engaged him in the enterprise, but he woudn't Satisfy me at this time. but pointedly denied that D[unmor]e was any ways concernd. After landing his arms & ammn. he was to return with fresh Instructions, before this time, but has not yet appeared. Come when he will he will be exposed before the Indians & dismissd for a Needy Vagrant. As he knew that a negotiation was pending here with the americans & a truce subsisting I expect he will Steer another Course, tho if he brings his Supply I will first make Sure of that.

159. Charles Weatherford; see document 110, *infra*.
160. Forwarding this letter to the captain general, Miró urged the calling of a congress of the Creek chiefs at Pensacola the ensuing May. He offered to preside over it in person, though it would occasion him an extra expense of 1500 to 2000 pesos (Miró to Ezpeleta, November 18, 1788, AGI C 1394). On December 1 he retracted this request and asked merely for authorization to call a congress if absolutely necessary (*ibid.*).

You my freind I observe has a touch about peace making. What in the name of God makes you all Mad in that vein, when the americans do not discover an equal earnestness, indeed such orders have come to me from the Westward[161] in such a peremptory tone & unconditional mode as carries an appearance of great uneasiness to us. It tempted me to imagine that the americans & Spain had resolved to Share the Spoil. The Talk to me is "make Instant peace with america but reserve your trade to Spain" for this reason I thought it proper to demand an explanation especially in what regarded our trade, which at the very time was newly burthend & heavily restraind at St Marks, which causd Panton to resolve to throw up the trade, & was it not reasonable for me to require that our trade Shoud be placed on a liberal & unalterable footing before I answerd the above mandate, particularly as Gov. Miro Confessd that he had no power to assure us a permanent trade on the footing we desired which I believe was on that which you have at St. Augustine or is offerd elsewhere.

What is most Curious is that he has Conceivd that I wish to give our trade & Influence of this Nation to Georgia. He has before now noticed my rooted aversion to those people, & it is absurd in him to imagine it, he may precipitate us to that measure by harshness of usage but I woud not willingly.

ONeils heat & violence on a late occasion has renderd it Impossible for me to act as an officer of the kings which I had at first accepted on much entreaty. & what was the great matter I did to offend them, why it was accepting an immediate Supply in a Case of Necessity when the people who had Stipulated in treaty to give us assistance went the length to threaten us if an Instant peace was not made, at a period too when the Georgians were declaring themselves averse to peace, Notified in papers Stuck up on trees on all the roads leading to the Nation. & if the donations had been tacked with any Conditions Injurious to Spain, or made with a View to Slacken the chain of Connexion between us & these Governments, then in that Case I Shoud have deemd myself dishonorable in accepting it—but no such terms were ever hinted.

In how different a manner did our Worthy freind Gov. Zespedes conduct himself on the Same occasion. There was no violent Suspicions no confining drunken wretches to extort Confessions, but he took a true politic mode to gain what he wishd. I can bend to a freindly admonition, but a Contrary Conduct produces from me Very Contrary effects.[162]

161. That is, from Miró and O'Neill.
162. Writing to Zéspedes on December 8, McGillivray covered the foregoing points with somewhat more of formality than here. He also mentioned that the Creeks had gone to the rescue of the Cherokees in the fighting against the Franklin

I have some dispatches from So. Carolina Since I wrote the Governors letter. I find from Pickens that Congress have Set themselves in good earnest into rectifying abuses which the Indians Complain of: as a first beginning they have come to Strong resolutions to do Justice to the Cherokees, & have resolved to use the Continental troops to aid them to put the resolves in force, so that I have some prospect now of Settling our disputes with Georgia as I wish our rights secured & causes of future quarrel removed to a great distance.

Bowles is not in the Nation that I can learn, but when he appears I will have the whole truth out of him, which you shall have when I get it, tho he Stickled hard before to me that Lord D[unmor]e was no ways concernd. Having had some personal acquaintance with him when in Garrison at Pensacola last war, I cant treat him as a felon, but will give him wholsom advice & dismiss him. Shall say no more on this Subject, but that I hope the period is not very distant which will terminate the Contest with Georgia which will no longer attract the attention of Vagrant & Needy Men, allured with prospects of Mending broken fortunes by plunder to be gaind in war will no more obtrude themselves into our Nation, to the great discontent & uneasiness of our Freinds.

My Western freinds are busily engaged in a design to overthrow both the Authority & Influence which I possess in this My Country, & say that they will soon take me down from the Man of Consequence which I am fond of acting. They had better not go to far in this favorite scheme of theirs, tho I can overlook trifles, yet they had better not urge me too far. The Man of Consequence has feelings which may be hurt & then they will find him to be what he is called. However I must Confess I cant help thinking myself so, being at the head of a Numerous brave Nation, & of a Confederacy of the other Nations dreaded by & formidable to some who think much of their power. By our arms we have drove one half of Cumberland from threatening the Spanish possessions to the Necessity of seeking Shelter & Soliciting to become its Subjects, & great numbers are received both at Orleans & Mobile. At the latter place they are Sent to Settle between the Chactaw Nation & ours, the propriety of which measure I have not yet questiond. A deputation from Cumberland was here this Spring offering any Condition for peace & another is now in my house for the same purpose. They bring me Notice that I am Complimented by that State with a lot & buildings in Nashville, with a large tract of land, & hope to have

settlers under Sevier and Martin (LC EF 114J9). Zéspedes drew upon this letter to Leslie when he wrote to Ezpeleta on January 14, 1789; he expressed full confidence in McGillivray (AGI C 1395).

the honor of enrolling my name among their Citizens. What think you of this?

A Colo. Moore, Commissioner from Virginia, writes me that he finds that "I render Succour to the Cherokees to defend them against the white people, & as their disputes are Settled, hopes that my future aid will be unnecessary & hopes I will use my Influence to free the Virginians & back country from hostillity. Concludes thus, "I have been Induced thus to address you being well assured by those Gentlemen with whom you Correspond in this Country of your humanity & benevolence. *They assure me that you wish to be at peace,* from your Character I may with Confidence request you will use every exertion to prevent *your people* from committing hostillities on the people of Virginia."

"Shoud be exceedingly happy to Cultivate a Correspondence with you & Shoud you think proper to oblige me direct to me in Richmond Virginia."[163]

From this & much more,[164] if I do assume the Man of Consequence am I to blame? Have no more news for you, the rabble that were Invited to pensacola to hold an election for New Masters of the talks are not yet returnd. I remain at home this winter to forward the pending Negotiations for peace, & do not go to Pensacola. After adding the French Kings Compts. & wishing you all prosperity remain

Yours most affectionately

ALEX: MCGILLIVRAY [*rubric*]

108. *Zéspedes to Ezpeleta, December 2, 1788*
[Spanish original in AGI C 1395]

SEÑOR CAPTAIN GENERAL:

There are here twenty-six deserters from the party of the infamous Bowls, of which I reported to you in my last unnumbered letter of the 24th of last month, to wit: two Germans, three Americans, and twenty-one British. The first five, subject to your approval, I would release, sending them shortly to the United States. But I find it difficult to decide what to do with the twenty-one Englishmen, who ask to be returned to the dominions of their sovereign. I would send them also

163. For McGillivray's reply see ASP IA, I, 19.
164. See, for example, Joseph Martin's plea for the return of several horses which the Indians had run off (*State Records of North Carolina*, XXII, 787). The commissioners, Winn, Pickens, and Mathews, protested this robbery in their letter of November 28. They also listed the following damages by Indian raids: Liberty County, between 25 and 30 negroes, and several large stocks of cattle; Effingham County, one man killed; Wilkes County, from 6 to 10 horses plundered; Greene County, from 21 to 27 horses plundered; Washington County, 6 horses plundered; Franklin County, from 16 to 20 horses plundered, one man wounded. "Congress," they warned, "will not look on in silence, and see any part of the Union robbed of its citizens" (ASP IA, I, 30).

to the United States, except that the Americans would not admit them at their ports but would oblige their conductors to bring them back here. . . . .

Their declarations have been taken,[165] and from them it appears that Bowls, helped directly by John Miller and secretly by the governor of Providence, had hostile intentions against Apalache and this place, if he could induce the Indians to help him, though he did not reveal these intentions until after the landing in Florida. But the desertion of his men (he was left with only five) together with his not having brought the tenth part of the goods, flour, and munitions that he promised on his first journey to the Indians, has resulted, I think, not only that his infamous project has fallen to the ground, but also that Mac-Gillivvray has killed him. I eagerly await the mestizo's reply so that I may be able to inform you promptly of everything.

May God preserve you many years. St. Augustine, December 2, 1788.

VIZTE. MANL. DE ZÉSPEDES [rubric]

Señor Don Joseph de Ezpeleta.

109. Miró to McGillivray, December 13, 1788
[Copy in AGI C 201]

NEW ORLEANS the 13th Decemr. 1788

SIR

I receivd the answer of Captn. General Dn. Joseph de Ezpeleta authorizing me to Sattesfie you & your Nation according my desires, & as it might appear most convenient to His Majestys Service; in consequence thereof I can assure you it is needless for you to look after extraordinary means to obtain the Supplys you shall want, & which by this oppertunity I give orders to the Commander at Pensacola to be delivered to the Indians you could send thither as a Present.[166]

At the same time I Counsell you to make your utmost endeavours

165. Voluntary declaration, signed by Hugh McDonald, John Lovern, Moses Duir, Wm. Maiben, and Wm. Lymmery (AN EI 598; Spanish translation in AGI C 119); and printed by Lawrence Kinnaird in the *Florida Historical Society Quarterly*, X, 79-85). These deserters declared, in essence, that they had been enlisted under false pretences. They thought their expedition had government backing and that it was aimed against the Georgians, whereas the real aim of Bowles, Miller, Bonamy, and Dunmore was to despoil Panton and Leslie's stores. When the recruits learned this and found that the Indians for the most part were not friendly, they deserted and surrendered to the Spanish officer on the St. Johns.

166. Miró to O'Neill, December 16, 1788, AGI C 5. Writing to Valdés on November 19, Ezpeleta had reported Miró's changed attitude toward McGillivray as indicated in Miró to Ezpeleta, September 16, 1788, AGI C 1394. The captain general stated very bluntly that he knew that McGillivray was Indian and English at heart and properly so, and that the Spanish officials should act "so as neither to displease the Indians nor exasperate the commissary" (AGI C 1418). See also Ezpeleta to Valdés, November 20, 1788 (AHN E 3887), and Valdés' approval, dated February 25, 1789 (*ibid.*).

to settle the Peace with the Americans in the next Spring under the terms expressed in my letter of 8th July last, in which His Majesty will be highly pleased as his generous mind woud procure that to the human kind in general. Although the King himself has already declared he will Undoubtedly Continue his protection to that Nation Supporting it in case the Americans still continue to Vex them, My Capt. Generl. & I two approaves very much your insisting upon their relinquishing their encroachments upon your Lands, before any treaty Should take place between Your Nation & them.

In the mean time it is highly Convenient to explain myself fairly to you, on the expedition arrived from Providence to Mosquitos under the direction of an English Captn. Bowls. You have not fulfilled the trust I have in you, when as it was consonant with our Friendship, you did not give me a particular account of this affair immediately, expressing from whence, how when & on what purpose the aforesaid Expedition has been made, & you only wrote me very confusedly, without particularizing any thing when you was already acquainted we were not ignorant of an English Vessel arrived to Mosquito from Providence, which, to sette on a good footing the trade with you brought in present arms, & ammunition. This step is against the agreements of the Congress held at Pensacola in 1784 the Trade of the english Vessels in the Coast of Floridas can give room to the greatest displeasure between Spain & England, Since the latter have given up to the former East & West Floridas, by the last Treaty of peace to this is contrary any attempts made by the English on the Said Coast: Consequently Your generous Sentiments, & noble way of acting will Naturally induce you cautiously to avoide any thing that may produce a misunderstanding between two such respectable Nations.

You pretend to get a shelter because we have induced you to make a peace with drawing the Supplys promised to You, which has not been the case, for I did not refuse them to you absolutely, neither can you show me a word in any of all my letters to you, which may give the least hint of this moreover you [have] been acquainted of our most Gratious Sovereign's intention to induce you to make a peace. Your answr. was you was also inclined to the same upon which I found needless to furnish you with the Supplys you were not in want of being now ready from my part to Comply with this. Since you acquaint me the truce is broken by the Georgians & that they are far from being willing to remoave from the usurpt Lands acknowledging therefore convenient you should be furnished with arms & ammunition in which we do more then was agreed to in the aforementioned Congress of 1784 as will be plain to you by the 13th Article which I desire you to read—

now you plainly see that the arrival of the Said Vessel to Mosquito River has given room to many false reports among others several Indians told that in this Vessel were an hundred armed Men, & that with those some of the Tensaw, & your Indians you attempted to attack Pensacola, which in my mind was despisd, being sure this was not possible, & thus I wrote to the Captn. Generl. telling him, you was not capable of acting so ungreatfully,[167] availing myself of the same reasons given by you, to convince us that this was not possible when you known you was suspected nevertheless this has been an evil, originated from the Said expedition without several others who might arise for the future, if any other English Vessel should appear on the Coast consequently Making no doubt that this letter will re-establish the good hormoney that has been interupted & that from thence you Shall firmly trust we will not give up Your Nation in any pressing emergency, I expect you for Your own part will exert all your utmost endeavour to strengthen it in not admitting any Brittish Vessel, & aquainting the Indians of what Moment such a conduct is.

I will end telling you that it will be very hurtfull to our Court to punish as you Mean the Trader Timothy Lane since he as Spanish subject is bound to give notice of every matter that by any means Should concern the Spanh. Govrt. & Consequently I flater myself you will forget every resentmt. against him to keep our harmony in the most strong Vigour I wish you might enjoy good & perfect health answering me by the bearer hereof according to my well grounded expectations & remain with the greatest sincerity Sir Your Most obedt. & hbe. Srvt.

ESTEVAN MIRÓ

Alexr. McGillevray Esqr.

110. *O'Neill to Miró, December 22, 1788*

[Spanish copy in AGI C 38]

Bowles also landed some cannon, the caliber of which is not indicated; he made some presents to the Indians, and one of the latter named Periman, whose daughter is or has been the concubine of Colonel Brown in Providence, shows himself to be very active for the introduction of goods and in favor of the Englishman Bowles, and openly declares himself enemy of the Spaniards.

Alexander McGillivray came to the town of Covitas to confer with Bowles, and several Chiefs of the Lower Creeks. These Indians vary

167. Miró had shown more confidence on this point than had O'Neill (see note 147, *supra*), but the whole truth would have been that Ezpeleta was the one who had placed most trust in McGillivray.

as to where the fort will be established; some say near the town of Covitas, but it is to be presumed that it will be rather on the coast so as to protect its communication with Providence.

The general rumor in the nations is that this spring or earlier peace will be made with the Americans, in order to establish better his trade or commerce with the English of Providence. William Panton is informed about this, but until the present he has not said anything about it to me.

Alexander McGilbray had a sister of his wife marry the mestizo son of Colvert,[168] Chickasaw trader, and I suspect that it is with the intention of forming an alliance with that nation.

My two informants, John Linder[169] and Charles Westerford[170] entreat me not to divulge that they have been the first to give me these reports, for it might result in their complete ruin.

111. *McGillivray to Linder, December 28, 1788*
[AGI C 52]
LITTLE TALLASSIE, 28 December 1788

SIR

I found here on my return from the Lower Towns my overseer Mr. Walker, who Informed me that the occasion of his Visit to me is owing to a process which You are commencing in Law against him on account of a Certain Molatto wench who calls herself Rachel now at my plantation under his management, which Molattoe wench I claim in Virtue of an american Bill of Sale. If You have any grounds for Such a procedure, You ought to direct Your attack at me personally & not at my Substitute, who has no right or claim in her. However a regard to my own Interest obliges me to advise You to drop this affair as You may rest assured that You must be responsible for the consequences of a Contrary Conduct. I am given to understand that You have enterd on this affair at the Instigation of another Molatto wench called Pegy Evans, who pretends to be a relation to the other & this Peggy was brought Some Years ago into this Country from Georgia by a William Oates, as an Indented Slave. She was detain by the then Brittish agent Mr. Taitt, & after he went away, at least when he was at Strachans plantation near Tensaw, he Consented to & saw a bill of Sale executed for Peg Evans, from the Said Oates to Cor. Sullivan, So that She is hereself at this time the property of the Sullivans & the Bill of

168. See note 12, *supra*.
169. A note to O'Neill, dated August 13, 1788 (AGI C 38), is subscribed by John Linder, Jr., "in confinement for not having told the whole truth about the landing of the British at Indian River."
170. Weatherford.

Sale for her I have seen & is now in some part of this Nation. Upon enquiry I have no doubt to find it out when she shall be restord to her proper owner.

I am Compelld to observe that Your Settlement in general have manifested on all & various occasions, an unfavorable disposition toward the Settlements which I had formd at & about Little River & have been Continually teazing & embarrassing my overseers & people in their employments & crossing their duty to my Concerns, for what reasons I know not, & you ought of all Mankind to be the last person that shoud encourage or adopt Such a Conduct, for reasons which Your own heart can best acknowledge. I formd the Settlements on my own ground without the Spanish limits. I chose a man of acknowledged good Character to manage my Stock affairs. He was always acknowledged to be amenable to Spanish Laws whenever he shoud Infringe them, & the Kings Commanding officer at Mobile has never in any one Instance had occasion to Call him into question on that account, altho several in the Settlement have endeavourd to bring him into such difficultys by absurd misrepresentations which the Moderation & Candour of the Commandant to his praise always despised. & as to my own part, I have given no Cause. I have not looked with a Jealous eye on the extensive & growing encroachments which the Settlement is daily making on our Lands, which if I had been earnestly disposed to do, the Nation woud have soon Convinced You of the Flimzyness of the rights which You pretend for them, & which You acknowledge to derive them for trifling presents of Taffia to Vagrant & beggarly alabamons. You are Short sighted Indeed or You woud Carefully avoid the giving any the least occasion for a discussion, which woud Certainly in the end prove unfavorable to Your Settlement.

As to the Mollattocs their Ingratitude Justifys me in the determination to Suffer the claims on them to take effect, & Instances of the Same from those who better was expected from will prove a Caution to me in future for whom I will Interest myself for. So that on the whole I conclude that my Settlements are in the way of Sinister designs, which they have formd. If so their wishes shall be Compleatly gratified for I have orderd the Instant removal of all my Stock & property back into this place, & the barrier which I was forming as a Cover to Your Settlement, Shall be no more as an eye Sore to Some. The Subject of this letter will be thought a reproach & I am much Concernd that occasion has not been given me for it, & I cannot be Justly blamed for it & more. I remain with wishing a more honest disposition to those Who Stand in Need.

ALEX: McGILLIVRAY [rubric]

213

112. *McGillivray to Panton, January 12, 1789*

[Copy in AGI C 202]

LITTLE TALLASSIE 12th Janry. 1789

DEAR SIR

I am lately returned from a Tour thro' the Lower Towns. My motive for the jaunt at this disagreeable wet Season was to have had a Conference with Tim. Barnard lately arrived from Georgia & coming up very Sick he Could not come here: he had as he writes me a message from the principals of that State. At my arrival at the Cowettas I was dissapointed for he had gone to Burghesses after his family where he had left them when he went to Georgia. Before I left the Lower towns several of the Cussitahs with their young King, some oconnee's &c &c. had arrived from Pensla. in a very ill humour. They said that being invited by the Tame King to hold a talk with the Governor, they went with that Expectation, but they found themselves mistaken and dissapointed besides being ill treated &c &c. and those up in this quarter differ but little in their accounts and say that the only Talk they heard from the Governor was levelled at me & Bowles. I am Surprised to hear from the Indians that I was represented to them as a public Enemy and ought to be drove from my post with marks of resentment and Contempt &c &c. If the Governor is Serious in hopes to Effect my disgrace with my Nation he will find every attempt he may make prove as abortive as the Late one, for this late affair has only the more attached my friends to me with the whole Lower towns.

Bowles is again on the Coast with a fresh quantity of Goods[171] which no doubt will produce a fresh hubbub at Pensacola, but it will be all in vain, for it is impossible to Convince an Indian that it is a Criminal action in him to receive a present from any one. I, that know them So well, Shant attempt it, and it would be a wise measure in others if they winked at Such things, if they dissaprove of it, instead of raising a fruitless Clamour which can only tend to Create Jealousy and alarm, heat the minds of the Nation and make the name of a Spaniard as odious as at any former time, when they had just begun to be reconciled to their new acquaintances. This they may depend upon and which they well know—that the Tame King's influence or power is very Small and is followed by only worthless beggars and the reason of so many being in town lately was the assurances given them by the Brother of the above

171. Reported also in Forrester to Panton, December 24, 1788, AGI C 201. Panton wrote to Miró on January 9, 1789: "As Mr. McGillivray is now fully informed of that adventurer [Bowles] as well as of the wicked views which he and his unworthy employers had for entering on this business I would not wish you to be uneasy for I make not the least doubt that he will turn him about his business" (AGI C 6).

214

fellow, that he was Shewn two Houses filled with Goods, Said by the Interpreter to be intended for the Tame King and all that would follow him to Pensacola. To Sum up the whole the Warrior King of Cusstah said openly "What does the Spaniards mean by all this Bustle and noise about our receiving presents from an Englishman? Did not the Governr. send a paper to the Holloing King that he would give no more ammunition to us. This Shows that the little he gave us was meant only to get us to draw the americans upon our Nation that we might fall an Easy Sacrifice to themselves. It now appears plain their Talks are now both alike and we are treated as no people." It is of much importance that ideas of this kind do not prevail among the majority of the Indians. I have done my Endeavours to quiet Such apprehensions at this time. I feel the disappointment of Xmas Cheer from Black John losing his horses, the Complaints of horse Stealing about Pensacola is become General, the Spanish Pen keepers take many. A valuable mare of mine was stole from Walker and was seen with a Spaniard. Should not these robberys be Stopped.

The exceeding wet weather and high waters keep back a good many Pack Horses tho ready to Set out.

I hear that some letters from Mobille are at little River for me and Supposed to be from Orleans,[172] which I believe, as Govr. Miro promised to write me the Sentiments of the Capt. General whenever he received a letter from him which he expected to be in two months from the time he wrote me last, which was in August.

If any English news by Capt. Forrest pray Let me know. I am truely glad that the Ship is arrived for more reasons than one, among them is I hope to Share in the Good things.

I remain Dear Sir Yours as usual

Signed ALEXR. MCGILLIVRAY

Wm. Panton Esqr.

113. *McGillivray to Panton, February 1, 1789*

[Copy in AGI C 202]

LITTLE TALLASSIE 1 Febry. 1789

DEAR SIR:

A variety of occurrences have offered since I wrote you last; I think I will give them to you in the order that they Came in. First I reccived an Express from the Commissioners accompanied by a Letter from Governor Pickney of Charlestown by Whitefields Companion last Summer the Terrapin a Cherokee Warrior. Copys of them I have

---

172. Doubtless document 109, *supra.*

215

inclosed as well as my answers to them.[173] I shall trouble you my Dear Sir to cause Copys be made for His Excellency Govr. Miro, thro' the Channel of Governor ONeill reserving the originalls to be Sent back to me or kept with my other papers.

When you see my answer to the Commissioners you will approve of it, for Considering every thing it could not be otherwise. As to Pinckneys Talk it is good, if he would act the impartial and unprejudiced mediator, in which Capacity he Steps forth, but from the Language of it I doubt His Excelly wants a pretext for quarrel and to join against us.

In Consideration that His State would be a large gap amongst those folks, in Case that they could be brought to act as they have hitherto done, I have taken some pains to inform him very Circumstantially of the origin and rise of the present Contest between us and Georgia, for, tho' I know that the Majority of the So. Carolinians are far from being friendly disposed towards Georgia, yet I am uncertain how far a resolve of Congress may tend to make them our Enemys; I have However put on a firm Countenance and have given him a hint of our Connexions to the Westward.

The resolve of Congress that accompanies this, will Surprise you as much as it has done me, considering the report of the Committee which I shewed you and Copy of which was Sent to Govr. Miro. It Says "it has been the opinion of this Country Supported by Justice & Humanity that the Indians have just Claims to all Lands not fairly purchased from them," and again "there is Sufficient Evidence to Show that those tribes do not Complain altogether without Cause; an avaricious disposition in Some of our people to acquire large tracts of Land which they endeavour to Compass by unfair means" &c. &c.

The foregoing is what principally Concerns American Talks, and I look upon them as Calculated to bring on a general quarrel. If my Conjecture proves true, why let the Hardest fend off.

I am favored with a letter from His Excellency Govr. Miro of 13th Decr.[174] which I take to have Come by Mr. Forbes. Its Contents are of an Explanatory Nature and give me the Highest Satisfaction. He assures me that the Court are determined not to give us up or desert us on any Emergency, and that I may rely upon a proper Support to make Good our Stand against the Americans, this is what I allways wished for. He finds fault with my having had recourse to Extraor-

173. The commissioners' letter of November 28, 1788, is described in note 164, *supra*. A copy of Pinckney's letter of November 6, 1788, is in AGI C 202. In reply McGillivray stated the case of the Creeks against the Georgians at great length, roundly criticizing the Georgian actions at the several so-called treaties of the post-Revolutionary period. A manuscript copy dated January 26, 1789, in AGI C 202, is not identical with the version erroneously dated February 26 in ASP IA, I, 19-20.

174. Document 109, *supra*.

dinary means for Supply &c. I have assured him in return that if I had not Construed the Royal orders and His injunctions for us to make peace on the most unconditional terms, and in a State amounting almost to menaces, I Should never have had recourse to Extraordinary measures to obtain that Supply, which I imagined was refused to us by our Friends.

As the Americans Seem resolved to persist in their Encroachments, a Continuance of the War appears to be inevitable. However I have resolved to Sacrifice my expectation of a Certain Supply both of men, arms and ammunition from another quarter, that all Cause of Apprehension may be removed from the minds of our Friends. An immediate Supply is now Wanted by me that we may be prepared to meet the Enemy upon equal ground. I have accordingly required Six thousand lbs of powder 1200 [*sic*, 12,000] lbs of Ball, about one Hundred Sized Brass kettles, fifteen Hundred Stand of Arms, (not Such as have been usually furnished us, which besides being too Small in the Bore, burst after a few discharges, but English Trading Guns which are Good and will last more than two Years in Constant use) Hatchets, Knives, flints, &c all of which to be ready for us by 15th or 20th April next.

I have likewise declared that, in the event of a certain protection and Support being given to us by the King, I had not the Smallest desire to Separate myself from them, and to Satisfy them, tho I would not promise to Shed the Blood of Bowles, yet I would dismiss him from this Country for ever, and that he was now at the mouth of Flint River expecting a vessel with Goods, which I understood is partly on a Trading Voyage. When they are Landed he is to give me notice, I Shall then send a man and party to divide the Cargoe and Send him to Seek adventures in other Climes.

I Send you a Letter from our Friend Leslie in which he confirms the frequent notices I have received of the Georgians being bent on my distruction. It is not my intention to run any Risque, I am not so much their dupe as to meet them on the vague Ground they wish, "*to investigate and found the Right of Claim.*" No! let them Come here with an honest and Sincere Heart and we Shall Soon Settle every thing. Tis not so hard, tis all comprehended in a Childs Bargain, *Let us alone, and We'll do the Same.* Do not Congress, all America, and all the World know our grievances and discontents, and that for motives of Self preservation we have taken up the Hatchet?

In Some of Your letters you Suggest that your opinions have not been attended to. I am very far my dear Sir from undervaluing your talk but the Gloomy Aspect of our affairs for the last twelve months, have

217

So deranged and torn my mind that I have often been almost half distracted.

I am now informed that I had mistaken the real intention of our protectors, that the requisitions for arms made by me Some time ago was only refused because deemed unnecessary as I was upon the eve of making peace with the Americans in Compliance with the Royal order, that as soon as we Complained of the terms the Georgians insisted on an order was issued to Supply us. I feel myself happy that I have been mistaken, that my apprehensions and doubts of protection were entirely Groundless.

It is likewise a matter of the greatest Comfort to me that His Excellency the Capt. General and Govr. Miro approve of the requisition I make, that the Georgians give up the territory in question as a preliminary to form the Basis of a Treaty upon. This demand being a Second time formally and pointedly refused by the American Commissioners is in effect a declaration that a Continuance of the War is their Choice.

Upon this occasion I have not the Smallest doubt but my request for a Supply of arms and ammunition will be Complied with. You perceive that for the present I have been moderate.

The only difficulty I have remaining is with respect to Lane, who as a Spanish Subject Governor Miro Says Cannot be punished for what he has done as it will be prejudicial to the interests of the Court. I observe in return that the fellow does much mischief; being patronized in Pensacola he insults every Indian he pleases and more particularly my relations. You remember my Dear Sir that tho' Weatherford was allied to me, I gave him up to the Laws he had violated, and in like manner I expect that Lane will be removed from Pensacola. This would be Sufficient, and I ask no more.

The Indians began to imagine there must be Something Serious in my not paying my usual visits to Pensacola but I am determined to persist in it untill that Raskall is removed.[175]

In yours of the 20th ulto by Taylor, you appear very well Satisfied with the Good intentions of Government towards fixing Your Commerce on a liberal and Solid footing, which I Shall be happy to See accomplished. While that matter is doubtfull and unstable it keeps myself and all the Headmen in a very dissagreeable State of Suspence.

Milfort[176] is this moment returned from attending Bowls. I Sent him

175. Compare with document 114, *infra*.
176. Louis [LeClerc] Milfort was a Frenchman who came to the Creek country in 1776. He became a war leader, a brother-in-law of McGillivray, and a valuable assistant to him. After McGillivray's death Milfort went back to France, where in the spring of 1796 he was made a general of brigade. In 1802 he published his

as a Spy upon his Conduct and intentions. He very artfully wormed a good deal out of Richmond[177] who is at Enmity with him. He says Bowles has greatly deceived His Nassau friends about opening a Trade to Rival your House. Your Commercial Situation is greatly envied there, tho God knows with What reason.

Bowles has too many irons in the fire and has Conducted himself of Late very foolishly. Whenever the Goods do arrive Kennaird[178] will take a good Cargoe to pay himself and perhaps I will Send Milfort for a Share So that if a greater quantity Comes than 1 imagine, they will be very quickly disposed off.

This Strictly Speaking, is not just, but as he and His Employers have attempted to deceive me, they do not deserve better at my Hands. He has in no instance obeyed any instructions So that I have a good handle on him.[179]

A Large Body of Adventurers Could I am Certain be got from Nova Scotia, if I thought proper to pursue the affair, but I now entirely abandon all thought of it only in Case of an American War, I think I ought to be allowed a Good Troop of Horse paid by our Friends.

The 13th Article which Govr. Miro refers to, does not Say that they have a Right to make us act in all Cases agt. our interest, but I see the article which Says "We do in His Royal Name promise to guarantee to the Nation all their Lands, Territorys &c. according to the Rights by which they Claim them."[180]

The Governor appears to have forgot the information Conveyed to me by Governor ONeill in his letter of 21 April which mentions that the King approved of Govr. Miro's Conduct in refusing me arms to

Mémoire ou coup d'oeil rapide, a record of his experiences among the Creeks. Though a man of spirit, he was, according to Roosevelt, "a braggart," and according to Turner, a "hopeless liar."

177. John Richmond was John Miller's secretary. See document 116, *infra*, for a further description of how Milfort pumped Richmond. The *Lucayan Royal Herald*, on August 15, 1789, printed Richmond's denial that Bowles had any such purpose as the deserters at St. Augustine had declared; see note 165, *supra*.

178. Jack Kinnard was an illiterate but influential half-breed who lived among the Lower Creeks. Panton gave him qualified endorsement as a possible successor to McGillivray; see documents 207 and 209, *infra*. See Swan's description in Schoolcraft, *Indian Tribes*, V, 260-61.

179. When Bowles first appeared McGillivray spoke of him as a gentleman; see document 99, *supra*. Later on, his disapproval was to be violent, but in February, 1789, it was merely moderate. "As for the adventurer Bowles Your Excellencys humanity does not require his blood to be Shed in this Country, but I will assure you that he shall be compelld to leave this nation never to return to it" (McGillivray to Miró, February 1, 1789, AGI C 204). "No foreign Strollers shall have any future encouragement to Interrupt the Good Harmony that shall henceforth subsist between us. As for Bowles he is even too insignificant for Contempt, however he Shall be Compelld to leave the Country to seek fresh adventure in other regions" (McGillivray to Howard, February 10, 1789, LC EF 114J9).

180. These references are to be Treaty of Pensacola, document 13, *supra*. McGillivray was also quoting Article 13.

make war on the United States. However I do not wish to enter into a Discussion on the Subject. On the Whole I am happy that a Good understanding and Harmony will Succeed to the late interruption.[181] God Bless you my dear Sir and give You every good thing, I Remain
Yours most Sincerely

ALEXANDER MCGILLIVRAY

Wm. Panton Esqr.

P. S. The Commissioners Seem to resent some expression of mine towards the Congress which I am not Sensible of. I think I have been allways in the Habit of Treating public Men and Bodys with Studied respect. I imagine they must allude to some expression in my Letter to Whitfield. Laughing with him Something has been wrote that displeased them. I believe on one occasion I was a little free in remarks when he was puffing them up.[182]
Yours

A. M.

114. *McGillivray to O'Neill, February 2, 1789*

[AGI C 202]

LITTLE TALLASSIE 2d February 1789

. . . .I never had a doubt of Your Excellencys friendship for me, & my reason for keeping away from Pensacola is owing to that I dont chuse to Suffer Insult & Indignity from that Vagabond Lane, who has frequently abused my Indian relations,[183] & no Notice taken of him, & he has told a Number of falsehoods to the Indians & I chuse not to meet him in Pensacola, & if he is Sent away from that place I woud not be long be absent from Pensacola in a Visit to my friends. It has been owing to the fellows fault altogether for when Your Excellency & Mr. Panton wrote letters in his favor to me, if he had Come to me all woud have been over but instead of which he went to his own house & began to abuse me & Sayd it was Your orders that he Shoud be at my defiance & Your Excellency well knows every man in Authority will Not Suffer it to be trampled upon by his Inferiors. He then run away & keeps in protection at Pensacola, which has Made him more Insolent & I know my own disposition so well that if I was to meet him

181. McGillivray wrote similarly to Miró on the same day (AGI C 204). He wrote more briefly to O'Neill on February 2, and in detail to Zéspedes on February 6; parts of these letters appear as documents 114 and 115, *infra.*
182. It would be interesting to know just what McGillivray had said. The Congress under the Articles of Confederation was a very much handicapped body, and it would have been easy to hold it up to ridicule. Compare, for example, with the judgment passed by John Fiske in his *The Critical Period.*
183. McGillivray had asserted to Miró on February 1, "My relation MacPherson had nearly resolvd to kill him, he abused my Sister & others in Mr. Pantons Yard" (AGI C 204).

in Town that on his least presumption a dissagreeable Consequence woud ensue. Therefore I keep out of the way of it, so in Justice he ought to be Sent out of my way. I refer You to the papers that Mr. Panton will Shew You an examination of Bowles's Crew that deserted to Augustine. I remain with respect & esteem

Your Excellencys obedt. Servant

ALEX: McGILLIVRAY [rubric]

115. McGillivray to Zéspedes, February 6, 1789

[LC EF 114J9]

LITTLE TALLASSIE 6 February 1789

. . . .I have seen a declaration[184] made by Bowles Vagrants, on their arrival at St. Johns, & not worth Notice, as to what they declared about an attempt to be made upon the Stores of my freinds, for madness itself coud not Suggest such folly to a man wholly unknown & unsupported by all the Neighbouring Indian Villages or any of them & unprovided with means to Carry off peltry Goods &c. &c. It is more like the truth that two or three other told me, that on landing & marching several days the periodical rains came on & drownd the whole face of the Country Spoild & damaged their provisions &c. & renderd marching so extremely dissagreeable wading to the waist in water, some got Sick others died, which made the rest take the first opportunity to desert, & that they were engaged at first against the Americans & were promised great emoluments from Plunder &c.

On the whole I think the Vagabonds are very well disposed of, one of them named Simmons is an old offender & was sent out of the Country by the brittish agent in Irons to Pensacola, afterwards he was one of Col. Browns troops & deserted from him to the americans & married how he got to providence I never learnt, but here he Shoud not have Stay'd a week if he had come up.

I have wrote to Governor Miro agreeable to the foregoing as well as my freind Gov. ONeil, who is apparently more disturbed about it than any else. And I hope it will have the effect that I wish for, to wipe away every cause of distrust, from between us & that a true good harmony may again be perfectly reestablished, & which was only Interrupted through a Misapprehension of each other. My best wishes, etc.,

ALEX: McGILLIVRAY [rubric]

184. Summarized in note 165, *supra;* compare also with the declarations of Milligan and Hopper at Havana, February 7, 1789 (AHN E 3887); and of Keating and Dalton at Havana, February 17, 1789 (AGI C 1418). See also Ezpeleta to Valdés, February 12, 1789 (AHN E 3887).

[Spanish translation in LC EF 114J9]
LITTLE TALLASSIE 8 February 1789
DEAR SIR:

From my heart I thank you for your favor of last December by Edward Forrester. The Georgians having complained of predatory excursions from the Lower Towns as infractions of the stipulated truce, I went down to effect a remedy, and being there, I received report of the arrival of Bowles a few days journey from me. Shortly after, I was interceded with for him, his situation was miserable; he accused the pack horse men and his recruits of treason etc.

On this occasion I asked him very circumstantially about his supporters, and on what authority his present enterprises were based. In his reply he by no means expressed himself clearly, but persisted in assuring with vehemence that no one had joined in fitting him out except Miller, Bonamy and Company, that this company had provided him an armed schooner belonging to a certain Johnston loaded with supplies and goods etc., and on this point he produced papers which convinced me that an abundant and effective help and aid was destined for me.

He proposed then to go to the mouth of Flint River to meet the ship, there to unload and bring up the goods by that river to the place called Bullys, or to the house of Burgess or Perymand. I agreed to the proposition and proposed to my Frenchman (whom you know) to accompany him in order to keep off impertinent Indians. I charged him very particularly to use the greatest skill, in order to learn from Bowles or Richmond, the treasurer of Bonamy, (toward whom I knew he had the sharpest animosity because he treated him as a domestic) every material circumstance relative to the nature and true object of his visits, etc. Consequently, they went in a boat from Perrymand's new house to the mouth of the river, where they arrived on December 21, and waited there into January without the ship's appearing. Then Bowles lost patience and determined to return with Perrymand to his house. The Frenchman proposed that he and Richmond wait another week with two Indians. Bowles agreed and went off.

Meanwhile Richmond and the Frenchman Milfortt were together. Richmond spoke of Bowles without reserve. The Frenchman learned from him that Bowles had frequently visited Miller's house because he was known by his brother, boasting of his former experiences in the Indian country and among other things insinuating that Panton and Company enjoyed an interesting trade in the Floridas, and that nothing could be easier than to supplant them and take this trade away from

222

them, and that he was sure he could do it by his own influence if the execution was left to him. And in order more surely to wrest this trade from its present monopolist, he proposed to offer, or better to subject me to the necessity of opening a port in one of the many channels or bays with which the coast abounds, and that he must attract by presents the people of the continent to join me, and that, in short, he would acquire such a number that the project would inevitably succeed.

I feel that the thing is plausible; nevertheless, Bowles has not spoken to me explicitly on this matter but by insinuations and half words. *What can be proved appears not impossible*, etc., etc.

It seems to me that his backers have chosen an instrument not at all appropriate for such undertakings. He could pass, eating and drinking like the other sons of his mother, but he does not seem to be suited to great things. As to what his deserters divulged at St. Johns, you must take into account that it was directed only to procure a suave reception and good treatment. Bowles never could have had the schemes that they charge him with, and I am sure that he had in his company three true devotees to your interests; the Warrior of Coweta and the man of my assembly would never have allowed such an attempt. Bowles spoke in so high a tone and promised so much so that he could induce them to go to meet him at Indian River. On mature reflection I believe that Richmond's statement of Bowles' projects and his backers comes nearest to the truth.

I have just this instant learned that the ship that Bowles awaited, after having passed the port, has rounded the cape and entered the river, and that the important papers have arrived. She brought munitions, etc., but not one vara of drygoods of any sort, which is fortunate for Bonamy, for if he had sent a shipment of fifty thousand pesos it would all have been needed to fulfill Bowles' promises to the Indians, without the proprietor's benefitting to the extent of a single bit. He has promised me that within ten days he will tender me the documents. If the originals fall into my hands, new light may be shed on the business. Enough of this adventurer Bowles. . . . .

117. *Howard to [McGillivray], March 28, 1789*
[Draft in LC EF 114J9]
 St. Augustine March ye 28th 1789

My dear and much esteemd Sir

The Contents of your two last Letters to his Excellency and Mr Leslie, as also your favor of the 10th ulto. have afforded me real

223

Pleasure and furnish me with an agreeable occasion of congratulating you on the pleasing Prospects that begin to open before you and your Nation.[185]

Give me leave to differ with you in opinion regarding the object of the Plan of Bowles and his Patrons: to plunder the Georgians was undoubtedly the ostensible Plan propos'd to his ragged followers, perhaps even Richmond, Wellbanks[186] and Robbins were unacquainted with any other; but depend upon it that the revenge and avarice of the Principal Projector had in view the ruin of your Friends. Moreover that Bowles intended to take goods at St. John's store, on his Bills which were not worth a farthing, or pr. force is clear to me as daylight by concurrent Testimony of the twenty eight wretches who deserted him, the greatest part of whom were certainly Scoundrels, but it is not less True that some few were simple honest men, who had suffer'd themselves to be deluded by specious Promises. However the Matter can be better clear'd up by John Galphin and the two Randalls. The former of whom Payne and other Indians did not approve or rather oppos'd the plundering from the aforesaid Store. It may also appear problematical to you that Bowles on his landing at the mouth of Indian River gave out that you had ceded to him the Command of the Creek Nation; This however He appears to have deny'd in Presence of Galphin who it seems examin'd him about the Truth of the report; Bowles denying the fact, and alledging that he had only said that He was to be your second.

I have strong reasons to suspect that a spanish youth of about twenty calld Luke Perez,[187] who speaks tolerable French and English, and who had come Down with Pack horses to wait for Bowles at the head of Indian River, from whence He deserted to this Town, was frightn'd away from Hence by some Rascals who dreaded He would discover there manoeuvres here with the Indians, on whom they impose by exchanging brandy against skins and Horses to the great Prejudice of the Health and interests of your People. This is a growing abuse that may be attended by bad Consequences, therefore I have to request, you will please to contribute to the remedy, by prevailing on said Luke to come to this Town, where upon my Honour far from having anything to fear, He will meet with a most favourable reception. In case He does not chuse to come, endeavour at any rate to find out and acquaint

185. See documents 115 and 116 and note 179, *supra.*
186. George Wellbank was a rough character who came from the Bahamas with Bowles in 1788. He stayed with the Indians when Bowles left in 1789, rejoined him in 1792, and came into possession of his papers and some of his influence when Bowles was arrested that same year.
187. Pérez had made one deposition on October 28, 1788, with respect to Bowles' first expedition to the Mosquito Coast (AGI C 1395).

his excellency, without mentioning my Name, with the real cause of his flight from this Town and also if Possible the Names of the Persons who Urged him to that step, by so doing, and excusing this Trouble, you will conferr a very particular obligation on My dear Sir your warm admirer and affecte humble servant

CHARLES HOWARD

118. McGillivray to Miró, March 31, 1789
[AGI C 202]

PENSACOLA 31st March 1789

SIR

Being desirious to receive Your Excellencys answer to my last letter[188] & requisitions Containd therein, before we held or opend our general Convention for the ensuing Spring, I was expecting the arrival of Gov. ONeil who I imagined woud bring me Your answer, but which I find that Your Excellency has already Sent to the Commandant Mr. Cruzat, Your Instructions in that affair as well as Your letter to Mr. Panton to Inform me of it.

The american Correspondence which Mr. Panton at my request Sent to you the Copys of Woud Satisfy Your Excellency that the americans Insist upon their own terms of Peace & which we from a due regard to our own Interests cannot accede to, this together with the threatening resolve of Congress make it very necessary for us to be prepared for Continuing the war. Mr. Panton has not many Indian Guns here, but I have engaged those he has at St. Marks being convenient to our Lower Towns. The Number falls very Short of what we want, but I am given to understand that Your Excellency Intends to provide the remainder from Orleans which I Shoud be glad if it Coud be done, & Sent here in all next month—or Sooner.

I coud have remained at my house in the Nation & have obtaind by letter the Information I wanted, but as I observd that my long absence from this place had given great uneasiness to the Inhabitants, as Supposing it to proceed from an Intention in Me to Injure them; but as my heart is free & clear of any Such designs, I came to this place to banish & clear their apprehensions from imaginary danger, & I hope that they are now Satisfied.

I thank Your Excellency for the Candid & Confidential Communications, which You have given me & be assured Sir that I am fully Sensible of the advantages which my people derive from the Spanish Government, & I entreat of Your Excellency that untill you know that I have taken leave of my Senses, that You will be pleased to treat with

188. Of February 1; see note 181 and document 113, *supra*, which cover the same points.

Contempt every Insinuation which may be made to You of my dissaffection.

Mr. Philip Nowlan whom Your Excellency Sent last Summer to me to be forwarded with Guides to Cumberland & Kentucké, I Sent as you directed. I furnished him with a good horse &c. the account of which I have sent to my friend Mr. Hodge to be presented to Your Excellency. Some people from Cumberland this winter Informd me of the arrival of Nowlan there from the Chactaws.

I have been awaiting Govr. ONeil ten days & the wind Continues unfair, & am this Morning Setting off for the Nation as I promised to meet the Chiefs in assembly this moon.

I am with great Esteem & regard

    Your Excellencys obedt. Servant

                ALEX: McGILLIVRAY [*rubric*]

his Excellency Governor Miro

X

FRONTIER CLASHES

119. *McGillivray to Folch, April 22, 1789*

        [Spanish translation in AHN E 3887]

                LITTLE TALLASSIE, April 22, 1789

SIR:

I received at Little River by Durand your favor, and I would have had particular satisfaction in seeing you and talking with you at the Tensaw, which certainly would have happened if I had received your letter in time, but my enforced long detention at Pensacola kept me from it. Eight or ten days had passed after I reached Durand's house before you could have had reports of me, and it is urgent that I must be in the Nation to participate in the assembly of the Lower Creeks or Talapuches and the Semanoles or Rovers, this month, according to the notice that has been given them. A messenger having just arrived from Cahuita with the report that the chiefs of these districts have assembled and await my presence, I propose to set out within three days for the town of Cahuita.

I must tell you of an affair which has just come to my attention and which causes me anxiety. It is that the tribes of Alabamas established well down on this river, roused by the complaints of the Choctaws,

226

because a large number of Americans has been introduced into their lands on the Tombigbee River and its branches (who greatly alarm and inconvenience them), have decided to work together soon to evict and plunder the greater part of the settlers of these districts.[189] This is a thing that I always feared would happen ever since I first knew the intention of the government to introduce Americans. Knowing the disposition and temper of the tribes located along the river, I strongly opposed this intention, writing to my friend Governor Miró in order at least to restrict the settlement to a few of the larger and better proprietors, but he did not give full attention to my warning.

I have always spoken of the disposition to usurp that the Americans have if once they are allowed to establish themselves, and of a truth the Indians have real reason to complain. Last winter the Indian hunters drove away three whites who were marking lines ten miles from this village and the Coosadas. These whites said that they came from the Tombigbee River and that they intended to establish themselves on the land they were marking and to build a trading house there. This episode has roused among the Indians great fear of the Americans, against whom they have the greatest animosity because of their disposition to usurp, and they now begin to say that the Americans have formed a plan of surrounding them, a friendship having arisen from Cumberland to Tombigbee and even to this district.

Two Choctaws are now in the villages next to the Alabamas forming a party to plunder the American settlers. Some persons in the party came to ask my permission, which is how I came to know about it. Consequently I prevented them from proceeding further. They told me that it was too late to stop the party of Alabamas, who because of the distance of their villages could not be warned so promptly. These tribes, it is true, have removed themselves in the hope of freeing themselves from being watched by the Talapuche Nation, and thereby they do many things of which we do not know until much later.

My visit to the Lower Towns will be of some duration, and on my return I shall assemble the chiefs of the Upper Towns and tell them then about these occurrences. As I have observed before, the Alabama chiefs seldom present themselves at our assemblies, protesting their great distance away. This is why they cannot be notified in time. And therefore I am of the opinion that you should not lose any time about calling the chiefs to Mobile to confer with them on this matter. In the same way some steps ought to be taken to diminish the number of

189. Corroborated in Favre to Folch, April 28, 1789, AHN E 3887. But in James to Folch, April 27, 1789, and Fraser and Perry to the settlers of Tombigbee, same date, *ibid.*, the Creeks are blamed.

Americans who are gathering at Tombigbee, and to restrain and control those who are already settled.

The principal reasons for the steps that the Indians are taking are that when they go to the settlements they abuse each other reciprocally, calling one another Virginians, a name or an insulting expletive which they give to the Americans. The Indian who considers them as enemies has no idea that they are subjects of another crown, and they are not, though they have been made Spaniards. The fact is that the Americans and the Royalists ought not to be gathered together in one settlement, because I know that disputes are already being fomented around Tombigbee with as much violence as in the American States, which can produce much trouble and bother for the officials sent to govern it.

I wish that you would communicate this to Governor Miró, to whom I shall send some recently received American correspondence by a trader who must go to Pensacola in a few days. I remain, Sir, with all respect, your most obedient servant.

ALEXANDER McGILLIVRAY

To the honorable Captain Don Vizente Folch, Commandant of Mobile.

120. *Miró to McGillivray, May 11, 1789*

[Draft in AGI C 2352]

NEW ORLEANS 11th May 1789

SIR

Dr. Vizte Folch has sent me the original letter you wrote me dated the 22nd April last[190] to which I answer now.

I am surprised at news you give that the Alibamons are marching toward the tombecbee, & Tinzas Settlements to attack the Americans established in that Quarter induced by the complaint of the Chactaws. I am likewise surprised to hear from you as a positive reason without exception that the cause of their resentment proceeds from seeing the said Americans fixed themselves in the Indian territory.

1° I am sure that you are not well informed of the Chactaws having formd any complaint on this account, since almost all the Nation came to this Capital this last Winter, & undoubtedly they would have mentioned it to me, which they did not.

2° It seems imposible to me that after the strict orders I have given to the Commander of Movila he should have permitted any American to settle on the Lands situated out of our Lines; but even when any of them should have done it, what I do not believe, have the Alibamons any reasonable right to come in arms to expell them from them? After

190. Document 119, *supra.*

the good treatement they have received from Government, if they had any complaint, should they not come to the Commander at Movila, or to me to represent it.

In the Month of January 1788, when four Alibamon Indians robbed one Abraham Walker which affair was made up, and offered by you that the theft should be returned, it was agreed, that Dn. Vizte. Folch with four or Six Chiefs of that Nation should go to mark out well the limits agreeable to the constant posesion and right that Great Britain had formerly, and belongs to us by right of Conquest, which I advised you of, & yourself answered me on the 12th June of the said year that the Alibamons had no Right to mark out Limits, because it concern the Creeks: for this very reason that the Indians may never complaints against us it would be very convenient that you and some Chiefs of your Nation, & others of the Alibamons should if it be posible should present yourselves in Tombakbee to point out & aknowledge a boundary line, & if absolutely they cannot agree upon it, represent me the pretensions of the Indians.[191] But if the line is clear, as I expect, and you are in accord, Don Vizente Folch will have any Americans who are found beyond our limits retire within them.

I have no doubt that you will show me now how loyal you are to Spain and how much inclined toward peace in general, and also that you will take the trouble to make the journey mentioned above to help conclude this affair to the satisfaction of both parties.

You also say that I acted in a manner most strongly against the intention of the government in establishing Americans in this place. To this I reply that you must agree that the first families that came were from St. Augustine, and you yourself recommended that they be admitted. Don Enrique Grimarest then commanded Mobile, and he was not under my orders. He promoted this settlement on his own authority, the development of which I have permitted subsequently.

It would be a disgraceful subjection, and one contrary to the rights of all mankind, that because the Indians do not approve the settlement of some lands that do not belong to them, we should have to refrain from developing and populating them, and it would also be a dishonor to the nation were we to permit the destruction of these settlements, when all these persons have taken an oath of fidelity to his Catholic Majesty and made themselves his subjects.

Under these principles, my decision in the present affair has been to send a reenforcement to Don Vicente Folch, so that with it he could establish a fort within our territory at Tombigbee or Tensaw, which-

191. The rest of this letter is supplied from a Spanish copy in AHN E 3887. The English copy is illegible.

ever seems more appropriate, and that there he should call together the disgruntled chiefs to make known to them the reason, showing them how the honor of Spain is pledged to sustain those new subjects, and making them understand that from the instant that they took the oath of fidelity they were as much Spaniards as we, and inducing them to agree to wait for you for the marking of the boundaries.

How unfortunate it would be if our own powder and ball, for they have no other, should be used to spill our blood. I do not doubt that such behavior would irritate our Sovereign so much that, though it would pain him greatly because he always wishes the Indians well, he would order me to provide myself with a large enough force that it could not be opposed. But in the meantime, I am persuaded that I have enough to protect these settlers, and I shall use them, and go in person to give the deserved protection to the settlements of Tombigbee and Tensaw, unless those that I am sending now to Folch are enough, in conjunction with the settlers, to prevent all hostilities.[192]

I remain with all respect for you, your most attentive servant.

[ESTEVAN MIRÓ]

Alexander McGillivray

121. *McGillivray to Folch, May 14, 1789*
[AGI C 52]
LITTLE TALLASSIE, 14 May 1789

SIR

I have to Acknowledge the receit of Your two letters of April & one by an alibamon of May, all deliverd at same time. I hearing some reports among the Indians that the chactaws had Invited the alibamons & others to Join in driving off the american Settlers who Inhabited above & outside of the former English Boundary, I Judged it proper that You Shoud know of it directly that the proper precautions might be adopted, I accordingly wrote You of it as will appear from the date of my letter. Just as I heard of the Intention, being on the point of going into the Lower parts of this Nation to hold the usual Conferences with those chiefs, I gave Instructions in the mean time to the Coosada Chief Red Shoes to keep a Strict look out that no partys shoud go off to Tombegbee untill my return from the Lower Towns, & to detain the two chactaws, who was urging the alibamons to go with them, untill I returnd to hold the Conference in this part of the Nation. The whole chiefs of the Cherokees Nation who have claimd our protection was at our Conference which delayed me a good deal, & am but Just arrived at home as Your Messenger gave me Your letter of 1t May &c.

192. See Miró's instructions to Folch, May 10, 1789, AHN E 3887.

230

As You have I suppose received the letter I mention, by Durands Negro, I enclosed to Young Linder, Containing the above Information, as well as my Sentiments of the old Walton, I have Nothing farther to say on his affair.

I have heard some imperfect report of the affair of old Walton & Jenkens, but being engaged as I am always at this Season of the Year with a Multiplicity of Business with the Americans & Indians, that I did not attend to it. Jenkens merited his Fate for engaging in a lawless design. The others may be Strolling about the Nation, which every one knows is extensive, & a great number of Settlements. To I have little leisure to Search about for them. Nor have I chains or dungeons to Confine in nor a Military guard to go on Such duty. My expences are already too Great, & I cant afford to execute public business on my own charges, which I have hitherto done without a recompense.

As You Say that You will represent my Conduct in these affairs to Governor Miró, You no doubt will do it as You like. If he is King in Louisiana I am one in the Creek Nations. However I am well assured that his Excellency is Satisfied that I Shall never be found remiss or Neglectfull on any occasion wherein the true & essential Interests of the King of Spain is Concernd, however I may pass over trifling objects.[193]

I entirely agree with You that the growing evils of lawless people shoud be crushd, but I beg leave to observe that Your people gave the example in the Murder of Laurence. When I wrote You by Dyer being early next morning I had not an opportunity to enquire into the affair, which was that I had been from home which is often the case, that Laurence did not come to report himself, but as soon as he heard of my being at home he Came as far as my Sisters house on his way to mine. The two assassins with others rushd into the house & fired their Guns across her face at Laurence. She being at the time pregnant & near delivery, She fainted & was Carried out & was with difficulty restored to life, & it farther appeared that Dyer & Johnston instead of coming to me with their dispatches was waylaying or watching the roads to my house for a day or two for Laurence, which plainly Shews that they came not with a design to Carry him a prisoner but to murder him, as a reward was offerd for the Compleating of it.

This & the Circumstances of it as Soon as I knew it, I considerd as a most daring outrage, & Immediately Sent after to apprehend them which if my messengers had effected, I Shoud not have waited for the result of Complaint but woud have hanged them on the Spot.

193. In his letter to Folch on May 10, 1789, *ut supra*, Miró did express confidence in McGillivray.

Laurences affair has produced a Similar one at Pensacola las winter a Shawnoe half breed was fired upon & wounded by Dr. Ruby & his Molattoes on account of a trifling debt of thirty Dollars. Exasperated at this & the loss of five horses Stolen from he killed a Spanish Cow hunter near the Town. So that all persons guilty of such outrages shoud be brought to tryal & if acquitted by Law or punished, others woud not entertain notions of retalliations.

The Cherokees have alarmed this Nation much with accounts of their Stopping some american officers in that Country & taking their papers away which provd to be Commissions to Inspect the Tombegbie Lands, & who were to be followed in the Summer by all those that the american Congress were driving from the Cherokee hunting Grounds, amounting to some thousand familys, & this past winter three men were found marking lines near one hundred miles this side of Tombigbie, all which has roused a ferment among this Nation & even among the Indolent Chactaws. Two Chickasaws are this moment arrived on some business, but as I cant have an Interpreter till tomorrow, will defer to give You an account till next opportunity. Mean time I advise that people of property on that river Secure it, as some party may Join the chactaws & so elude my Care & Vigilance.

I am Sir Your Most Hble. Servt.

ALEX: McGILLIVRAY [rubric]

122. Miró to McGillivray, May 22, 1789

[Copy in AGI C 2352]

SIR:

On the 11th of this month I replied to the letter that you wrote to Don Vicente Folch on April 22 last,[194] in which you set forth the bad intentions of the Alabamas against the settlements of Tombigbee, saying that although you tried to stop them from going farther you were told that it was too late to stop the party of Alabamas. The Alabamas, you said, had moved away in the hope of freeing themselves from being overseen by the Creek Nation. In all this it was clearly implied that if it had been the Creeks who had offered this insult to the Spanish nation, you would have remedied it. Therefore, though two other letters from persons who live in the Choctaw Nation report that it was the Creeks, I did not believe it, and in this opinion I have written to the commandant of Mobile.[195]

But I have just this day received a letter from the commandant of Natchez, by the translation of which you will see that he asserts that

194. Document 119, *supra.*
195. See notes 189 and 193, *supra.*

there are Creeks in the Chickasaw Nation killing all the whites that they find living there or passing through there, that it is their plan to cross the Mississippi and on its west side destroy a settlement begun at L'Ance a la graisse, and from there to descend to the Natchez district to kill any Americans they find.

I suspend judgment on the truth of this declaration, and I am inclined to believe that it will prove wholly false, for it is not possible that without your knowledge your Nation would have launched upon such an outrage. Yet some small party might have taken advantage of your absence at the Lower Towns. If this did happen, I have full confidence that you will immediately take the most effective means to stop this disorder, and in order that you may the better convince your people that they have no right to oppose the settlements that his Majesty has ordered to be made by Americans admitted as his subjects. I shall tell you succinctly the reasons for so doing. . . . .

These will suffice to induce you to try to undeceive the Alabamas, and also the Talapuches, if it should happen, as I do not believe, that they are involved in the hostilities committed, and I do not doubt that all the chiefs of good intentions will be convinced by this reasoning and will separate themselves from the hostility, for it is a rule of mankind that an entire nation responds to resist a wrong done to a part of the nation.

Under these principles, you will see clearly that if the evil is not remedied, I must begin by interrupting all the commerce and the distribution of munitions and by preparing myself for a general war with all the Indians who do not enter into confederation with me, or who do not at least remain neutral. Otherwise they shall not obtain munitions from me, which they could pass on to my enemies.

I shall await anxiously for your reply that you will of course calm these disturbances, because you will thus be enabled to induce the chiefs to contribute toward the true remedy, that they will try to restrain not only the Creeks, if the accompanying report was true, but also the Alabamas, who without doubt started the hostilities at Tombigbee. This will contribute toward the general welfare both for you and for Spain.[196]

May God preserve you many years.

ESTEVAN MIRÓ

Alexander McGillivray.

196. Making report to Valdés on May 20 concerning this war scare, Miró justified the proposed fort on the Tombigbee, chiefly because it would prove to the Indians that although the settlers there were "Americans by birth," they were now "true Spaniards" (AHN E 3887).

123. *McGillivray to Miró, May 26, 1789*

[AGI C 52]

LITTLE TALLASSIE, 26 May 1789

SIR

I received Your Excellencys letter of 11th Instant,[197] by the hands of Monsr. DeVille from Capt. Folch, & I take due Notice of the various Matters therein Containd.

The first article Concerns the Information which I gave of the reports of the alabamons Intentions of driving the american Settlers from Tombegbe river & Tensaw Settlements as it is said however I certainly mentiond nothing of the latter people.[198] It is very true that I used my Interest with Your Excellency's favor to procure an establishment for the most part of the present Inhabitants of Tensaw, & it is equally true that I objected to the Intention of Introducing americans into the Neighbourhood of our hunting grounds under any Shape. If my objections were not directly presented to Your Excellency Yet they were to a Kings officer Mons. Grimarest, the then Commandant of Mobile who I naturally Supposed woud give You the Information. The objections which I made was founded on a report that John Turnbull who always was & is now an unalterable enemy of the Spaniards had by the assistance of freinds obtain leave from Your Excellency to bring & Settle a Number of Americans his friends upon Tombegbe & Tensaw. Your Excellency never favord me with any Information or remarks on my letters. Several on Interesting Subjects having never been answerd has often occasiond a long Silence & Ignorance on my part.

Having ever disdaind practising Falsehoods to any people on any occasion, I have ever Corresponded with You in truth, & You May beleive me when I repeat that the Chactaws or some part of them are Stimulating our people to attack the Tombegbe, & one is actually now in the Town of Coosada. However I have taken proper measures to restrain our people from such hostillity, & the few horses that have been brought in from there that I hear of, Shall be returnd to their owners. I have Sent the principal chiefs of the alabamons to Mobile to Satisfy the Commandant of the peaceable Intentions of their tribes in this matter.

I cannot at this time go with the chiefs to ascertain the Limits as You propose to me being engaged to meet the Commissioners of Congress on the 20t of next month to treat of Peace. Their Talk of Invitation is herein enclosed[199] & for Your Excellencys Information I offer

197. Document 120, *supra*.
198. This is correct; see document 119, *supra*.
199. Pickens and Osborne to the Creek Nation, April 20, 1789, copy in AGI C 182.

234

a few remarks. The Commissioners Say they wish to renew peace & freindship with us on our Land, the So. West Side of Oconee. This having no appearance of a relinquishment of all of the disputed territory, I Shoud have rejected the Invitation, but in the present posture of affairs with us, it is very necessary for our Interest to Conclude a peace with the americans, even at the expence of Considerable Concessions on our part to purchase it.

I had pledged the Spanish good faith & my own Credit for the Certainty of a farther Supply of Ammunition & arms to enable this Nation to obtain a Safe & honorable peace. At our Meetings the cheifs are pressing me for Information on the Subject. I tell them I have Your promise for it, & I have long expected to hear that it was all ready at Pensacola agreeable to promise, & am much dissappointed. We cannot prosecute our claims with our private resources, & our expectations in our freinds & Protectors are frustrated in their harbouring doubts & Suspicions of our attachment & freindly disposition & in the moment for active operations, the means is withheld from us. These are powerfull reasons & tho extremely reluctant to the measure I deem a peace with the americans absolutely necessary for this Nation under our present Circumstances. I go not to dictate the Conditions of Peace as was always my desire, but to Submit to & receive their Impositions. [200]

Having wrote to Capt. Folch by DeVille [201] which Your Excellency will See, I am Constraind to Conclude this letter from an Inveterate head ake & pain in the eyes, contracted by long Sittings & Smoking tobacco at our late Conventions.

I am with respectfull regard
    Your Excellencys most Hble. Servant
        ALEX: MCGILLIVRAY [rubric]

124. *McGillivray to Miró, June 9, 1789*
            [AGI C 202]
            LITTLE TALLASSIE, June 9, 1789
SIR

Just as I am on the point of mounting my horse this morning to go to the American Treaty, Your Excellencys favor of 22d May [202] is put into my hands.

I have most attentively perused Your Excellencys dispatches & as they relate to some affairs which has been the Subject of disenssion

200. See also McGillivray to George Galphin, May 18, 1789, ASP IA, I, 35; John Galphin to Osborne, May 23, 1789, *ibid.*, p. 36; George Galphin's report, May 27, 1789, *ibid.*, pp. 35-36; and John Galphin to Osborne, June 1, 1789, *ibid.*, p. 36.
201. Document 121, *supra.*
202. Document 122, *supra.*

between us, & I have wrote you Some days since by Mr. DeVille who came here from Mobile with letters from the Commandant, & I hope that at his return there every thing will assume its usual good harmony, as I have been at extraordinary pains about the matter, & I earnestly wish that my letters may be well attended which will prevent future differences. I Shall drop the Subject with assuring Your Excellency that the Chactaws were the Instigators of the late trouble & alarm—& permit me Sir to take the liberty to Caution You from placing a Confidence in Tales fabricated by designing americans within Your Government with a View & hope to Involve our Nation in a War with Spain. Such things are exceedingly disagreeable & in some measure embarrassing to me.

In the Mean times it gives me pleasure to observe that Your Excellency Nevertheless entertains a Confidence in My Integrity & honor, which is So clearly evinced in the Orders which You have given to Mr. Cruzat to Issue out the promised Supply of arms & ammunition. The threatening parts of Your [letter] I Shall make no farther Comments on than that they were Suggested by a belief in you that our Nation had hostile Intentions toward Spain. I again repeat to Your Excellency that Considerations of Sound Policy loudly dictates to us the necessity & propriety of maintaining the strictest friendship with Your Government. This Nation always distrustfull & Jealous of the americans, are apt to Shew it in an irregular manner & the wide extent of Country & distant Situation of the Villages often put it out of the power of the Chiefs to prevent disorderly actions.

It is not the kings Natural Subjects that the Indians dislike but it is the Americans: who are pouring into Louisiana & W. Florida. I Shall not trouble you with any political predictions, but it does not require any extraordinary powers to foresee what they aim at & what will happen Sooner or later.

Having appointed the time & place to meet the Commissioners of Congress, I am Setting out to Meet them. The knowledge of a Certain Supply of arms &c. revives our hearts & we Shall of course Insist upon the Most favorable terms & in Some Measure dictate them.

I am with great respect & esteem
    Your Excellencys obedt. Servant
                        ALEX: McGILLIVRAY [rubric]

125. *Folch to McGillivray, June 14, 1789*
                        [AGI C 52]
                    FUERTE DE SAN ESTEVAN, 14 June 1789

SIR

236

I received your letter 14 May.[203] Shall only answer the articles which personally concern me and leave the rest to be answered by Governor Miro the chief of this Collony.

Yn the first place I thank you for your care in puting a stop to the parties which purposed coming to ruin the Ynhabitans on Tombigbe, and Should any of them have made their appearance here notwithstanding your vigilance, they shou'd not have evaded mine.

Yt seems very strange to me that the death of Laurence happening on the first of March, your Sister did not faint away untill the middle of May; because if the like had be fallen her before, it was natural to think you wou'd have made mention of it in the different letters you wrote me during the interval.

The Orders which I gave Dyer and Johnson were presented to you to which you should give more credit than to the rest of your Nation; according to your manner of explaining yourself in your letter, you give me to understand, I gave orders by word of mouth different to them you have seen, this duplicity you would not accuse me of, if you knew me perfectly.

You have sense enough to know that the late Story, which has been propogated concerning this affair, was invented by a number of Wreches, who find shelter in your Nation, with no other view than to exasperate you, and by these means render themselves securer.

Yn consequence of Laurence's having plundered Negroes, and threaten'd to return to repeat the same, all the Ynhabitants of my District offered to pay Dyer and Johnson the expences of their journey. This is the recompense you make mention of.

That you may the more manifestly behold to how many mistakes they are exposed who too readily are influenced by credulity, I shall cite you the following instance: the diference between the Death of Laurence and that of the Spanish cow keeper commited by Savana Jack in Pensacola were not thirty hours. Now is it possible, the distance being three hundred miles, that the one should be the effect of the other.

I have lately examined the circumstances of the whole affair, and find that those you call assassins, did not deviate in the least from my orders, for which reason you would have done ill to hang them, and my advice to you is never to do the like to them who have passports, because the consequence may be dangerous.

Finally, shoud you notwithstanding my remonstrances to undeceive you, continue to prefer the Welfare of such like Wretches, I shall be under the necessity of renouncing your friendship (tho' my Country

203. Document 121, *supra*.

may not) which, as I have hitherto seen, I cannot preserve without obtaining that of a class of peaple, to look at whoom only I should think myself degraded.[204]

I am Sir your most hble Servt.

V. FOLCH [rubric]

126. *McGillivray to Miró, June 24, 1789*

[AGI C 202]

LITTLE TALLASSIE, 24 June 1789

SIR

When I had last the pleasure of writing Your Excellency I was on the point of Setting off for the Cowetas in the Lower Towns on my way to meet the commissioners of Congress to treat of Peace, at their request. When I arrived at the Lower Towns I found the Chiefs assembled in meeting when they gave it as their opinion that I ought not to proceed to the appointed place of meeting the Commissioners for the reason that as in the last month we had generally resolved to recommence the War & were actually prepared to take the feild, & some partys had actually Set off to war when the Talk of Invitation arrived to us, & those partys were Just all returnd having killed several & took some prisoners, which no doubt would provoke the Georgians to offer us gross Insults if not make some hostile attempts upon our persons at the Treaty, therefore it woud be most proper to Send an express to them with our reasons for declining the proposed Treaty in the present Circumstances of things & to assure them of our Willingness to treat personally of Peace after a few Months had elapsed, giving time for our Minds to cool when we coud confer & treat in temper & moderation. After having dispatched an express[205] I arrived here from the Cowetas, two days ago.

The above reasons only shoud not have deterrd me from proceeding to the Treaty, but the matter which weighd most in my mind was the result of a conversation which I had a little before with my friend Mr. Jas. McGy.[206] who lately arrived here from the South of Georgia after some Negroes who had ran off & came here. He told me that the Congress had lately given Instructions to their Commissioners, that

204. The manuscript in the Spanish archives appears to be the original, which may mean that this insulting letter was not sent. In his letters there is no indication that McGillivray received it, yet it surely would have called forth a sharp rejoinder. But Miró took note of it and of the charges in Folch's letter of June 13 (AGI C 52). He ordered Folch never to write to McGillivray again (document 127, *infra*).

205. The letter carried by John Galphin is in ASP IA, I, 37. See also Pickens and Osborne to the Creeks, June 29, 1789, *ibid.*, and a personal letter to McGillivray, *ibid.*, pp. 37-38.

206. Not a near relative, so far as I know.

in their negotiations with us, they were to conduct themselves agreeable to the desires of the Georgians, & in the event of our refusing to accede to their decission, the whole was to be referrd to General Washington, (who is vested with nearly royal Powers,) for his Judgment the result of which woud be adopted by Congress.

The wishes & Intention of the Georgians are well known to be these first to compel us to a concession of all the territory which they want from us, a part of which cuts deep into East Florida, their Second object is to force our trade from its present channel the Floridas into their own hands which will at once make them our dictators in all matters.

Possessd of this Information, we coud not consistently with our prior engagements with You proceed to treat with them on terms so contradictory with those with You. Your Excellency may rest assured that it shall be my Study & endeavor to maintain good faith with you, however what Interested & Insidious men may urge to you to the Contrary. As Your own good Sense & a clear knowledge of our Situation will point out to Your Excellency the Impossibility of our acting in any manner which may risque us the forfeeture of the kings Guarantee, which while extended to us is our chief dependence for Security & Safety.

In the meantime as we are threatend hard by the Americans with the displeasure of their King Washington,[207] to be prepared for every event & to be guarded against the effects of it I have despatched the Cowetas Cussitahs & Some other Towns in the Lower Nation to proceed to Pensacola to receive Your Excellencys bounty of ammunition & arms & am Sending off others from here for that purpose.

About three weeks Since a party of our Warriors returnd from the Cherokee Nation. They being on the frontier of North Carolina fell in a considerable party of Americans, directing their course toward the Cherokee Country & our warriors, Judging them of hostile Intentions toward that Indians attackd & routed them, as they made no resistance killed but few. Among the killed was two Chickasaws. By their papers it appears that they were the Father & Son the name of the former was Panss. Fallayah or long hair a relation of a very troublesome fellow named Poy. Mingo. This latter has Sent as messengers to Congress with a letter Containing the Strongest professions of freindship to the Americans requesting a trade of Goods, offering to admit them to Settle & build a fort at Chicasaw bluffs on Wolf River. A great

207. Pickens and Osborne had written on April 20, 1789, "We are now governd by a President who is like the old King over the great water. He Commands all the Warriors of the thirteen great fires" (AGI C 182). The opponents of ratification of the Constitution had inveighed against it on this very score.

number of letters was found among the baggage, the whole of which was taken when the Americans fled & left it. They are chiefly private & on trifling matters only one mentions a Colo. Morgans Settling or building a Town called New Madrid the Settlement of which has given rise to much Speculation among the Western Americans, & they mean to throw every obstacle in the way of its Settlement as they beleive Such an establishment will be prejudicial to the others. It has they say Already taken away all but fifteen familys from the Illinois Settlement.

The Chicasaws can have little to say for the fall of their Countrymen as tis a maxim with all Indians to have no regard to any found in an enemys Camp, & if they resent it, they will be Soon destroyed between this nation & its Indian allies, who are all eager to chastize the Chickasaws for their defection from the general league, & this Nation so well practised in arms by the American war, they have provd themselves equal to the best American Militia in the feild & of course an over match for an Nation who keept aloof under pretence of a Neutrality, as the Choctaws & Chickasaws have done.

In Your Excellencys letter of 22d May is anexd an affidavit made before Monsr. Grand Pré, by certain Americans, concerning a design of our people to attack & disperse New Madrid & the whole of which is founded in American finess, for the reasons as aforementiond. The letter I allude to is written by a Mount Florence, to Colo. Hawkins. If I can find it by this opportunity it shall go to Your Excellency with this or by Some other opportunity, Indian Information in general ought to be Suspected as they carry Tales to encure a good reception & to obtain presents. Franchimastile is no freind to Spaniards to my knowledge. A Tuckebatche Indian being in the Chickasaw country was affronted by them on account of the Americans, on which he killed the first of them he saw Shortly afterwards, & that is the whole truth of the matter.

The Alibamons have not given Your Excellency more cause of vexation lately than myself. As soon as Red Shoes & the others come home which will be Shortly I will give them a Talk Sufficient to Set them in their proper Senses. As for the Creeks they are pretty well under controul & I can answer for their Conduct. I wish Your Excellency to believe that my best endeavors Shall be used to maintain & promote the best harmony possible, between the Kings Colony & this Nation.

I am with True Esteem & regard

Your Excellencys most obedt. Servt.

ALEX: McGILLIVRAY [rubric]

240

127. *Miró to Folch, June 29, 1789*
[Spanish copy in AGI C 56]

It will be best for the service of the king that you never again write to Alexander McGillevray. When you have any reason to write to his nation you will tell it to me so that I may carry it out or do whatever seems best to me, for although there may be some delay it will never be so harmful as that which McGillevray found so offensive, as he wrote me, which could have had the worst consequences.

You do not know the antecedents, because of which I am sure that he is not the one who caused the present disturbances. On the contrary, I am positive that he will endeavor, as he promises, to stop them.

As regards the peace that he is going to make with the Americans, I have for some years, in accordance with the royal orders, tried to persuade him to do so. But this made him distrust us with some apparent foundation, for he feared that we were going to abandon his nation to oblige it to make this peace. This led to the appearance of the Englishman Bowles who brought merchandise to Mosquito River, but McGillevray, already disillusioned, promised to confiscate them from Bowls, and the latter escaped knowing that no good awaited him there.

I do not say by this that McGillevray may not change or that he will always be faithful, because I know he is too sensitive, which can at the last moment give rise to some real controversy. It is in order that you may not be the principal cause of such a change that I have issued the above injunction.

With this are answered all the letters that you have written to me about McGillevray.

May God preserve you many years. New Orleans, June 29, 1789.

ESTEVAN MIRÓ

Señor Don Vicente Folch.

128. *McGillivray to Cruzat, July 2, 1789*
[AGI C 202]

LITTLE TALLASSIE 2d July 1789

SIR

I did myself the pleasure to write You by Mr. Milfort who I Sent to Pensacola to see to the delivery of the arms & ammunition. Being at the time of writing much hurried it did [not] occur to me to Inform You that the Vagabond Timy. Lane who fled this Nation & is protected in Pensacola, Continues to behave in a Very disorderly manner to many Indians that go there, particularly of this Town, one of whom he much abused & hurt, & threatens to Continue Such outrages upon every

241

friend of mine that he meets with & it appears that he is sufferd to
Commit Such Actions with impunity. I have Now to request of You
Sir that he may not be Sufferd to go about the Streets during time
that the Indians that go for arms &c. remain in Town, for fear that
his Insolence will draw upon him the treatment which he deserves from
every one of my freinds. He woud not have been Sufferd so long but
that I Constantly enjoin every Indian to Conduct himself in Pensacola
in the most Civil Manner to the Inhabitants & others. The fellow Lane
is Much Complaind of by the Indians in general & he will Certainly
meet with some Mischief, the Creeks will not bear abuse & Ill treatment
at least those that Now go are Very Seldom in that Town & will be
most apt to Chastise his Insolence.

I had agreed to drop my resentment at Lane at the request of my
friend Governor Miro, which Circumstance I believe has occasiond
him to assume fresh arrogance & Insolence, & I now for peace Sake
Wish him removed from Pensacola to New Orleans. I Sincerely am
with Much Esteem Sir Your Most obedt. Servant

ALEX: McGILLIVRAY [rubric]

Honorable Francisco Cruzat Esqr.
Commandant of Pensacola &c.

129. *Folch to Miró, July 2, 1789*
[Spanish draft in AGI C 52]
FORT OF SAN ESTEVAN, July 2, 1789.

MY DEAR SIR:
On this occasion the same thing happened to me as to the boy who
found some scissors and set out to cut flowers; he lost the best part of
the goods without knowing the consequences.

To see McGillevray so proud and haughty and the Indians so un-
grateful is the cause of the fervor with which I have written in my No.
161. I believed, however, that I was writing to you and not to the court.
Nevertheless, if at any time it happens that I displease you, in spite of
all my care, I shall also fail in my wish, which is and always will be
to do whatever I can to contribute to your satisfaction. . . . .

According to my way of thinking, McGillevray hopes to obtain
a seaport in order to escape the tariffs. When he gets it, he not only
will be no longer dependent on us, but will endeavor to attach to himself all the other Indians. Even now it is time for us to set watch on
him and not to let him escape from our sight, because the disease of
wishing to be king has possessed him as a great delirium. . . . .[208]

208. Folch had gotten some of his ideas about McGillivray's projects from
Cornell, the interpreter. See Folch's letter to Miró, June 13, 1789, AGI C 52.

XI

ROCK LANDING

130. *Miró to McGillivray, July 22, 1789*
[Spanish draft in AGI C 184]

MY DEAR SIR:

I have received your letter of June 24 last,[209] in which I see with regret that you have suspended your going with the chiefs to the treaty of peace with the Americans because of the recent hostilities committed by your warriors, who had set out before you received the last letter in which the American commissioners agreed to form a treaty of peace.

At the same time you tell me, that if there had been no other reason than the above, you would not have failed to go to the treaty, but that you are informed that the commissioners have orders to satisfy the Georgians, and that the latter do not wish to cede the usurped lands, and also that it is the intention of the commissioners to force your nation to establish a trade solely with them.

I know that in this you have proceeded with a desire to show me how much you are devoted to deserving the king's protection by standing up for the articles of our Congress of Pensacola in 1784. Nevertheless, it seems to me that it would promote the tranquility of your nation and that in any event the world would know the reasonableness of your part, if it is necessary to continue the war, if you renewed the conferences, showing in them that the Creeks are a free nation that can not be obliged to cede the lands that the Georgians have usurped or forced to form a commercial treaty with anyone unsuitable, or made to break pledges contracted with another party. If under these just conditions the Americans do not want to form a treaty their injustice will be made manifest, and the nation will be better in position to defend its rights. Spain will then have a better right to protect you, for after having urged your nation to offer to make this peace, as I have done in various letters and as is the intention of his Majesty, if the Americans do not wish to concede it on just terms and without the condition that you separate yourselves from the protection of his Majesty into which you entered at the Congress of Pensacola, then the Americans can have no complaint if his Majesty helps you to defend yourselves and to protect the lands that belong to you.

I wrote to you on July 8, 1788, on these same points. All that I ask of you is that you take note of that letter, making known to the commis-

209. Document 126, *supra*.

sioners what I said in it about the alleged treaties of Hopewell and Seneca with the Choctaws and Chickasaws.

I wish you good health and that you will give me opportunity to serve you, praying meanwhile to God to preserve you many years. New Orleans, July 22, 1789.

131. *McGillivray to Miró, August 10, 1789*
[AGI C 202][210]

LITTLE TALLASSIE, 10 August 1789

SIR

In my last letter[211] I related some occurrences to you and told you that I had answered the proposal that the commissioners made me to treat with them on the 20th of last June. Some ten days ago I received an express from these commissioners in which they acceded to my wish to postpone the treaty until a more opportune time for us.[212] They proposed to me the 15th of September for the commencement of the treaty, and to this proposition I consented, for I constantly desire to prove my disposition to put an end to this bloody contest, whenever we can do so with security. I shall consider myself fortunate if I can induce them to conclude a peace on terms that will entirely remove all cause of future complaints and assure my Nation the peaceful enjoyment of its rights.

It is well & generally known that the War in which we have so long been engaged in with the Americans was of their own Seeking. Intoxicated with high Ideas of National Consequence from having unexpectedly gaind the establishment of their Independency, they Vainly Imagined themselves what they affected to Stile themselves, Conquerors of the old & Masters of the New World. In this dream of greatness & Power they fondly thought that they coud Seize with Impunity every foot of Territory belonging to the Red Natives of america & that it woud be easy to exterminate them if necessary to the accomplishment of such Iniquitous Views.

That we have in part if not wholly defeated the wicked intentions of the americans is known to every people & that we have brought these haughty republicans to bend & Sue for peace from the people whom they had despised & marked out for destructing.

At the same time I acknowledge with the warmest Sentiments of Gratitude, that we accomplished this chiefly with the Generous aid & Support which we received from our great Protector the King of

210. The first paragraph and the last two are supplied from a Spanish translation in AHN E 3887.
211. Document 126, *supra*.
212. Pickens and Osborne to the Creeks, June 29, 1789, ASP IA, I, 37.

244

Spain whose Interest has likewise been benefitted by our rescuing from the americans an extensive Scope of Territory which they were adding to their Southern State of Georgia toward East Florida.

It is probable that in the treaty we shall be able to end the dispute over boundaries, since they have already abandoned half of their usurpations. But they will be determined to have our trade again, fully convinced of their own power to win over and attract the Indian Nations. A peace concluded with them without stipulations concerning trade will have very little stability.

In the event that we postpone either or both points, of arranging the boundaries and of trade, which I shall not hesitate to do if it is necessary, I shall count on you to render me the most effective and decisive assistance for carrying on the war. I trust that we shall never be exposed to the risk of last year, when at the moment that our adversaries were making the most vigorous efforts you refused to give us any more aid or support and told us to make peace. Permit me to call to your attention that if we are really forced to make peace with the Americans, they will take every advantage of our situation.

ALEX: McGILLIVRAY [rubric]

his Excellency General Miro,
Governor of Louisiana and West Florida.

132. *McGillivray to Panton, August 10, 1789*
[Copy in AGI C 203][213]

LITTLE TALLASSIE 10th August 1789

DEAR SIR

There being no pack horses going for Pensacola of a long time past, I had no opportunity to answer your last letters, the Bearer on my promising him two Kegs Taffia has undertaken to Carry these to you.

Galphin whom I sent to the Rock Landing with a Talk declining the Treaty of June last, returnd about a Fortnight since, & I find that they are resolved upon holding the Treaty; in order to accomodate us they the Commissioners are Complaisant enough to postpone it till 15th Next Month, and one of them the late Chief Justice Osborn, remains all the time at the Rock Landing. Pickens returnd for the Cherokee Treaty, but in that I took measures to disappoint him, for those Chiefs would not meet. The people being all at home and the grand Ceremony of Kindling the New fire being Just over I deem it the fittest time to meet these Commissioners, & have accordingly made

213. An inaccurate copy is printed in Pickett, *History of Alabama*, pp. 389-95, and still more inaccurate excerpts in Foreman, "Alexander McGillivray," *Chronicles of Oklahoma*, VII, 111-12.

the broken days, of which nine are left to Set out in. In Conducting the Business of the Treaty, I will as you observe Confine it to the fixing our Limits & the Acknowledgement of the Independency of my Nation. This I deem very necessary as the Americans pretend to a Territorial Claim or Sovereignty over us in Virtue of the late peace, this being Settled will in a great measure be doing Away every Cause of future quarrel between us. You Well know how Customary it is, in all Treatys held with Indians, to agree on a Commercial one likewise, it being Absolutely necessary as it more firmly Attaches them to friendships formed, as without Stipulations of that Sort in a Treaty of peace none will be lasting. However in this Instance I will agree to None, as you have a prospect of being enabled by the favor of Government to Supply this Trade on as Moderate terms as the Georgians can do, & here let me observe to you that in the Affair of Trade, the Americans will push hard for it, & it will be for us the most difficult part of Whole Negotiations to decline it, but I will risque the Breaking off the Conferences before I will give in to it. On the Whole if I find that the Commissioners Insist upon Stipulations that will in their Operation Clash with those that we have already Entered into with Spain, I Shall not hesitate to Cut Short the Negotiation,[214] & support the Connexion which we have with Spain, it being more Safe and reputable than those republicans can make us, but at same time, I must Insist upon an Equal resolution in them, our friends the Spaniards to afford us their decided Support by every means in their power & not under any pretences to repeat the Conduct of last Summer, in the very moment for vigorous exertion to refuse a further Aid & Insist & menace us to make a peace right or wrong with the Americans, which if we had done at the time, we Should have been drawn into hostilities with Spain before this day, & I repeat to you what I have frequently done to Governor Miro that if we are obliged for want of Support to Conclude an Unconditional peace with the Americans, it will prove essentially hurtfull to the Kings Interests.

The Amunition and Arms given us by the King we have not yet been Able to fetch Away, it is a good Store in hand, to make our hearts firm in treating with the Americans, but I am miserably disappointed in the Guns, these, my people who have ever been accustomed to the best English guns, find the greatest difficulty to use, being entirely unfitt either for the purpose of hunting or War, they may say they have no other, but I pointed out where they were to be got, & if our friends resolve to Support us, they might do it with what was good. A Chief of the Coosadas named Red Shoes is lately returnd from Orleans very

214. This is what was to happen.

246

well Satisfied with his reception & treatment there, & has brought a very good talk with him, and I am equally Satisfied that the Western Horizon is again Cleard up and looks fair; & so it will always continue if the intention of adopting as good Spaniards the restless American is intirely given up. I mean in our neighbourhood between us & the Chactaws. I have observed to Govr. Miro that the reasons he gave me for Settling Americans on the West Side of Mississippi is founded on real political principles, & I truly wish'd that it was in the Compass of our power to drive them all from the Ohio & Cumberland to Seek the New Asylum as being moved out of our way, our Warriors never would follow them there.

The Coosada Chief Red Shoes being disgusted with Capn. Folk on Tombegbe resolved to go to Govr. Miro who Satisfied him. Between you and [me] I believe that Folk acts rashly, if he had Spoke to an Assembly of Creek Chiefs, as he did to the Alabamons & Challenged them to war & Shewd them his Swivels, &ca &ca, he would have been directly taken at his word.[215]

My friend the Govr. is likewise possessd with the belief that all the damage done the Settlers below is done by us, but it is wrong the whole was a few Horses & Mares taken & my Sister Durant took back the most of them from the Coosadas, but at present the Chactaws is the favorite and all the Outrages which they Commit is all fully turned upon us, by their partisans. It is notorious that the Chactaws are discontented, & Indians never fail to manifest it, in either taking Scalps or Committing depredations, which last they do, for it is Common for them to Kill horses & Cattle &c. on Tombegbe & this Summer even about Mobile, but all this is Conceald from Govr. Miro by them, & Charge us with falshoods.

Ben James,[216] who is so much Confided in is privately an American Agent & has Actually a Commission which he received from Georgia to Act with Davenport &ca & I know Could he be Supported with any necessarys by the Americans he would thow off the mask; he was even weak enough to address me for leave to open a Trade with the States which I refused him as well at his application this Summer to go to the American States. As a proof of my Assertions respecting the Chactaws Folk sent them a Talk this Summer Menacing them with a stoppage of their Trade untill they made Satisfaction. I am ever ready to make allowance for a momentary impression, by false report, but it would be better that they were more guarded aginst such, & not

215. See note 204, *supra.*
216. Ben James had violently denied any connection with the Americans on the occasion of the meeting at Yazoo. See Palabra dicha en el Yazú, March 19, 1787, AHN E 3887.

made the ground of making differences which might produce a Serious Effect. The late Menaces which were thrown out to me Created no great anxiety in my mind, because I could have directly Opend the Eastern door, where large magazines of goods &c have been Stored for some time past awaiting it to be opend, but for peace and quietness Sake, hope there will be no Occasion now for it, as everything is fallen into a Calm so let it remain, & in all that I have done or said was Solely to discover & Shew the means to preserve it, I hope for ever between us. The Chickesaw Nation are Content (whatever pio Mingo Can Say to the Contrary) to put up with the loss of that Chiefs Brother & Son as having [   ] fallen in Bad Company. This will be a warning to [   ]217 Convince them that they will not be permitted with Impunity to Act and Encourage hostile designs against us or Concert with any people.

Now let me touch a little upon my private affairs. I wish I could lay my hand upon their last letter to Send you, & a Very Curious, & to you not an unentertaing Carolina Newspaper, just receivd, but they are both Swallowd up in a Multitude of papers. You know how it is with me in the paper way. The Commissioners Say it would give them great pleasure to have a private Conversation previous to our Entering on the business of the Treaty, as it would tend to make it go on agreeably and with more ease. I need not Interpret that paragraph to you when already you know that they have for some time past been endeavouring to Stop my mouth & hands with my family Estate which to your knowledge is more than £30,000 sterling, the offer of which is now I expect to be pressd upon me, & there has since I Saw you last arose a Considerable Conflict in my mind, in revolving these matters over. Here am I an Absolute Heavy Tax upon you218 for several years, and in fact not only for my private Support, but for all extra Expences of this department, and although my dear Sir I know that I can Still depend upon your generosity and in your friendship that you overlook the heavy Expence I put you to, yet you well know how hurtfull it is to the feeling heart to be beholden to Subsist wholly on the bounty of private friendship. Thus Situated I ask & wish you to give me your opinion. On the one hand I am offered a restoration of property and more than one Hundred Thousand Dollars at the least Valuation, and on the other not Wherewithall to pay an Interpreter, & I find that Letters is Still address'd to me as agent for S. C. Majesty when I have some time ago renounced the pittance of a Common Interpreter that was Allowed

217. The fraying of the manuscript here corrects what appears to have been a split infinitive.
218. Unless allowance was made for the direct and indirect contributions that McGillivray made to Panton's business ventures.

248

me as being a Consideration disgracefull to my Station. If they want my Services, why is not a regular Establishment made as was done by the English with a Competent Sallary offered and allowance for two Interpreters, one in the Upper & one in the Lower Towns, for hitherto I have had to pay them myself, or Shall I have recourse to my American Estate to maintain them & myself. I wish you to advise me what I had best do.

Although I have no Solid ground to hope a Compleat adjustment of our dispute with the Americans, I am resolved to go if it is only to wipe off the Suggestion[219] made to me by our friends that I was Actuated by unjust motives and unreasonable prejudices against the Americans, as the ground of hostilities Against them; but if they on the other hand Should find a body of people Approaching their mines would not they Say what Business have you here, Do you not know that these are grounds, from which we draw the Chief Sources of our Conveniences and happiness, and we Cannot Suffer you to participate of, & of depriving us of them, and if then encroachers Should refuse to withdraw, would they not Commence and Support an Inveterate hostility untill they Should Expell them? The fellow Romain who madam Vallin writes of was a great Liar. He came here from the Chactaws with a great quantity of Silverware and a few goods & wanted Nicks. White to join him in purchasing Negroes to Carry to & Sell at New Orleans. After roving About some time he had a difference with Milfort, who threatened to Send him in Irons to Orleans, which terrified him Apparently, and he went off to the Cherokees and from thence either to the lakes District or the American States. I expect our Treaty will be over by the middle of September, if we return Safe Expect a Visit early in October from Dear Sir

Yours most unfeignedly

(Signed) ALEX: McGILLIVRAY

133. *McGillivray to Miró, August 15, 1789*
[Spanish translation in AHN E 3887]
LITTLE TALLASSIE, August 15, 1789.

SIR:

I have just now received your letter of July 22,[220] whose contents have caused me great satisfaction, the more so since it arrived at the moment when I was going to set out to meet with the American commissioners in order to commence the treaty. But had I not been certain about the matters that your letter contains before going to this assembly,

219. See document 130, *supra.*
220. Document 130, *supra.*

249

I would have been most embarrassed to conduct the negotiations, but the assurances of his Majesty's support in all our just rights and your last news concerning our future trade have decided me clearly to insist at the treaty upon stipulations that will assure us our rights and pretensions, preserving at the same time in its entirety the treaty subsisting between the crown of Spain and our nation, whose ruin is the principal object that the Americans have in mind when they assemble to treat of peace. But in the state in which we find ourselves they will be altogether disappointed in their wishes, and consequently the objects of the treaty between them and us reduce to a very few issues. For the only thing that I can say to them is: Give us what we ask for justly, return to us the territory that you have usurped, and the war on our part will cease. We need nothing, nothing from you as a favor. We have already formed a treaty of alliance and friendship with a just and generous power, whose protection has furnished us an abundance of goods and an adequate trade. Therefore, in justice, we only need from you recognition that it has been the true cause of the long war that we have had with you. If you refuse to accede to our request, you will find us determined to insist upon and protect our rights.

It is probable that in hopes that the new congress will force matters in their favor against us, the commissioners will try to intimidate us into acceding to their demands, but if they pretend such a thing, I shall immediately break off the conferences, relying firmly on our great protector. . . . .[221]

I remain, with sentiments of the most perfect respect and esteem, Sir, your most obedient servant.

ALEXANDER McGILLIVRAY

Señor Brigadier Don Estevan Miro
Governor and Commander in Chief of Louisiana and West Florida.

134. *Panton to Miró, August 31, 1789*

[AGI C 203]

MUCH ESTEEMED SIR

The enclosed letters[222] for Your Excellency arrived lately from the Nation and I forward them by Miguels Boat which is the first occasion that has offered since I received them.

McGillivray is gone to meet the Commissioners of Congress at the River Occonnie. His Conduct there will afford Your Excellency a sure Criterion by which to judge of that Gentlemans disposition towards this

221. McGillivray had written a very similar letter to Miró, three days earlier (AHN E 3887), on receipt of Miró's letter of July 13, 1789.
222. Documents 131 and 132, *supra.*

250

Government. I expect him back in all the next Month when he has promised to come and see me & Your Excellency shall be duly informed of the result of this Congress which I wish may end to the satisfaction of all partys.

His letters to me which accompanyed those to Your Excellency Contain several matters of moment which I wish he had addressed to You himself, but as he may not have laid his mind before You so freely as he has to me I think it right that You Should see him in his native Garb & without disguise. I therefore send You duplicates which is intended for Your private perusal *only*.

You will perceive his Strictures on my Friend Mr. Folk is severe. I impute that difference to the mischievious disposition of Some Incendiarys who in every Country are ready to widen breaches betwixt Friends by Carrying Malicious tales from one to the others. Do You my Dear Sir tell Don Vicenti Folk to be guarded against such & leave the other to me and I shall not rest untill I make them good Friends.

I sincerely wish Your Excellency good & am with much Love and veneration

Your obliged Servt.

WM. PANTON [*rubric*]
PENSACOLA 31st August 1789

His Excellency General Miro

135. *McGillivray to Panton, October 8, 1789*
[Copy in BL LC]
LITTLE TALLASSIE, 8th October, 1789.

DEAR SIR

I arrived three days ago from the Oconee, sick, disgusted & fatigued to death. From this beginning you will imagine that matters did not go on to my mind; however I will proceed with my story, and you will see.[223]

After a tedious journey down, I made the first halt at 18 miles from the Rock landing, when Commissioner Osburn, Colonel Clark (Son to the General) and some other Officers arrived in my Camp, welcoming my arrival. Osburn informed me that Genl. Pickens was not arrived, but would be on the ground at the time appointed. A few days after the General arrived, and the next day they received an express from Augusta, informing that a new appointment had been made by Wash-

223. McGillivray gave much the same report to Zéspedes, December 1, 1789 (LC EF 114J9), and to Miró, December 10, 1789 (AGI C 202). For the version of the American commissioners, see their correspondence and report (ASP IA, I, 68-79), and Humphrey's letters to Washington, September 21, 26, and 27, and October 1, 1789, in F. L. Humphreys, *Life of David Humphreys*, II, 4-14.

ington & Congress, that Genl. Lincoln, Col. Humphrys an Aid of Washingtons & a Mr. Griffin late President of Congress, were the new Commissioners.[224]

Jo Clay in a letter to Billy Clark observed that "so respectable an Embassy and the Troops accompanying them would no doubt obtain an awfull impression on the minds of the Indians, as would be productive of the best consequences; at same time no doubt but they would proscribe the late iniquitous proceeding of the Land Speculators, who had brought on the Indian War." To be plain with you, my expectations on the occasion were sanguine, that such an appointment was purposely made to give us full and ample satisfaction in regard to our Land grievances, and that we should conclude a peace on as broad a bottom as one of Fox's or Shelburnes; but mark the end.

After the ceremony of mutual visits at our respective Camps, we proceeded to open the treaty, which I insisted should be conducted and concluded in my Camp; to which with some reluctance they assented, and the next day they came over to our Camp, when Genl. Lincoln gave out his Talk, and then put it, a Copy of his Commission and a draft of the intended Treaty into my hands, to consider of at leisure and give an answer. In the evening I assembled the Chiefs in my Tent, and explained the whole to them, together with the exceptionable parts of the Draft of Treaty. My particular objections were naturally enough pointed at the 2d Article, which ran that all Tribes and Individuals of the lower & upper Creeks, the Chiefs for themselves & Towns, & Tribes within the limits of the United States, do acknowledge the Creeks to be under the protection of the United States, and of no other Sovereign whosoever; and also that they are not to hold any Treaty with any State whatsoever. This I objected to, on the ground that it tended to annull the Treaties which we had already concluded with Spain, by which we held and enjoyed the most essential and im-

224. Washington appointed Benjamin Lincoln, Cyrus Griffin, and David Humphreys to act as commissioners (see their instructions in ASP IA, I, 65-68). They sailed from New York on August 31, reached Savannah on September 10, and set out at once for Rock Landing. They carried on a correspondence with the governor of Georgia and with their predecessors as commissioners, Osborne and Pickens (ibid., pp. 68-71). Benjamin Lincoln of Massachusetts was one of Washington's most trusted generals. He was severely wounded at Saratoga. At Yorktown he received Cornwallis' sword. In 1787 he led the force that put down Shay's Rebellion. Besides this Indian commission, he was sent in 1793 to try to arrange a treaty with the Indians north of the Ohio. Cyrus Griffin's chief claim to fame is that he was president of the Congress under the Articles of Confederation in 1788. David Humphreys had a reputation as a poet and a friend of Washington. He had been an aide-de-camp to the general during the Revolution and then accompanied him to Mount Vernon. From 1784 to 1786 he was in London and Paris as secretary of legation for Franklin, Adams, and Jefferson. Later he was first United States minister to Portugal. Brown and Dartmouth conferred upon him the degree of LL.D.

portant benefits and advantages; as well as it went to overthrow every pretension we had to an independent situation and while they demanded important sacrifices from us, they on their part held out to us, not the shade of an equivalent advantage for it.

The 3d Article related to boundary: to which I objected, on the ground that it by no means tended to remove our discontents; as not only that they insisted on a confirmation of all the Oconee Lands and the Southern branches, the encroachments on which by the Georgians was the sole cause of the contest between us; but that they went farther and demanded over the Georgian pretensions to the River St. Marys, including all the Islands & Streams of said River, the branches of which intersected the waters of St Johns in East Florida on the one side, and the branches on the other, spread out to the midst of the Semanolia Villages, and all Oka Finnoka swamps &a. &a.

In the morning I sent over a letter stating that we all concurred in objecting to the 2d. & 3d. Articles: upon which Col. Humphries came over to argue me out of my objections, but he did not succeed, and came over the two following days; and having no communication with Lincoln & Griffin, I concluded that they pitted that Gentleman against me, being fluent of Speech, and a great boaster of his political knowledge, and his assisting at the former Treaty with the Courts of Versailles, Berlin, &a. He shifted his ground, modes of attack in various shapes. The arts of flattery, ambition and intimidation were exhausted in vain. I at last told him by G——— I would not have such a Treaty cram'd down my throat. On his departure I told my Warriors that it was in vain to expect to bring them to do us the justice we wanted; my opinion was that as we came in a body, so we should retreat as peaceably as we came, and not to be laying there wrangling with them, lest bad consequences might ensue: So the next day I removed back to the Okmulgee where I was overtaken by Genl. Pickens, Cols. Few & Sanders, with the Holloing King. We had a long conversation, but I would not by any means consent to return to the Rock Landing, without they would pledge themselves that the Commissioners would consent to treat us as we wanted on equal terms:[225] This they could not do, so I remained obstinate to my purpose and came on.

Pickens I take to be a worthy moderate man: We got well acquainted, and I am sure if he had remained in his appointment, we should have come to some agreement.

On the whole I trust that our friends will approve of my conduct

225. Unless "the officers would pledge themselves that the Commissioners would make the Restitution of the Encroachment the Basis to conclude the Treaty upon" (McGillivray to Miró, December 10, 1789, AGI C 202).

in this late Negotiation, as I was resolved to be the honest man, and not sacrifice the interests of our friends and our own political good faith, to private interest and mercenary motives. I had notices that Washington had sent me various valuable presents, as a mark of his friendship, but I would receive nothing. To spare myself the mortification of a disagreeable interview, I decamped without the ceremony of taking leave. As I had a letter from Knox[226] the American Secretary at War as I left the Nation, I have to answer it; and I will communicate thro' him to Washington the whole particulars of the late Negotiation, and the cause of its being interrupted; advising that I shall be ready to renew them in the Spring in the Nation, and not out of it.

My Warriors behaved with great propriety; I forbid any to accept the least present, if we did not wholly agree.[227] I had nine hundred chosen men with me, and not a man would accept of any thing: The Commissioners had about four hundred men in arms with them.

I must confess that I was much attended to by all ranks there, and made many who had always professed themselves my bitter Enemies, change their Sentiments after a short acquaintance. I did not see McQueen, but I saw Billy Clark & he was desirous to get out again to Beards Bluff, and fifty more Adventurours if peace had been fully concluded.

The operation of the new Constitution is much dreaded by most of the better sort of the upper Gentry. In conversation with some of them, they asked me when & where I was going to settle my new State, for there was above 1500 families waiting my pleasures in Georgia. I trifled with and amused them. Three or four Colonels & Majors have bound themselves to correspond with me, and give me the soonest and best information of every public occurrence of their Country. A General and some Colonels, the most troublesome of our Neighbours, asked my opinion of coming out Westward. I encouraged them, as it is better to have them behind us than in our way. In short I have made one half traitors to their Country. What a sett of———![228] This Talk is a short warning: expect me early in November Dear Sir—Yours most truly ALEX: McGILLIVRAY. Tom Black has just given me yours.

136. *McGillivray to Leslie, October 12, 1789*
[Spanish translation in LC EF 116L9]

226. Knox to McGillivray, August 12, 1789, copy in AGI C 202. This letter contains an emphatic guaranty by the United States for the complete security of the Creeks who should attend the meeting at Rock Landing.
227. McGillivray therefore requested that Miró send fifty pieces of Limbourg, twenty dozen shirts, and twenty pairs of blankets to give to the chiefs and warriors who had attended this meeting (AGI C 202).
228. See also document 136, *infra*.

. . . .In a few days I came to be very popular with the generals, colonels, and majors of the tidewater people. Although I am not a sorcerer, I could manage them as I pleased. They are extremely ignorant and unpolished; each sentence that came from my mouth they took for pure gospel. They got it into their heads that I was going to establish a new state, and 1500 families were ready to present me petitions on this particular and to become my subjects. I amused myself and juggled with them until we parted.

One day before leaving home to go to this treaty, I received a despatch from Governor Miró[229] with favorable report of the benign condescension of our great protector King Charles IV, conceding us our trade on terms as advantageous as the Americans could or would wish to do, and even better, and confirming the guaranty of protection stipulated in the treaty of peace, friendship and alliance held in Pensacola in '84. These reports made me (to use the Indian expression) stout in my heart and strong in my mouth. Without these assurances I would have been in an embarrassing and painful situation dealing with Lincollen and Company. . . . .[230]

137. *Miró to McGillivray, January 12, 1790*
[Spanish copy in AHN E 3887]

NEW ORLEANS, January 12, 1790

I have received your letter of last December 10th.[231] I deeply regret the indisposition you have suffered, and I hope that this will find you entirely relieved and recovered.

I read with particular attention the account of the occurrences in September between the American commissioners and yourself with regard to the treaty of peace, and I observed then that the generous protection that his Majesty has so graciously afforded you has been well repaid by your unwillingness to accede to the 2d and 3d articles of the proposed treaty, which were contrary to those agreed upon and stipulated in the Congress of Pensacola. Nevertheless, I fear that your having broken off the conferences of the treaty, in the fashion that you did, will only enable the commissioners, misrepresenting your inten-

229. Document 130, *supra.*
230. But in another letter, McGillivray laid the failure of the treaty to the influence which Georgia had exerted upon the American commissioners (McGillivray to Miró, December 10, 1789, AGI C 202; see also document 138, *infra*, and Bowles to Carondelet, March 14, 1792, AGI C 2371). Writing from Lexington, Kentucky, on January 26, 1790, Wilkinson told Miró that the treaty failed because McGillivray insisted on a free port on the Atlantic. He advocated that McGillivray be ordered to make peace for four, five, six, or seven years, and that the time be used to diminish his authority (AGI C 2374). The commissioners in their report, *ut supra*, make no mention of a demand for a free port.
231. AGI C 202.

255

tions, to persuade the United States that you have taken this pretext to continue the hostilities, not being really disposed toward peace.

In any case I can do no less than approve your proper conduct in not giving them occasion for other complaints, having retired in good order without committing any hostile acts. You thus avoided putting any obstacles in the way of renewing the negotiations next spring, if the President of Congress is inclined to do so.

As there is time for it I am reporting everything to the captain general so that in view of what has happened he can give me the corresponding orders and I can, as he desires, advise you how to regulate your conduct in case the conferences are renewed, though by all indications it appears to me that there is little or nothing to add to what I have written to you, explaining the orders of his Majesty on this matter.

I have already given the necessary orders for 785 guns to be delivered to you, and by this opportunity I send the order to Pensacola. I have no doubt that you will be satisfied, for they assure me that they are of superior quality.

In respect to the fifty pieces of Limbourg, the twenty dozen shirts, and the twenty pairs of blankets that you request as presents for the chiefs and warriors who accompanied you to the last treaty, since this is an extraordinary present, it is necessary to await the orders of the captain general, which I will communicate to you as soon as I receive it.[232]

Wishing you all happiness, I remain, with the greatest esteem for you, your most attentive and constant servant,

ESTEVAN MIRÓ

Señor Don Alexandro McGillivray.

XII

THE TREATY OF NEW YORK

138. *Hawkins*[233] *to McGillivray, March 6, 1790*
[Copy in AGI C 203]

SIR   NEW YORK 6th March 1790

The communications I have had with you on several occasions and

232. Domingo Cabello, the new captain general at Havana, approved and transmitted this report to Valdés on March 5, 1790 (AHN E 3887). The Junta de Estado approved on June 14 (*ibid.*), and a royal order was issued on June 19 (AGI C 1431).
233. See note 41, *supra*.

my general Conduct will evince the Sincerity of my desire that the United States Should be on the most friendly terms with the Southern Indians & that the Connections Should be formed on principles of mutual advantage, properly Compatible with justice & humanity. If it were possible that any doubts remained in your mind respecting my former intentions, the subject of this Letter ought to banish them entirely.

You well know that I am intimately acquainted with the principles of the disputes between the State of Georgia & the Creek Nation; and all the various representations made by You & the Lower Creeks to the United States in Congress assembled, or their several Agents against that State.

Judge then of my Surprise when I learned that the mission of three uninterested dignified Characters Commissioned by the President of the U. States to enquire into & adjust the disputes between the State of Georgia & Creeks have proved abortive! That the cause of the disappointment appears principally to be a disinclination on your part & the other Chiefs to form any Treaty with the U. States & that your Conduct on the occasion fully Supported this opinion. By your thus refusing to treat with the U. States when so solemnly invited thereto you have placed yourself & Nation in a new & Critical Situation. The U. States have offered to interpose & settle the disputes on terms of mutual advantage which had arisen between part of their Citizens & your nation the Creeks, & you have apparently refused to Submit the disputes to a fair hearing & decision.

The main purport of this Letter is to place before you and the Creek Nation in Strong Colours, the exigence in which the Nation is involved, & to endeavour if possible to point out those evils which are impending & which you & the other Chiefs seem only to have power to Avert.

The U. States cannot advance one Step further, they have already proceeded to the utmost lengths that could be required of them either by the principle of Justice or humanity, and they will not be responsible for any Consequences that may ensue however dreadfull.

You and the other Chiefs seem desireous to preserve the peace. But you understand too well the feeble restraints your people are under to believe Seriously you can prevent partial hostillities, hence arises the extreme danger to which the Creek Nation is exposed. If you Strike, the U. States *must punish*, it will then become a Contest of power the events of which may be dissagreable and expensive to the United States, but the result must be ruin to the Creeks.

To prevent the Calamities which will ensue to Your Nation from

257

a war, well deserves your anxious Concern. Reflect well upon the Creeks & Compare their force with the power of the United States.

The U. States have the means of estimating properly the value of your Character. They are disposed to be favorable and friendly to You, but they Cannot Sacrifice their national Dignity and Justice. If then You Should be Seriously desireous of extricating the Creek Nation from their present embarrassed Situation, Manifest Candidly your disposition for that purpose, Come forward Yourself with a few of the principal Chiefs of the Upper & Lower Creeks to the President of the U. States, lay before him a real State of the Case, & I will answer with my Honour & my life that you will be received & treated with, on the footing of Justice & humanity.

Altho I am a Senator of the U. States I write entirely in my private Capacity. I feel the strongest desire to be instrumental in Averting those evils which according to the present train of things appear to be inevitable. Acting under the influence of these principles of humanity in which I shall ever Glory I have applied to the president of the U. S. for a passport for You and such other Chiefs as may be thought proper to accompany you. It has been granted me solely on the Condition that if you Should decline using it for the purposes intended, that it Should not be delivered. Should you on reflection judge that the measure proposed is one that would greatly benefit your Nation you will find that every Security & facility will be afforded you to embark at Charleston for this place.

Receive this Letter with the Candour it is written & let your Conduct thereon be open & undisguised. Artifices of which your Enemies accuse you would at this time be ill advised and immediately detected, & the result would be as pernicious as the most bitter Enemies of the Creeks could devise.

Colo. Marinus Willet[234] the bearer of this Letter is a Gentleman of Honour with whom I have fully Communicated on the subject of its Contents, and you may therefore Converse with him freely. I am persuaded that he will experience from You every attenention which his Rank & situation may require.

Remember that the United States are disposed to be favorable and friendly to you and that I Shall rejoice if my efforts Should prove Serviceable to your Nation.

I am with Sincere Esteem

234. Marinus Willett is well characterized in this and the following document. His Revolutionary activities were chiefly in western New York, at Oriskany and Oswego in particular. He was for a time sheriff of New York and subsequently mayor. See *A Narrative of the Military Actions of Col. Marinus Willett*, prepared from his manuscripts by his son (New York, 1831).

Sir

Your most obedt. & humble Servt.

BENJN. HAWKINS

Alexr. McGillivray Esqr.
Principal Chief of the Creeks.

139. *McGillivray to Panton, May 8, 1790*

[Copy in AGI C 203]

LITTLE TALLASSIE 8th May 1790

DEAR SIR

I acknowledge with pleasure the receipt of Your Letters of 19th & 22d ulto. At the request of our Upper Chiefs I was making a tour among their respective towns as well with a view to business as recreation, but of the Latter I found but little as I was pursued thro' all my rounds by the Rambling Agents of the Yassou Companys, some of whose Letters I inclose for your information.[235]

I have answered Moultrie &a. that I thank them for their good will & attention in offering me a Share in their entended Establishments but being of opinion the Sovereignty to these Lands would be contested by affairs & would be a main obstacle to my accepting of a Share or indeed to any one reaping any benefit from a Scheme of the nature he mentioned, besides our disputes & war with Georgia not being brought to a Conclusion their rights of Territory were still in dispute with us.

I am pleased to find that my arrangement with these wild Speculators is approved of. The Tennesee Companies Grant includes every foot of our, the Cherokees & Chickasaw Hunting Grounds. I drew my information from one Gordon a very Sanguine Talkative Chap, who was entrusted by Cox the Manager to Cajole me into measures by the most profuse and wild promises he could invent; Take Notice that the Tennesee Grant begins on the Great Bend of that River and down the River to the Mouth of Bear Creek below the Great Shoals and up the Creek to the Head, which interlocks with the head of 20 Mile Creek of the Chickasaw Nation a main Branch of Tombegbie & down to the main River, West to the Yassou and Mississippi. The Settlement is to Commence directly at Mouth of Bear Creek. One Hawkins a violent fellow with a pack of Desperadoes are to attempt it & this Grant I must

235. A. Ingles to McGillivray, February 19, 1790, AGI C 203. See also Alexander Moultrie's letter to McGillivray, February 19, 1790, *ibid.*, printed in the *Mississippi Valley Historical Review*, XVI, 391-94. It goes into more detail about the schemes of the land speculators and about the advantages that McGillivray might derive from accepting a share in the company. Documents 139 and 140, *infra*, indicate McGillivray's hearty disapproval.

directly oppose in force. The Virginia Grant is next N. E. of the latter. Such is the Sketch of this business. These fellows must think me as mercenary, base & unprincipled as themselves by presuming to address me on such a Subject. I had given an opinion of these Grants to Govr. Miro & I hope it will have the effect I desire to guard our Common Interest against these Vagrant Emigrants. It is the avowed intention & view of the Georgians in this business to effect a Strong Settlement at our Backs & as we may be hemmed in among them for purposes needless for me to explain to those who know any thing of our Situation and affairs; but I am determined to resist them (even if our allys & friends give their Sanction to them) at every risk.

Let me now turn your attention to another affair that engrosses mine at the moment; I have to announce to You the arrival of an Ambassador from New York a Colo. Marinus Willet expressly sent by the president Washington. This officer during the War was particularly distinguished for enterprise and success, & has since filled respectable offices. I find him just as Genl. Pickens a Candid and Benevolent Character, possessing abilitys but without Show or parade. His being Commissioned I find is in Consequence of that puppy Humphries report to the president, it being a very unfavorable one and asserted that I would not treat on any terms whatever, & gave as a proof my abrupt departure from the Treaty Ground without any reasons. So I find that my different notes to them objecting to certain Stipulations were never produced to the president; as for Lincoln he never Set foot in New York but kept on to Boston where he was first heard of.

Colo. Willet saw the report which was given out to have filled 300 Sheets of paper by those Enemies. He Says it only filled a Quire! there being other matters in it than the Treaty Transactions, Such as remarks & observations on the Country, proper places for fixing a Chain of forts, &ca. Numbers of Indian Towns one hundred & more.[236]

The report gave much Concern to all our Northern Friends which gave occasion to Genl. Washington Willet & others to read over all my Correspondence with Commissioners &ca. relative to our disputes with Georgia. It was agreed in opinion that the writer of those Letters from the Manner of reasoning in them, could not be such a man as was represented in the report, & it was proposed that some person who might be more agreable should visit me in person to learn the true State of the Matter & to renew those professions & assurances in the name of the president that were Contained in Genl. Knox's Letter & that as so many Commissioners for Concluding a Treaty of peace had failed

236. Printed in ASP IA, I, 78-79, and preceded by related correspondence, *ibid.*, pp. 68-78.

thro Error or misconduct; & it being the Sincere desire of the President & Congress to bring about an amicable & equitable accomodation of our Disputes & to assure us that not one acre of Land shall be asked of us, but rather restore whatever is usurped, the attempts to that purpose of any State to infringe on Indian Rights by force are Strongly reprobated & Washington wishes before his Career closes to see formal peace pervade the Land on all Sides.

We were Speaking last night of the Late act of the Georgia assembly of disposing of those Grants & of the ill tendency of them in regard to Indian hunting Grounds, that such measures would tend to frustrate every endeavour of the President to effect the General peace he has so much at heart. He informed me that the accounts had reached N. York with the addition that I was deeply concerned in them, this was not believed & it was recommended to the Georgians to revoke the Grants as it would farther embroil Matters & it appeared there was a view by that measure to drag the U. States into an Indian War, which if successfull after much loss of Blood and Treasure Georgia would reap the whole advantage. It is in this light that the Conduct of that State is looked on by the Northern States & that he Willet was instructed to assure me that Congress would by no means Countenance the prosecution of the intended Settlements, but that it depended much on my decision, for if I Supported it, it would be difficult for Congress or the president to Cancel the Grants in question as they wished. After arguing the foregoing & adding further Encouragement he pressed much on the Necessity of my Accompanying him to N. York with a few Chiefs. Such a measure would certainly give us peace and Security; for a Treaty concluded on at N. York ratified with the signature of Washington and McGillivray would be the bond of Long Peace and revered by Americans to a very distant period.

The foregoing being the substance of Colo. Willets Commission[237] I conceive his Communication to be of the highest importance & as there is not the most distant insinuation of a wish on their part to draw us into any engagements that may tend to operate against those we have already entered into with Spain, but on the Contrary to give Congress an opportunity of Defeating the late Grants to those Companys & to restore to & secure to us our Rights of Territory.

With these prospects held out to my view 1 have not hesitated to accept of the invitation. A month or two [of] Bodily fatigue is no con-

237. There is some question about the land grant issue being the sole or principal motive for inviting McGillivray to New York. Washington's published papers are not enlightening on this point. The explanation, however, seems plausible, and it does not appear to be the sort of explanation that it might have occurred to McGillivray to fabricate (see Panton's comment in document 143, *infra*).

sideration against the obtaining & securing the blessings of peace with its advantages for my country. To avoid the importunities of the Caro. Compy. I shall avoid a passage by Sea from Charleston. I take a land route from Genl. Pickens's who has a Company of Horses to escort me to Salisbury & then relieved by others on to Richmond Virginia, thence by Stages to N. York.

I herewith write Govr. Miro on the subject.[238] This decision of mine Cannot afford the least Ground of Alarm or Suspicion to my Friends. My Conduct on every occasion has evinced to them the integrity & uprightness of my dispositions toward the Engagements we Entered into & which now Subsists between my Nation & theirs. I have hitherto resisted every private Consideration of Interest that have been so often offered me with a view to Warp me from my present Connexions & as the Governor has always encouraged me to make peace with the Americans & preserve our alliance & Treaty, clear of them, I am Certain he will be pleased at my going to N. York, and Satisfied with the objects I have in view by Undertaking that Journey.

These Companys have had the other day a Taste of what they have to expect. Three Large Boats with Swivels full of Hawkins Settlers coming down with the intended Settlement, a party of the Creeks & Cherokees attacked them during which one of the Boats drifted near Shore where She was boarded & 27 Men were found Killed & five Wounded. The Admiral with Small cannon coming up the Indians Could not destroy her.

Those that escaped had a quantity of ammunition for the Chickesaws. A number of Piomingo's men met the Cherokees & abused them much for Spoiling their talk, & threatned soon to be Supported in War against them & the Creeks. Every thing urges to a speedy issue with Washn. or at least an attempt to it.

I refer you to the inclosed for Your information & Amusement;[239] the Broken days are gone to the Cowettas for a meeting. I sett out in Eight days, & the bearer can be back a few days after my return from thence.

May God preserve & prosper You is the Constant Wish of Yours

ALEX: McGILLIVRAY

Wm. Panton Esqr.

238. AGI C 203. The letter is very similar to this one to Panton, but with the addition of a request for $20,000 annually in goods to encourage the Creek warriors to defend the western territories. He represented that it would in the end prove a great saving to the king, for it would "procure as much Service or more as from ten regiments of Troops." See also the postscript to document 140, *infra*.

239. A. Ingles to McGillivray, February 19, 1790, AGI C 203.

140. *McGillivray to Leslie, May 20, 1790*
[Spanish translation in LC EF 114J9]
COWETAS IN THE LOWER CREEK NATION, 20 May 1790

. . . .Osborn's propositions in the Georgia Assembly were made on his own initiative and without my concurrence. I have no more ambition than you or Panton for the honor of being granted citizenship among such vagabonds. As Osborn is one of the western speculators, I took his ideas in what he did. All the individuals cited above as my correspondents have set forth how much they have tried to procure me the right of citizenship and the restitution of my rich estates. In that event I would certainly be opulent and independent, but I will make no sacrifice to attain it, notwithstanding that my present means fall far short of abundance. For I am only considered worth the miserable pay of an interpreter, and if it were not for my connection with the house of Panton, Leslie, and Company I would literally die of hunger in the service of a powerful king. I have suggested repeatedly, without effect, the necessity of a liberal Indian establishment. . . . .[240]

[P. S.] I cannot refrain from availing myself of this cover to remark that all the eagerness which Washington shows to treat with me on such liberal terms is not based, I am persuaded, on principles of justice and humanity. Rather I believe that his true end is that of restraining the malevolence of the northern and eastern states against the southern, and although I would prefer to conclude the negotiations in my own land, I think that it would be better for our interests and for those of our friends for me to go to New York. There is still time for Spain to protect her western possessions. If she does her part we shall do ours. An expenditure of 15 to 20,000 pesos annually would get the most effective services of the red warriors, worth more than ten regiments of whites in this sort of warfare.

A.M.

141. *Leslie to McGillivray, May [31], 1790*
[Spanish translation in LC EF 116L9]
ST. AUGUSTINE, FLORIDA, 13 May 1790[241]

DEAR SIR

Yesterday Gray brought me your favor of the 20th instant.[242] He

240. The portions of this letter here omitted resemble very closely document 139, *supra.*
241. This date is obviously incorrect, since the letter is in answer to McGillivray's of May 20. It probably was written on May 31.
242. Document 140, *supra.*

tells me that you will doubtless be *en route* to New York before he could return to you; in consequence that it is useless for me to write to you by him.

But I can now avail myself of this opportunity to answer your favor by the bearer, our mutual friend Captain Carlos Howard, who by chance is about to make an excursion, which he has contemplated for some time past to the northern States in order to get for his health a change of climate and the benefits of the sea air.

It being highly probable that you will meet in New York, and although you can be held acquaintances and friends (since this had arisen only by written correspondence and the great understanding you each have of the other's character) I cannot allow this occasion to pass without availing myself of the pleasure of being the introducer of you to each other, thus making possible for both of you a communication more familiar than that which has been feasible between two persons separated by a distance of more than five hundred miles.

I know that Don Carlos, on his part, has had for some years past a sincere appreciation and veneration for your public character, and has frequently shown an alert desire to know you personally, and to give you proof of his esteem and friendship. He has seen much of the world, and to his experience of men and things he has joined an equally general and extensive knowledge of books and of the various branches of literature, which makes him with people of education an agreeable and diverting individual of society, whenever the state of his health and strength permit him the full exercise of his talents.

If you meet in New York, it will be in his power to introduce you to the Spanish minister in case you do not carry letters from the Governors, Miró or ONeille. Anyhow you will find him useful in other ways, for I am persuaded that he will be most happy to render you every possible service in any affair in which you conceive that he can contribute to further your views or facilitate your wishes, especially in connection with any communications that you may have to make to the Spanish governors or even to the court at Madrid.

He has seen your letter of the 20th instant, and at my request he has communicated its contents to Governor de Zespedes, who approves and agrees with your explanation of the generous conduct of General Washington, hoping that there will result from it equitable and decorous conditions of peace between your nation and the United States, and that through it the future pacific and unmolested possession of your hunting grounds and territories, as also your own property, will be assured on a permanent footing by virtue of the reciprocal pacts which he (the governor) is confident will not be opposed to or even interfere with those which you have already entered into with Spain, which, I must say, has seemed to me invariably since the last peace to be (in preference to any other power) the most natural friend, ally, and protector of the southern Indians.

For my part I wish and I pray God from the innermost part of my heart that you will have all success in your negotiation, and I flatter myself (whatever other advantages of a public or national nature your prudence and conduct can achieve in this crisis) that an occasion now offers to add a new luster to the reputation and importance that you have already acquired, through a further exhibition to the world on a theater so public and in a negotiation so arduous and interesting, of the ability and wisdom with which God has endowed you, as also of the honor and good faith which have thus far marked and distinguished your political career.

You can readily understand how anxious I shall be to learn something of the progress of your negotiation, but especially of its happy termination. Consequently, permit me to ask you to do me the favor (whenever an opportunity by sea offers and you are not too busy in New York) to write me something on the matter, as much to inform Panton as me. And with this request, I close, wishing you, after the happy completion of every object of this journey, a happy return to your own country, accompanied by applause and renown. I am with great appreciation, Dear Sir, your most obedient humble servant.

JOHN LESLIE

Señor Don Alexander MacGillivray.

142. *McGillivray to Miró, June 2, 1790*

[AGI C 203]

LITTLE TALLASSIE, 2d June 1790

. . . .Your Excellency will see from this Communication[243] that there is a fair prospect of terminating our long & disagreeable Contest with Georgia in a Manner favorable to our Interests, by removing the Causes of our discontents, & I am of opinion that I ought by no means to reject the propositions now offerd, as the ground of treaty between our Nations & the United States. I have good reasons for desiring to Conclude a good Peace. A number of our frontier towns are getting weary of a Contest & war that diverts their attention

243. Willett's arrival is reported in the first paragraphs, here omitted. In the final paragraphs, McGillivray asked Spain to assign the Creeks twenty thousand pesos annually. Miró concluded that this request was due to the importance McGillivray believed he had acquired by having been invited by Washington and Congress. Miró urged additional commissaries for the Southern Indians (Miró to Valdés, August 10, 1790, AGI C 177).

for so long a time from their Indespensible occupations, & we can promise to ourselves no Solid or real advantages by wishing to maintain an eternal Contest & War, in preference to Peace. I am Sensible that we coud rely on Your usual Support in a just Cause at Same time I could not expect to draw You into countenancing our Nation in mad hostile measures. Thinking as I do, I have not hesitated to resolve to accompany the Commissioner Colo. Willet to New York, & in the event of my concluding a treaty of Peace with the United States I shall adhere to the Caution which You have repeatedly given me & containd in your last letter "transact Your business with the United States so as to be at Peace with them but no other connexion the least woud give umbrage to our present good Intelligence."

The Intelligence which Your Excellency gives me of the present disposition of the Infatuated Chickasaws is exact & agreeable to the Information I have received from other quarter. The Agents of the New Western Companys, (of whom I informd you in a former letter) are assiduous in drawing over the foolish Chickasaws to assist their Schemes of usurpation. In this Situation of affairs Your Excellency woud do well to observe to the Chickasaw & Choctaw Nations, that You see with Surprise & regret the mad & foolish Conduct of certain of their people, who were forward in assisting the Schemes & designs of the Americans to encroach on & usurp the western waters, & of their pretending to dispose of a Country not their own, that they had no longer the pretence that necessity for want of trade was the Cause of their encouraging American Settlers & encroachments, as the King had orderd Stores of Goods for their Conveniency at the usual places of trade & if they did not alter their mad Conduct, You coud easily Convince them that You were the only people they coud obtain a trade from, & that the allys & friends of the King the Creeks & their Confederates were determined to Support & defend their claims & rights to a free use of the hunting Grounds on the Western Waters, against the Americans & their Indian friends & that in such a Case You coud not think of permitting them to receive any ammunition etc. from Mobile & &, so that they must perish &c. Such language will I think have its good effects.

I have endeavourd to obtain every Information on the Subject of the foundation of the three new Companys, & I find from good Authority, that the Grants of the Western territory was an act of the Georgians, in their private Capacity that Congress was not consulted about the measure & they have not approvd of it, & that Congress had advised the Georgians to revoke their act, which has raised a ferment in the minds of the Interrested, & the State was much agitated & divided about it. However one thing is certain that the Agents or Managers of the Companys are making the greatest exertions to effect a Speedy Settlement of their respective Grants that by the aid of the Chickasaws they may hold possession against any resolve of Congress to the contrary. In Consequence of such measures I am apprehensive that a rupture must soon take place between us & the Chickasaws which makes me desirious to close matters as far as possible with the Congress. The offers which are now made us by the President of the U. S. I do not consider as resulting from principles of Justice & humanity but on the Contrary as proceeding from their poverty & Inability to Support & maintain a Vigorous Contest to reduce us by force. It is better to treat with an enemy under Such circumstances, than a more powerful one.

My letters from Pensacola of 20' Ulto. gives me no account of the arrival of any Goods from You on our account. If they Shoud after this arrive they will be kept till my return, which I propose God willing to be in October next. I go by Land through the American States for my Curiosity. Independent of other Considerations I think I can best serve our own & the Kings Interests by the Joureny. Tho I do not pretend to the ability of a Machiavel in Politics, Yet I can find out from my Slender abilities pretty near the disposition of the American Politics so far as they respect the Spanish Nation, & Your Excellency may depend on receiving a faithfull account of every matter whenever I may return. . . . .

143. *Panton to Mir6, July 12, 1790*
[AGI C 203]
PENSACOLA 12th July 1790

MUCH ESTEEMED SIR

I wrote Your Excellency a long letter on the 4th Instant and I now mean to finish my narrative as briefly as I can.

From the Chickasaws to the Creekes is a distance of three hundred miles and upwards, and after taking so long a Journey, to see McGillivray, You will easily Conceive how much I was mortified to find him from home, but it seems he despaired of my perseverance at so hot a Season and therefore Yielded the more readily to the persuasion of the Envoy from the President who urged his departure with marked Sollicitude.

I enclose You duplicates of his letter to me that he wrote on the eve of his departure from which and Mr. Hawkins's letter[244] Your Excellency will learn his motives for this unexpected Expedition. If he suc-

244. Documents 139 and 138, *supra.*

ceeds in the objects he has in view, and obtains a reasonable peace without infringing on his prior engagements to Spain, I shall most sincerely rejoice, but I confess to You that I doubt it much.

It is very true that the President, and Congress too, may be opposed to those Georgia Grants, because they Consider all the western Lands within the limits of the United States as the property of the Union, and not belonging to any particular State, and therefore on that principal they will Contest the right that Georgia claims to sell those immense tracts of Land, but as neither of their pretentions are considered as fully valid, without a cession from the Indians, both partys are striving who shall be first in obtaining that title, so that their pretension to Justice and humanity is all a buble and it is obvious to me that McGillivray will find it so before he returns. I wish I had seen him before he went, but I have nevertheless Confidence enough in his Steadiness to rely that he will reject any overture which may be made to him, that can be Considered injurious to Spain or disgracefull to himself and friends.

I enclose You duplicates of two letters to him from Carolina Gentlemen, which, while they lay open the whole scheme of those Companys they will also Show You their uncommon Sollicitude to obtain his Sanction and to get him to partake in their Speculation. Even I, have had my offers, and the Georgians would remove my name from their Confiscation and banishment Laws if they could be but certain of its being agreeable to me and that I would join them in their favourite scheme. This hint I have had from a Man who proffesses himself my friend. The proposition not coming from Men in authority I take no notice of it, but if they have the presumption to make it to myself, You shall see it, with my answer. In the meantime be You satisfied that they have not wherewithall to bribe me to come into a measure my mind disapproves of, no, not even for Washington himself, had he the thirteen United States in his Belly.

In Mr. Moultries letter Your Excellency will perceive that he brags of having a chactaw Grant for the front of the Yassou Lands, and I enformed You in my last that I had reason to believe such a deed had been Signed by a few chiefs in the Year 1785. This Circumstance however ought not to retard any measure You may deem proper to prevent those Speculators from taking possession of the Lands. By right of conquest the Land is Yours, as far as ever the English possessed, & moreover I have allways understood that the chactaws made over the sovereignty of all their possessions to the King of Spain at the Congress of Mobille in the Year 1784. If therefore Your Court resolves to establish Your right, do not hesitate [to] go as far as You mean to support.

America may grumble but she is not in a Condition to strike and the best natural barriers that I know of in all america is the mouth of the Ohio. In the great bend of that river where the Cherokee river falls into it there is an old French Fort standing which might soon be repaired and made sufficient to command both rivers and would effectually prevent any bodys of Men from falling down them to molest Your Settlements below. There is the proper spot to build Your new City, from thence You may carry on Your Commerce with the Americans above You, all Communication betwixt Your Settlements below and the americans would be cut off. Those rafts of Enemys who pass through the Indian Nations would be stoped, and the Inhabitants of Kentucky Cumberland Holstein French Broad &c being by the nature of the Country Separated from the Eastern States would find it their Interest to live on good terms with You. The Cherokee river would then become the line of division betwixt Spain and the United States, and that Nation would of Course become the Carrier of the whole produce that will be made on the River Mississippie.

These are hints which occured to me in the course of my Journey and I give them to You with the freedom of a friend. If Your Excellency sees any of them worthy of attention; well—if not, Consign them to the flames and forgive me for taking up so much of Your time. One thing more before I conclude, there is Doctor O Fallen[245] who is Soon to be round at New Orleans, his rout is by way of Kentucky. That Man altho' now unacquainted with Mr. McGillivray or our House expresses an uncommon degree of friendship for both. He says that he is known to the Governors of Luisianna and East Florida and writes something of his being employed by the Court of Spain. Yet at the same time, You will see by Mr. Moultries letter that he is very intimate with those Land Speculators. The Man writes well, is intelligent and has given McGillivray some hints respecting his Personal Safety on a former occasion which I believe were genuine, but his proffessions of friendship seem too profuse and indicates design. If Your Excellency knows him to be a good man be so good as to let me know him also. You will notice that Mr. Moultrie Writes of their having agents in Kentucky, Yassou, and in New Orleans. If they are open agents they cannot do much harm, but if Secret ones Your Excellency will no doubt detect them. Congress is Said to be very Secret in what concerns the South Western territory.

245. As agent for the South Carolina Yazoo Company, James O'Fallon carried on an extensive correspondence with Miró. Proceeding to Kentucky, he sought support in that quarter, and acquired a measure of it by marrying a daughter of George Rogers Clark. Washington issued a proclamation against him in 1791; two years later he was associated with Gênet's conspiracy. See J. C. Parish, "The Intrigues of Doctor James O'Fallon," *Mississippi Valley Historical Review*, XVII (1930), 230-63.

Whenever any thing is argued relative to it the Gallery is cleared and the doors closed. It is reported that 20,000 men is voted for the service of the Year and that the President is moreover empowered in Case of an Eventual War to increase the Army to 70,000 Men besides Militia on his own Authority, but this wants Confirmation. It is likeways mentioned that John Jay is gone to England to negotiate a treaty of Commerce and eventual Union but this is all hearsay news.

It is a pity Your Court and that of England do not unite in keeping down the growth of those spurious upstarts whose influence and example has already had such banefull effects on the Power of Kings. But here I must stop for I find my letter is Spinning out to an unpardonable lenth and I have already transgressed too far on Your Excellencys time.

I am with the utmost Esteem
    Dr Sir
        Your Obliged & very Humble Servt.

                Wm. Panton [rubric]

His Excellency Govr. Miró

144. *Howard to McGillivray, July 18, 1790*
       [Spanish translation in AGI C 182]

              Philadelphia, July 18, 1790.

Dear Sir:

When I got permission, about the middle of last May, to come to this country for a change of climate (you will recall that since the beginning of our correspondence my health has been delicate) I little thought that this would facilitate the long desired pleasure of dealing with you personally. Consider, then, how agreably surprised I was, two days before I started on my journey, to know the contents of your letter dated May 20[246] which you wrote to our mutual friend, announcing your meditated trip to New York. This letter, which I have read and reread, clearly demonstrates the integrity and disinterestedness of your intentions, but permit me to ask: are you certain that those that invited you are motivated by principles equally generous? To tell the truth, your letter answers the question, for you state expressly that you do not believe that liberality or humanity could have played any part in the invitation. To urge this subject further to a person of the penetration for which you are known, would be a reprehensible presumption on my part, and even more so to propose to offer him advice. Nevertheless, wishing nothing but good to you and your friends, and may I add

246. Document 140, *supra.*

270

without flattery, esteeming you for your persistent patriotism, I submit the following suggestions for your mature reflection.

Spain, as the enclosed letter clearly shows, is the only ally and natural protector of the redskins of the south: without reserving to herself any emolument, she has granted them a trade equal to all their needs and free from any tariff; she has not asked for, and will never ask for the cession of an inch of ground. The Americans will not act thus. They are an industrious people, stingy and commercial, although weak and still lacking in strength; therefore, they will aspire to enrich themselves with Indian trade; but this they cannot do without raising considerably the current prices of the merchandise that you need. Very little of such merchandise is manufactured in America; hence it must be imported and a tariff must be paid; to this must be added the increased cost of transporting by land to the Indian borders.

You will easily understand that the route through which up to the present time your nation has received the necessary supplies is less troublesome and more rapid than any which could be supported by the United States.[247] Perhaps they will lead you to understand that this route will be cut in case there is a rupture (of which there are already rumors) between Spain and Great Britain. But even in such a case you must keep in mind that since the beginning your friends took the precaution of stipulating neutrality with respect to Indian trade.

As far as territorial rights are concerned I do not doubt that you are aware that it is possible and even probable that for the present they will concede to the Indians the full and peaceful possession of all the lands that they are disputing, and to you, your particular claims; but it is also evident that at some future date, when your territory will have ceased all its present relations with Spain, not only the disputed lands, but also the last foot of the Creek territory will be gradually usurped, until you will cease to be a nation. Turn your eyes toward the north; reflect on what those tribes were in past times, and realize what they are today. The English and the French were in truth the first usurpers, but the Americans have already begun to imitate them, and will continue to do so until they have reduced the Creeks to the same level in which are now those who were once powerful, their now almost annihilated northern brothers.

Do not imagine, esteemed sir, that I even remotely wish that there should not be a permanent peace between your nation and the United States: far be it from me to have such thoughts! In all that is compatible with the duty of a good Spaniard, my personal inclinations are in favor

247. The reverse was more nearly true. See Panton to Miró and Navarro, May 9, 1787, AGI C 200.

of the Americans and of their illustrious president; moreover, my sovereign is on friendly terms with the United States, and if they have as honest intentions as Spain has, and I have no reason for believing the contrary, they will not attempt or even desire through a treaty to adopt measures which will destroy the connections have that existed for a long time between the Creek nation and the Spaniards. They are not ignorant of the nature of these connections. You have made them known to them before now in a letter to the Governor of South Carolina,[248] and later, still more clearly to the commissioners of the Congress at Rock Landing on the Oconee River. For saying all this I have no other authority nor impulse than that inspired in me by the sincere esteem that I have repeatedly professed for you and your people; of whom, you will readily agree, for more than six years I have shown myself to be a disinterested friend in all that has depended on my small influence. The same esteem has led me to seek an explanation in New York as to the object and consequences of your trip, from the distinguished Baron Don Josef Ignacio de Viar, provisional successor of his Excellency, Don Diego de Gardoqui, whose maxims, always favorable to you and your friends, he has adopted as his own. This gentleman has assured me that he will gladly, and without delay, address to his Excellency the Secretary of State whatever new propositions you may have to make to the Court at Madrid, and he does not doubt that they will receive due attention. I give you my word that I am of the same opinion, and I firmly believe that you will do well to take advantage of this opportunity. I do not know whether I will be able to have this letter and the one enclosed delivered to you within or outside of New York; however that may be, I will introduce you to Don Josef in that city, if you so desire. It will be very wise for you to communicate to him in writing, either through me, or by any other means that you deem convenient, all the questions that may be treated by you and the Congress or its commissioners. I will appreciate your sending me your reply in the proper form, and with the same reserve as you receive this one: it would be a sure way of arousing jealousy in the hearts of many, although God knows that neither your attitude nor mine is inimical to the United States or opposed to concluding peace. For a a long time you have been aware of my character, which, I take leave to say, is that of a man of honor and of a friend. Please keep this in mind, and let me know in what ways I can be of service to you, and you may be sure that I will strive to prove that I am your ever faithful servant and passionate admirer.   CARLOS HOWARD

Señor Don Alexandro McGillivray.

248. See note 173, *supra.*

145. *McGillivray to Howard, August 11, 1790*
[Spanish translation in AGI C 182]

NEW YORK, August 11, 1790

DEAR SIR:

The serious illness which has troubled me ever since my arrival has prevented me until now, from replying to the subjects suggested in the paper that you put in my hands in Philadelphia.[249] I now take advantage of this leisure moment to write you something in answer to that paper. Our friend Mr. Leslie has good reason for saying in his letter to me that Spain is the natural protector of the Southern Indian Nations. This is not only my opinion but also the general one of those who are fairly well informed about our situation; all consideration of a sane policy should dispose her to such a protection. It is of equal importance for the interests of the Indian Nations that they be closely connected with Spain; according to these principles I negotiated and concluded a treaty of peace and alliance, with the officials of the king authorized to that effect, which was founded on the permanent basis of reciprocal convenience; and it is not my intention or my desire to sacrifice said treaty to new projects.

I certainly should not have hastened to accept the invitation to make a treaty in this place if our situation were such as to encourage me to run the risk involved; anyway, I am sanctioned in this measure by the advice of Governor Miro and others to whom I have always communicated our public affairs without reserve, and of whom I have asked at all times advice for my government. He has repeated to me his desires that I conclude peace with the Americans, respecting at all times our treaty with Spain; which treaty (I inform you in passing) was never confirmed or ratified, as he himself has confessed, and the aids and helps which have been given us to sustain and carry on our claims and rights were, after a fashion, snatched by force; for on an urgent occasion, these aids were lent me scantily and with reluctance. Our trade, in truth, is put on an equal footing with the extension of our desires; and it has been of infinite utility to my nation.

For this we are duly grateful; nevertheless, having reflected on everything maturely, I feel justified in concluding a peace with the United States, although it is not equal to our claims and desires. My refusal of the American propositions of peace at Rock Landing last September came near to causing very serious consequences, and in spite of the fact that the proceedings of the Georgians toward us are generally condemned, my hasty refusal was considered by the President as an insult to the dignity of the United States, and if I had not come to this city,

249. Documents 141 and 144, *supra.*

Congress would have undoubtedly declared war against us; in which circumstances we would have had much to fear situated as we were, especially since the new government is established on a basis which renders it capable of making war on us in a fashion that would assure them a complete success. In that case the terms prescribed to us by the Americans would leave us very little or nothing; and we could not very well count on the efficacious measures in our favor on your part, for as the offered and stipulated guaranty had never been confirmed we had no solid basis for supposing or hoping that Spain would go into a war in order to sustain our claims.

These motives have led me to agree to the following articles of peace[250] to end our disputes. The first stipulation required of us was an unqualified recognition of the sovereignty of the United States over us. I opposed this article. After much debate it was modified, to extend over those parts of our nation which lie within the boundaries of the United States. It did not seem to me worth while to cavil on this point, being persuaded that Spain would sustain and maintain her claims against the pretension that the United States makes to 31° north latitude on the Mississippi, etc.; therefore, we would remain in our former state. Another stipulation was directed toward taking our trade from its present source. After much debate it was decided to defer the consideration of this point until the end of two years;[251] and it seemed to me the best way to escape this article, the most difficult point to adjust. It occupied us several days, because the Georgians and other interested persons insisted that the cessions made to them should be confirmed on the part of our nation. These lands had been alienated and populated and could not be restored except by force, and force could not be employed against the citizens, nor their blood shed. I agreed that an arbitrary line should be drawn on the Oconee River for which the United States should make us immediately a compensation of ten thousand dollars in merchandise, and two thousand dollars annually; the United States surrendering all claims up to the new Georgian line, from the branch of the Alatamaya to the source of the St. Marys River and its various springs, the old British boundary over that river being included, and the United States being a guarantor of all future usurpations on the part of their citizens.

These articles, with some regulations to maintain good order between us, compose the treaty, and everything considered, I am thankful that it did not turn out worse.

Being in general little influenced by personal considerations I did

250. A fair summary of the treaty as printed in ASP IA, I, 81-82.
251. See the secret article, *ibid.*, p. 80.

not stipulate anything with respect to my estates in Georgia and South Carolina, although I will ask said states to return them to me, and if they do not do so the union will compensate me. Some time ago those of Carolina left my estate at my disposal. I resisted, as much as I decently could, accepting the honorary badge of Brigadier General; finally, tired of being repeatedly pressed to do so, I agreed to add this plumage to my cap.

The foregoing is an exact compendium of my negotiations here, which I give with candor and without reserve,[252] and I flatter myself that no part of the treaty can give just motive for suspecting that I failed to fulfill my obligations. Now I must repeat a plea which I have made many times; to wit: that the true aims and dispositions of the ministry in respect to our affairs be communicated to me. The time is critical and it is absolutely necessary that there exist between us a clear, explicit, and confidential communication in place of the vague and ambiguous procedure which up to the present has existed between us, and which has only served to perplex my mind and to embarrass our public affairs. Let certain articles and stipulations be formed and agreed upon, which must be duly confirmed and ratified by the King; let us have a certain rule by which to govern ourselves to our satisfaction, through lack of which we have been induced to adopt certain measures which otherwise might not have been adopted. I refer to the stipulations, to the guaranty of offensive alliance and commerce of the Treaty of Pensacola of the year '84.

And let there be a liberal establishment of officials of the department in the nation. It is a well known fact that I am not greedy, but a former ruling hurt my feelings, when I was placed on the same basis as a common interpreter, a stipend which long ago I have refused to accept. We lack two interpreters with comfortable salaries.

I was almost forgetting to say that I protested strongly against the behavior of the new western companies, in the terms in which Georgia has formed them, and I have the word of the government that said companies will be broken up.

Having concluded all our affairs in this city, I desire to start my homeward journey at the end of this week for the St. Marys River. I end this letter wishing you a happy, agreeable trip to St. Augustine, begging you to give my regards to our friend Mr. Leslie, since I have no time to write to him now. This letter is written in terms which will give you to understand that it was finished after various interruptions.

252. McGillivray did not mention that he had been put on a salary of $100 a month, or that he had taken an oath of allegiance to the United States.

With the most affectionate expression of esteem and attention, I remain, Dear Sir, yours as usual,

ALEXANDER McGILLIVRAY

Señor Don Carlos Howard, Captain of the Regiment of Hibernia, etc.

146. *Viar to Quesada,*[253] *August 13, 1790*

[Spanish original in AGI C 1436]

DEAR SIR:

As I have already been informed by your official letter of the 17th of last month that the former governor of that place, Don Vizente Manuel de Zéspedes, set out for Havana on the 16th of that month, I reply to you saying that the Captain and Secretary by commission, Don Carlos Howard, who, as announced in your previous letter, was to come here, arrived the 14th of last June and delivered to me the official letter of that governor. It contained a translation of the letter of the mestizo, Alexander MacGillivray, which was written to John Leslie of that city, and the original letter of the latter to the mestizo, which he brought with him, enclosed with the official letter.

It seemed to me very convenient that Don Carlos should go to Philadelphia to wait for the mestizo in order to deliver the letter to him together with one that he has prepared for him.

In spite of the fact that the said Don Carlos was reputed here and at Philadelphia to be a suspicious character and that he always had people around him,[254] he took advantage of an opportune occasion to hand them to McGillivray, who received him with great joy, and promised they would see each other in this city.

On the 21st of last month he arrived at this city with three kings and twenty-seven chiefs of his Creek Nation, and they were received hardly less highly than royal persons.

The next day he came to visit me, together with General Knox, the Secretary of War (whom the States have appointed as commissioner to effect the treaty that we know about) and Mr. Jefferson, Secretary of State.

I returned the visit as it behooved me, and in the houses in which I have seen him since, he has been very cordial to me, as well as to Don Carlos, to whom he has promised to reply to the letter of John Leslie, and if he does so, I will communicate at once what happens.

253. Juan Nepomuceno de Quesada succeeded Zéspedes as governor of East Florida while McGillivray and Howard were in New York. He seemed to be less warm toward McGillivray than his predecessor had been.

254. Hamilton said of Howard, "We have every reason to think that he has been using endeavours to check or even to frustrate our negotiations with the Creek Indians, and with this view he has made them large presents in this city; this we consider as perfectly unwarrantable" (*Canadian Archives, 1890*, p. 150).

276

In spite of the fact that these people have guarded him closely,[255] and that he has been ill for a few days at the home of General Knox, where he has lodged since his arrival, we have been able to speak to him occasionally, taking advantage of all opportunities that have presented themselves. Up to the present he has appeared to be attached to us, but time will tell.

On the 10th instant at the home of the President he assured Don Carlos that he had concluded his treaty, that he had planned the reply to John Leslie's letter, and would deliver it to him on the evening of the 11th at the home of General Knox. If this happens thus, I will notify you at once, adding that he was uncertain whether he would depart for the St. Marys River and that if he did he would pass through your town.

If this does happen, I hope that you will know how to treat him, for I expect that his friendship will be very useful to us. This is not only my opinion, but it was always also that of the envoy Don Diego de Gardoqui, as you will see in the official letters that he wrote on this matter to your predecessor Don Vizente Manuel de Zespedes.

I consider very wise your predecessor's determination to have commissioned Captain Carlos Howard to carry that letter, not only for security, but also because in the present affair I could not have had at my side a person more trustworthy nor better instructed concerning all transactions and able to throw light on all matters that come up.

Finally, although the mestizo has not replied to the letter that John Leslie wrote to him from your city, he has done what is equivalent by addressing one to Don Carlos, which the latter is taking with him in order to present to you.

By this letter, and by the account that Don Carlos gives you, you will be informed personally of all that has happened in relation to this mestizo during his stay in this city.

May God preserve you many years. New York, August 13th, 1790.

JOSEF YGNACIO DE VIAR [*rubric*]

Duplicate

P. S. Today, August 13th, the treaty has been ratified in the House of Representatives. Little do they suspect that I know its contents.

Señor Don Juan Nepomuceno de Quesada

255. Major George Beckwith was at New York for the British in 1790 in a capacity not unlike that of Howard for the Spaniards. His request for an interview with McGillivray, to inquire whether Bowles and the Indians with him at Quebec were authorized representatives of the Southern Indians, was answered by Alexander Hamilton, who said that the United States was not satisfied with the conduct of the Spanish agent Howard and therefore might not find it consistent to give Beckwith such permission. The interview, however, was arranged (*Canadian Archives*,

147. *Extract from the* Pennsylvania Packet and Daily Advertiser, *August 18, 1790*

[Printed copy in AGI C 2362]

NEW YORK, August 14—Yesterday the treaty of peace and friendship between the United States and the Creek nation was solemnly ratified by the contracting parties, in Federal Hall, in the presence of a large assembly of citizens. The vice-president of the United States—the great officers of state—his excellency the governor—and of several members of both houses of Congress.

At 12 o'clock the President of the United States, and his suite—general Knox, the commissioner; the clerks of the department of the secretary of war; colonel M'Gillivray, and the kings, chiefs, and warriors of the Creek nation being assembled, the treaty was read by the secretary of the president of the United States.

The president then addressed colonel M'Gillivray, the kings, chiefs and warriors; he said that he thought the treaty just and equal; and stated the mutual duties of the contracting parties: which address was communicated sentence after sentence, by Mr. Cornell, sworn interpreter, to all of which the Creeks gave an audible assent.

The president then signed the treaty, after which he presented a string of beads as a token of perpetual peace, and a paper of tobacco to smoke in remembrance of it: Mr. M'Gillivray rose, made a short reply to the president, and received the tokens.

This was succeeded by the shake of peace, every one of the Creeks passing this friendly salute with the president; a song of peace, performed by the Creeks, concluded this highly interesting, solemn and dignified transaction. . . . .[256]

1890, pp. 150-51 and 153-56). The Spaniards were also concerned about the Indian delegation to Halifax, Quebec, and London (see Las Casas to O'Neill, July 25, 1790, AGI C 105; and Miró to Las Casas, August 21, 1790, AGI C 1446).

McGillivray described Dalton more circumstantially in a subsequent conversation as a loyalist who had gone to Nova Scotia, and thence in a small craft with fish to the Bahamas, where he was cast away. He came over to the Indian country. McGillivray told him to leave, but excused him on the score of sickness for five months. Then he escorted him to the seacoast and saw him on shipboard bound for the Bahamas. Dalton went to England and "plagued" the ministry. "I was very much surprised," McGillivray continued, "to find him here on my arrival; we met in public on my landing, he has been plaguing me very frequently by messages and notes from day to day, and I was not able to get rid of him, until General Knox left directions for him to be told that if he came again he would be sent to Jail."

256. The same issue of the *Pennsylvania Packet and Daily Advertiser* contained a copy of the treaty and a list of its signers: Knox, McGillivray, and the twenty-three Creek chiefs, on August 7, when the document was witnessed by Richard Morris, chief justice of the state of New York, Richard Varick, mayor of the city of New York, Marinus Willett, Thomas Lee Shippen, John Rutledge, Jr., Joseph Allen Smith, and Joseph Cornell (by mark), the interpreter. On August 13 it was signed by Washington, Jefferson, and Knox.

278

August 16—Last Thursday evening, the St. Andrews Society, of the State of New York, held their quarterly meeting at the City Tavern— The Society, anxious of shewing their respect to the character of Col. M'Gillivray, availed themselves of his presence in this city, and unanimously elected him an honorary member of the Society; and immediately after a Committee was appointed to conduct him to it. The Colonel was introduced to the presiding officers in their places, and received the compliments of the Society. When the business of the Society was finished, he partook of a collation provided for the occasion, and mingled with great affability in the festivity of the evening. An occasional song was prepared and sung by a visiting friend, and addressed to the chief, in terms so artless, and yet so affecting, as touched the hearts of the members with sensations uncommonly pleasurable. The Society were honored with the company of the Hon. Samuel Johnson, Senator of the United States from N. Carolina, who had previously been elected an honorary member, by a meeting of the Society specially called for that purpose.

XIII

RECEPTION OF THE TREATY

148. *McGillivray to Quesada, September 6, 1790*
[LC EF 116L9]
St. Patricks on St. Marys River 6 Sepr. 1790
Sir

I have the pleasure to acknowledge the receit of Your esteemd letter by Captain Howard.

I beg to apologize to Your Excellency for not Accepting of Your Kind Invitation to Visit You in Augustine at this time.

Our Journey to New York provd tedious & fatiguing, & was on My arrival there seized with a Violent indisposition which held me a long time, & before I was perfectly recoverd I embark for this place. The heat being excessive, I fear a long Journey now (& my Visit to St. Augustine woud greatly lengthen it) Woud tend to Indispose me more are reasons why I decline it.[257]

I Shoud have been pleased if I Coud have had the Satisfaction to

257. See also McGillivray to John Leslie, September 3, 1790, in which stress is laid upon the impatience of the Indians to return to their families (Spanish translation in LC EF 116L9).

have fully explaind in person to You the Nature of our late treatys with the Americans. In the mean time You may be assurd that no Stipulations or Articles of it any way Clash with or tends to Militate against those we have Subsisting with Spain & you may farther rely on my best exertions to promote & Maintain the good Harmony & Friendship that Subsists at present between our Nation & the Kings Provinces of the Floridas & Louisiana, which assurances I have repeated to the Gentlemen who you did me the honor to Send.

I beg leave to Conclude this letter with Intimating to You my Intention to Visit you early in the ensuing Spring. Mean time I remain

Your Excellencys Most obedt. Servt.

ALEX: McGILLIVRAY [rubric]

His Excellency Dn. Juan Nepomuceno de Quesada.

149. *McGillivray to Leslie, September 13, 1790*
[Spanish translation in LC EF 116L9]
PLANTATION OF COLONEL MARBURY, 13 September 1790

DEAR SIR

I am at this place on my way home; we are making little progress in gathering horses on the opposite bank.[258] The colonel has provided for me abundantly, for which reason I have drawn on you in his favor.

The day before yesterday I received official letters from the Yazou Company on the old story, advising me among other things that the grant (the lands on the Yazou are meant) is confirmed and approved, and wishing to know my final decision. Ynglis insinuates that I would reap many advantages by joining with them; he points out the commercial, agricultural, etc. benefits, and adds that if any consideration could induce me to go back into business after fifteen years' recess, it would be to establish a connection of this nature with him and his friends.

I observed that these gentlemen are all anti-federalists in their views. This resolution originally was caused by the act of congress assembled at New York, at the time I was there, which act was drawn up deliberately against all the schemes of the land speculators. I regret that I cannot send you the letters, because when I received them I packed them up and I cannot get at them without unpacking everything, which I am not able to do in my present situation.

I replied to these gentlemen, particularly to Ynglis, that as I realized that there were always the same difficulties for the fulfillment of their projects, and since it also seemed to me that their proper government

258. In James Alling to John Leslie, October 2, 1790, is further information about the difficulty in getting horses for the trip (*ibid.*).

280

was opposed to the entire business, my determination was not favorable to them, moreover, that much of the land included in the grant is within the Spanish limits and there is no hope that the king would renounce his rights, and that while I would not hesitate to enter into projects to better my fortune, nevertheless I would not embrace any that might compromise my nation in new disputes and deprive me of the repose and tranquility that I so greatly desired after having passed the flower of my life in contentions and wars. But on the other hand, if they could surmount these difficulties and obtain a free and indisputable right to the Yazou River, I would not hesitate to accept any share that they might wish to give me. I made this reply publicly because I thought it necessary since the company has made wide use of my name in this affair and the idea that I am interested in these grants has been gaining ground without much profit to me, as I have been informed on good authority. The boat being almost ready, and I to embark on it, I close this letter with my respects to Captain Howard, and believe me to be always affectionately yours

ALEXANDER McG.

Mr. J. L.

150. *Howard to Quesada, September 24, 1790*
[Spanish original in AGI C 1436]

DEAR GOVERNOR:

As soon as John Leslie and I, in compliance with your order came to the Florida bank of the St. Marys River, we sent on the first of this month, by way of precaution, a trustworthy person to the new Georgian town of St. Patricks, situated on the opposite bank, with a letter to deliver to the mestizo Alexander McGillivray as soon as he should arrive, telling him that we were waiting for him in that neighborhood. He answered on the third, notifying us of his landing in that town the day before, and inviting us to go to see him, and in fact the next day we arrived at St. Patricks, where the mestizo received us joyfully; and the civil magistrate James Seagrove as well as the military commandant of the post, Captain Purbeck, with great politeness, although I suppose they would have dispensed with our visit.

We stayed there, John Leslie three, and I four days, during which time I was able to see that the site that has been selected for the new town seems very low and liable to be flooded during spring tides, that the detachment consists of seventy soldiers with one captain (the above mentioned) and first and second lieutenants, both of whom are absent and that at present work is being done in the construction of a fortification all made of wood, with a palisade, the commandant intending to

281

mount on it three pieces of bronze artillery of six-pound caliber which he brought with him for that purpose.

In view of your letter McGillivray was at first inclined to come to this city, but having consulted the other Indians on that particular, these being tired of their sea voyage, and desirous of joining their families as soon as possible, and already finding themselves in a country where they felt at home, they disliked to make such a great circuit. In the conversations without witnesses which I had with McGillivray, he signified that he had not fulfilled everything that my letter dated July 18th indicated to him, particularly that of seeing and communicating often with the Charge d'Affaires and with me, because of the suspicion that was aroused in the American government not only by my presence in New York, but also by that of a British major who came from Canada, during the critical time when President Washington was secretly waiting for him (McGillivray). The heads of the union, not satisfied with never leaving him one instant alone, under the pretext of being obsequious, also appointed people to watch and follow my footsteps and those of the mentioned major, the government having gone so far as to fear that the purpose was to destroy the promised effectuation of peace. McGuillivray was convinced that my presence and that of this official contributed to the fact that the Americans did not insist on an unqualified recognition on the part of the Indians of the sovereignty of the United States as well as that a secret article concerning the settling of the question of Indian trade was deferred for two years.

Whereupon I must inform you that I found out from McGuillibray himself that the previously mentioned English official managed to speak to him alone, but I have not been able to discover the subject of their conversation.[259] I found out directly although reservedly from McGuillibray that President Washington, as well as Minister Knox, tried to destroy completely his connections with Spain. And when they asked him what motives he could have for being so tenacious in refusing to agree with their solicitude, he replied that the Spaniards had always been good neighbors to the Creeks, while the contrary was true of the Americans who were notorious for their hostile incursions and usurpations of Indian lands, and they had been the aggressors in the war to which an end was now going to be put. He asked the President what guaranty the latter could offer as to what he would now stipulate with the United States, if McGuillivray agreed to break without just cause the connection which he had a long time ago contracted with Spain.

When it came to settling the question of Indian trade McGuillivray

259. See note 255, *supra*.

declared that he could not agree to any proposition which would be harmful to the interests of his close friends and protectors, Panton, Leslie, and Co. This having been heard by the President and the Secretary, they proposed to admit the company in question into American territory (naturalizing moreover the individuals) and to place it on the same footing as the court of Madrid had permitted it. McGuillibray replied that he was certain that neither the said company nor its correspondents in England would ever give up the advantages that Spain offered them, to become American citizens. As a result of all this, according to McGuillivray, it was agreed in the said secret article, to defer regulation of Indian trade for two years.

As I noticed that the mestizo was not accompanied by a nephew of his, ten or twelve years old, whom I saw with him in New York, and who spoke English well, I inquired of McGuillibray as to his whereabouts. He replied that Minister Knox had taken him under his charge in order to give him a cultivated education. I could not forbear replying that to give over one's nephew in that manner to the Americans was to manifest a decided predilection for that nation. He answered that in reality he felt more inclined toward Spain than toward the United States, that his only consideration in leaving his nephew with the minister was the boy's own good, and that with pleasure he would give over another nephew to be brought up as a Spaniard; the only difficulty occurring to him being that the latter would forget the English language. I said that this difficulty ceased to exist if one kept in mind that there were Irish regiments and commercial firms in Spain.

When I took leave of the mestizo he told me in the presence of the American commandant that he would not fail to fulfill his promise to you made in the letter that I carried, about visiting you next spring, and taking me aside, he said that he clearly could see that the Georgians had formed an erroneous concept of the treaty of peace, believing that he had separated himself from his connections with Spain and that he would only permit Americans to enter the Indian nation, and to undeceive them from this mistaken concept, he was determined to publish in that region a notice under his signature, declaring that he would not permit any individual to enter his nation for the purpose of carrying on commerce without a previous license from him, without which requisite he would confiscate all the goods introduced. He added that as soon as he landed some Georgians rushed to meet him with joyous faces, and as if to ask him for a reward for the news that they gave him, that there had begun a quarrel up the river between the Spaniards and the Indians, and that they (the Georgians) hoped soon to have all the trade of the Creek Indians. At this point I consider it my duty to

283

inform you that I have no doubt but that these particular Americans and even the government itself dedicate directly and indirectly all their efforts to sow discord and to prejudice the Indians against us.

Finally, I should make known to you that an American captain named Swan[260] came accompanying McGuillivray from New York and continues traveling with him up to the Indian nation with the ostensible intention of filling the office of Superintendent of Indian Affairs (there was such a post in the time of the English), but I believe that his true purpose is to supervise the actions of McGuillivray and gradually to inspire in the Indians affection for the United States, at the same time destroying their attachment to the Spaniards.

May God preserve you many years, St. Augustine, September 24, 1790.

CARLOS HOWARD [*rubric*]

Señor Don Juan Nepomuceno de Quesada.

151. *O'Neill to Las Casas, October 2, 1790*
[Spanish original in AGI C 1445]

. . . .About three years ago I distrusted the behavior of Alexander McGillevray. At that time a rupture with England was feared, which no doubt caused the Captain Bowels mentioned by Don Luis Bertucat to go to the Mosquito River on the east coast of Florida with a levy made at Providence of seventy soldiers, some arms and munitions of war, including four very small cannon, and some salt and other articles. He conversed secretly on that occasion near the Indian village of Casista with Alexander McGillevray, who alleged that at first Bowels had only come with some presents from the king of England for his friends the Indians, that the Indians would accept presents from any power that gave them, and that it would be useless for us to oppose it. As a result of everything a long time passed without his coming here. Nine months ago, when he was here, he tried to make excuses to me on this matter, which I overlooked, and it seems that he has succeeded in accomplishing it with Don Estevan Miró.

I have not the least doubt that McGillevray has a preference for the English. He is sagacious and reserved, with sufficient capacity to combine in an agreement the interests of England, and to foster them

260. Caleb Swan was a Revolutionary soldier, who stayed on in the army and became its paymaster-general, 1792-1809. Following this excursion to the Creek Nation he wrote a paper entitled "Position and State of Manners and Arts in the Creek or Muskogee Nation in 1791," which was published in Schoolcraft, *Indian Tribes*, V, 251-83. Milfort remarks, "combien ce M. Souanne desiroit posséder de bonnes terres" (*Mémoire*, p. 147).

with partisans among the Americans, particularly some emigrant establishments of the latter on the Cherokee River, the Cumberland River and in Kentucky, or even the company that is formed among the Americans to buy from the United States the lands between those establishments and the Mississippi, and in this way also to gratify the contentment of the Indians. . . . [261]

ARTURO O'NEILL [rubric]

Señor Don Luis de las Casas.

152. Miró to Las Casas, October 16, 1790
[Spanish original in AGI C 1440]

By a boat that left St. Augustine with families for this province, and touched at Providence, I have acquired the Gazette of that Island in which is found the peace treaty made August 7th between the United States of America and the Creek or Talapuche Nation.

Articles 2, 4, and 12 are opposed to the treaty made in the congress over which I presided at Pensacola in 1784, inasmuch as they accept the gifts and protection of those states.

I am of the opinion that McGillivray and his chiefs want to keep on the good side of both parties, and that they will maintain themselves in our friendship, the former receiving his pension and the others presents, while at the same time they enjoy all the advantages furnished them by the states.

I see that in this treaty the question of trade has been kept silenced, thus avoiding speaking of the one they have established with us, which leads me to suspect that McGillivray has perhaps explained reservedly to them the situation in which he finds himself with us on this point, perhaps promising them to consult with Panton about separating himself from it if he can convince him to place himself under the protection of the United States. What makes me think so is that it is notorious that the chief purpose of the Americans is to get the trade of the nation, which is the best way to foment its friendship. [262]

You are thus informed by all that I have communicated to you, and by the official letters about McGillivray and his nation that I have sent to your predecessors, of all that is necessary in order to make you realize the importance of preserving his devotion to us. Therefore you will be able to give me the instructions that you may judge convenient

261. In the paragraphs here omitted O'Neill promised to see if he could learn anything about the delegation of Indians that Bowles had taken to England. He also promised to "pump" out of McGillivray the latter's designs.

262. A shrewd deduction; see Howard's account in document 150, supra.

285

about the way in which I should conduct myself in the matter of this treaty.

May God preserve you many years.

ESTEVAN MIRÓ [rubric]

Señor Don Luis de las Casas.

153. *McGillivray to O'Neill, November 2, 1790*
[Copy in AGI C 203]
LITTLE TALLASSIE 2d November 1790

SIR

On my arrival from New York I had the pleasure of receiving two letters of yours written in my absence, and dated the 28th May Containing Information of the very unruly & Improper Conduct of Milfort; when he was in Pensla. on the Business I sent him for. Knowing something of his rashness of temper I always Strictly Charged him to Conduct himself in a Manner that Might not give any room for Censure either on his own account or mine, & on which Subject I have been very free with him & he Shall no more be in any Situation which Shall give Your Excellency any future umbrage. The other letter of 25th June gives me Information of the arrival of the Articles which I had formerly requested of Governor Miro & this being the Season when little bountys are needfull to the deserving people, I have Sent the bearer David Francis to receive some of the Articles Such as ten pieces of Stroud eighty Blankets, fifty white & fifty Check Shirts, & some kegs of Taffee. The remaining goods will be managed as necessary, by which time I Shall have the pleasure of Seeing Your Excellency in Town. . . . .[263]

ALEXANDER MCGILLIVRAY

His Excellency Arthur O'Neill Esqr.
Brigr. General & Governor of West Florida.

154. *McGillivray to Quesada, November 10, 1790*
[LC EF 116L9]
LITTLE TALLASSIE 10 Nor. 1790

SIR

Your Excellencys dispatch of 14 Oct. by express was handed to me Yesterday. In answer to which I beg leave to observe that some days before I left St. Marys several people had Complaind to me concerning

263. The letter goes on to describe the negotiations at New York and the dissatisfaction of the Georgians, in which connection see document 154, *infra;* McGillivray to John Leslie, November 10, 1790, Spanish translation in AHN E 3889 bis; and the Protest of the Legislature of the State of Georgia against the Treaty of New York, ASP IA, II, 790-91.

the matters Containd in your letter together with his dishonest Intentions toward my freinds Messrs. Panton Lesslie & Co. upon which I was resolvd to reprimand him, but he kept out of my Sight on the american side of the River, always drunk. He sent his man to me with some horses excusing his non-appearance.

It was rather unfortunate that Kinnard was gone to St. Mark to Visit Mr. Panton when I was at his house but I Spoke a great deal to his family & likewise left a written talk for him Concerning his imprudent Interference about Allens affairs. The principal Indians were assembled in Numbers, waiting my approach in the Flint River Villages, to whom likewise I Spoke to on the Subject of a peaceable & freindly behaviour towards the Inhabitants of the Floridas. It appears to me that Allen means to fix himself on the american Side for the purpose of sheltering himself from future prosecution for debt or misdemeanor. I have advised Mr. Leslie in a letter by the Oussitche Chief to endeavor to seize allen & I will take it upon myself as my own act, in which case his Indian freind will Scarcely murmur.

The Goods which You Mention to have been Sent to allen came I believe from Mr. Seagrove the American Collector at Patrickston, as I knew Allen was Collecting horses bought with the Goods of P. & Co. to pay Seagrove a large debt which he had contracted with him, but those I intercepted & returnd to Kinnards family with orders to pay nothing to Allen without Mr. Lesslies particular order.

It is my Intention Strictly to adhere to the resolution of not giving licenses to trade to any persons on the American Side, tho I did give one to Seagrove on Condition of his bartering for horses, only which he Ships to the Spanish & French Islands. In case of my refusing this, it woud have raisd much clamour & woud have made Seagrove & others a troublesome Set.

I return Your Excellency many thanks for Your kind enquirys about our late Journey. It was Certainly a very dissagreeable one, & distressing in having many of our horses drownd, some died & others tired on the road, such disasters are to be expected in travelling the Roads of East Florida in which there is but the one Season & that but a Short one for travelling with any tolerable Comfort.

If our restless Neighbours the Georgians will permit I Shall endeavor to do myself the pleasure of Visiting Your Excellency next Spring, but am Concernd to See that those people are taking measures to frustrate the good Consequences of the late treaty of Peace with their Government. Instead of being Satisfied with the Concessions which we made to Secure a peace, a party in Georgia Calling themselves a Combined Society of freinds, are pursuing Schemes which if persisted in must

287

assuredly Compel us again to take up the red hatchet of war against
them in defence of our Territory. There were Stipulations in the late
treaty which I never Woud have consented to if I had been properly
Supported & encouragd. A little time more will disclose the disposition of the Georgians, & if I find War unavoidable I Shall address the
king for ample aid & support, which if granted to us May in the end,
prove of great Consequence to his dominions here.

    I remain with respectfull regard Sir
        Your Excellencys obedt. Servt.

ALEX: McGILLIVRAY [rubric]

his Excellency Governor de Quesada

155. *McGillivray to O'Neill, January 13, 1791*
[AGI C 205]

LINDERS HOUSE, TENSAW, 13 January 1791

SIR

    I arrived here on New Years day on my way to Pensacola. The next
day I was unlucky enough to Scald my leg with hot water which has
laid me up since which to add to my misfortune the Rheumatism has
attackd me in my feet & all together it has given me a fever which I am
affraid will keep me Confind for the rest of this month. However as soon
as I can ride I intend to See Your Excellency in Town. Having brought
some horses down I mean to have them return soon as possible after
getting some more of the articles in Store to pack them up. Therefore
I wish Your Excellency to let the bearer have eight peices [strouds]
20 pair of duffle blankets, as Much Taffia [as he] can take—2 doz
Shirts 1 doz to be white.

    Wishing you the Compliments of the Season I remain
        Your Excellencys most affectionate & obedient servt.

ALEX: McGILLIVRAY [rubric]

His Excellency Arthur ONeil

156. *McGillivray to Miró, February 26, 1791*
[AGI C 184]

PENSACOLA, 26th February 1791

    . . . .Among other assurances that Colo. Willet was authorized to
make me, I found that the overthrow of the associated or Yasou Companys was in my power. I Judgd it a favorable moment to accept of the
Invitation to treat with the American Congress, & accordingly I proceeded to New York. On my arrival there I had the Mortification to
learn that Mr. Gardoqui was gone to Spain so that I had it not in my
power to avail myself of his advice & assistance. I was much concernd

in finding that Your Nation was on the eve of War with England, which I dreaded well knowing in that case that it would be inconvenient for your Nation & its allys to have disputes with the americans, & this Consideration made me less Inflexible in some points than I otherwise would have been.

Peace was accordingly Concluded & the terms of it You will see expressed in the enclosed paper, & which differs in nothing from the Original Articles excepting what relates to the Sovereignty, which in the Original it is printed & conveying the meaning strictly that the American Sovereignty is to extend no farther than to *such parts of the Creek Nation* as shall fall within the limits of the same.[264] I was very particular in that matter, & on that article we had nearly broke off, Congress persisting in having (as at the Rock Landing) an unqualified acknowledgement of its Sovereignty over our whole Nation & myself as obstinate in rejecting it as being totally Inadmissible & Contrary to our Treatys with Spain, & here permit me to observe that it was a well Judged measure in Governor de Zespedes to send Capn. Howard to New York where his presence was so unwelcome & suspected as to Induce them to set Spies on his Conduct, but he found means to elude them in advising me in letters which they could not detect. It is my beleif that his being there caused them not to be so tenacious on the point of Sovereignty & other matters as they otherwise might have been. The Secretary at War, the Commissioner for treating with me, after many Consultations with the President, at length agreed to fix the Sovereignty on the terms I have mentioned. That point being got over there was less difficulty in settling others. In asscertaining our Limits I recoverd the encroachments of the Georgians on the side of East Florida, & altho' the Sacrifice on our part in giving up so much land was great, Yet considering the then Situation of the times, I Confess I was glad to close with them on the terms I obtaind, especially as I have it fully in my power to prevent future encroachments, & to put a Stop to the designs of the Associated Companys, who were ready to pour into their pretended purchases a deluge of emigrants which if Congress had given a Sanction to the Georgia Grants & Sales to those Companys it would have been difficult if not impossible for me to prevent.

On the whole I hope His Majesty will approve of the terms & stipulations of the Treaty of Peace which I have concluded with the American Congress, & I request of Your Excellency to forward a dupli-

264. This is not the exact wording of Article 2, but it is the sense (see *ibid.*, I, 81-82).

cate of this Letter to the Minister of State, that it may reach his Majestys knowledge.[265]

Before I conclude this Letter I beg to observe that in the course of my negotiations at New York, I endeavord to obtain the restitution of the Valueable possessions in the State of Georgia belonging to my family & myself, but was Informd that the Congress had no right to exercise any such powers over the legislature of that State, & Confessing my Case without remedy from them, but being much disposed in my favor they proposed to Grant me the Sum of Twelve hundred pr. annum to Compensate me in some measure for the losses of my family untill the State of Georgia coud be prevaild on to restore me to the enjoyment of my rights. To this it was proposed to give a Commission of a Brigr. General, but finding that an Oath calculated to bind me down to the american Interest would be required of me on accepting such Commission, I did not hesitate to give the offer a strong rejection. I mention this matter to your Excellency, in order to Gaurd you, & my other friends from entertaining a belief of the reality of any such Circumstance. So likewise it is currently reported, & generally beleived the I have the honor of a Colonels Commission in the Spanish Service which Your Excellency well knows to be Intirely groundless, & between you & me I conceive that my Station as Chief of my Country is far Superior to the first, & your Excellency is certain that the latter was never offerd me, & as it is a matter of Indifference to me in what manner I am addressd in so I never think it worth my While to Set people to rights.

That I might not incur the most distant Suspicion of duplicity, I inform Your Excellency that the President of Congress agreed in a Seperate Article, that if a War should unfortunately break out between Spain & England (which was then deemed Inevitable) so that a Stop Shoud be put to the further Importation of the Necessary Supplys for our Trade, it was Stipulated that I should have a free Port, in St. Marys River or thereabout, to import our Necessary Supplys in, without exempting one Article Whatever, or restricting us to any particular part of the World, the Imports & exports free from dutys. But as peace is now fully Concluded on between your Court & Eng-

265. The court, after considering this letter, issued a royal order that McGillivray's friendship be cultivated—by increasing his pension, if necessary, and that he should be kept distrustful of the Americans (Floridablanca to Miró, October 26, 1791, draft in AHN E 3889 bis). See also Lerena to Miró, December 25, 1790, in which Miró was authorized to assign McGillivray two thousand pesos a year, and if necessary, to double the amount, "since he is at the same time being courted by the United States and by the English" (AGI C 177).

land, I have no Wish to avail myself of that Indulgence. The trade will therefore flow as it has hitherto done. . . . .[266]

157. *McGillivray to Miró, June 8, 1791*

[AGI C 2371]

LITTLE TALLASSIE 8' June 1791

SIR

I had the satisfaction of receiving Your Excellencys letter of 29' March.

The Copy of the Treaty alluded to by me in my letter of Feby. was an American publication & which was forgot by Mr. Panton, At same time I observed that the american Copy was not exact, herewith I send Your Excellency the Articles Constituting the basis of the Treaty. Having wrote very fully in my letter of Feby.[267] concerning my Motives for Concluding peace with the American States, I shall in this letter give Your Excellency the Occurrences of this Spring past.

In April last I had authentic Information that the Tennessee Company had assembled an armed body of one hundred & fifty men, at a place called French Broad to proceed to the Muscle Shoals on Cherokee River & there to erect a fort to be mounted with a few small pieces of ordnance, & when this was effected greater Numbers of Familys were to Settle the country under the protection of the Fort. This Measure of Messr. Cox Gilbert & Strother &ca leading of that Co. I conceivd to be a flagrant Violation of the treaty, because Congress had pledgd themselves Not to Countenance the Georgia Grants to the Yasou & Tennessee Companys & left me at liberty to act hostilely against them if they shoud presume to Settle the Countrys in question.

Accordingly upon receiving the Information that an armd body of Men were Intending for the Muscle Shoal I Immediately Sent out a

266. Pickett states that the secret articles also provided for handsome medals and an annual salary of $100 each to six of the principal chiefs and for McGillivray's commission as brigadier general at a salary of $1200 annually. For confirmation see the itemized statement in ASP IA, I, 127. Pickett mentions another provision to the effect that Creek youths, up to four at a time, would be fed, clothed, and educated in the north at the expense of the United States. Partial confirmation is afforded by McGillivray's leaving his nephew with General Knox (see document 150, *supra*, and Knox to McGillivray, April 29, 1792, copy in AGI C 177). Pickett's statement is vouched for by Professor A. P. Whitaker, on the authority of Professor S. F. Bemis (see the *North Carolina Historical Review*, V, 298). On February 14, 1791, Wilkinson reported to Miró, probably erroneously, that the secret articles provided for a donation of $20,000 (AGI C 2374). He went on to offer this gratuitous advice: "I am of the opinion the Peace which has been made, cannot last long; the Interests of the Indians & that of the Citizens of the adjacent States are so opposite & irreconcileable, and both Parties are so vindictive, licentious & ungovernable, that their inherent animosity, must soon burst forth in mutual aggression; Spain should wait patiently for this Event and be ready to take advantage of it."
267. Document 156, *supra*.

Considerable party of my Warriors to attack & destroy such settlement. These Americans not being found at the places, our people have returnd. However I have desired that a good look out shoud be kept on the Cherokee Swing & about the Chickasaw Bluffs, as those Infatuated Indians at least a part of them are much in the Interest of the Tennessee & Yasou Companys. This last Company having lost their principal Manager Major Thomas Washington who was hanged two Months ago, being Convicted for forgerys to an immense ammount, of Course the Yasou Company appears to be in a Slumber.

Our Eastern Neighbours the Georgians have frequently Violated the late Treaty in Several Instances they have lately murderd a Coweta Indian & I am apprehensive that the peace will not hold long. The Georgians have reprobated the terms of the Peace in most Clamourous & Indecent manner, their Conduct of late evinces that they desire to break the Treaty. Such being the State of our affairs, I warn Your Excellency in time, that in the event of a New rupture we shall stand in Need of his Majestys most gracious support in defending ourselves & defeating the inordinate ambit[ions] of the american emigrants Westwardly, encroaching on the Territory of the King as well as on ours.

However it shall be my Study to avoid rashly commencing a New War, being at same time Carefull to keep the americans within their due bounds, & if this moderate Conduct provoke them to acts of hostillity we will expect Your Excellencys Support.

The principal articles are as follow

1: There shall be a perpetual peace & freindship between all the Citizens of the United States of America & all the Towns & Tribes of the Upper, Middle, & Lower Towns & Tribes Composing the Creek Nation.

2d. The said Chiefs headmen & Warriors do acknowledge *all parts as are Within the Limits of the United States* to be under the Protection of the United States & of No other Sovereign.[268]

Some other Stipulations respecting a regulation for preserving mutual good order between us & the States. Satisfaction for Injurys to be mutually given with good faith, all Intruders on Indian Lands to be at the descretion of the Indians. No White hunters permitted to kill game in the Woods.

Separate Article

268. The exact wording in all printed copies is: "The undersigned kings, chiefs, and warriors, for themselves, and all parts of the Creek nation within the limits of the United States, do acknowledge themselves, and the said parts of the Creek nation to be under the protection of the United States of America." McGillivray interprets the meaning accurately.

Whereas the trade of the Creek Nation is Now wholly carried on through the Territorys of Spain & obstructions may happen thereto by War or prohibition of the Spanish Government it is therefore agreed between the Contracting Partys that in the event of Such obstruction happening it shall be lawfull for the President of the United States to designate certain persons to Introduce into & transport through the United States to the Country of the Creek Nation any quantity of Goods, wares & merchandise free from any duty or Imposition whatever, but subject only to regulations for guarding against abuse.[269]

Having given Your Excellency the principal articles of the Treaty Concluded at New York I hope that they will not be deemd clashing in any manner with the articles of the Treaty of Pensacola.[270]

You will be pleased to observe that the Sovereignty of the United States is to be acknowledgd only in such parts of our Country as shall Come within their limits, but Resting in full Confidence that the King in maintaining his claim & Rights from the americans, No part of our Country will fall within the United States, & as it is I have not given its Citizens any power to exercise any Authoritys or Commerce in any part of our Nation, & Your Excellency may be firmly assured that while I breath in this World my best exertions shall be to fix my Nation Steadfastly in the Kings Interest against all other people. I shall Inculcate the same principle in the Youths of my family whom I educate.

I receive with most gratefull acknowledgements the Notification that Your Excellency gives me of the late donation of his most Gracious Majesty to me & am Content to receive it in the mode which You mention.[271] I am extremely sensible of what Efficacy Your Excellencys recommendation has been to me & of which I Shall ever retain a most gratefull remembrance.

The bearer requests the favor of some Taffia & Salt. A number are gone as I understand theres no keeping them back. With most respectfull & Sincere Esteem I am

Your Excellencys Most obedt. Serv.

ALEX: McGILLIVRAY [rubric]

his Excellency B. Gen: Stephen Miro

269. Compare with the printed form, ASP IA, I, 80, and with Pickett's description, note 266, *supra*.

270. Miró's answer was to request a complete copy of the treaty (Miró to McGillivray, July 6, 1791, copy in AGI C 1446). The new captain general, while promising to work whole-heartedly in the interest of the Creek Nation, regretted that "sight had been lost of various articles of the treaty held in Pensacola." He hoped that he would be able "to avert the coolness" which he expected this would engender at the Spanish court (Las Casas to McGillivray, July 7, 1791, draft in AGI C 1484).

271. The reference is to the increase of his annual salary to $2,000 (see Panton to Miró, April 18, 1791, AGI C 40).

158. *McGillivray to Miró,* [*June 8, 1791*]

[AGI C 2370]

SIR

I must inform your Excellency that one Pope[272] who arrived here from Orleans & Pensacola on his way to South Carolina & Virginia. Since his departure Im informed that he had different drafts of the fortifications at Natchez, Orleans & Pensacola that he was Sent by Genl Clark at Kentucke for the purpose, as Clark was Secretly preparing a Strong force (Secretely Sanctioned by the State of Virginia) to fall upon the Spanish posts on the Mississippi.

The letter for a Mr. Wilcox that accompanys this may probably throw some light on the affair at least I deem it prudent to cause it to be put into Your Excellencys hand.[273]

I recollect that one evening Pope was talking at random about the Americans & said it was reported that Clark was to apply to me for a Strict Neutrality of the Indians in case he was ripe for an attempt on the posts of Spain. Such things have been so long & often the common topic that I only laugh'd at him, but Since his departure my frenchman tells me he wanted to shew him some drafts. They happen'd to meet two days journey from this place. The time for Clarks operations are before next Spring etc.[274]

A. McGILLIVRAY [*rubric*]

272. In his *A Tour through. . . . the Creek Nation* (Richmond, 1792), Pope furnished one of the best descriptions of McGillivray and his ménage. He found McGillivray building a new log mansion with dormer windows. He reported fifty Negroes, and large stocks of horses, hogs, and cattle. He described McGillivray's wife as "a Model of Prudence and Discretion," but of olive complexion, and their "two lovely Children, Alexander and Elizabeth," he complimented upon their expertness in speaking English. Writing of his host he said: "This Gentleman to Appearance is at least Five and Forty, tho' in Fact only thirty-two Years of Age— Dissipation marked his juvenile Days, and sapped a Constitution originally delicate and feeble. He is subject to an habitual Head-Ach and Cholic, notwithstanding which his Temper is placid and serene, and at Intervals of Ease quite joyous. He possesses an Atticism of Diction aided by a liberal Education, a great Fund of Wit and Humour, meliorated by perfect good Nature and Politeness" (*ibid.*, pp. 46-51). McGillivray seized the opportunity offered by Pope to despatch a couple of letters to acquaintances he had made at Manchester and Richmond, Virginia (*ibid.*, pp. 51-52).

273. John Pope to Wilcox, June 4, 1791, Spanish translation in AGI C 1436. The letter appears to have been purposely worded ambiguously, but it hints at a plot to attack Spain's posts.

274. Copies of this letter, of document 157, *supra*, of Pope to Wilcox, June 4, 1791 (Spanish translation in AGI C 1394), and of Miró to McGillivray, July 6, 1791 (copy in AGI C 1446), were forwarded to Las Casas by Miró with a cover letter dated July 17, 1791 (*ibid.*). The captain general replied that Pope seemed to be merely a "despicable adventurer," but that the Louisiana and Florida commandants who had been so careless as to allow a stranger to make sketches of their forts should be reprimanded (Las Casas to Miró, August 12, 1791, *ibid.*).

159. *Miró to McGillivray, September 17, 1791*

[Draft in AGI C 204]

SIR

I received your letter of 28th August in answer to mines of 9th June, & 6th July, & perfectly acquainted with their contents I find the reasons you give upon the robberis committed by the vagabonds of that Country well grounded, & *a propos:* I am equally satisfyd with the answer of topalca; & your exposal upon the emigrant from the united States.

I am indeed very sorry at the causes who prevents you from sending now a copy of the treaty of New York; but at the mean time I will be extremely pleased with your arrival here in the beginning of November (as you said) & accordingly, I send orders to the commander of Movila that the King's schooner might be ready for you whose arrival shall be seasonable as the Baron Carondelet[275] mi appointed Succesor will be then here, & wee consult together about those matters.

I am very glad of the treaty concluded between the Cheroqui Nation, & Govr. Blount in the name of the united States of America, being extremely satisfyd with the Stipulation thereof, since the things remaining in that points the Companys will not think of their Settlements on that Quarter.

I communicate all those transaction to our Captain general & am with due esteem & regard—

[ESTEVAN MIRÓ]

XIV

THE RETURN OF BOWLES

160. *Panton to Miró, October 8, 1791*

[AGI C 203]

PENSACOLA, 8 October 1791

MUCH ESTEEMED SIR

On the 6th Instant I troubled Your Excellency with a letter. I have

275. Francis Hector, Baron de Carondelet, has been characterized as the worst possible successor to Miró as governor and intendant of Louisiana. He did know French and he was a brother-in-law of Las Casas, the captain general at Havana, but he did not understand the border problems that he would have to face, and he was not temperamentally suited to meet them. His impetuosity in plunging into action frequently threatened Spain's position with the Americans and with the Indians. For an illustration see his confession in document 198, *infra*. Whitaker discusses Carondelet in his *The Spanish American Frontier*, pp. 153-70.

now to enform You that Mr. Robt. Leslie arrived last night from Saint Augustine & brought me an extract of a letter from my Partner Mr. Thos. Fobes in New Providence to my Partner Mr. John Leslie in Sain Autustine and I now send You a Copy of it for Your enformation. The same day that Mr. Leslie received that letter he laid a Copy of it before the Govr. of Saint Augustine, who emmediately fitted out some Armed Boats in hopes of catching Bowles;[276] but it seems they were unsuccessfull, for Mr. Robert Leslie saw him at a village on Flint River, where he had collected a number of worthless Vagabond Indians with whom he meant to proceed up to the Coweta Towns, where he was to give out his talks. Mr. Robert Leslie hastened on to Mr. McGillivray's, to whom he had letters from the Governor of Augustine, and he set off immediately for the Lower Towns on purpose either to drive that vagabond out of the Land or to take his Scalp. I am of opinion that McGillivray will dispose of the fellow, and that we Shall hear no more of him; but if he does not; the Black Guard is Capable of doing mischief and You had best give pointed orders to have him knocked in the Head.

His History from the time of his being drove from the Nation in the winter of 1789,[277] is somewhat extraordinary, and is a proof of his enterprise and perseverance. When he went off he had address enough to prevail on two three half Breeds of the cherokess & a Couple of Young fellows from the Creeks to accompany him to New Providence where he was soon after his arrival put in jail for debt; But having got out of Confinement from the influence of Lord Dunmore he with his Indians escaped over to the Florida Point, where it is said the Indians had resolved to kill him, and would have done it for the deception he had practiced on them, if accident had not preserved him by throwing a Spanish vessel ashore near where he and his Indians were encamped. The crew of the vessel & passengers having left the wreck Bowles and his people took possession of Her wherin they found a Considerable booty, and among other things some suits of very Rich Gold laced Clothes with which he equiped his party and having hired a fishing Boat that happened to be there catching Turtle he proceeded to Nova Scotia where he introduced his Indians & himself to Govr. Parr as Men of the first rank & Consequence of the Creek & Cherokee Nations. And So artfully did he Conduct himself, that the Governor listned to his Storry and believed it. From Nova Scotia he was Sent on to Lord Dorchester, the Governor Genl. of Canada, and from thence he was Conducted to England, and was Carressed and entertained at the Public

276. Quesada also wrote to warn McGillivray on August 20, 1791 (LC EF 116L9).

277. Panton wrote 1779, but this is obviously a slip.

expense. I am pretty certain that Mr. Pitt was not ignorant of Bowles's being an Imposture, Yet, it suited his purpose during the dispute with Spain, and he was passed upon the Spanish Ambassadore as a Man of the greatest Consequence among the Southern Indians. After these disputes were settled the minister packed him & his Party out to America. It is Said they were accompanied with handsome presents but to what amount I know not.[278]

This is all that I know about him but as I expect to hear from McGillivray soon we shall see what he does with him.

I remain, Dear Sir

Your most Obedient Servant,

WM. PANTON [rubric]

His Excellency, Governor Miro

161. [*Miró*] *to McGillivray, October 15, 1791*

[Draft in AGI C 204]

NEW ORLEANS 15th October 1791

SIR

The Commander of Apalache writes to me in a letter of the 26th September last that Captain Bowles was in the River Canard[279] with a Schooner ladden with goods, who by the aforesaid Bowels are being given at present to the Indians under the promise that in a short time he should receive one Vessel bigger. I make no doubt that you will by all means carry out what you offered to me on the said Bowles in your letter of the 1st of February 1789[280] as well as to show how dear is to you his most gracious Majesty's protection as to procure the Indians the necessary tranquility since it must be highly prejudicial to them to be divided by partys one in favour of Bowels trade, and another in favor of Mr. William Pantons by whom the concurrence of the former undoubtedly will hurt very much.

I Desire you to acquaint me as soon as possible of every thing in this transaction, wishing you good health, & being always sure of the esteem and regard with which I am Sir

Your most obedient humble Servant.

[ESTEVAN MIRÓ]

Alexander McGillevray Esqr.

278. For a sketch of his London experiences see F. J. Turner, "English Policy," *American Historical Review*, VII, 706-35, and VIII, 78-86.

279. Panton's schooner went with the government launch under Bertucat in search of Bowles (Forrester to Panton, October 10, 1791, AGI C 1436).

280. Document 113, *supra*.

162. *McGillivray to Panton, October 28, 1791*
[Copy in AGI C 2362]
LITTLE TALLASSIE, 28th October 1791

SIR

We are here not without our troubles, for that fellow Bowles, aided & protected by Philatouchy & Perryman and their freinds, is making a great noise in the Chetaws, & has perfectly Confused & distracted the foolish & inconsiderate part of the Indians thereabout. This however Cannot hold Long, for he has fortunately brought nothing of Consequence with him, for all the presents he obtained in London if I am rightly informed, does not exceed a few horseload of ammunition, about Twenty Guns, a few horse Swords & pistols and a piece or two of Scarlet Cloth, & of which he has distributed a few Blanketts to those fellows who has made all this Clamour.[281]

When I went to the Lower Towns, I endeavoured to draw him from the Factor Philatouchies house, but without Success, for his father in Law Perryman Suspected me & would not Let him Come & finding the Indian unwilling to use violence in a friends Town, as they Call one an other, and as I did not Choose to Indulge the Factor, by going to See a Stranger whose business was to wait on me I returned without seeing him. From the best Information I can get from White People who have seen him, he pretends to show a Commission from Mr. Greenville Secretary of State in England appointing him Superintendant & General, & he tells the Indians that he has Come to rescue them from the americans & from Panton & McGillivray, who, he accuses of having Sold them & their lands, a part to one Side & a part, to the other. He asks for a tract of land at the mouth of Oakalagany, or flint river which he is to fortify & to Carry on a General Piracy in the Gulph & be an other Blackbeard.

From this and by his Continuing to harp at you, it appears, that he Still maintains the design of Suplanting you in the Indian trade & no Doubt must be encouraged to the attempt by those who Sent him first, & you may depend that the said Philatouchy & Perryman will be aiding to all his designs however base & injurious they may prove to their Country in the end. It is one Comfort however that their Influence does not extend beyond the Villages of Oussitchie & Chetaws. The Eufaullys & all the Villages round Saint Marks are all your fast friends & Complain much against those desaffected Gentry.

On his arrival this last time he acted with the Policy of a Cunning

281. After the return of Bowles' boat to New Providence, Thomas Forbes wrote that the stories of bronze artillery and thousands of arms were fabrications and that Bowles "would not find credit for one hundred dollars' worth of goods" (Forbes to Leslie, November 2, 1791, AGI C 1436).

imposture, for he took Care to leave on board the Vessell he Came in every person who Could Speak a word of Indian or English, so that he had the Telling of what Story he pleased without danger of being Contradicted. Tom Lewis, a half Breed boy (whom he Seduced away when last here) at last got on Shore, but so fully had Bowles prepossessed the Indians with his own Story & the Indifferent Character he gave them of the half breed boy in regard to his veracity, that when he Came to tell the real truth, he was Scouted as a great Liar.

The Boy's account, is, that in England where Bowles was not known, they were all treated with extraordinary Kindness; but when they arrived at Bahamas where he has been known before, he Bowles was treated as a Vagabond, except by Lord Dunmore, John Millar & one or two others his Lordships friends.[282]

I Sent three Warriors to dispatch the Vagabond, but they are Just returned without effecting it, he is so well guarded by the Factor & Perryman, but in a little Time I have no doubt of his being Killed, for the new things he brought will soon be gone & then the Dreams which his lies has occasioned will Come to an End.[283]

The half breed Tom Lewis informed me that Bowles's vessel[284] made a hasty retreat from where She lay at the mouth of Ockalagany & was put to Sea before Bowles got his despatches on board, so that he missed of writing his friends this Trip. Why in the Name of Heaven did not the Commandant at St. Marks Seize the Schooner; & why after what has happened, is not an armed boat kept there, to prevent Such Villains as he from Circulating lies & trash to disturb the peace & tranquility of the Nation?

The Gentleman who was sent to me from New York[285] to see the land run agreable to the treaty made there, is gone back & will Carry an account with him of Bowles's proceedings & as the Terms of the Treaty

282. This corroborates Forbes' statements (Forbes to Panton, Leslie and Company, September 12, 1790, AGI C 1436; Forbes to Leslie, August 1, 1791, *ibid.;* and Forbes to Leslie, November 2, 1791, *ibid.*).
283. "I have proclaimed a reward of one hundred Dollars for him or his head all over the Nation, & I am sure that he will be killed in less than a Month." This was McGillivray's report to O'Neill, October 28, 1791 (copy in AGI C 1445). "So that he must be taken or killed or run away before long," runs the prediction in McGillivray to Miró, November 15, 1791 (AGI C 204).
284. "A schooner of about fifty tons, very dirty on the sides, and as a whole it seemed to be falling apart; its shape was so flat that it could not be a swift boat; its two masts are almost perpendicular; and besides the ship's boat Bowles plans to take a large canoe almost as long as the schooner." Bowles brought a flag of new design and a great seal for the Indian nation (Declaration of Edward London, August 8, 1791, AGI C 1436).
285. John Heth came with $2,900 in gold, the balance due the Creeks and McGillivray (ASP IA, I, 127). He was instructed "to impress upon McGillivray.... the necessity of the Creeks delivering up all prisoners" and of running the line (see Knox to Heth, and Knox to McGillivray, May 31, 1791, *ibid.*, pp. 125-26).

is not Complyed with, in my opinion an american war against this nation must be the unavoidable result of Bowles's intrigues. It is no difficult matter to persuade a few Indians to Commit mischief on the frontiers of Georgia, but it will be no easy matter to get them out of the Scrape after they are involved in it, & it will furnish the americans with an excuse for insisting on further grants, which the posture of their affairs will enable them to inforce. Then, Bowles, if he is alive will push off to Providence; the Factor & Perryman will fly to their former lurking places in time of danger, & as for me I am firmly resolved to move myself family & negroes down this River to little River; I am absolutely worn down with the Life I have lived for ten years past, & what is most provoking, these lower Town Indians seem wholly insensible of the destruction from which they have been saved by their friends;[286] as yet I have no reason to be so much dissatisfyed with the upper towns.

I have had a Severe return of the Rheumatisme which has Kept me in torment for some time past. I am at present a little relieved & Shall Set out Shortly for Mobille where the Kings Schooner waits by Governour Miro's order to Carry me to new Orleans. I wish you Could make it Convenient to accompany me.

163. *Statement by Middleton,*[287] *December 21, 1791*
[Spanish translation in AGI C 1436]

[Middleton described a meeting at the Half-way House attended principally by chiefs of the Lower Creeks. Bowles' talk was presented: he promised to write to the great king and also to Georgia demanding the return of the usurped lands and to England asking for aid; he urged the Indians not to steal horses or resort to violence; he said he had 6000 men at his call in the islands, and when he brought them the Indians could join or remain neutral. The Indian who took the letters on to McGillivray found him ill, but he promised to answer the next day.]

Mac-Gillivray said that the Indians had thrown his talks aside, that they had shamed him in his own country and made him out a liar before the white people, that they had admitted the talks of a stranger and thrown his aside, and now that he had abandoned theirs, they could look for someone else to formulate their talks and write their letters, and he added that he would leave the nation. Many of the chiefs of the towns begged him to stay, but he paid no attention to them.

286. Compare with Middleton's statement, document 163, *infra*.
287. Middleton had been entrusted with letters for McGillivray, but at Augusta was advised to send them on by Indian carrier. His statement was made at New York.

Those among them, he said, whom he had considered gentlemen, had admitted the talk of a stranger, of one who had deceived them once, coming as a man of importance, and when Mac-Gillivray asked him for his credentials, he replied that he had left them at home: *that by next spring he expected to see them all dead, or exiled from the country, and that then they would be glad to listen to his talks;* for when the great king was here, with all his people, and had besides the aid of all the Indians who wished to come, the Americans had expelled him and his people; and what could they (the Indians) expect to do with only a handful of men against the United States; that he, Mac-Gillivray, had preserved them for a long time in peace, but that they would not experience this in the future.

164. *McGillivray to Miró, December 30, 1791*

[AGI C 204]

PENSACOLA 30th December 1791

SIR

In a former letter which I wrote to Your Excellency I proposed to myself the pleasure of Seeing You as in November in Orleans, but a Severe & long attack of the Rheumatic Gout has prevented my purpose & am now very unwell & the Season being far advanced & Bowles being Yet in the Lower part of the Nation gives cause of uneasiness to my freinds here I Judge it expedient to hasten home & take the necessary measures to rid the Country of him.

From every account which I can learn of the Views of this Desperado is that he is aided & encouraged by Lord Dunmore & Miller the Merchant in the diabolical design to endeavor to accomplish the destruction of the Trading establishment of the house of Messr. Panton Leslie & Co. as well as Causing the Indians to be dissaffected to their Neighbours, in which designs he will not Succeed, as his party is Confined Solely to Indians in two Villages of the Lower Creeks & they Consist of two chiefs of the Second Class & Men who are unable to Support themselves by hunting Game in the Woods, to whom he has made promises of great presents to be given on the arrival of two Ships with Goods, which he tells them was to arrive in all this Month on the Coast, & as I am persuaded he comes from no higher Authority than Dunmore & Miller I Judged it for the best to Suffer him to remain where he was in the lower Towns untill the time he told the Indians the Ships woud arrive was elapsed in Order that they might of themselves be Convinced of his Lies, before I took any Sanguinary measures & as I have no Conception that he will be able to make good his

301

promises to them, the Imposition will make them more Cautious how they listen to Strangers in future.[288]

I think it Needful to advise Your Excellency to have an Armd Vessel Mounting four Cannon a Six pounder at the head & Stern & two four pounders in the Waist & of an easy draught of Water to be Stationd at St. Marks & to Cruise along the Coast to the Mouth of the Apalachicola near which is an Island where the Vessel can lay occasionally in order to Guard the Coast & to prevent Intrusion of Smuglers & Vagabonds who land on the Coast to Confuse & distract the Indians, who Inhabit the Country at least five hundred Miles from my residence. The distance often prevents my getting timely notice of such people.

Bowles has lately wrote a letter to Governor ONeil[289] in which he Impudently assumes an Importance with a View to force himself into the Notice of the Governors of these Provinces, & with equal effrontery has had the presumption to Write a letter to the Marquis Florida Blanca & desires it to be forwarded to Court. The request of the Vagabond Imposter ought not to be Complied with & Your Excellency should open the letter that we might be better acquainted with his Views & designs. This is what I woud have done if the letter had fallen into my hands.[290]

This is all I have to Communicate on the Score of business, & what Remains for me to say is of an Interesting Nature to my feelings. Your Excellency is about to leave Your Government & this perhaps is the last occasion that I shall have to address a letter to You as Governor of Louisiana. Accept therefore my warmest thanks & acknowledgments as well on my part Individually as in behalf of my Nation for the Many proofs You have given us of Your attention to our real Interest & happiness & I Sincerely pray that the Superior being Who has given You a benevolent & good heart may preserve You & Your family on Your passage & that You may have a happy meeting with Your Sovereign & our great Protector whose Interest & Views you have so well promoted.

It is to You Sir that the Creeks are greatly Indebted for their forming a Just opinion of Spanish honor & good faith & be assured that Your

288. A similar account is included in Panton's letter to Miró, December 11, 1791, AGI C 203.
289. Bowles to Miro, December 4, 1791, AGI C 2371. See also Bowles to the state of Georgia, October 26, 1791, in which he demanded recognition of the Creeks as "a free and independent nation" and protection of its territorial integrity. A treaty, he warned, "should be a national act, approved by the legislative council of the nation, and not a clandestine agreement with an individual of no consequence, such as the supposed treaty with Alexander Gillibray" (AGI C 1436).
290. McGillivray repeated the foregoing to O'Neill, January 1, 1792, AGI C 1436.

Name will not be soon erased from our Minds. Wishing that You may be long happy, I remain with Sincere & great Esteem
  Your Excellencys Obedient Servant
                              ALEX: McGILLIVRAY [rubric]
  his Excellency Brigadier General Stephen Miro
  Governor & Commander in Chief of Louisiana &c.

165. *Seagrove to McGillivray, January 14, 1792*
                    [Copy in AGI C 206]
                    ST. MARY IN GEORGIA, 14th January 1792
DEAR SIR
  With exceeding Concern I have received the disagreeable information of the distracted State the Creek nation has been in for Some months past, owing to the attempts of *Mr. Bowles* a desperate Vile adventurer.
  I feel as a friend for the very unpleasant Situation you have been in, in Consequence of his intrusion; but I have reason to hope that your Sufferings are nearly at an end, that your Country will Soon be freed from so grand an impostor as Bowles, that peace, tranquility and happiness will Shortly be reestablished throughout the Creek nation, never again to be disturbed by Such a Vile Character.[291]
  I have now the pleasure to inform you, that I have just received dispatches from the president of the united States, the Contents of which are of the utmost importance to yourself and the Creek nation— the Communication of which to you through me, must be by a personal interview—and as I am at a loss to know where you are at present, I have dispatched this to our friend Jack Kinnard, with an earnest request that he will provide a trusty person to deliver it to you with all possible Speed.
  As I am ordered to the Rocklanding on the river oconee, I have to request that you will meet me at that place, or as near as you Conveniently can, and in as Short a Space of time as possible. What I am commissioned by the united States to Communicate to you, as well as the dispatches you will receive when we meet Can not fail to give you Satisfaction; I hope you will therefore use all possible dispatch in meeting me.
  Should any thing detain you for a few days, in Setting out, please dispatch an express or two (the moment you receive this) to meet me at the Rock landing, informing of your rout & the place you propose for our meeting.

  291. Writing to Knox on the same day, Seagrove revealed that this hope was based on word from Jack Kinnard that Bowles was losing the respect of the Indians who had been fond of him and that Kinnard now considered him a liar and an imposter (Spanish translation in AHN E 3894 bis).

I should be more particular but do not Conceive it prudent, as this may chance to fall into improper hands.

With every Sentiment of Friendship and respect I remain
Your obedient Devoted & hble. Serv.

JAS. SEAGROVE

The Hon. Alexander McGillivray

166. *Carondelet to McGillivray, January 19, 1792*
[Draft in AGI C 205]

SIR   NEW ORLEANS, 19 January 1792

To give you a convincing proof of the disposition with which I have taken the command of this Province, as likewise of the desire I have to do everything in my power to oblige you as an unequivocal mark of the regard and consideration I have for you, as soon as I received the intelligence communicated to me by the Govr. of Pensacola of the reason that for the present moment deprives me of the satisfaction of seeing you in this capital I gave immediate orders to fit out one of the King's Schooners mounting six six pounders well manned and commanded by Dn. Joseph Hevia officer of the Royal Navy with orders to station his cruise about the Ysland of St. George to intercept the two Vessels expected by Bowles from Providence.

The said officer has my orders to combine with you the means of seizing the said Bowles dead or alive,[292] in case he be found as it is thought at the entrance of the River Apalache, and to enable him to put in execution this design, has on board of this vessel twenty well determined Soldiers commanded by an officer fit for the purpose, & an armed boat with Swivels to go up the River if necessity requires it.

Be so kind as to inform Mr. Hevia by some of your confidents that will meet him at St. George's Island, of the intelligence you may have of Bowles, as likewise if his two vessels are arrived, and particularly if Bowles is or not on the river Apalache, at what distance from its mouth, and any other mark that may exactly describe the place of his existence, adding every other direction you may think fit to surprise and take him, mentioning at the same time if you can assist him in this enterprise.[293]

I remain with the greatest regard & esteem, Sir
Your Excellency's etc.

292. Compare with the American attitude as expressed in Knox's instructions to Seagrove, February 20, 1792, that his first duty was to have Bowles' "impostorship properly exposed, and his person either secured or banished" (ASP IA, I, 249-50).

293. Writing to Las Casas on January 18, 1792, Carondelet said that if this detachment failed to capture Bowles he would employ a man at Natchez who had offered to kill him if promised "a good reward" (AGI C 1441).

167. *Leslie*[294] *to Panton, January 30, 1792*
[Copy in AGI C 203]

FORT ST. MARKS, 30th January 1792

DEAR SIR

In consideration of the State of affairs among the Indians since I was last with you, the Following disagreable narrated will not Seem so extraordinary.

On the night of the 15th Instant John Hambly arrived at Appalachy with a Hard Talk to the Indians against Bowles, on the 16th we had sent an express to Mickasucky for their chief and his attendants to come down to us, in the mean time I came down here with Governor Quesadas letters to the commandant & to know how we might concert measures for our mutual good; but before I got back to the Store *Bowls, a major Cunningham*, with about a Hundred Indians had made themselves master of all the property about the place, & have been in possession of it Since that time,[295] they *generously* permitted Hambly & *myself*, to depart the place; Hambly went home, I came here. N[ed][296] they kept with them under pretence of allowing him 125 Guineas a year; I have been endeavouring to see you, or to write you ever since, but without success; I had got as far as St. George's Island in an open boat with 5 Spaniards, but the weather obliged us to return, when two or three days after, Julian brought me your letter of the 4th Inst; as by it I find we may expect McG[illivra]y this way soon, as also the ship Mary, I have determined to stay here to see the End of this matter. Although the Indians are outrageous against you & your house McG-[illivra]y & all who are opposed to their *Genl. Bowls*, yet I think they will not destroy the skins which may amount to about 28 thds unpacked, & 27 being packed before Xmas. Hence your Loss will be but a bagatelle to some I have known you sustain.

Some days ago Bowles and Cunningham differed and Cunningham afraid of his life, came to the Fort for Protection & is now in *el Sepo*. This morning *Ned* came here with all the Books and old papers, having heard some threats against his life. Just before he left that, Bowls was joined by G: Wellbank, whom he immediately dubbed *Major Wellbank*.

This Scoundrel had the assurance to deny that he was the same

294. Robert Leslie, younger brother of John.
295. For description of what happened January 9-25 see the statement of William Cunningham, April 2, 1792, AGI C 2371; for the period January 16-28, see the statement of Edward Forrester, February 28, 1792, *ibid*. Both have been published, together with an excellent discussion by Lawrence Kinnaird in "The Significance of William Augustis Bowles' Seizure of Panton's Apalachee Store in 1792, " *The Florida Historical Society Quarterly*, IX, 156-92.
296. Edward Forrester.

Forrester knew as Col. Stewart's overseer; as I am not certain whether this may not miscarry I shall deferr being more particular untill some vessell leaves this for you. In the meantime it will be necessary to Send us (when you are assured of things being settled this way) provisions for our People, who are now living among the Mickasucky Indians. The ship will I suppose bring us goods enough to Keep us jogging, at least, till we have time to look about us. Government will no doubt take up this matter now, & I hope in the end, it will be no loss to the House, perhaps for its Good. That it may be so is the Sincere wish of Dear Sir, with respect & unfeigned esteem,

Your most obed. humble Servant

ROBT. LESLIE

List of people said to be under Sentence of proscription by Bowls: William Panton, John Leslie & Robt., Edward Forrester, Tom Perryman, Tom Carr, James Loveitt, James Burges with others I Forgett.

R. L.

P. D. Altho' the Commandant is writing his chief fully on these matters, it may not be amiss, for me to say that as far as I could learn from these robbers while two days their closely watched prisoner, there are a number of them whose immediate intentions are to succeed each other in Case of any falling in the attempt, and their ultimate Intentions, are to embroil the Indians & the Spaniards, to put the two Floridas in as much confusion as possible, for the motive of Introducing the Kentucky & Cumberland people, to open the Mississippi, as also all the harbours & ports this way & throw the Spaniards out of the Country; when the conquest of Mexico & Peru is to be tried next.[297]

If this man can not be laid hold of soon, I mean to open Store in the fort & endeavour as much as I can to Collect the Debts of this House, which amount to at least 40,000 Drs., but of this matter you will write me fully.[298]

297. Bowles explained his purpose differently. He assured the commandant of St. Marks that he had no intention to bother any Spanish subject or to let any Indian do so (Bowles to Guessy, January 4, 1792, AGI C 1436). The same day he proclaimed his intention to open the Creek and Cherokee ports to the vessels of all nations (AGI C 2371). On January 16, he told Guessy that he had seized St. Marks because Panton had affronted him by offering two thousand pesos for his assassination (AGI C 2362). On January 31, he declared that Panton had taken possession of stores that belonged to the public and had also attempted to stop his trade; consequently he confiscated the stores at St. Marks for the benefit of the Indians (*ibid.*). To Durouzeaux also he wrote that Panton was a traitor (January 31, *ibid.*). So likewise in his letter to Burgess, February 7 (AGI C 2371; see also document 171, *infra;* and Bowles to Carondelet, March 14 and 17, 1792, AGI C 2371).

298. For other descriptions of the seizure of St. Marks see Guessy to Quesada, January 18, 1792, AGI C 1436; Robert Leslie to John Leslie, January 31, 1792, *ibid.*, the testimony of John Leslie's Negro, Frank, *ibid.*, Robert Leslie to Christine, May 3, 1792, AGI C 152A; the declaration of Henry Smith, May 9, 1792, *ibid;* and his testimony, June 12, 1792, AGI C 2362. On June 24, 1792, Robert Leslie,

168. *Carondelet to McGillivray, February 6, 1792*

[Copy in AGI C 205]

NEW ORLEANS, 6th February 1792

SIR

His Majesty highly interested in the welfare of the Creek Nation has been gratiously to appoint Lieutt. dn. Pedro Olivier[299] to reside among them in his Royal name that been more particularly acquainted he should represent in the behalf: I accordingly send you the afore said Lieutt. with this credential trusting he will be received & treated with the Satisfactory distinction his most gratious Majesty shows to your Nation.

The above Lieutt. Olivier is particularly charged to promote & support the credit & authority you acquired among the Creeks, as well as to endeavour to oppose Bowles, knowing the weight, & consideration [it] shall give to your Character having by you a Resident appointed by his Most Catholic Majesty has been the Real cause of hastening Olivier's departure from thence: Wishing you all prosperity and health untill I may have the pleasure of being personally acquainted with you, I remain, Sir

Your most obedient humble servant,

EL BARON DE CARONDELET

169. *Panton to McGillivray, February 9, 1792*

[Copy in AGI C 203]

PENSACOLA 9th February 1792

DEAR SIR

By the forementioned duplicate of a letter[300] from Mr. Robert Leslie, you'll See our Situation at St. Marks, & that the vessels which Bowls expected are neither more nor less than the Goods in our Store, which were placed by us for the purpose of maintaining that trade, which the whole nation promised & engaged to protect. Now Sir, I Call upon you as the first chief & the principal one in the Land, who was the means of my Settling that Store at St. Marks, & I beg that you'll Call together all those chiefs that were at Pecolata, & I demand of you all to know what I have done to merit this inhuman treatment. When you were all poor & naked I voluntarily relinquished ease & the

---

Edward Foster [*sic*, Forrester], and John Innerarity certified that Panton's loss through Bowles' seizure of the store at St. Marks amounted to 2674 pounds, 1s. (ASP Public Lands, IV, 161).

299. Pedro Olivier was sent in reality as a check upon McGillivray. Miró had recommended the step (Miró to Cabello, October 1, 1789, AGI C 1425, and to Las Casas, August 12, 1790, AGI C 1446). The court approved on October 26, 1791 (Floridablanca to Miró, draft in AHN E 3889 bis). For Olivier's instructions issued by Carondelet, February 8, 1792, AGI C 122A.

300. Document 167, *supra*.

pleasures of refined Society to live amongst you for no other end than
that of administring to your wants. I have been the means of your
closing your women & children for seventeen years past who must
otherwise have gone naked. Many hundred of your people have I fed
when they were Starving, & when you had enemies to Contend with,
you all know that my exertions were forever in your favour, & for all
these favours your people have Joined with a Scoundrel to destroy me.
I demand Satisfaction from the Nation in General for this outrage;
I do not expect that the Nation will be able to restore to me what
I have lost, but I demand the Life of that Villain Bowls, who has been
the Cause of all this mischief, or that he may be taken & delivered
over to the Spanish Garrison, in order that he be tried according to the
Laws he has so wickedly broke through.

 I am
   Dear Sir Your most Obedient Servant

            WM. PANTON [*rubric*]

Alexr. McGillivray Esqr.

170. *Panton to the Kings, Warriors, & Headmen of the Cussitaws, Cowetas,
Brokenarrow my Friend John Kennard & all the rest of the Lower Towns,
February 19, 1792*

       [Copy in AGI C 203]

FRIENDS AND BROTHERS

 By a letter which I have received within these few days past from
St. Marks, I am informed that Mr. Bowles and another Vagabond,
who Stiles himself Major Cunningham, aided by a number of your
people of the Coweta & ofsuky Towns, on the 16th of last month did
enter my Stores at Appalachy and with force of Arms have robbed me
of all the Goods & Skins which I had at that place.

 As it is now more than a month Since that happened, you have all
had time for reflection & I send this to James Derousseaux your Lin-
guister, that I may be informed from your own lips what it is that I have
done to deserve such inhumane treatment.

 You all must remember what passed between you & me at Piccolato,
and that it was at your own request I settled a Store at Appalachy,
which you the headmen of the Nation promised in the most Solemn
manner to protect. I could have had soldiers enough to have guarded
that place but I considered myself amongst my friends and Brothers,
and thought myself and family and property as Safe amongst you as
if I had been in my own Land.

 You cannot but remember, when I Came first amongst you, that
I did not Come in the Garb of poverty and wretchedness as Bowles

  308

Came, nor did I lead you with lies to the Sea there to gape at the Wind, looking for Vessells that will never arrive. No! My Vessels Came before me loaded with Goods. I Filled Appalachy with Goods for the supply of the lower Towns. I settled Pensacola for the conveniency of the upper towns; and the chactaws & Chickasaws are Supplied at my Magazines at Mobile. From these places you have been enabled to cloth yourselves & Familys during a long period when you could get them no where else.

You all know when you had ennemys to Contend with, my advice and assistance was forever exerted in your favour & when a moderate peace was offered to you, I was amongst the foremost to advise you to accept of it & Keep it. When you were hungry you all know that I have fed thousands of you for nothing. When you had enemies Mr. McGillivray & myself saved you from destruction, and now that you are at peace with all around you, you have afronted him & Joined with a Scoundrell to destroy me.

Brothers if this is the way that you Serve your friends, if you should want them again who will Serve you on Such Conditions.

Brothers you have not acted right, but I do not blame you so much as I do your adviser, nor is it yet too late to regain my Good opinion; Mr. McGillivray Served you faithfully, & whoever tells you the Contrary is a liar & the Truth is not in him; I advise you to go to him and appologize for your behaviour, he is generous & will forgive you.

As to me and what you have done to me I must have Satisfaction & the only Satisfaction that I wish or seek for is the punishment of that Villain that Prince of Liars Bowles, whom you must bring here dead or alive; and then the Talk will be Straight between us. He calls himself an Englishman, but be assured he is none; he tells you that he Came from the King of England, but when did you See an officer of that King Come to you in poverty & rags. I believe you all know me to be an Englishman, and if that Country has any intentions of redressing your wrongs (if you have any) I have Ships that left England long after Bowls Came from New Providence, and must have heard it Sooner than him; but I assure you on the word of an honest man I have heard no Such Talk, and believe me when I tell you that the English are at too great a distance ever to be of any real use to you.

This wicked man has come to deceive you, he wishes to throw you head long into a War with the Spaniards & the americans & once he has accomplished that, then he will run off to his lurking places amongst the Bahamas, & you be left without a friend in the world.

I beg to hear from you as soon as possible. I have my ship at St.

Marks with the yearly Supply of Goods and there is more than enough here.

Wishing that the Great giver & Taker of Breath may restore such as are mad amongst you to reason right on what they have done, withdraw the film from their Eyes, that they may See & know their friends from their Foes, they will then perceive that I am Still their Friend & Brother.

WM. PANTON [rubric]

PENSACOLA 19th February 1792

*To the Kings, Warriors, & Headmen of the Cussitaws, Cowetas,
Brokenarrow my Friend John Kennard & all the rest of the Lower Towns.*

171. *Bowles to Carondelet, March 13, 1792*

[AGI C 2371]

NEW ORLEANS March 13th 1792

SIR

I am informed since my arrival in this Town, that it was reported I had an intention to commence hostilities Against his Catholic Majestys Subjects in this Country. It has been the misfortune of this Country, for a long time, to harbour some interested and designing persons, who have carried on the most artfull and dangerous intreagues, tending to involve the Spanish Nation in a War with the Creeks, by industriously reporting the most gross falshoods to both sides. But the Creeks would not break the peace without an absolute violation of all Friendship by an open attack upon them, which has been declaired by those people to be the intention of the Spanish Government, and I myself have been continually threatened, and repeated attempts have been made to assassinate me, which has also been reported to be the orders of his Catholic Majestys Governors. This I conceived to be false knowing the intreagues of those people therefore dispised them, and have steadily adhered to what I concieved to be the true Interest of the Creek Nation, and not enemical or prejudicial to his Catholic Majestys Interest, or the Interest of his subjects.

In the latter end of the year 1788 proposals was secretly made to me, by the People of Cain Tuke & Cumberland (who are the remains of the American and tired of their Situation in the interior parts of the Country are ready for any enterprise) to prevail on the council of the Creeks, to recieve them under their protection and to attack his Catholic Majestys Subjects on the Mississippi and the Floridas, with an offer to support me with 10,000 Min.

This I refused concieving it the interest of the Creek Nation to keep those Adventurous Americans from geting posessions in their Country.

These proposals being thought not safe to be trusted in the Breast of a Person so hostile, as I on that occation declaired myself, some plan must be laid to get rid of me and in the Month of March 1789 several attempts was made to cut me off.

In this situation was affairs when I went to england upon some business which I shall hereafter declair to your Excellency. During my absence from this Country fresh proposals were made to Alexr. McGillivray, who taking upon himself the title of Chief of the Nations, Subjugated those people to the United States and entered into a privat contract with those people, in order to get posession of the Country as far as the 32d degree of North latitude, and have actually obtained grants for those lands from the Legislative body of the State of Georgia, Copys of which I have in my posession. These people hearing of my return and knowing they could not get posession of this teritory against my will, came forward not three months past with a proposal, which was to invite me to the command of the Whole. This also I have refused, and reported the Whole business to the Council of the Creeks, who taking the business into consideration passed sentence of Death on McGillivray.[301]

And the Chiefs in Council conciving that it was requisite and necessary that immediate and viggorous exertion should be made to save the Country from confusion, which could not be done without the executive power, being vested in one person they therefore appointed me Genl & Director of the Affairs of the Nation. My first step upon entering into the office of Government was to declair our disapprobation of the measures adopted by the subjects of the United States, and that we would oppose with our swords all operations that might tend to give them posessions in our Country, and in the mean time I put the Nation in a state of defence and ordered all american subjects to depart the nation.

I next presented an address to his Catholic Majestys ministers stating the situation the designs the wishes of the Creek Nation in all openness and sincerity, with an offer to Unite in a common cause upon principals that will tend to establish an everlasting peace and be a secure covering for his his Catholic Majestys Collonies in America.

This being done I had hopes of peace at home, but one object still remained, and that the most dangerous of all, which made every effort to sowe the seeds of discord and breed confusion. This was the house of Panton Leslie & Co we knowing these People to be under some contract

301. If such action was taken it was merely by a small coterie of Bowles' supporters. Quesada stated to Floridablanca on March 25, 1792, that McGillivray was supported by "most of the chiefs and the greater number of the people" (AHN E 3889 bis).

311

with Spain and concieving there might be a difficulty with the court of
Spain in removing those people, they being British subjects and as
such placed in our Country (as they reported) by the English in order
to supply us with articles of Commerce for our convenience, But who
on the contrary have taken every advantage, that the privalidge of a
monopoly could give them, and have misrepresented the nation, to his
Catholic Majestys Governors, & thereby have done us every injury,
knowing also that those people were engaged in the designs of our
enemies as they payed the Ynterpreters who was engaged by Mr.
McGillivray to act in behalf of the Confederacy he had engaged
himself in.

The Nation being acquainted with all these circumstances could not
refrain from removing so dangerous and so active a set of people, and
therefore ordered the stores of Panton Leslie & Co to be siezed which
was accordingly done on the 19th January.[302] This oppression being
removed by the Creek Nation Alone, will save the Court of Madrid the
trouble of recieving and answering any remonstrance that might otherwise be made by *the Court of London*, had the subjects of Spain commited
such an act, and has opened the way for peace to be established between
the Creek Nation and Spain, which those people have spared no pains
to prevent, by reporting every falsehood which their mischievious
Imagination could invent and brout the Nation on the Brink of a war.

Having thus given your Excellency a brief state of the policy hitherto
pursued by the Creek Nation and the disignes of the people engaged
in the Country, I will submit to your Excellencys judgment, whither
the Creek Nation deserves the attention of his Catholic Majesty, whither
they have acted impolitic, injudicious, or unwise, & whether the
Governors has not been imposed upon in the most scandalous manner
to answer the ends of a designing set of Vagabonds.

It is my most earnest wish to establish peace between the Creek
Nation and their Allies, and His Catholic Majesty for that purpose
I accepted your Excellencys invitation[303] and came to this Town in
order to make such arrangements as will prevent any misunderstanding
taking place or any accidents happening, untill answers are returned

302. Actually on January 16.
303. See Carondelet to Bowles, January 31, 1792; Carondelet's passport and
safe-conduct for Bowles, February 3; Hevia to Bowles, February 22; and Hevia to
Bowles, February 24; copies in AGI C 2362. Bowles was guaranteed a safe return
to St. Marks. Bowles left another letter for the captain of the ship he was expecting,
authorizing him to unload and either wait or depart (copy in AGI C 2371).
Wellbank feared that he would be carried off. He and the Indians took "what they
thought proper" from Panton's store, left the rest, and went home to remain quiet
until Bowles returned (Wellbank to Bowles, March 6, 1792, AGI C 152A). Quesada
reported to Las Casas on May 8, 1792, that McGillivray sent one hundred armed
Indians "to undeceive and disperse" Bowles' followers (AGI C 1436).

from El Conde de Florida Blanca[304] to the address of the Nation and not to answer any charge that may be brought against the Nation by Mr. Panton Leslie &c.[305]

I have the Honor to be your Excellency most obedient and very humble Servant

WM. A. BOWLES *Gnl. Dr. Aff. C. N.*

His Excellency the Barron Carondelet.

172. *Carondelet to Las Casas, March 22, 1792*
[Spanish original in AGI C 1446]

. . . .I have written to Pedro Olivier, commissioner at the side of McGillivray, to find out what effect was produced on the Creek Nation by the imprisonment of Bowles.[306] I have addressed another letter to McGillivray to urge him to persuade the principal chiefs to come to see me. My intention is to win their good will by means of presents, to strengthen their union with Spain, to make them see that the safety of their nation depends on their reunion with the Cherokees, Choctaws, Chickasaws, etc., with the support of Spain which will protect them against the usurpations of the Americans their natural enemies, whenever the latter are the aggressors, and finally to prepare for the commissioner of his Majesty, Pedro Olivier, the means to win the confidence of the Creek Nation in such a way that the government can in the future get along without the support of McGillivray and be promptly informed of all that should occur among those Indians, at present more powerful and civilized than any other savage nation.

As I understand it, it is convenient to cut off all communication between the partisans of Bowles and Providence, until the tranquility among these Indians is entirely reestablished, since it is certain that Lord Dunmore and the traders of that island, determined to support him and to destroy the firm of Panton, will try to irritate these savages against the Spaniards, and will perhaps induce them to commit some hostilities. Two frigates, establishing their cruise from Santa Rosa Island

304. José Monino, Conde de Floridablanca, was at this time the king's chief minister. During the war with England he had sought to protect Spanish America by erecting a buffer Indian province east of the Mississippi. After 1783 he continued his efforts to prevent American expansion. It was really Floridablanca who decided upon the policy of forming alliances with the Southeastern Indians, of counter-colonization in Louisiana and the Floridas, of closing the Mississippi, and of asserting Spain's claim to the region as far north as the Tennessee.
305. Bowles addressed two more letters in this same tone to Carondelet, March 14 and 17, 1792 (AGI C 2371).
306. See document 173, *infra.* The Spanish chargés at Philadelphia reported that the news of Bowles' capture "occasioned singular pleasure" among the heads of the American government, and that the secretaries of state and war immediately came to question them (Jaudenes and Viar to Floridablanca, May 11, 1792, AHN E 3894 bis).

313

to St. Johns River, would accomplish the double purpose of preventing this communication, and of watching over Pensacola in case the rumors of an early invasion by the Americans against the dominions of his Majesty should come true.

May God preserve you many years. New Orleans, March 22, 1792.

EL BARON DE CARONDELET [*rubric*]

173. *A Talk from the Kings, Chiefs & Warriors of the Lower Creek Nation to Captn Pedro Olivier Comisario Español, July 3, 1792*
[Copy in AGI C 2371]

COWETAH OLD TOWN, 3d July, 1792

FRIENDS & BROTHERS,

We have a short Talk to give you & hope you will pay attention to it. Our Beloved Friend & Father, (Genl. Bowles) is in your Land—he has been gone from us a long time—we can hear of his being sent about from Place to Place, but cannot hear of his returning—our Hearts have been heavy & overburthened since his departure—we wish you to send for him, that we may see him once more in our Land to revive our drooping Spirits. We have heard your Talk, but can give you no Ansr. to it until we see our beloved Father, therefore the sooner you have him sent to us, the Sooner you will know our Minds. It is our intention to abide by your Talk, if you send back our father, but should you refuse our Talk we will refuse yours, nor never listen to it while we have Breath. We hear so many stories about him, that we are almost distracted, therefore let him be sent back & our Hearts will be streight— but if you refuse our Talk we know not what will follow. If any of your People come into our Land, we feed them & protect them & let them go when they please, it does not seem to be so with your People, or why do they keep our friend from us to distress us. Two of us, who are in this Talk, (Okillissa Chopka & Tustunie Opoia) have at our Breasts a Medal of his Catholic Majesty, as a token we do not forget him. We hold the English by one hand & the Spanish by the other. We expect you will make no excuses about our father, but have him sent to us as soon as possible, as we are uneasy about him & impacient to see him. The Land your people live on at St. Augustine, St. Marks & Pansacola is ours & only lent by us to you, should you refuse this our request we do not know how much longer we can lend it to you. We have no more to say, only to send this Talk to where our father is, that he may be sent back, when you will find our Hearts Streight & as you would wish.

314

XV

INTERFERENCE FROM CARONDELET

174. *White to McGillivray, March 5, 1792*

[Copy in AGI C 203]

OCONEE 5th March 1792

DEAR SIR

This will be handed to you by James Randon (my interpreter) who from motives to serve you, I consented should undertake to deliver the letter, which will accompany this, from our worthy friend James Seagrove, Esqr., who Congress has authorised fully to reistablish you in the Nation, & see the late treaty at New York carried into full effect. Your presence is absolutely necessary, to bring about this desirable revolution with the Creeks, who have taken such unwarrantable Steps, under the direction of Mr. Bowles.

The presents for the Creeks, that have already arrived (some of which Randon has seen) are very considerable, & on the treaty being fulfilled, & you again restored to your former influence, & Authority (which the President seems determined to bring about) every Individual in the Nation will feel the bounty of Congress.

Mr. Seagrove desired I would write to endeavour if possible, to induce you to meet him, & that I might write with certainty, shew me his orders from the Secy. of War by command of the President, which were so favorable to you, that as a friend, I should be very sorry, you should delay one moment & on your arrival am convinced you will be fully compensated for the trouble, or fatigue, you may have on the tour, in fact you are to be consulted on all occasions, & whatever you, & Mr. Seagrove, think necessary, to settle all our affairs amicably the President has directed shall be done. However as Congress wants nothing from the nation, it is expected all matters may by you, be easily accommodated.

Probably you have already recd. information from Mr. Seagrove by way of Kenards, as he wrote in January by that route.[307] Mr. Seagrove requested that Randon should be returned with all possible speed, to give him information of your intentions, when I should be extremely happy in a line from you, & when you arrive in this quarter,

307. See document 165, *supra.*

shall do myself the pleasure to wait on you, to conduct you to my habitation, if you think it an eligible situation.[308]

I am Dear Sir with respect
Your Most Obt. Servt.

(*Signed*) EDWD. WHITE

Brigadier General Alexr. McGillivray
Chief &c. &c. Creek Nation Tensa, West Florida

175. *Carondelet to Panton, March 24, 1792*
[Copy in AGI C 214]

NEW ORLEANS, 24th March 1792

SIR

In answer to your letter of the 6th instant I must tell you that William Bowles being in our power the measures, which you said McGillivray would take to get him, are useless. Indeed I wonder at the indifference and slowness of McGillivray in an affair so much more important to himself than to us, since his life and credit were involved in it.

As I am informed by McGillivray of his resolution to conclude the treaty about the boundaries of the Creek Nation this summer, I can only express my surprise that you as a close friend of his could not dissuade him from a resolve so much against your interest and against his own. Therefore as an Englishman, as a protectee of Spain, and as Mr. Panton, you ought to make every attempt to prevent the conclusion of a treaty so contrary to the interests of the Creek Nation, to those of Spain, to those of England more closely connected than ever to Spain, and to your own; for that treaty, making the Creeks absolutely dependent upon the Americans, will indispensably bring forth commercial relations, which will surely deprive your House of the advantage it draws from trade with the nation.[309]

My most gratious Soverign cannot look without concern on the repeated encroachments of the Americans, who successively become Masters and possess themselves of the Lands belonging to the Indian Nations his Allys; the English for their part have a particular interest in setting bounds to the States, ambitious neighbors to the rest of their possessions on this continent, who mean to invade everything they see convenient to them.

That is the very reason that prompted the British Government to help secretly the Tribes of the North against the Army of General St. Clair, which was routed at the end of last year.

308. For McGillivray's answer, see ASP IA, I, 295-96.
309. Document 178, *infra*, reveals how well Panton carried out these instructions.

316

Too just to excite the savages against their neighbors, his Most Catholic Majesty cannot but help these Nations his Allys, provided they are not the aggressors. In these terms I have spoken plainly, and I shall always do so. Whenever they are attacked unjustly I shall support them openly and vigorously, being unafraid of the Boasting of their Foes, and shall avail myself of the advantages these Provinces can afford for their defense, if properly managed.

Accordingly it becomes us to cooperate without loss of time to destroy the treaty between the Creeks and the Americans. To this end you must use your influence with McGillivray, giving him to understand that he exposes himself to lose the pension appointed by our most gratious Sovereign, (which can be augmented, which, I pledge my word, I will do without consulting the Minister as soon as he relinquishes the pension allowed him by the united States, and breaks every connection with them), or that if we have no other recourse left we can oppose him with the aforesaid Bowles,[310] who certainly will throw every obstacle in the way of the conclusion of the treaty, as he did the preceding year, and would procure us undoubtedly the most intimate connection with the Creeks, whose separation McGillivray seeks so unjustly.

You can assure him that should the Americans attempt to seize by force the lands they have been trying to secure by cheating and negotiating, that I not only will help the Creeks openly and powerfully with arms and ammunition, but will engage the Cheroquis, Chactaw, Chicasaw, and Sawanaw in the same contest to confine the Americans within due bounds.

Do me the favor to send the enclosed letter immediately to Don Pedro Olivier, King's Commissary in the Creek Nation, and to confer with him on the success of the affair with McGillivray. Make your best endeavors to prevail on the principal chiefs of the Upper and Lower Creeks to come and speak with me upon this business, which, I believe, will be highly advantageous for our negotiation.

I trust from the faithfulness, friendship, and attachment you must have for the Spanish Nation that you will exert your best efforts to conclude everything favorably.

I remain, etc.

310. Though made prisoner Bowles was shown some deference, apparently in the hope that he would become a Spanish agent. For example, his guards were instructed to guard him carefully on the way to Havana but with "imperceptible vigilance" (Carondelet to Trudeau, March 22, 1792, AGI C 122A; see also Bowles to Alcudia, July 14, 1793, AGI C 2371). Two months after Bowles' actual arrest, the Spanish government ordered efforts to attract Bowles to the Spanish party, and this failing, his seizure by any means necessary (Bajamar to O'Neill, May 23, 1792, AGI C 176). For his subsequent career see note 130, *supra*.

[AGI C 204]

LITTLE TALLASIE 10 April 1792

SIR

I have the Satisfaction to acknowledge the receit of Your Excellencys much esteemd favor of 19 ulto. I am very happy to find that the Infamous desperado Bowles is now in the Situation to be rewarded for his daring Villainies.

I am told that he had the Impudence to charge me with disaffection to the Spanish Nation & of being a Secret favourer of the Americans, & pretends to have Intercepted letters of mine to prove it.[311] It is well known that all my Correspondence with the Americans was always publishd in their News papers, of Course every people is in possession of them. Nor was he ever in a Situation with the Americans to have an opportunity to Intercept any of my letters. I believe that he pick't up some printed papers of the Yasou & Tennessee Companys, who a Year or two ago made so much noise & wherein those people took the liberty of placing my name at their head in order to delude people of property to Join their Schemes, & if they did so without my Authority it was not my fault, but I took the best measures to Convince the World that I was No favourer of the Companys in my Negotiations with the american Congress, as the destruction of the Companys was made the basis of the Treaty of Peace & the President of the Congress publishd a proclamation respecting it in July 1790. Last Summer the american Govr. Blount of Franklin gave me Notice that Certain Persons of the Tennessee Company in defiance of the late Treaty were proceeding to make establishments on the Muscle Shoals of the Cherokee River & that I might take what Steps I pleased on which I sent off Partys from this Country & dispersed them, since which no further attempts have been made by the americans to establish New Settlements in those parts. On the whole I trust that all who know me are Convinced that Neither my private character Nor political Integrity needs any Vindication from the foul aspersions of Such a Miscreant as Bowles.

It may appear Surprising that he was able to accomplish the mischief that he did, but then it is to be considerd that a great many young Indians have been raisd in the american War & have been so accustomd to War & depredation that a regular life is dissagreeable to them, & they will eagerly listen to & follow any one that holds out the temptation of plunder to them & of getting goods at an easy rate. So the party of Bowles was not Considerable as to Number or rank in the Country, Of Course his progress was not much attended to by any one,

311. See document 171, *supra.*

& he Committed the outrage upon Pantons Store at the Season when all the people of Note were hunting in the Woods, for among the Indians all ranks & Conditions depend for Subsistence on hunting in the Woods except they have property. It is Certain that if he had a Strong party he woud have plunderd the Inhabitants of the Floridas & Georgia. Now he is gone I cannot hear a Murmur of discontent on that account expressd by any Indians.[312] This affair however it has affected the Interest of Panton & Co. will have its good consequences in guarding against future adventurers.

The limits between us & the Americans of Georgia was to have been markd in October last but the great promises of Bowles having an English Fleet & army to assist the Indians persuaded them not to agree to mark the line at the appointed time. The American Commissioners have applyd to have the affair settled this Spring & as they have declared to the Nation that they will not do any business with them without I am personally present, I am prevaild on to go to the Frontier River to set matters to rights, as I wish to prevent any fresh differences between the americs. of the South & this Nation on the Score of Lands. But being of opinion that a good look out ought to be kept on the N. W. frontier I instructed the hunters that if they saw any appearances of Settlements on those rivers or bodys of Americans, that they shoud attack them. My orders have been a little exceeded, as they have destroyd some boats who had passports from Governors & totally obstructed the Navigation of the rivers during the past Season.[313]

I am lately Informd by Col. White[314] the Commt. of Pensacola that some deserters had killd an Indian & much abused a Woman who is dangerously ill. It appears that the Indian in attempting to take up the deserters was killed by them. They were since apprehended, the relations of the deceased are Calld to Pensacola to [see] them executed & this will Satisfy them.

Being soon going to the lower Towns to meet the chiefs of that quarter in assembly I will explain to them Your Excellencys desire, as I do not intend to make any Stay at the Frontier after two or three days Conference with the Commissioners, on my return we shall have a meeting here to Introduce Lieut. Olivier to this upper Nation, & afterward I will do myself the pleasure to see you in New Orleans.

312. Bowles did have his partisans; see document 173, *supra.*

313. See documents 182 and 183, *infra;* also Blount to McGillivray, May 17, 1792, ASP IA, I, 269-70; and the statements of James Ore, *ibid.*, p. 284, Richard Finnelson, *ibid.*, pp. 288-91, and Joseph Deratte, *ibid.*, pp. 291-92.

314. Enrique White was acting governor of Pensacola in the absence of O'Neill, whom he was to succeed later in the year. From 1795 until his death in 1813 he was governor of East Florida.

I am respectfully, Your Excellencys Most Obedient Servant

ALEX: MCGILLIVRAY [*rubric*]

the favor of a present of Taffia, ammn. Salt &a. is requested for the bearer of this letter.

his Excellency El Baron de Carondelet
  Governor & Commander in chief of Louisiana & West Florida.

177. *Olivier to Carondelet, April 10, 1792*

[Spanish original in AGI C 25]

As a result of the duplicate of your official letter which I have just received, dated March 15th last, I shall tell you that on the 19th of that month I announced to you my arrival at this destination, where I have been quite well received by Alexander McGillivray who has given me as my lodging place a house which he has in the region called Little Tallassie, about three leagues farther up from his present residence called Hickory Ground. . . . .[315]

I cannot tell you on this occasion anything with regard to my reception in the Creek Nation, since I have not yet been presented at the general council of this Nation, as I have requested of Alexander McGillivray, and as I communicate to you in my official letter, in which I explained to you the reasons alleged by Alexander McGillivray which did not permit it until the middle of this month. This circumstance, together with the lack of an interpreter who should be at my disposal, has prevented me from presenting myself in the villages, even in the neighboring ones, from which some chiefs have presented themselves to me. After I had communicated to them the ends for which I had come to live among them, they have shown me that they do not dislike this development, but are as anxious as I to see the time arrive for the general meeting in order to hear my talk.

In the few days that I have been here I have not received notice to the effect that the council of the Creek Nation has resolved to have a war against the Americans, nor that the latter are making preparations for the establishment on the Yazou River. Therefore I think it impossible at the present. . . . .

Shortly after my arrival Alexander McGillivray told me that he would have to make a journey to the region named Rock Landing where he had been called to determine, with some delegates of the United States of America, the boundaries which should be fixed between the domains of the latter and those of the Indian nations of this continent.

315. See the deposition of John Ormsbay, May 11, 1792, ASP IA, I, 297-98.

May God preserve you many years, Little Tallassie, April 10, 1792.

PEDRO OLIVIER [*rubric*]

Baron de Carondelet

178. *McGillivray to White, May 6, 1792*
[AGI C 205]

LITTLE TALLASSIE, 6' May 1792

MY DEAR SIR

I had the pleasure of Your letter of 23d March. From about that time & untill very lately the extraordinary freshes of the Spring had totally obstructed our Communication with Pensacola the roads being impassible to Pack horses & otherwise I Should have done myself the pleasure of answering Your letters much earlier. Just before Yours Came to hand the Indians of the Mucklassah Village came to me with a report [that Red Shoes'] Nephew was killed by the Spaniards about Pensacola. Being much engagd at the time I did not much attend to them but gave them a line or two in great haste to enquire into the truth of it. A woman that was much abused with the Man still Continues dangerously ill & is expected to die soon.

As the Indians will insist on retalliation, No doubt but his Excellency the Baron will Satisfy the expectation of the Indians in Causing the offenders to be Capitally punishd.

Our friend Panton Surprised me exceedingly some days ago with an unexpected Visit. He was ten days on his Journey & got a Severe ducking in a full Creek, & excepting a Small touch of the Rheumatism in one foot he is in good Order, & being recoverd has proceeded on to the Cherokee Country, Six or Seven days ago & expect him back in a fortnight.

It was fortunate that the high Waters detaind me from going to the Oconee River untill Mr. Pantons arrival as it has Savd probably some unpleasant discussion had I been gone as I at first intended.[316] How soon Mr. Panton returns here from the Cherokees I propose to Visit the Baron at New Orleans respecting these Matters. I have not

316. But to the American commissioner James Seagrove, on May 18, 1792, McGillivray professed real regret that the line could not be run. He went even farther and laid much of the blame upon the Spanish official Olivier, who had told the Indians that he was sent to prevent the running of the line (ASP IA, I, 302). See also McGillivray to Knox, May 18, 1792 (*ibid.*, pp. 315-16), and the account of the meeting held this same day at Rock Landing by Seagrove and a delegation of Lower Creek chiefs (*ibid.*, pp. 299-301). Seagrove stated very clearly that Washington recognized McGillivray as the "great chief and director" of the Creeks and as such would aid and support him. On May 21, Seagrove wrote a long letter to McGillivray, regretting that he could not attend the meeting, promising him support, and offering him asylum at his home if he felt a temporary removal was necessary (*ibid.*, pp. 298-99).

321

heard that our freind the Governor has arrived Yet from Orleans, if he is please give him my best Compliments. I remain with most sincere esteem & regard, Dear Sir

Your most obedient servant,

ALEX: MCGILLIVRAY [rubric]

Henry White, Esq.
Pensacola

179. *McGillivray to O'Neill, May 12, 1792*
[AGI C 205]
LITTLE TALLASIE, 12' May 1792

SIR

I had the pleasure of Your Excellencys letter by the bearer Antonio Garcon. I am extremely glad to find that you are arrived in Pensacola in good health.

A long attack from the Rheumatism & the exceeding great Rains & high waters prevented me from going to the Oconee River about running the line untill Mr. Panton arrived here. Besides there is a great Confusion among the Indians of the Lower Creeks. Some that were Bowles freinds who still believe that he is an English officer & others our freinds who are upbraiding them about Robbing Pantons Store. There is one Welbank & another who have Bowles papers among some of the Lower people, & they have been all very earnest at me to Settle Matters with the American Commissioner for them, but I have all along refused untill they deliver up Welbank & the papers to me in my house. I propose to go & visit his Excelly. the Gov. of Orleans, for which purpose I will be in Pensa. as soon as possible. Mr. Panton is gone to the Cherokees to look after his affairs & expect him back in ten days, but I dont wait for him. I remain

Your Excellencys most affectionate etc.

ALEX: MCGILLIVRAY [rubric]

Governor Arthur O'Neil

180. *McGillivray to O'Neill, May 22, 1792*
[AGI C 205]
LITTLE TALLASSIE 22d May 1792

SIR

I wrote Your Excellency a few lines by Antonio Garcon, but as he has been detaind by Mr. Olivier to Interpret Talks for a meeting that is now on hand, You may be Surprisd in not hearing from us. I Shoud have been very near down to Pensacola by this time but my Constant Companion the Rheumatism has made a fresh attack upon me. Mr.

322

Panton has gone from here this three weeks to the Cherokee & is not returnd Yet but expect him every hour.

We have no news here. The americans are Constantly sending expresses for me to go to the Oconee. Ive told them at last that I had particular business at New Orleans & I was going there directly. I expect to get better in a few days when I will set out for Pensacola & if an opportunity is not Convenient then I must go to Mobile. One of the Kings Schooners is Commonly laying there.

I remain Your Excellencys Most affectionate & obedient

ALEX: McGILLIVRAY [*rubric*]

These upper warriors observe that they never get a drink of Taffia or a present in their lives & now beg the favor.

His Excellency Brigadier Arthur O.Neil
Governor & Commanding in Chief &a. Pensacola

181. *Seagrove to Knox, May 24, 1792*
[ASP IA I, 296]

. . . .General McGillivray's conduct in this business with Bowles, resembles that of Britain with America, during the early part of the late war, by undervaluating the power of their adversaries. . . . .

The words of the Great Natchez warrior, when answering some of my *talks* made in favor of the General, were: Bowles laid our beloved man, Gen. McGillivray, on the ground, and made him of no more consequence than a child, but we will raise him up again; and, from the talks we have now heard, we are convinced he is right; we will therefore put his enemies under him. . . . .

I never could scan the General's motives in affecting to treat Bowles' usurpation, and the confusion his country hath been in for near a year, with such indifference; there must be a hidden cause, but which cannot long lie dormant. I am again impelled to repeat my want of faith in this man's integrity to our country; the whole tenor of his conduct is a flimsy appearance of friendship, but not one pointed or spirited exertion in favor of the United States. I wish I may be deceived, but I fear you will not find him, in the end, the man you wish him to be.[317] A man, to preserve his reputation, ought not to serve many masters; the General has many, and I am convinced the United States are not

317. Carondelet had just voiced comparable doubt of McGillivray's attachment to Spain (document 175, *supra*). Knox's opinion seems to have been much more favorable, as expressed in his letters to Seagrove (ASP IA, I, 253-55), and to McGillivray (April 29, 1792, copy in AGI C 177). The latter closed with this message: "I have the pleasure to inform you that your Nephew is well, that his growth is great, that he learns as expeditiously as could be desired, that he is contented, & that his morals are irreproachable—as a specimen of his learning, he writes you the inclosed." Unfortunately the enclosure has not been preserved.

the favorite. A Spaniard, or an Englishman, is respectable all through the Creek nation, but it is very dangerous for any person, known to belong to the United States, to travel, or be in that country; and, I am sorry to find, that no pains have ever been taken to remove that unjust prejudice. . . . .[318]

182. *Hoggarth to McGillivray, May 25, 1792*
[AGI C 177]

CUMBER LAND, 25th May 1792

DEAIR AND HONORABLE SIR:

I am verey Sorrey to inform you that our good and worthey frend ganiral Robrtson was wounded yesterday by the indians so bad that his life is dispard of the Indians has been verey Troubelsom heair this spring they had Stold a number of horses and kild a good maney of our peeple thay destroyd one hole fameeley by the name of Thomson thay kild the old man & his wife and ownded one of his daughters & toock hir sum distance from the Hous and kild her and toock another Sister prisoner together with a Marid Woman and child in case Sir those weoman ar braught in to your Nation pray try and get them if in your power and keep them till you have an oppertunity of leting me no and I wil Send after them & if you cant git both pray try and git Miss Alcey thompson She has one brother Still a live who will pay Every Expenc you are at in giting hir in horses or good rifels as for the other pore creathre thay have nothing but Deair Sir if She is in the nation try and git hir and if aney caust I will See that it Shal be pade I was in hopes that the creeaks wood have been frendly with us thar was an old Cheeaf of yours in to see us and we treated him very well and he promist to cum and See us again, but he never cum back. I hope he was not afrunted we tryd to treeat them as well as in our power o that you could by Sum means give us pees from that Nation. I was very Sorey my Der Sir to hear that A Boles that imposture gave you So mutch

318. In the following paragraph Seagrove spoke disparagingly of Olivier's being stationed at Little Tallassie, reported that Carondelet had sent out an invitation for a meeting, and remarked that Panton had "more influence over McGillivray than any person living." See also Seagrove to Washington, July 5, 1792 (ASP IA, I, 304-5), in which still sharper criticism of McGillivray is voiced. Acting upon this information and that in the deposition of James Leonard, July 24, 1792 (*ibid.*, pp. 307-8), Thomas Jefferson as Secretary of State lodged a formal protest with the Spanish chargés at Philadelphia against the sending of an agent within the limits of the United States without its consent. The chargés referred the matter to their court, where it came before the Council of State in November, 1792. The Council, having before it a long report on American, Creek, and Spanish inter-relations, approved the sending of Olivier to the Creek Nation but recommended prudence to Carondelet and Las Casas. Jaudenes and Viar were instructed to lay a copy of the treaty of Pensacola before the American authorities, "so that they may see how long ago those Indians became our allies." There is an expediente on the subject in AHN E 3887.

trouble as he did. I congratulat you on you being reinStaited and am in hopes that them fulish mad peeple See that thay cant Live with out you. may the Lord bless you my frend pray Rite by the furst oppertunitey & let me no if them wimman is in you Nation or not. Mrs. Brown is well & gives hir complyments to you.

JAMES HOGGARTH

Collo. Alexander McGillivray

183. *Jane Brown to McGillivray, June 4, 1792*

[AGI C 177]

CUMBERLAND, June 4, 1792

SIR

I give you this trouble to acknowledge the many obligations I am under to you for the many kindnesses you have done for me which no other hand could have done and when my calamities threw me upon your mercy. Be assured Sir they Shall never be forgotten though words can never express the sense I have of your goodness. I have at last reached Cumberland and settled in tolerable circumstances with four of my children the eldest being to the northward and the youngest dead lately. My little Betsey remembers you most affectionately and gratefully. She is now at School.

My numerous losses have reduced me in my circumstances but my mind is perfectly reconciled to my lot. I am fully disposed to bear every calamity with composure except the captivity of my little George. I have the utmost confidence in your obliging proposal to procure him for me and am persuaded you will use every prudent measure to release him and send him to me. Yet I cannot help feeling such impatience and anxiety to see him that time hangs heavy upon my hands till his safe arrival may crown all the enjoyment I have in life. I have the pleasure to be with the utmost esteem & respect Sir

Your obliged humble Servant

JANE BROWN

P. S. It would greatly oblige me if you would take the trouble to write me whether there be any probability that my son will be obtained soon.[319]

General McGillivray

319. Willett and Pickett have left a record of Mrs. Brown's thanks to McGillivray on an earlier occasion. It was at Guildford Courthouse, North Carolina, when McGillivray was on his way to New York in 1790. Some years before this the Creeks had killed a man named Brown and captured his wife and children. McGillivray ransomed them from slavery and entertained them at his house for more than a year. When the widow heard of McGillivray's arrival at Guildford, she "rushed through

184. *Olivier to Carondelet, May 29, 1792*

[Spanish original in AGI C 2362]

I reported to you yesterday the 28th in which is described the meeting of the chiefs of the Upper Towns to introduce myself to them and to inform them of the reasons why I came to live among them, with which they have shown themselves to be satisfied. After the discourse on this particular, I gave them to understand that this provision by the king was a slight token of his paternal love for the Creek Nation.

At the same time I let them know how prejudicial it would be to the nation to conclude the treaty that has been started with the Americans, as also the cession of the immense territory to which they pretend, the fatal consequences that would result if they were to condescend to surrender their title to it and permit the line to be run as the Americans solicit, and the opposition which our sovereign has to the termination of such a treaty, which would be the certain ruin of the Creeks.[320] I told them that fortunately for them this report had reached your ears in time to make them see what they had done when halucinated, and that it was to their interest to follow your advice and to accept his protection, which he offered them with all necessary assistance to defend their lands and lives. I showed them that the Americans want to oblige them by force to conclude the said treaty. That consequently they must anticipate by forming an alliance with their brethren the Cherokees, Chickasaws, and Choctaws, who would be equally assisted in such case, for which you would offer to hold a meeting of the chiefs of these nations whenever it would best suit them, in which they would treat of these points to conclude a defensive alliance under the protection of Spain.

On this, Alexander McGillebray (knowing the effect this discourse might produce in the minds of the majority of the Indians of this nation, who have never been very favorable toward the said cession of lands) took the opportunity to say to the assembly that the treaty with the Americans in which they had ceded a portion of their lands had been with the approval of your predecessor, whose having been relieved by another who had a different opinion of this treaty was the cause of this new proposal. Therefore the conclusion of the treaty should be suspended until after having conferred with you.

---

the large assembly at the court house, and, with a flood of tears, almost overpowered him with expressions of admiration of his character, and gratitude for his preservation of her life, and that of her children" (Pickett, *History of Alabama*, p. 404). Roosevelt gives Sevier credit for rescuing Mrs. Brown and her children (*op. cit.*, III, 321-23).

320. A sharp criticism of Olivier's anti-American actions is contained in Seagrove to Washington, July 5, 1792, ASP IA, I, 304-5.

In the same assembly it was decided that the meeting could be held in Pensacola for the Creeks and Cherokees and in Mobile for the Alabamas, Chickasaws, and Choctaws as was formerly done, but Alexander McGillebray observed to me that it could not take place until the first days of next September, because of the work that the Creeks had to do in their harvesting and the festivals that they are accustomed to hold in the summer months, and also because he must first confer with you on this matter.[321]

In a fortnight the express will return whom I advised you I sent to the Lower Towns to learn the effect that the arrest of Bowles produced in his party. Not having met anyone here who has come from there, I cannot say anything on this subject, except that they remain quiet as concerns Bowles, who wrote them after he was arrested that he would return shortly. This report has been confirmed to me by a chief of Cowetas, one of his principal partisans who came to see me six days ago on the part of the town of Cowetas and others nearby. He said they wished to see me and hear my talk and to let me learn their attitude about it. He also told me that Bowles had proposed that they make war on the Americans, offering to be their general and to help them in this undertaking with two ships and 600 English soldiers, and much merchandise for presents, and to provide a trade much more favorable than what they have today, to which some chiefs agreed provided that what he promised should be fulfilled.

I shall wait only until Alexander McGillebray sets off for New Orleans to go myself to the Lower Towns. May God our Lord preserve your Excellency many years, Little Tallassie, 29 May 1792.

PEDRO OLIVIER [rubric]

Sor. Baron de Carondelet

185. *McGillivray to Carondelet, May 30, 1792*
[AGI C 205]
LITTLE TALLASSIE 30' May 1792

SIR

I have to inform Your Excellency that a general meeting of the Chiefs of the Upper Creeks have been held by Capt. Pedro Olivier & the Chiefs propose to meet Your Excellency in Congress in Pensacola in all July or August next. Mean time I am preparing to Set out to go to Orleans either by the way of Pensacola or Mobile to have the Satisfaction of a Consultation with You on Indian affairs. I expect to be with

321. In his reply Carondelet deplored "the inaction and irresolution with which McGillivray, under frivolous pretexts, like that of a journey here, strives to hold the Creeks." He insisted that the Creek attack on the Americans should be begun within one month (Carondelet to Olivier, June 13, 1792, draft in AGI C 2371).

Your Excellency sometime in Next Month if I can obtain a convenient opportunity from either of the places I have mentioned. I am with most respectfull regard

Your Excellencys most obedt. Servt.

ALEX: McGILLIVRAY [*rubric*]

his Excellency El Baron de Carondelet
Governor & Commander in chief of Luisiana & Florida

186. *McGillivray to O'Neill, June 6, 1792*

[AGI C 205]

LITTLE RIVER, 6th June 1792

DEAR SIR

After Mr. Pantons arrival at my house in the Nation I woud have set out directly to go to Orleans but I got another fit of the Rheumatism. When I got a little better I came off to go by Pensacola but the Weather being very hot & the flies tiring some of our horses I was obligd to put in here & tomorrow I am going to Mobile by Water to take passage in the Kings Vessel to Orleans. I have missd of receiving two letters from his Excellency the Baron the Indians taking different roads from the one I came in.

I causd a meeting to be held in the Nation for Mr. Oliver to give his Talk to the Chiefs, & when it was agreed upon that a general meeting shoud be held after their husk was over that is when the Corn work is all done which will be next month when the Corn is ripe. I am going in all haste to see the Baron to have matters prepard. & to return directly to have the meeting come on.[322] Mean time I am with great affection

Your Excellencys obedient Servant,

ALEX: McGILLIVRAY [*rubric*]

Governor Arthur O'Neil

187. *Olivier to Carondelet, July 5, 1792*

[Spanish original in AGI C 25]

. . . .Only what you inserted in your official letter about insisting anew with McGillebray to persuade him to abandon entirely the party of the Americans will not be, for the present, fulfilled as I should have wished, since he went away from here the first of June saying that he would go to Pensacola and that from there he would go to embark on the boat at Mobile to sail to New Orleans. I do not know whether he

322. Concerning McGillivray's trip to New Orleans, Ben James wrote: "It is not for the good of the States of America that he is there, nor yet for the nation" (James to Blount, June 30, 1792, ASP IA, I, 284).

has done so, since I have not had any news of him except that he had not as yet appeared in Pensacola by the 12th of that month, which leads me to believe that he must have taken the road by Little River. This man's method of procedure gives ample grounds for believing that if he is not strongly in favor of the Americans, at least he wishes to be agreeable to them.[323] I have noticed on all occasions when I discussed this point with him, that he was very much interested in fulfilling the treaty that he has made with them. . . . .

May God preserve you many years. Little Tallassie, July 5, 1792.

PEDRO OLIVIER [rubric]

The Baron de Carondelet

188. *Carondelet-McGillivray Treaty, July 6, 1792*
[AGI C 2362]

Francis Baron de Carondelet, Colonel of his most Catholic Majesty's Armis, Governor, & Intendant general in & over the Provinces of Louisianna, & West Florida, & Alexander McGillivray, General & principal Chief of the Creek Nation: being very desirous of strengthening by every means upon firm, & solid grounds the peace, friendship, and reciprocal union which happily subsists between the Spanish, & Creek Nation, & their Allys, & to remove at once every obstacle, which might impede the entire & absolute fulfilling of the Treaty agreed upon by both Nations at Panzacola in 1784: paying attention, and considering also that the treaty made with the United States in 1790, has been followed by numberless disturbances, & great uneasiness among the different Chiefs of the Nation, the greater part of whom are decided to reject the said treaty with the United States, 'till his most gratious Majesty's pleasure should be known about extending his Royal protection, & Guarantee to all Lands of the Tallapusee, or Creek Nation: We have agreed upon the following articles, which are to be considered as explanation of our former Treaty in 84, to which in every other respect must be attended to.

Article the 1st.

His most Gratious Majesty, wishing to keep a perpetual peace & good harmony between the United States, & all Indian Nations her Ally's, the Chiefs, & Warriors of the Creek Nation, ought to avoid

323. Compare with Seagrove's observation, also on July 5, "I fear General McGillivray is not faithful to the United States; and I have my suspicions, that, if any mischief is brewing, he is deeply engaged in it" (Seagrove to Washington, July 5, 1792, ASP IA, I, 304-5; see also document 181, *supra*). Gayoso de Lemos, writing to Aranda, also on July 5, observed that McGillivray went over to the American side (at New York) for lack of Spanish support, and he added that this was the same reason why James Wilkinson was no longer working for Spain in Kentucky (copy in AGI C 177).

carefully every violent action, or any hostility against the Americans settled on their Lands under pretence of aforesaid treaty of 1790, or any other Treatys, but recommends that the Chiefs should in peremptory terms demand that all Yntruders on the Lands of the Nation should retire with their effects, within the term of two months, within the limits granted formerly to the Brittish Nation.

Article the 2d.

His most gratious Majesty will guarantee all the Lands belonging to & actually possessed by the Creek Nation, at the forming, & concluding of the Treaty of Panzacola in the year 1784; & on the same principles of reciprocal union, & friendship the Talapusee, or Creek Nation will Guarantee the Lands of his Most Catholic Majesty in the Provinces of Louisianna, & West Florida.

Article the 3d.

His Catholic Majesty will, to show his good & gratious disposition towards the Creek Nation, furnish them & their Ally's with ample, & sufficient Supplys of Arms & ammunition, not only to defend their Country, but even to regain their encroached Lands, should the Americans refuse willingly & peaceably to retire in the time pointed out, or in case of the Creek Nation being unjustly attacked by any People whatever unprovoked.

In witness of all, & every thing herein determind between the Contracting parties, they have hereunto set their hands, & Seals, in the City of New Orleans this sixt day of July, in the year of our Lord one thousand seven hundred ninety two.

ALEX: McGILLIVRAY [rubric]

(seal) EL BARON DE CARONDELET [rubric]   C. C. N.

ANDRES ARMESTO [rubric]

Secy.

189. [Carondelet] to McGillivray, July 6, 1792
[Spanish draft in AGI C 205]

In reward for your good services, by which his Majesty is confident you will continue to keep the Creek Nation loyal to the Spanish Nation, and in peace and harmony under the rules and the convention that we have signed; in the name of his Majesty, who authorizes me to act for him, and by virtue of his royal order, I have resolved to increase the pension that you now enjoy, of 2000 pesos annually, by 1500 pesos, on the same terms, commencing from the first of this month. May God, etc. New Orleans, 6th July 1792.

[EL BARON DE CARONDELET]

Alexander McGillivray, Esquire.

330

190. *McGillivray to O'Neill, July 16, 1792*

[AGI C 205]

MOBILE, 16' July 1792

SIR

I embrace this opporty. to Inform Your Excellency that I arrived here Yesterday from Orleans, & as I must be delayed for a little time between this & Little River before I can go to Pensacola, I enclose a letter from his Excellency the Baron de Carondelet to You & which I intended to have deliverd in person, but expecting the letter to Contain Some Matters of advice I think it proper that Your Excellency shoud get it as Soon as Coud be Convenient.

As the Intended Congress with the Indians is to be managed by Your Excellency & myself I offer my opinion that You Shoud Instruct Mr. Olivier that as Soon as the Indian husk is over in the Upper Towns that he shoud give notice to the chiefs to repair to Pensacola & he with them, & I will be there in Time for it.

I should not have remaind so long in Orleans but I was in the daily expectation of Mr. Pantons arrival there, but his long delay & not giving me any notice of his Intentions that way I left Orleans after waiting near a Month as the Sickly Season was coming on.

The Commandant Lanzos not being here I must wait here for a boat from my plantation to go up the River & from thence I shall proceed to Pensacola. I left Mr. Maxother[324] very well in Town. With best wishes for Your Excellencys health I remain with most sincere & respectful esteem

Your Excellencys obedt. Servt.

ALEX: McGILLIVRAY [*rubric*]

Governor Arthur ONeil

191. *Carondelet to McGillivray, July 18, 1792*

[Copy in AGI C 205]

NEW ORLEANS, 18 July 1792

SIR

By the inclosed copy of the talk directed by General Washington to the Chactaw Nation[325] you will see how the United States are affraid that the Indians our allies should unite together with those of the North to make War against them, and you will likewise take notice of the snare they put to them that they should engage in a War against each other to banish away our projects. I will do my best endeavours to make

324. I am uncertain whether McGillivray meant Maxent or Mather or Strother.
325. The same proposition as outlined by Knox to Seagrove, April 29, 1792, ASP IA, I, 253-55.

known to those Nations their true interest & that of the United States in inviting them to the Treaty of Cumberland, and after to join their Army. They have no other idea but to engage the young Warriors in a Battle with the Northern Nations to fight a bloody War between them to separate them from our alliance.

I am persuaded should the Creek Nation send a talk to the Chicasaw & Chactaw Nation directed to convince them that the attempt of the Americans are only directed to deceive them with some presents, and to sow [dissension] and division the Nations to improve the moments of disunion and dislike falling upon them when Spain abandons them, that talk might have a greater effect than all I could send.

I shall be very glad to hear of your safe arrival home.

With every esteem & regard

Your most humble & obedient servant,

EL BARON DE CARONDELET

Alexander McGillivray, Esq.

192. *McGillivray to Carondelet, July 22, 1792*
[AGI C 2371]

MOBILE 22d July 1792

SIR

I have the pleasure to acknowledge the receit of Your Excellencys letter of 6' Inst.[326] in which You are pleased to Notify to me that You have augmented my pension to fifteen hundred dollars pr. Year more than it was last Year. I cannot but feel in the liveliest manner this fresh mark of his Majestys most gracious Consideration for me, & I beg leave to assure Your Excellency that my best endeavour shall be always exerted to merit the Continuance of his Royal favor & protection as well as to deserve the Confidence of their Excellencys his Governors of his provinces. This addition to my pension making me more easy in my Circumstances, I resolve on the measure of relinquishing every pecuniary Compensation made to me by the American Congress for my property Confiscated by the State of Georgia. It is far from my heart to wish to have the least dependence on a people whom I know to be the Natural & determined enemy of all the Indian Nations & whom it is Incumbent on us to resist.

I have learnd since my arrival here that the Americans that had come into the chactaw Nation to Invite those Indians to go to Cumberland had gone off with much precipitation & that no one of any Note woud go with them.

I have the Satisfaction to observe that it appears that our Creeks by a

326. Document 189, *supra.*

332

Spirited Conduct on this occasion compelld these Commissioners to a precipitate retreat from the Chactaw & Chickasaw Nation & likewise warnd those Indians of the danger attending all those who shoud be found in the American Settlements as two considerable partys of Creeks were on the way to endeavor to Intercept the Americans on their return to Cumberland.

I enclose to Your Excellency two letters which I received a few days Since by a chactaw one from an old lady whom I ransomd from slavery about four Years since & who has still a child of hers in our Country, the other from a man formerly an Indian Trader.[327] This letter will give Your Excellency an Idea of the present State of the american Settlements on the Western Waters of the Ohio River & I expect that our Creeks will keep them in a State not to have leisure to think of distant expeditions.

I find that some alabamons on their return from Orleans have plunderd some american Settlers up this river, & they assert that they received orders from Your Excellencys Interpreter to do so & Macpherson tells me that he heard Fonneret giving such Instructions to some Alabamons. The Captain Commandant Lanzos is not Yet returnd from Tobegbe I hear that when he was informd of the Intention of the alabamons, he disapprovd of it & when the accounts arrived he was much displeased but if he was here I woud explain to or Inform him of the Nature of the Indian that he will pay no attention to any officer in Contradiction to what he Conceives to be the order of the Commander in Chief, through his Interpreter.

Having wrote to Govr. ONeil to send Instructions to Mr. Olivier to assemble the Chiefs & their warriors & to Conduct them to Pensaca. I Set out in short time for that place & from whence I shall have occasion to write. Mean time I am with great & respectfull Esteem

Your Excellencys Most Obedient Servt.

ALEX: McGILLIVRAY [rubric]

His Excellency El Baron de Carondelet
Governor & Commander in Chief of Louisiana & W. Florida &c. &c.

193. *McGillivray to James, August 10, 1792*
[Copy in AGI C 205]

LITTLE TALLASSIE, 10' August 1792

SIR

I Wrote you a Lettre by Mr. Bellow which I expect you will have received before this. You no doubt, as well as Some Others, have been Alarmed on Account of the mischifs done by our people on your quarter

327. Documents 182 and 183, *supra*.

but as I mention by Bellow the Indians are not altogether to blame. False reports have been made to the Gov. of Orleans that the Americans were building forts on your River. There Agent here Sent the Indians out to Attacke every Amn. they Coud meet & the Chactaws have always piloted them to Certain houses where as if the Chactaws woud always deny that Ams. were living about there Our Indians woud return. However on my Comming home this fall I found five Gangs Going to Start to plunder all above the Spanish fort. I Stop them all but One Gang that had Started who brought in Mrs. Baker. The Indians woud [give] her up for a ransom, but the Spanish Officer wont give one & as it was not my talk that Sent them out, I wont interfere as I have often Ramsoned persons & have met with little tanks or Gratitude. I let this work its Own Course.

As there are but few of our Indians but wat know you I Assure you that you may be in perfect Security at any of your places, As I have Spoke much of you & Rober Welch &c as being Old hands in that part of the world.

Busy & Medling persons may have told you things of me as I have heard that you always took Occasion to Speak very disrespectfull of me which if you did, you were very wrong. It is very far from me to Injure my own honor & Conscience to turn a mean Assassin to Set Indians to Revenge me & Spill the blood of a man whom the my friends before me used to Esteem. So as I have Given you my word think of me as formerly before my dispute had happend, as we are like to be Indian Countrymen, for our lives so let us Advise the poor indians to keep what they have got. The Chactaws & Chickesaws by Only Speaking can keep off any new Settlement being made this Side of Cumberland & by Sticking to the Spaniards they will hold there Contry Longer than Otherwise.

Commissionaries are now treating in Madrid in Spain about Settling the Claims of Spain & America & the Indian Countries will be Secured in a [perfect] measure if the are not Inprudent enough to Give it away before the affaire is Settled.

I remain etc.   ALEX: McGILLIVRAY [rubric]
BENJAMIN JAMES

194. [Carondelet] to McGillivray, August 19, 1792
[Spanish draft in AGI C 205]
NEW ORLEANS 19 August, 1792
DEAR SIR:
I have just received a report that the Americans have established a fort in the territory of the Chickasaws some forty leagues above Tom-

becbe in the region where the French had one. The consequences of this step will not be hidden from your penetration, nor how convenient it is that they be driven off from this establishment, which will shortly grow powerful and ruin Mr. Panton's trade. I am informed that this work is already in a respectable state of defense against Indians, and is garrisoned adequately but without any artillery.

The sure way to destroy it will be to send parties of Indians to relieve each other successively in blockading its garrison and preventing its having any communications.

Don Arturo O'Neill still insists on a congress, and I persist against having one, for the reasons that I have expressed to you, and inasmuch as Don Pedro Olivier has written to me that measures are already commenced on the part of the Americans against the frontier towns [and you] must not absolutely abandon them, for they certainly would take advantage of your absence for their total destruction.

I have told you that I would never urge upon the Creek Nation anything risky or contrary to its interests. As Don Pedro Olivier has written me that two thousand guns will be needed to arm the nation quickly, and since I cannot supply more than one thousand now, and in view of the fact that Mr. Panton, Mr. Durnfort, and the others cannot furnish those I have ordered before November, it would be convenient to defer driving the Americans from the usurped lands of the Creeks as much as you can, but still without running any risk of the line being marked, for which there would be no remedy.

The American expedition on the Ohio received another blow as a result of a great foray which it undertook in the vicinity of its camp. I remain, etc.

[EL BARON DE CARONDELET]

General McGillwrai

XVI

A GENERAL INDIAN CONFEDERATION

195. *McGillivray to Carondelet, September 3, 1792*
[AGI C 205]
SIR   PENSACOLA, 3d September 1792
Since my arrival here I have received Your Excellencys letters of 18' July of [this] & 19' ulto. & a duplicate of the latter.[328]

328. Documents 191 and 194, *supra.*

In the first I found some papers respecting the late transactions of the americans in the Chactaw & Chickasaw Nationes, from which I find that they were soliciting those Nations to go to a Congress at Cumberland & to receive presents. I have since heard that they have Succeeded in seducing poymingos party & some Chactaws, & here I must observe that the desire of getting presents is so strong among Indians, (the custom having been long establishd) that no remonstrances against the practice will be attended to. However the partys that are gone to Cumberland does not consist of chiefs of note or Warriors who can Influence the bulk of their Nation & I shall not fail to exert the Influence & power of my Nation in opposition to the measures & Views of the americans in the Chickesaw & Chactaw Nations.

Some chiefs of our N. W. frontier are arrived here who Inform me that the chief Mingo of the Chickasaws had come into that part of our Nation in June last or early in July expecting to find me at home. He came for the express purpose to apologize for the bad conduct of Poymingo & declared that for himself as head of the Chickasaws in general he woud exert his Influence & authority to prevent his people from adopting any measures which might tend to interrupt the good harmony at present Subsisting between our Nations. A chief of Natchez has lately arrived from the Chickasaws. He Informs me that the americans offerd to make an establishment on the Cherokee River for the purpose of carrying on & supporting the Chickasaw & Chactaw trade. The offer was accepted of but observd that the Creeks woud not admit of it. The americans said that they woud build forts to protect themselves. It is by such Insidious Arts that the americans of Cumberland & Kentucky hope to possess the Indian Lands, without rousing their suspicions untill they gain their ends but they shall not be sufferd to effect their Schemes without meeting with Vigorous opposition from us & our allys. I believe I can venture to assure Your Excellency that the american fort on Tombecbie of which You have been Informd has no existence, for my people have been too Vigilant to be ignorant of such a Circumstance, besides Tombegbie is not the present object of the americans. It is Bear Creek which emptys into the Cherokee River at the Muscle Shoals & which is in the list of Congress for an establishment. The Muscle Shoals is the passing place to my people when they go a hunting or to War & my people by my orders have frequented those places all this past Spring & Summer & they will at the end of this month Swarm out there in going to attack Cumberland & the other Settlements in that quarter.

In Your Excellencys letter of 19' ulto. (the duplicate of which I have lately received) You advise that the peace shoud Continue with the

Georgians untill November next. I am of Your opinion & that we Shoud not precipitate hostillitys with that State for the reason mentiond in Your letter, that Mr. Olivier had made a requisition for a Number of Guns to Arm the Nation, the whole Number of which Your Excellency coud not at present procure, & what arms are now in Store here will serve to fit out a Number of my people for a present expedition to the Ohio & Cherokee River, & in the mean time I will take measures *to differ with the Georgians* & I need not take much trouble about that matter as I clearly perceive that they will furnish me with an occasion, which I wish much for them to do as in all my political measures with them hitherto I chose rather for them to appear as the aggressors to the World & more especially as I had so recently Concluded a peace with them & that You may See clearly that I did not Seek the peace'myself I enclose Your Excellency a duplicate of a letter from Gov. O Neil,[329] which will I hope convince still further that the Suspicions that existed against me on account of that treaty was not well founded.

It never was my Inclination to be on good terms with the americans. I very early preferrd & Solicited for the Freindship & protection of the gracious Monarch of a powerfull Nation to which I will steadily adhere & will inculcate the same principles in the minds of my people.

Having recoverd of the fever I now Set out soon for the Nation to assemble the chiefs & explain to them the Nature of the Communications which I have had with Your Excellency & to Concert a plan of Operations for the ensuing Season & the Winter.

I am with perfect esteem & regard
    Your Excellencys most obedient Servant,
        ALEX: McGILLIVRAY [rubric]

His Excellency Baron de Carondelet

196. *Carondelet to McGillivray, September 14, 1792*
[Copy in AGI C 205]
        NEW ORLEANS, 14 September 1792

MY DEAR SIR

Having carefully perused your letter of the 3d instant, I agree with you in every measure you propose [to] prevent any establishment being made in the lands of the Chickasaw Nation, or of our other allies. I persist in my former opinion that you should by no means appear at the Congress at Rock Landing, nor even permit the boundary to be run, since they are now treating about this at Madrid, and in the

329. Not found. Unfortunately, O'Neill's letters to McGillivray have not been preserved. Hill's *Descriptive Catalogue* lists none in the Papeles de Cuba. Document 86, *supra*, is the only one that I have located.

definitive settlement of our boundary by the plenipotentiaries appointed for that purpose by the Congress of the United States and our Ministry, the boundaries of our Indian allies will, of course, be included. It is therefore your business now to convince the Creek Nation that it is to their true interest to postpone indefinitely the demarkation of the boundary, since they may be confident that without resort to arms they will regain possession of part if not all of their encroached lands, which will undoubtedly be the case after the conclusion of the negotiations of the Great King their protector. For the same reason it is advisable that they remain under arms and ready to repel the Georgians should they attempt to run the line by force, but without committing hostilities unless the Georgians attack or enter their territory. Notice hereof is sent to the President of Congress by the King's envoy at Philadelphia.

My intention never was to employ Milfort except in expeditions which require more handwork than headwork. He fancied that I allowed him five hundred dollars from the day of his arrival in town. In truth I promised him that sum in case he should be useful on an occasion to be indicated later, but his arrogance toward Don Pedro Olivier to whom he is by no means obedient, according to information from Governor O Neill, though Olivier is commissioned Royal Commissary of His Majesty in the Creek Nation, displeased me exceedingly and dissuaded me from employing him in the future.[330]

The complaints of the Chicasaw chief Atakabe Olactá cannot be groundless, as you will see by the enclosed notice of the present made him. That Nation is already much contaminated by the deceptions of the Americans who will make them pay dearly for their confidence; but the Chicasaw Mingo does not fall into this error, and Franchimastabe sent to the Governor of Natchez two medals he had received from the American commissaries. Finally, the Chicasaw chief Ugula Yacahe promised that he was going to Cumberland only to learn what would be proposed in the Congress, and that he would communicate everything on his return.

197. *Leslie to Quesada, October 2, 1792*
[LC EF 116L9]
St. Augustine E. Florida 2d October 1792

May it please your Lordship

Having lately received intelligence, which in general I believe to be

330. Quesada wrote to Las Casas on May 8, 1792, that when McGillivray sent one hundred armed Indians to disperse Bowles' followers, Milfort accompanied them, and that after eight or ten years of intimate friendship with McGillivray and marriage to his sister he had broken off relationships and intended to go to Europe (AGI C 1436; also see note 176, *supra*).

well founded, through different Channells, but Chiefly from our Agent at the Indian Tradg. House establishd last year by your Lordships desire upon the Bank of St. Marys River; I Consider it my duty to lay the same before your Lordship, as it may prove in Some degree interesting to this Government.

It Seems that two white men, whose names I have not learn'd[331] Came down some time ago, from the Creek Country, to the State of Georgia; & there reported that My Partner Mr. Willm. Panton, who resides at Pensacola, had this last Summer, made a tour through the Creek Nation, visiting the principall Towns, & holding Conferences with all the Head Men & Chiefs of the Country: in which, (they Add) he every where dissuaded the Indians from adhering to the Treaty enterd into between them & the Americans at New York, telling them that they ought not to permitt the Boundary line between their Lands & Georgia, to be Cutt & Mark'd as that Treaty Specifys: And That they need be under no apprehensions from the Americans, as the King of Spain Considerd them under His Royal Protection, & would assuredly support & maintain them in the possession of their Lands and just rights. That from the Americans they had little to expect, as they were a poor people, & Could not affoard to give them presents of much Value, but that he endeavourd to persuade the Chiefs of the Nation, to go down & Visit the Governor of New Orleans, who would receive them kindly, & give them handsome presents, besides ammunition, musketts & other warlike Stores in Abundance, wherewith to defend themselves and their Lands, Against the Encroachments of the Georgians.[332]

The Said two white men, further reported, that a French Gentleman had lately been Sent by the Governor of New Orleans, to reside in the Creek Nation, & that he had accordingly taken up his residence at Mr. McGillivrays House there, in quality of Superintendent of Indian Affairs, on the part of the Spanish Government, & was Constantly giving & Sending out Strong talks among them, of the Same tenor & purport as those Mr. Panton had given them before; adding that Shoud they be Attack'd or disturb'd in their possessions by the Georgians, they might have a firm reliance on receiving timely, powerfull, & effectual Support from the Spanish Governments, Not only of Arms

331. Weatherford and Leonard; see the deposition of James Leonard, ASP IA, I, 307-8, and Seagrove to Washington, July 5, 1792, *ibid.*, pp. 304-5.
332. Compare with Panton's own account of his excursion through the Indian country. "There is in each nation a considerable party inclined to peace; but the one that is for war is composed of men that. . . . have a great influence. . . . . Next spring, if you wish, you can start the bloodiest war that the southern states have ever experienced" (Panton to Carondelet, November 6, 1792, Spanish translation in AGI C 177).

& Ammunition &a, but that a body of Spanish Troops would also be sent to Assist & Act in Conjunction with them, for their better devence. That in Consequence of these Talks & perswasives, more than Two thirds of the Nation were Already disposed to Brake with the Americans, & to throw themselves entirely upon the protection & friendship of Spain; & that the other third would also probably soon accede to the Same Counsel. These two white men, I am further informd, were at Savannah, examind by order of Govermt., upon oath, as to the truth of their reports; & had made long & Circumstantial afidavits to the above tenor, but doubtless Containing much other Subject Matter, of which I am not inform'd, having heard that their declarations reducd to writing, fill'd up more than Twelve Sheets of paper. That the intelligence Containd in them, was Considerd by the Government of Georgia, to be of so important a Nature, that rather than wait for the departure of a Vessell then loading at Savannah, for Some of the Northern States; they had Charterd a Schooner on purpose, to Convey the information to Congress as Speedily as possible, & in her had also Sent forward the Said two men, to Corroborate at Philadelphia the truth of their relations, or for further examination there. That President Washington had in Consequence made representations to the Court of Madrid, & to the Captain General at Havana, upon the Subject. I am further inform'd that the Georgians have Sent to invite the Head Men of the Creek Nation, down to Mr. Seagroves on St. Marys in November, to receive presents, & to induce them if possible, to preserve peace, but its thought few or None of them will go down there in a friendly way. That on the Conterary the people of Georgia are greatly alarm'd under the apprehension of an immediate Commencement of hostility agt. them by the Indians, and in the Meantime are furiously & desperately enraged & incensed against our House & Connection in general, but more particularly against Mr. Panton, whom they bitterly rail at, with the most inveterate enmity, and Continually load with most dreadfull & horrid execrations & threats: thinking him to be the principall instrument of Alienating the minds of the Indians from their late peaceable dispositions towards the Georgians; & of persuading them to throw themselves altogether into the arms of Spain; & upon the dependance, protection & favor of our Lord the King.

Reflecting on these Circumstances I have lately been extreamly Uneasy & disturbd in Mind, for the Safety of our property at the before mentiond Indian Trading House on St. Marys; dreading that some of the Lawless Vagabonds of Georgia, impell'd partly by the desire of Plunder & partly Also from Motives of revenge against our Firm, May Steal ofer the river in the Night time, & Seize our Goods, Negroes,

& other effects there, destroying what they may not be Able to take away; & Murdering perhaps, Some of the white people, our dependents there. For which reason, I humbly Submitt to your Lordships Consideration, before I take any effective Steps in the business, my purpose of Withdrawg. our people & property from that frontier, and, with your Lordships permission, of erecting Some Buildings for the Indian Trade, at Picolatto, or any other eligible inland Situation upon the River St. Johns.

I have further to entreat your Lordship to excuse my making this representation in the English tongue, Not being yet so fully Master of the Spanish language, as to trust that I could express myself therein, with the precision Necessary on a Subject of this import.

I have the honor to remain with the most reverential respect, praying God to preserve your Lordship Many Years.

Your Lordships Most devoted & faithfull
       humble Servt.

JOHN LESLIE [rubric]

P. S. I have further heard that it is reported in Georgia that in General Washington's representation to Court, above alluded to, He mentions it to have been the most difficult & troublesome task belonging to his Administration of the Govermt. to restrain for Years past, the American Settlers on the Western Waters, whom he describes as an Ungovernable Sett of Men, from Attacking the Spanish possessions on the Mississipee, and its Understood that this Communication was Made, in a letter from a Coll. Hamilton, Minister of Finance for the United States, to some Gentleman in office, of the State of Georgia, But this being a Vague report, may not probably be Well founded.

Al Señor Don Juan Nepomuceno de Quesada Governador &ca. &ca.

198. *Carondelet to McGillivray, October 22, 1792*
[Copy in AGI C 205]
NEW ORLEANS, 22 October 1792

DEAR SIR

I am indirectly informed that you have taken notice of some talks delivered by Don Pedro Olivier to the Creek Indians prejudicial to your interests, which are as dear to me as my own; and desiring to banish every unfavorable impression your mind may have, I confess to you, with my natural frankness, that before I had the pleasure of being intimately acquainted with you I was angry with you on account of the steps you were said to have taken against the interests of our august monarch. I gave to Don Pedro Olivier proper directions to destroy the confidence of the Indians in you. Thus it is no wonder that in accordance with my suggestions the King's Commissary should have spoken to different chiefs to dissuade them from following your advice concerning the demarkation of limits as requested by the United States.

As I am deeply convinced by the conversations we had in this town of your loyalty and affection for the King's interest, my later orders are absolutely contrary to the earlier, and direct him to keep the best harmony and sincere friendship with you, and to follow your advice implicitly. I have not the least doubt that he has observed everything with the greatest exactitude since then. Perhaps Mr. Milfort mentioned to you something Don Pedro Olivier had said earlier to create disaffection against you; but this suspicion is groundless because the said Milfort wrote against Olivier, whose presence in the Nation is unpleasant to him, and in hopes that he may succed to the employ of King's Commissary. You can depend that nothing will be done or determined without your knowledge, as your interests will always be very dear to me.

The Talapuche chief Tomopa Mingo reported to the commandant of Tombekbe that some Americans met with five Creek hunters, whom they attacked, killing three and [wounding] two; but that this inhumanity could not fail of being properly chastised, since the chief of the town as soon as he heard of the atrocity went out with two hundred Indians after the Americans.

While the Indians are to oppose the running of the boundary line, we must prevent any unprovoked hostilities by the Creeks against the Georgians, until the result of the negotiations, begun at Madrid between our court and the United States, is known.[333] I am authorized to say that our court will act vigorously to preserve for our Indian allies the lands possessed by their ancestors; and if we should all unite toward the same desirable end, I am thoroughly convinced we shall make them entirely free from the oppressive and destructive system the Americans conceived and constantly followed from the infancy of their independency.

I hope that your health is better and that you will avail yourself of anything in my power, as I am earnestly desirous of being useful to you.

I remain, Sir

Your most affectionate & devoted Friend.

EL BARON DE CARONDELET

333. This was precisely the policy that McGillivray had been following. See his letters to Seagrove, May 18, 1792, ASP IA, I, 302, and October 9, 1792, *ibid.*, pp. 321-22. How he continued to do so is made clear in document 201, *infra.*

199. *Carondelet to McGillivray, November 11, 1792*
[Draft in AGI C 205]

NEW ORLEANS the 11th November 1792

MY DEAR SIR

By a letter of King's Commissary in the Chactaw Nation the Lieutenant Colonel Jhon la Villebeuvre, copy of which Mr. Olivier is ordered to show you, I am acquainted of the Murders commited by the Creeks upon the persons of a blacksmith of the name of McFarlan, & his children, whose Mother has been carried as slave to the Nation; I am told that at the same time they attempted to kill Ben. James, but a Chactaw of the town wherein he lives protected him: by a second letter I received yesterday in the night I am informed that those Indians have been send by Red shows Chief of conchate; those news vex in great measure the Chactaw, who are extremely incensed against the Creeks, the complaint of the chactaw is that the same arms, and ammunition furnished by the Spaniards are the instruments the creeks made use of to perpetrate those crimes; from that you will readily conceive how highly convenient it is to put a stop to such a disorder, which should be attended by a bloody war of one nation against the other in the very time in which the intime connexion and foederation of all the Indians is of the greatest interest for their own preservation & general welfare.

The Governor of Natchez has been obliged to call together a body of three hundred men at Bayou Pierre to shelter and protect the Americans subject of his most catholic Majesty, & inhabitans of that District who were greatly allarmed at the murder of the unhappy McFarlan. I expect you will reprimand the chief Red shows & the other warriors his accomplices in their mischievousness, obliging them to set at liberty McFarlan Widow, & giving them to understand that the Americans, who live within the limits of the Spanish dominions are subjects & like sons of the King are the Spaniards themselves.

The chicasaw King taska etoka will arrive here in two dais with a talk of the Creeks, Cherokis, Sawanos, & several other Northern Nations, Falanchimastabe with eight hundred wariors will come with him: I am told that they come on purpose to make a proposal of a defensive alliance, connexion, & reciprocal guarantee of their Lands under the protection of Spain: the chicasaw Chief Payemingo, Ugulayacabe, & two more are decided friends to the americans are expected here in few dais: I will flater the vanity & Pride of them all persuading them to forget their hate, & quarrels against the Creeks to be only interest to their general welfare.

It seems that the Minister of State of the Congress has presented to our court officially some complaints against me, all shall very easily be vanished, showing that every one of my proceedings has been consentaneous[334] to the good harmony which subsists between both Nations; having only counteracted their encroachments upon our allys, & endeavoured to form a defensive alliance between them all to guarantee mutually their Land, giving them in the mean time seasonable advices to prevent their hostilities, but to defend & preserve themselves.

I am confident that wee shall shortly receive orders from our court giving notice that all discussions are over by a fair treaty stating the proper limits in which our allys shall equally find their utility & tranquility.

I am with the sincerest esteem and regard.

Sir

Your most obedient

Humble servant.

[EL BARON DE CARONDELET]

General McGillevray.

200. *McGillivray to Carondelet, November 15, 1792*

[AGI C 205]

LITTLE TALLASSIE, 15' November 1792

SIR

I have the pleasure to acknowledge the receit of Your Excellencys much esteemd letter of 14 Sepr.[335]

I am very well Satisfied that Your Excellency is disposed to let me transact the political affairs of our Country after my own manner. No Wisdom or foresight can form any plan in the closet that can always suit to manage Indians, as nothing but a long experience & knowledge of them can direct them properly. I shall allways attend to the Ideas which You shall be pleased to Suggest to me concerning the Kings Interest, tho I may at some times act from my own discretion to avail myself of particular circumstances to effect certain objects. Yet Your Excellency may rely & be assured that I shall keep in my View the great object of my long labours to endeavor to disappoint our enemies from accomplishing their favorite schemes on the Indians Territorys, or that of our friends.

I have had a Visit from the principal Micos of the Lower Creeks, & they have agreed with us not to have limits markd as the Americans desire, neither to give Satisfaction for two americans that have been

---

334. In the Spanish translation the word is "opuesta," opposed, but Carondelet evidently meant "not opposed" (AGI C 205).

335. Document 196, *supra*.

killed on the Oconee this Summer by the Lower Indians. This Circumstance will be a Security for the line not to be run as I will keep the affair from being Settled & then no Indian will Venture his person among the americans, & beside this, I have orderd that all the Cattle & other Stock be all seizd upon & drove off. These measures will tend to widen the breach & answer our present purposes without proceeding to direct & open hostillitys.

I am very glad to hear that a negotiation is on foot to decide the respective claims of Spain & america to Territorys, an event that will I hope give peace & Security to these countrys, tho I fear that No agreement whatever can restrain the Western americans from continuing their encroachments. Altho they pretend to great moderation in their Talks to the Indians, as much as I can hear concerning the late treaty at Cumberland the americans only requested the freindship & neutrality of the Chickasaws & Chactaws, & did not ask for Land, but perhaps Your Excellency may have learnd more than I have done on that Subject.

As to the Chickasaws I do not well know what to think of them. Bellew was here & told me that he was applying to Your Excellency to employ him. I advisd him as being well known to the Chickasaws to go to that Country & endeavor to set up an opposition by Stirring up Colberts party of which the Mingo is principal against the american party, as dividing them woud have its good effects, & if he was Successfull in this measure I assured him that Your Excellency woud encourage & support him. I took the occasion to Set him out by sending a Talk by him to Chickasaw Mingo, in answer to one he sent me last month with tokens of freindship.

Bellew stands a good chance to Succeed at this time as I find the Mingo is much affronted at the americans because they do not take any notice of him, & pay all their attention to poy Mingo, & a little Courtship now to the old Mingo from our Side will I trust have its good effects, & an attempt will be made to get him & his freinds to pay Your Excellency a Visit.

I have reason to expect a deputation from the Northern tribes of Indians in here in the ensuing Spring for the purpose of animating the Southern tribes to exert themselves in the Common Cause.

There has been some Skirmishing with Various Success between some small partys of Indians & americans.

We have Just received accounts of the loss of three of our people Young Lads & from the Circumstances it is said that it was done by an Indian enemy & poy Mingos party is Suspected. If it shoud prove certain, the Chickasaws will be attackd. Some Indians of the Cowetas

345

have returnd from Bahama Islands, but I dont hear any thing of consequence. Wellbank it is calld to the Bahamas. I woud urge the propriety of having a good look out kept on the Coast of Florida to seize those little Vessels that are kept running between the Bahamas, otherwise we shall never have order kept up in the Lower part of the Country.

A Menace from his Excellency the Captain General to Lord Dunmore & his Islanders might have good Consequences as they actually attempt to make the Indians hostile to Spain.

I have been sometime laid up with my old Complaint & recover but Slowly. With most perfect esteem & regard, I am

Your Excellencys most obedt. Servt.

ALEX: MCGILLIVRAY [*rubric*]

His Excellency Baron de Carondelet

201. *McGillivray to Panton, November 28, 1792*
[AGI C 204]

LITTLE TALLASSIE 28 Novr. 1792

MY DEAR SIR

By this oppy. I have to acknowledge the receit of Yours of 10' Inst.

Im not much Surprisd at the Conduct of my quondam freind the little prince, for ever Since the affair of St. Marks I have been at No pains to Conceal my Sentiments respecting his Villainy & he in return has fallen on a Very paltry Shift to defame me. You did me Justice in giving the Lie direct to his Storys. You who have long known me & in many difficult Situations in public life never heard or at least never known my Political Integrity impeachd by the Worthy & Candid of Mankind. Little Calumnys No person in a public Station can escape, the experience of all times shows it & in such countrys as this at this time I am Certain is the Most difficult & perplexing to manage than any other in the whole Continent & it Cannot be done by the ordinary rules & Modes.

Having already wrote to his Excellency the Baron Concerning the result of the Visit made me last month by the Micos of the Cussetahs & Cowetas, from them I found that two Georgians had been killed in the Summer & a demand for Satisfaction was made by them. This Circumstance made the chiefs down there distrustfull, & Seagrove proposed to Meet them at the Indian Line on St. Marys an empty Country. There being a famine apprehended in the Lower Towns & Seagroves Informing them that hearing of that he had sent to Phila.

346

& a great quantity of provisions had arrived for them,[336] I found that they were rather disposd to go to him but woud first Consult me on it. After some Consideration I Judgd it Most expedient to give Consent to the Measure rather to Suffer them to go in a Secret or unauthorized Manner & especially as they promisd to follow exactly my Instructions.[337]

My principal Injunctions to them were to be decided against the running a line & to make use of the affair of Satisfaction to that purpose. That the Clans Concernd woud Not Consent to give up two of their people & that the Frontier americans were loud in demanding it, & of Course the personal Safety of any Indians who might be calld in to attend the running of the line Coud not be Assured by the Commissioners from those turbulent banditti on the frontier. In the Next place in order to Widen the breach I gave out in general orders that as the Georgians had put over a great Number of Cattle horses &a. into the So. fork of Oconee & erected hutts, that these Cattle shoud be all seizd on & the hutts burnt, which by this is in part accomplishd, & lastly I kept back every chief of these upper parts, & not one is gone. & as the Micos wishd to have their own Interpreter I desired Durouzeaux to go with them. I afterward Sent Alex Cornel who Speaks good English to attend attentively to every thing that Shoud be passing there.

It being on this train that I have placed matters there is no danger of the few chiefs that are gone to Meet can do any thing in favor of the Georgians, more particularly as [the] whole Upper Creeks are entirely devoted to me, & most of the Lower except the plundering gang, who are inconsiderable in respect to the others.

Welbank did not write an Insolent letter to me as you heard on the Contrary he beggd not to be destroyd, & that he was Soon to return to his *Native Land* & that in case he shoud be killd the papers was out of reach, by which I Suppose he has given them to some of the gang to keep. Perhaps the prince as he writes from his house & with whom he resides since old Barnet & his man gave him a Severe drubbing & turnd him out of his house. This Walton tells me who is Just Come up from there. W. told Walton that by the last Indians from Nassau that Lord Dunmore had Invited some more chiefs to go over & that his Son shoud accompany them provided he woud be protected from the Spaniards. But I dont find that the last party has given room for them to hope that Bowles promises are likely to be accomplishd, but the leader Keeps a Sullen Silence & the other, thro meer obstinacy,

336. The Creeks were told that there were five thousand bushels of corn and other important presents (Seagrove to McGillivray, October 8, 1792, ASP IA, I, 314).
337. But compare with the explanation offered to the American agent (McGillivray to Seagrove, October 9, 1792, *ibid.*, pp. 321-22).

Savage like keeps prattling the old [story], & it appears that the princes relation is to head the next party to go with Welbank. In my letter[338] to his Excy. the Baron I urged the propiety of the Capt. Genl. taking some decisive measures in this business to Keep Cruisers to seize on these Vessels, that L. Dunmore is Sending over, & exciting the Indians to be hostile to Spain & even to attack the fort of St. Mark in Concert with Vagabond Indians.

On my first Coming home I had so much to do I coud not leave it soon & the Cursed Gout seizing me has laid me up these two months nearly. Every periodical attack grows more Severe & longer in Continuance, It now mounts from my feet to my knees, & am Still Confind to the fire side or I Shoud Certainly have gone to the Lower Towns for none but myself in person can act with a high hand among those chiefs. One Indian will never offer Violence in anothers house, they cant be Induced to it. As for Milfort he I believe has never thought of W. or any other. I have Seen him twice in all my illness. Olivier is at home. [The horses of yours are] borrowed for the winter. (Indians never say they Steal, but they borrow.) Yours are on the pensacola road to be returnd you in the Spring. He must be very uncomfortable in his Situation, he can do Nothing in the way of business as he is to universally dislikd. He has askd leave to go to Orleans he says this Winter, & he may as well stay there as come back for what Service he is of.

You Say that if horse borrowing is not put an end to from the Cherokee people that you may Shut up Shop. If it was Stopt Yet You may go near it the destruction of horses has been so great in this Nation that there is Not above ten in a hundred Indians Now who can pack out his provisions to the hunting grounds & of Course there will be Very few Skins taken this winter. Add to this that runners are despatchd thro the hunting grounds to Call in all the hunters by the next full moon (this is now full) in order that the Wakokays may take Satisfaction of the Chickasaws for the boys that I mentiond in my last to You. One of them has escaped & was found after ten days nearly famishd. He tells that it was a party of Chickasaws in the Cumberland Service from the Circumstance of their going toward that Settlement after doing the mischief, & a large party of them are hunting in that Neighbourhood to Cover it.

The mountain leader has got four or five thousand lbs. ammn. in his magazine by which he rules the roost & turnd all except three Villages up. The old Mingo who is wandering *an exile* among the Chactows, a part of whom are in the Mountain Leaders Interest & may probably drive them into his War, if those Indians dont better them-

338. Document 200, *supra*.

selves. The Spanish Interest is Strong in that part of the Nation Called the Six Towns who are numerous & most warlike of the whole. From this account You See into what embarrassments You are thrown into as a Merchant & me as a Statesman. Your Interest must Suffer, but I am approaching to a despondy. thain I will drop the Subject. I will endeavor to See You before xmas, if my Complaint gives me leave. I hope the Ship has arrived from Bahama & Your Next will give me some News. I remain dear Sir most affectionately yours

ALEX: McGILLIVRAY [rubric]

To Mr. Panton

202. *Carondelet to McGillivray, December 14, 1792*
[Draft in AGI C 205]

NEW ORLEANS, 14 December 1792

MY DEAR SIR

I received just now your esteemed letter of the 15th November last, & its contents afforded me the greatest satisfaction, because they informed me of the wise measures you took to put off the running of the line between your Nation and the United States without proceeding to open hostilities. Before spring I hope to receive the decision of the negotiations on this question now in progress in Madrid between our court and the United States.

Being persuaded, like yourself, that no agreement whatever can restrain the Americans of the West from continuing their encroachments, I formed the scheme of uniting the Cherokees, Creeks, Chactaw and Chicasaws in a defensive confederation under Spain's protection. And availing myself of the casual meeting here of the Chicasaw Mingo, Franchimastabé with twenty-six great & small medal chiefs of this nation, Kilikaski chief of Cusitas, six Cherokee chiefs, the famous warrior Bloodyfello, and about a thousand Chactas, I proposed to them the said plan, which they embraced with eagerness, giving their word that they would propose it to their nations, and bring back an answer in the spring. It is evident that this plan is the only recourse left to the Indians to obtain from the Americans an advantageous settlement of the boundary, and at the same time to enforce them to observe it constantly.[339]

By the various murders which the Talapuces have committed in the

339. The plan is elaborated in Carondelet's agenda for an Indian congress, January 28, 1793 (draft in AGI C 2371). Carondelet admonished McGillivray that it was "of the greatest consequence" that he should attend and that he should first consult with him (Carondelet to McGillivray, February 1, 1793, draft in AGI C 2353).

territory of the Chactas, even in the Natchez District, against various Americans, may overthrow the projected plan, kindling a war between the two nations, of which the Americans will no doubt take the greatest advantage. I wrote to the Governor of Natchez, and to the King's Commissioner in the Chacta nation, Lt. Col. Dn. Juan de la Villebeuve, urging them to quiet the Chactas, and I expect you to do the same with the Talapuces.[340]

Two principal Cherakee chiefs and the Warrior Bloodifello have gone to the Chicasaws to persuade them to follow the common cause, and I am confident that the talk Bellew carries from you will have the best effects. When he was here I promised him that he would be rewarded if he behaved himself like a man, and so I will do. I am expecting Payemingo and three other chiefs of his party.[341]

Chicasaw Mingo misbehaved himself to the point of threatening me with his going to the Americans, quitting my table, and leaving my house in vexation because I would not permit Turnbull to open a store for the Indian trade at Yazou. I opposed it firmly. Nevertheless we parted very good friends, since he received from me a Great Medal, certainly a masterpiece in work and size among the Indians.

The Semanoles still make me uneasy at St. Marks of Appalachy, but I hope that Welbanck will soon be in our power, and that their connection with the Bahamas will be thus broken.[342]

Don Pedro Olivier has asked permission to come to this capital until the month of March.

I am infinitely sorry that you are tormented so frequently with Rheumatism. I have some famous powder invented by one Olivenza, to whom the King granted the exclusive privilege of selling it during his life. The powder is a specific against galico, venerian complaint, without being disagreeable and without requiring a tedious regimen. Should you desire to try it, I shall send you some with the prescription or a translation thereof, on the understanding that it be not displayed to any physician.

I remain with the greatest esteem, etc.

340. Advised by Villebeuvre that an American army of fifteen hundred was ready to attack the Chickasaws, Carondelet urged McGillivray to settle the disturbances between the Creeks and the Choctaws and Cherokees so as to avoid the disastrous consequences that would result if the Americans succeeded (Carondelet to McGillivray, December 16, 1792, draft in AGI C 204).

341. See the copy of Carondelet's talk to Pio Mingo, December 18, 1792, AGI C 2362.

342. An armed vessel was sent to patrol the coast in an endeavor to capture Wellbank with Bowles' papers. Five hundred pesos reward was offered, principally for the papers (Carondelet to Montreuill, December 13, 1792, BL LC).

203. *McGillivray to Carondelet, January 15, 1793*[343]

[AGI C 2363]

MOBILE, 15th January 1793

SIR

A long Indisposition hitherto prevented me from answering Your Excellencys esteemd letters of 22d Oct. & [21st] November last. Some [matters] relating to the affairs of John Linder who is lately dead & left me one of the [executors] of his Will & Testament, which has been [the cause] of my writing to Your Excellency from [Mobile].

In the letter of the 22d Octr. I [note] what is said respecting Cap. Oliver. It [was not my] Intention to prefer a Serious charge against [him] for that particular of his Conduct which [related] to Mr. Panton because I had the report [from] one chief among the Alabamons only & [he occasioned] me no disturbance, & I continued to Shew [him] the same attentions as I had ever done on [his] arrival.

I am much Concernd for the [outrage] committed on the persons in the Chactaws by partys of the Coosada Chief Red Shoes [whom I] questioned about these matters. [I returned from] Pensacola in time to prevent much greater [damage] as I found many partys on the point of setting out toward the Mississippi, & I trust that the measures taken will prevent future repetitions of like nature . . . .I am of opinion that Red Shoes had much [violated] orders. Nor are the Chactaws without blame. . . . .

I have been Informed by the Cherokee. . . . that a Number of Chactaws & Chickasaws arrived in Orleans on a Visit to Your Excellency [who also] Informed me of the very good advice You deliverd in a Speech to them,[344] & I sincerely [hope] that those tribes may Conduct themselves in future [with the] prudence which was recommended to them. [The] Chactaws perhaps may, but I am to well acquainted with the Stubborn disposition of poy Minto to believe that he will [break] his american Connexion by which his Vanity is gratifyd in being the leader & head of a [nation] & the americans will retain him in their Interest [at any] expence. The Mingo or Tuskatokah has in [general] a good character & was never very favorable to the americans, for which they shewd all attention to poy Mingo which enabled him to raise a great opposition. . . . . Your Excellency may rely [on this] to be the fact, whatever may be told to the contrary. The Injurys poy Mingos party had done lately to our familys will be retaliated, & so Matters may perhaps rest, if poy mingo does not [offer]

343. The manuscript of this letter, the last one extant from McGillivray's pen, is badly frayed at the bottom and edge. Bracketed words are supplied for some of the elipses but not for all.
344. Carondelet to Pio Mingo, December 18, 1792, copy in AGI C 2362.

further hostillitys, & which it is probable [he will] do, in the expectation of american support, [they] having already given him large & repeated [gifts] of powder & arms for the purpose of breaking [the peace] which if they are rash enough to do [will bring] a Severe chastisement on his Country, as [our] Northern Confederates will Join us in the [Spring] a Number of whom I expect to arrive in [our] Country early in the ensuing Spring to bind & Strengthen the Chain of freindship.

I come now to Your Excellencys letter of 21t Novr. which Covered a Copy of one [addressed] to Mr. Panton, on a Very Interesting Subject to him. I allude to Turnbulls application to Your Excellency for a license to establish a Trading House at Mobile in opposition to that of Panton & Co. established there. . . . .[345]

From Your Excellencys knowledge [of Indians] you will readily admit that it is no hard or [difficult] matter, for any designing person for a present .[to make] them say any thing, it being Indifferent to the [Indians] who it is that Carrys on the Trade provided he [gives them] presents & if Mr. Panton had been present & [rather] than Turnbull no Complaint woud have been [made on] the Score of trade. Therefore whenever requisitions [of that] Nature are made by Individuals when there exists [no good] ground of complaint, should be rejected for the reason [that they are] already amply Supplyd with every Necessary [facility for] trade, & the phantom of an american trade to [be carried] on from the Muscle Shoals has been Conjurd up by Interested persons merely to aid & effect their particular [ends]. That no permanent or profitable Commerce can be carried on from the american States thro that channel [is well] known to most traders, & Turnbull himself can [vouch] for the truth of this from his own experience, as on [the late] peace, tho an Inhabitant of this Province he [had] to Supplicate the favor of the Spanish Government [and] entered into Cumberland with all his effects & there he [attempted] to establish the trade of the Chickasaws & Chactaws [but he] found that he Sunk most of his property in the [venture] he then returnd to this Country. . . . . & he has already taken measures [against] the house of Panton & Co. by tampering [with] different Traders & Factors in the Chickasaw [Nation] not to make payment of their debts, to [Panton] but to wait for & purchase his goods. [All] this rivalry & clashing of Interests will

345. The governor had explained to Panton that he had granted Turnbull permission to open a store at Mobile because of the "obstinate application of the Chicasaw King." He assured Panton, however, that his house would have the government's "decided preference" (Carondelet to Panton, November 21, 1792, draft in AGI C 205). Carondelet also notified McGillivray, November 25, 1792 (ibid.).

produce most dissagreeable Consequences & vexations [to the] Government. . . . .

Before I left my house my Warriors had returnd from Seagroves Treaty at St. [Marys. From] them I find that the chiefs who attended the treaty had strictly Conformd themselves [to our] Instructions. Tho hard pressd by Seagrove to fulfill the terms of the N. York treaty they declind the business, & after hearing a Very pacifick Talk from Seagrove the meeting broke up. It appears that Seagrove had received positive orders to Visit me at my house. I anticipated his Instructions, which are to endeavor to Conclude a Commercial Treaty between our Nations & the United States. [When] I was at New York it was then attempted & much Solicited on that [point]. . . . .

ALEX: McGILLIVRAY [rubric]

XVII

McGILLIVRAY'S DEATH

204. *Panton to Carondelet, February 16, 1793*

[AGI C 203]

PENSACOLA 16th February 1793

MUCH ESTEEMED SIR

I received the Honour of Your Excellencys letter dated the 5th Inst. I have not heard a tittle of news from the Nation that can be depended on since I wrote You the 27th ulto. excepting that a small skirmish took place sometime ago betwixt a few Cherokees & Americans near to Cumberland in which the Americans were beat, 10 killed & a Captain made Prisoner who was afterwards put to the Stake and burnt. If this is true it is the first execution of the kind that has taken place amongst these Southern Indians since the peace of 1763.

It is with infinite Concern that I inform Your Excy. that Mr. McGillivray lies dangerously ill in my House of a Complication of disorders of Gout in the stomack attended with a perepneaumony and he is so very bad as to leave scarcely any hope of his recovery. I am, Dear Sir

Your most obed. Serv.

WM. PANTON [rubric]

His Excy. the Baron de Carondelet

205. *Panton to Carondelet, February 20, 1793*
[AGI C 203]

PENSACOLA 20th Feby 1793

MUCH ESTEEMED SIR

I wrote Your Excellency on the 16th Instant in which I mentioned Mr. McGillivrays illness and now it is my misfortune to announce his death to You which took place on the 17th at 11 OClock at night.

He made no other will than declaring before Governor O Neill that his Estate must go to his children & that Mr. John Forbes of Mobille and myself should act as his Executors & Guardians for his children.

Poor fellow he has left us at an untoward period but there is no help for it. It appeared to me a necessary measure to send immediately for the chiefs of the nation to come to Pensacola in order that Government may adopt such measures with them as shall be thought most Conducive to the good of the whole, and this step I recommended to my friend Governor O Neill. But as these meetings are always attended with expense the Governor declined acting in it untill he receives Your orders: But as I am awake to the advantage the Americans will gain by delays on Your part I have taken it upon myself to request of the chiefs to come down without delay and I am Convinced You must approve of this as soon as I have a moments time to state my reasons & which I shall do in my next.

Last night Cap Robert French in the Ship named the *Esdaile* arrived from London. He brought no letter for Your Excellency & had simply a passport from the ambassador. You will with Your usual expedition furnish another for Her return and which You will favour me with as soon as it is possible.

I can add no more the vessel is under way
Yours Dr Sir

WM. PANTON [*rubric*]

His Excellency the Baron de Carondelet

206. *Forbes to Durnford, February 23, 1793*
[AGI C 203]

MOBILLE 23d Feby 1793

MY DEAR TOM

Your Letter of the 4th instant went upon a Tour to Pensacola before it came here owing to Miguels having gone there before he came to this place. The articles were all Safely delivered unliss a Basket of Aniseed which had been pilfered & which Miguel promises to pay for.

By this vessell goes to Orleans four prisoners accused of Some Crimes of which we are ignorant here; but one of them owes our House Con-

354

siderably and as Some of his Negroes goes with him you must not lose sight of them as all his property will not be Sufficient to pay us. I have laid in a memorial on the subject which Lanzos Sends forward at my Request to the Baron. I hope he will order the property to be given us, as if it lyes on Expences it may be all eat up.

I suppose You will be this time have heard of the decease of our friend Mr. McGillivray. I assure you I have felt it as if he had been a near Relation.

I am My Dear Tom
Yours Sincerely

JOHN FORBES [*rubric*]

To Mr. *Thomas Durnford*
Mrch:
New Orleans

207. *Panton to Carondelet,* .... *1793*[346]

[AGI C 178]

MUCH ESTEEMED SIR

I wrote Your Excellency a few days ago when I had the painfull task of informing You of Mr. McGillivrays Death.

Knowing, fullwell, how ready the Americans would be to catch at every advantage, which this event may give them, I considered it immediately necessary and without waiting to Consult You, to send for the chiefs to come directly to Pensacola, in order that measures may be taken to secure a Continuance of their friendship, and that means may [be] found to carry on the business of Nation, without interruption, from this late misfortune.

The plan that I advise You to follow is to secure in Your Interest John Kennard, of the Lower Towns, and likeways the Little Prince of the Broken arrow. This last is the schoundrel who aided Bowles in his Robbery of me, but do not You mind that. I say secure him.

They are both Interested Men, but their ruling passion is ambition. I would have You therefore dub Kennard, with the title of Colonel, and if You Stile the little Prince Major or Great Captain it will flatter his vanity—and about 600 Dollars to Jack, & about 300 Drs. to the Prince yearly & during good behavior, would, I think with these titles, be their full price. There may be one or two more in the Lower Towns, that will require distinction, which I can better point out to Governor O'Neill when they arrive. The upper Towns are more orderly and it

346. Probably written late in February or early in March.

would be well to leave it to their own choice to name three or four of their most beloved Men on whom You ought to Confer titles & small pensions and if You appoint Mr. McGillivray's Brother[347] with their approbation chief over all untill His nephew McGillivray's Son comes of age, You will find Your interest in doing it. You will no doubt order the chiefs plenty of Provisions, & good presents, for untill the boundarys is settled between Your Court and the President of Congress it is indespensibly requisite to be at considerable expense. I imagine in a short time that the Chickesaws will cry out for peace, and as You ought to be the Mediator You will be able then to Stipulate Conditions and get them to relinquish their American connexions.

This letter will be delivered to You by a Mr. Mawbury, formerly a Lieutenant Colo. in the Service of America, who was encouraged by Mr. McGillivray to remove himself and his family to this Government. On his arrival here he found his friend on his death Bed who desired me to write to You in this Mans favour. He has brought his negroes with him with Two sons very handsome children, and proposes to return soon for his Wife whom he left big with child. As far as I can judge of a Man from so short an acquaintance, he appears to me a decent Person, & will no doubt become a good subject, & as Mr. McGillivray's friend, I execute his Will, in recommending him to You. . . . .

208. *Panton to Carondelet, March 21, 1793*

[AGI C 203]

MUCH ESTEEMED SIR

It was very kind in Your Excellency, to remit me the Passport for the return of the Ship *Esdaile* with so much Expedition. She is not Yet returned from Mobille, but I look for Her daily. If You have any Commands for the Ambassadors in England, they will be in time if here by the 5th of next month. Governor O Neill informed me that You wished to know, if amongst Mr. McGillivrays papers there be any thing that can give light of the present intentions of the Americans. In answer to this I have to mention, that, he had no papers here saving a letter from his Father, another from a friend in England, and some others of no manner of Consequence, nor do I believe since his return from New Orleans that the Americans had so much Confidence in him as to trust their Secrets with him. I shall however see them by & bye, and if there is any Communication which You have not already got,

347. The reference probably is to his brother-in-law, Louis Milfort. It may be to Dan McGillivray, though I have found no explicit statement that he was a brother.

that I deem any wise Interesting to Your Government, You may fully
rely on being informed of it. . . . .[348]

WM. PANTON [rubric]
PENSACOLA, 21st March 1793

His Excellency The Baron de Carondelet.

209. *Declaration of James Dearment, April 18, 1793*
[Spanish translation in AGI C 1436]

. . . .As the informant was passing through the Lower Nation, it
happened that the greater part of two days he camped close to the
house of Canard; and having heard of the death of his friend McGillibray, he asked in a conversation with Canard what he thought would
be the result of that death, and who would occupy his place in the
nation.[349] The mestizo replied that he knew nothing for certain; he
knew that young Alexander Cornel was clever and able, but he was
illiterate. Then the witness asked Canard if the Indians, who take
him for an educated man, would not elect him as successor to McGillibray. Canard replied that he was illiterate also, although he did not
know how well he would manage with the assistance of an amanuensis.
James Dearment.

NOTE: Said Alexander Cornel is a mestizo son of George, residing
at Tukabache, and a nephew of John Cornel, a white man, who was
interpreter with McGillibray at New York.[350]

210. *Milfort to Carondelet, May 26, 1793*
[French original in BL LC]

TUQUETBACHET, May 26, 1793

SIR:

I have the honor of informing your Excellency that I have just
received two letters from you, which are the only letters that I have
received since the one you sent me on the 24th of last October. The first
one, sent to me by Mr. Panton and dated March 25, I did not receive
until May 20.

Your Excellency has done me the honor of stating that you could see
by my letter that I was not unaware of McGilvrit's death. That is true.
You also tell me to send the principal chiefs to Pensacola, that Mr.
Olivier awaits them in order to arrange for the Creeks to make peace
with the Chickasaws.

348. In spite of several thorough searches McGillivray's personal papers have
not come to light. Possibly the suggestion in document 213, *infra*, is based on fact.
349. One rumor was that Panton was to succeed him (Seagrove to Knox, April
19, 1793, ASP IA, I, 378).
350. This note was contributed by Carlos Howard, who took down Dearment's
declaration. Joseph Cornell was the interpreter at New York.

I had sent 1200 men against them, when I received a letter from Mr. ONil in which he commanded me as follows: Mr. Olivier left here several days ago to go to Mobile to visit the Chi [Chickasaws] to see if he can induce them to make peace with the Creeks, and has Baron de Carondelet's instructions in this matter. My little army had left four days previously but I immediately sent an express to call them back and they returned. The Chis have just sent an envoy to ask us for peace and we are going to hold a conference for their accommodation.

You command me in the same letter to have Sigrot [Seagrove] arrested. I spoke of it to Mad Dog. He said that it would be necessary to see two other chiefs and if they approved, we would do it. I consulted them and all three promised me that if he came here they would deliver him to me. As for the northern Indians, they went back before I had received your letters.

The second letter was sent to me yesterday by Mr. Olivair and is dated December 12th. This rascal of a Woilbonque [Wellbank] ran away. I had given orders that he receive the punishment he deserved. He must have found out that he could no longer escape being punished, and ran away by the Cherokee, so Oquelocnay will be peaceable. But another rascal has arisen among the Lower Creeks. This is Golfain [Galphin], who, several days ago, having robbed the Americans, stole something from two of your inhabitants near St. Marys. He robbed them of everything, taking away from them their covers, sheets, mattresses, seven negroes, their cows and horses. There was also a little boy whom Golfain scalped. It is a little band of thieves, and the chief of the nation has abandoned it to anybody who wants to destroy it and no satisfaction will be asked for them. I heard that they were near the St. Johns River where they have stolen almost a hundred more oxen and cows.

You were kind enough to tell me that you had ordered Mr. ONil to give me whatever I should ask of him because you were too far away, but he did not have the kindness to let me know about it. That did not prevent me from serving you and I did not spare pain or money to serve you better, and I report that I have brought back three of the largest villages of this nation to your interest. I have also satisfied the fifteen chiefs whom I had sent to the Americans to prevent the line from being marked. In fact, I neglect nothing to serve you.

I know that I have several enemies who are trying to make my conduct seem to you as black as it is white, but I also know that you have too much intelligence not to see their malice. It is true that I did not show great friendship for Mr. Olivier last year, but I had reasons.

McGilvrit and I feared each other. I feared him because I knew his

358

spirit and the malice of his family, and he feared me because he knew how strong my influence was, being general of the nation and always ready to march at their head whenever it was necessary. But these fears do not exist today, and I shall be pleased to support Mr. Olivier, and consequently your interests.

Your Excellency was so kind as to write to me that my salary began from the moment I had arrived at New Orleans. This was, if I remember, the first of May a year ago. I take the liberty to ask you to invest me with this said appointment, or to have the kindness to send me an order and I will send to get it. As I believe that it will be necessary that I give a receipt, if you wish to send this money to Mr. Olivier for me, I will send him the receipt. You also did me the honor of writing to me that you had ordered that the 150 piastres which I spent in the king's service should be remitted to me. I also take the liberty of asking you to have it sent me. As for what I have spent since, I leave it to your generosity, and whatever you do will be right.

We have today set the day for a general meeting in order to see what your orders are. This meeting will take place on the 5th of June. I am living at Tuquebachet; the chief required me to. I am sorry that Mr. Olivier lives so far from me, and I fear with reason that something bad will happen to him, because McGilvry's family are circulating the rumor that he was poisoned.

Please give my thanks to your wife, I beg you to present her my humble respects. The Indian tells me that the bearer died en route. I shall do my best to find another.

I leave my interest in your hands and I want to be occupied only with yours. I ask your Excellency to believe me with deepest respect,

Your most humble and most obedient servant,

DE MILFORD[351]

Mr. le Baron de Carondelet.

[P. S.] I send this letter to Mr. Olivier so that he will get it to you.

211. *Panton to Leslie, August 28, 1793*
[Copy in LC EF 116L9]

PENSACOLA 28 Augt. 1793

The affair you mention of the plundering of Seagroves Store &c, has Created much ill blood Among your Neighbours & has put them to some expence: they Are Very Angry with me I Know, but with No Manner of reason; if they Act only on the defensive, the Indians will readily make peace, but on the Conterary, if they Come forward to

351. Milfort or Milford signed himself thus, but his American contemporaries and his Paris publisher wrote his name Milfort.

destroy the offending Villages, they Will Assuredly bring on themselves, Such an Indian War, as Georgia Never before experienced. I have been in the Nation all last Month, looking after McGillivrays Affairs & Notwithstanding his Sisters had divided the Negroes among them, Conformable to Indian Usage, I got them to Yield up All the Negroes & a part of the Cattle, for his children; & they are to be placed under a White Man of My Chusing to labour for their benefit. . . . .

212. *A Talk from the White Lieut. of the Ofuskees to his Friend & Brother, and also his Father the Governor of New Orleans, November 9, [1793]*[352]
[Copy in AGI C 188-3]

FATHER,—The Spaniards I only acknowledge to be our Father, & the first white people we red people ever saw or heard of, it was you who first took us by the hand when we were in an entire State of Nature & Ignorance, & under a Tree on the Seashore; to the great surprise of our fore Fathers, told them from whom & what manner they first came, & then existed, & that Talk has been handed down to us from them, that the Spaniard told them that the Maker of Breath with his own hands made one man out of the Clay after his own Likeness & put Life in him, & after that made one Woman out of part of the Man & put Life in her also, & soon after making them, he learned the Man by getting upon the Woman to make Children, & that all the people in the world sprung from them, from that time we remained in intire State of Ignorance, & I suppose were naked. We are told you frequently held Talks with us under a Tree on the place where Pensacola & Mobille now stand before ever there was a house built on either places. It was the Spaniards that first Gave us Guns Powder & Bullets, & learned us by hunting to cover our Nakedness, & in return we acknowledge you as our Fathers & Benefactors, being sensible of your Superiority & knowledge & abilities, & as your Traffick became greater we still became more sensible of the advantage of an Intercourse with you, & acknowledge you as Fathers & Masters by suffering you to build Houses & enjoy part of our Lands, & when the English came we looked upon them as your Brothers.

As to Seagrove telling you that we have thrown you & your Talks away, he is a Liar, & if you believe him you must think that we are Liars & madmen to throw away our friends & take people by the

352. This document is included chiefly as illustration of the decline in Creek leadership after McGillivray's death. The White Lieutenant was reckoned a man of ability; it was said that McGillivray's control of the Upper Creeks was largely through him (Barnard to Seagrove, July 2, 1793, ASP IA I, 400). But this letter reveals that as a negotiator with the whites he was a far cry from McGillivray.

hand that are Daily hunting our Lives & Land; so far to the reverse that I, as a redman that has a little more sense than the rest of my wretched Bretheren from the bad Talks sent to Governor White & Mr. William Panton of Pensacola, I am afraid you will throw us away & leave us to the Mercy of our Enimies who will soon extirpate us.

Great & Good Father this Talk is sent you by way of vendicating myself & Brethren Chiefs of this Nation from the Censure of some bad Talks invented by Seagrove who came unto our Nation & imposed upon us, by insulting our friends & Sowing Sedition amongst us. Such Talks is this Day explained to me by my friends Daniel McGillevray & Stephen Sullevan from a Philadelphia Newspaper, I never before saw nor neither heard of, & as for Seagrove he is a Liar, & his heart crooked & his Tongue forked for in so treacherous Manner to attempt our ruin by such vile Insinuations to insult our elder Brothers. But Great Father I hope you will look over the Insult of vile Tongues, & look upon us as a wretched part of Mankind that are liable to the Imposition of every evil minded person or power, & do for his Sake that your fore fathers informed & made us all, look upon us, & do all in your power for us, & altho' we are not all of a Colour yet we are all sprung from the first Two that were made. I hope as Fathers & Brothers you will protect us from these people who are daily Studying our ruin for the Sake of our Land. If we must part with our Land & you are even obliged to protect us with the Sword, better it would be for us to give it to our friends to protect us, than suffer our Enemies to enjoy it, who are Daily destroying us.

Notwithstanding what is passed thro' the Channel of Mr. Seagrove's Talks, I shall place my whole Dependence upon you; hoping shortly to receive a long Talk from you, directed to the Interpretation of some good man you may appoint for that purpose, & whom you & I can depend on.

Mr. Olivier was a very good man, & his Tongue was not forked, as for Milford & the man you sent last to us they are nobody & their hearts & tongues are not straight; there is now no beloved Man of yours amongst us, & I hope you will trust the Appointment of one to Governor White & Mr. Panton of Pensacola, who know what kind of a man will best suit both us & you, & that the Maker of Breath [w]ill inspire you with pity on us is the wish of your wretched Son & Servant.

TASKINIAHATKIE or WHITE LIEUTENANT

(Countersigned)
Menesses & Linguisters:
  STEPHEN SULLIVAN
  DANIEL McGILLIVRAY

N. B. Mr. Panton has always supplied us with Goods, & all other wants have been well supplied, he I wish to be always continued to supply us, for I believe him to be a good Man & shall use my endeavours to protect him always & his Traders.

TASKINIAHATKIE or WHITE LIEUTENANT

(Countersigned)
    STEPHEN SULLIVAN
    DANIEL MCGILLIVRAY

A True Copy from the original ordered to be sent to his friend & Brother William Panton Esquire, & accordingly sent by your friend et

DANIEL MCGILLIVRAY

213. *Obituary Notice in* The Gentleman's Magazine[353]

Feb. 17. At Pensacola, Mr. McGillivray, a Creek chief, very much lamented by those who knew him best. There happened to be at that time at Pensacola a numerous band of Creeks, who watched his illness with the most marked anxiety; and when his death was announced to them, and while they followed him to the grave, it is impossible for words to describe the loud screams of real woe which they vented in their unaffected grief. He was, by his father's side a Scotchman, of the respectable family of Drumnaglass, in Invernesshire. The vigour of his mind overcame the disadvantages of an education had in the wilds of America; and he was well acquainted with all the most useful European sciences. In the latter part of his life he composed, with great care, the history of several classes of the original inhabitants of America; and this he intended to present to Professor Robertson, for publication in the next edition of his History.[354] The European and the American writer are no more; and the MSS of the latter, it is feared, have perished, for the Indians adhere to their custom of destroying whatever inanimate objects a dead friend most delighted in. It is only since Mr. MacGillivray had influence amongst them, that they have suffered the slaves of a deceased master to live.

214. *Panton to Lachlan McGillivray, April 10, 1794*[355]

1794, April 10 PENSACOLA

353. Printed under the caption "Marriages and Deaths of considerable Persons," in the issue of August, 1793, London, Vol. LXIII, part II, p. 767.
354. The reference is to William Robertson, whose *The History of America* (London, 1777; 2 vols.) is the oldest English work on the history of Spanish America. I have found no other indication that McGillivray wrote something for Robertson's use. Such a manuscript, if it ever existed, and if it could be found now, would doubtless prove a most interesting supplement to Adair's *The History of the American Indian* (London, 1775).
355. Printed in Pickett, *History of Oklahoma*, 430-31, from a document found in the papers of the District Court at New Orleans.

. . . .Your son, sir, was a man that I esteemed greatly. I was perfectly convinced that our regard for each other was mutual. It so happened that we had an interest in serving each other, which first brought us together, and the longer we were acquainted, the stronger was our friendship.

I found him deserted by the British, without pay, without money, without friends, and without property, saving a few negroes, and he and his nation threatened with destruction by the Georgians, unless they agreed to cede them the better part of their country. I had the good fortune to point out a mode by which he could save them all, and it succeeded beyond expectation.

. . . .He died on the 17th February, 1793, of complicated disorders —inflamed lungs and the gout on his stomach. He was taken ill on the path coming from his cow-pen on Little River, where one of his wives, Joseph Curnell's daughter, resided, and died eight days after his arrival here. No pains, no attention, no cost was spared to save the life of my friend. But fate would have it otherwise, and he breathed his last in my arms.

. . . .He died possessed of sixty negroes, three hundred head of cattle, with a large stock of horses.

. . . .I advised, I supported, I pushed him on, to be the great man. Spaniards and Americans felt his weight, and this enabled him to haul me after him, so as to establish this house with more solid privileges than, without him, I should have attained. This being the case, if he had lived, I meant besides, what he was owing me, to have added considerably to his stock of negroes. What I intended to do for the father, I will do for his children. This ought not to operate against your making that ample provision for your grandson, and his two sisters, which you have it in your power to make. They have lately lost their mother, so that they have no friends, poor things, but you and me. My heart bleeds for them, and what I can I will do. The boy, Aleck, is old enough to be sent to Scotland to school, which I intend to do next year, and then you will see him.[356]

356. There are a few letters in the Panton papers that mention Aleck's schooling at Banff. John Innerarity of London, who acted as his guardian, wrote to Panton in 1798, "he bids fair to make a good scholar and what is better a good man." Four years later, however, John Leslie wrote to Forbes that "poor Aleck McGillivray labours under a consumption," and that the doctor gave him only three months to live (*Florida Historical Society Quarterly*, XIV, 116-19).

BIBLIOGRAPHY

I. MANUSCRIPTS

Manuscript materials bearing upon the career of Alexander McGillivray have been gathered principally from four repositories. The Papeles Procedentes de la Isla de Cuba section of the Archivo General de Indias at Seville contains the greatest number. These letters are scattered through several score legajos, of which 4-7, 15, 18, 25, 37-40, 52, 56, 88, 104, 105, 121, 150-52, 158, 176-78, 182-84, 196-206, 208, 214, 217, 597, 613, 1336, 1375, 1387, 1394, 1395, 1418, 1425, 1431, 1436, 1440, 1442, 1445, 1446, 1470, 1484, 2351-53, 2360-63, 2370, and 2371 are especially to be noted. In the Archivo Histórico Nacional at Madrid, several useful expedientes were located in the Estado section, legajos 3885, 3885 bis, 3886-88, 3888 bis, 3889 bis, and 3893-98. The East Florida Papers in the Library of Congress at Washington and the Louisiana Collection of the Bancroft Library at Berkeley, California, contain many significant items. These two bodies of documents are now in American hands, but their accumulation and early preservation was another service to historiography rendered by Spain as a colonial power in America.

Other archives have yielded lesser numbers of McGillivray items: The Georgia Archives at Atlanta, the Expedientes de Intendencia in the Archivo Nacional de Havana, the Historia section of the Archivo General y Público de la Nación at Mexico City, the Cuban transcripts in the Ayer Collection of the Newberry Library at Chicago, and the Knox Manuscripts in the possession of the New England Historic Genealogical Society.

The documents here printed are only a part of those consulted. It is believed, however, that they are representative of the entire group, and that they include the most significant items.

In the course of the preparation of his *History of Alabama*, which was published in 1851, Pickett made an intensive search for McGillivray's personal papers. Neither he nor Owen, who made a similar search some fifty years later, succeeded in locating any such collection. The presumption is that none exists.

II. PRINCIPAL PRINTED MATERIALS

Several of the printed works listed below consist in whole or in part of contemporary materials directly descriptive of McGillivray, his land,

365

and his people. Adair's vivid portrayal of Southeastern Indian life is for the period of McGillivray's boyhood. Romans, Hutchins, and Bartram published topographical descriptions. Willett and Swan wrote straightforward accounts of their trips to the Creek Nation; Pope's is a more gossipy travel book. Bowles put himself in the center of the stage in his *Authentic Memoirs,* while Milfort was such a braggart and so careless about misstatements that his book must be used with great discrimination, even though his long residence among the Creeks gave him exceptional opportunity to observe McGillivray through his entire career. Hawkins' accounts are really for a later period, but like Adair's, help greatly toward an understanding of the Indian problems. Volume VII of the *American State Papers* is particularly rich in documentary materials relative to the American negotiations with the Southeastern Indians.

Among later writers Pickett was the first to make a serious effort to compile the facts about McGillivray. He captured much traditional data in Georgia and Alabama that otherwise would have been lost, and he made use of the printed sources available in 1851. His account, in fact, was basic to practically all that was written about McGillivray in the next seventy-five years. Gilmer, Gayarré, Chappell, Roosevelt, Skinner, and Foreman added little to Pickett. In 1928 three valuable monographs appeared. Dr. John R. Swanton published two long papers on the social, religious, and medical practices of the Creeks which were a significant addition to our knowledge of their culture, and Professor Arthur P. Whitaker published a forty-page survey of McGillivray's career, based on extensive use of the materials preserved in the Spanish archives.

James Adair. *The History of the American Indians.* London, 1775.

American State Papers. 38 vols. Washington, 1832-1861.

William Bartram. *Travels through North and South Carolina, Georgia, East and West Florida, the Cherokee Country, the Extensive Territories of the Muscogules or Creek Confederacy, and the Country of the Choctaws.* Philadelphia, 1791.

Benjamin Baynton. *Authentic Memoirs of William Augustus Bowles, Esquire, Ambassador from the United States of the Creeks and Cherokees to the Court of London.* London. 1791. Reprinted in *Magazine of History,* Tarrytown, N. Y., 1916, pp, 103-27.

Jane M. Berry. "The Indian Policy of Spain in the Southwest, 1783-1795," *Mississippi Valley Historical Review,* III (1917), 462-77.

Herbert E. Bolton. *Arredondo's Historical Proof of Spain's Title to Georgia.* Berkeley, 1925.

———. *The Spanish Borderlands.* New Haven, 1921.

Caroline M. Brevard. *A History of Florida from the Treaty of 1763 to Our Own Times.* 2 vols. Deland, Florida, 1924-1925.

Douglas Brymner. *Report on Canadian Archives, 1890.* Ottawa, 1891.

Edmund C. Burnett. "Papers Relating to Bourbon County, Georgia, 1785-1786," *American Historical Review*, XV (1905), 66-111, 297-353.

Richard L. Campbell. *Historical Sketches of Colonial Florida.* Cleveland, 1892.

John Walton Caughey. "Alexander McGillivray and the Creek Crisis, 1783-1784," *New Spain and the Anglo-American West*, I, 263-88. 2 vols. Los Angeles, 1932.

————. *Bernardo de Gálvez in Louisiana, 1776-1783.* Berkeley, 1934.

Absalom H. Chappell. *Miscellanies of Georgia.* Columbus, Georgia, 1874.

Verner W. Crane. *The Southern Frontier, 1670-1732.* Durham, 1928.

H. B. Cushman. *History of the Choctaw, Chickasaw, and Natchez Indians.* Greenville, Texas, 1899.

Rachael Caroline Eaton. *John Ross and the Cherokee Indians.* Menasha, Wisconsin, 1914.

Carolyn T. Foreman. "Alexander McGillivray, Emperor of the Creeks," *Chronicles of Oklahoma*, VII (1929), 106-19.

Charles Gayarré. *History of Louisiana.* 2nd ed. 4 vols. New Orleans, 1879.

George R. Gilmer. *Sketches of Some of the First Settlers of Upper Georgia.* New York, 1855.

Andrés González Barcía. *Ensayo Cronológico para la Historia General de la Florida.* Madrid, 1723.

Marie Taylor Greenslade. "William Panton, c 1745-1801," *Florida Historical Society Quarterly*, XIV (1935), 107-29.

Peter J. Hamilton. *Colonial Mobile.* Boston, 1910.

Charles H. Haskins. "The Yazoo Land Companies," *Papers of the American Historical Association*, V (1891), 395-437.

Benjamin Hawkins. *A Sketch of the Creek Country, in 1798 and 1799.* Collections of the Georgia Historical Society, Vol. III. Savannah, 1848.

————. *Letters of Benjamin Hawkins, 1796-1806.* Collections of the Georgia Historical Society, Vol. IX. Savannah, 1916.

Roscoe R. Hill. *Descriptive Catalogue of the Documents Relating to the History of the United States in the Papeles Procedentes de Cuba, Deposited in the Archivo General de Indias at Seville.* Washington, 1916.

Frederick Webb Hodge (ed.). *Handbook of American Indians North of Mexico.* 2 vols. Washington, 1907-1910.

———— and T. H. Lewis (eds.). *Spanish Explorers in the Southern United States, 1528-1543.* New York, 1907.

Francis Landon Humphreys. *Life and Times of David Humphreys*. 2 vols. New York, 1917.

Thomas Hutchins. *An Historical Narrative and Topographical Description of Louisiana and West Florida*. Philadelphia, 1784.

J. G. Johnson. *The Spanish Period of Georgia and South Carolina*. Athens, Georgia, 1923.

Charles C. Jones. *Antiquities of the Southern Indians, particularly of the Georgia Tribes*. New York, 1873.

Lawrence Kinnaird (ed.). "American Penetration into Spanish Louisiana," *New Spain and the Anglo-American West*, I, 211-37.

———. "International Rivalry in the Creek Country," *Florida Historical Society Quarterly*, X (1931), 59-85.

———. "The Significance of William Augustus Bowles' Seizure of Panton's Apalachee Store in 1792," *ibid*., IX (1931), 156-92.

John Tate Lanning. *The Spanish Missions of Georgia*. Chapel Hill, North Carolina, 1936.

Woodbury Lowery. *The Spanish Settlements Within the Present Limits of the United States*. 2 vols. New York, 1901-1905.

James H. Malone. *The Chickasaw Nation*. Louisville, 1922.

Louis (LeClerc) Milfort. *Mémoire ou coup d'oeil rapide sur mes différens voyages et mon séjour dans la nation Crêck*. Paris, 1802.

William Edward Myer. "Indian Trails of the Southeast," in *Bureau of American Ethnology, Forty-Second Annual Report*, 727-857. Washington, 1928.

Thomas McAdory Owen (ed.). *Report of the Alabama History Commission to the Governor of Alabama*. Publications of the Alabama Historical Society, Vol. I, Montgomery, Alabama, 1901.

Thomas Valentine Parker. *The Cherokee Indians*. New York, 1907.

Albert James Pickett. *History of Alabama and Incidentally of Georgia and Mississippi*. 2 vols. Charleston, 1851. Reprinted in one volume, Sheffield, Alabama, 1896. Citations are to this one-volume edition.

John Pope. *A Tour through the Southern and Western Territories of North-America; the Spanish Dominions on the River Mississippi, and the Floridas; the Countries of the Creek Nation; and Many Uninhabited Parts*. Richmond, Virginia, 1792.

Alfred Wade Reynolds. *The Alabama-Tombigbee Basin in International Relations, 1701-1763*. MS, Ph. D. thesis, University of California, Berkeley, 1928.

Bernard Romans. *A Concise Natural History of East and West Florida*. New York, 1775.

Theodore Roosevelt. *The Winning of the West*. 4 vols. New York, 1896.

Henry R. Schoolcraft. *Historical and Statistical Information, Respecting*

the History, Conditions and Prospects of the Indian Tribes of the United States.
6 vols. Philadelphia, 1851-1857.

Manuel Serrano y Sanz (ed.). *Documentos Históricos de la Florida y la
Luisiana, Siglos XVI al XVIII.* Madrid, 1912.

————. *España y los Indios Cherokis y Chactas en la Segunda Mitad del
Siglo XVIII.* Seville, 1916.

Constance Lindsay Skinner. *Pioneers of the Old Southwest.* New Haven,
1919.

Caleb Swan, "Position and State of Manners and Arts in the Creek
or Muscogee Nation in 1791," in Schoolcraft, *Indian Tribes,* V, 251-83.

John R. Swanton. "Aboriginal Culture of the Southwest," in *Bureau
of American Ethnology, Forty-Second Annual Report,* 673-726. Washington, 1928.

————. *Early History of the Creek Indians and Their Neighbors.* Bureau
of American Ethnology, Bulletin 73. Washington, 1922.

————. *Myths and Tales of the Southeastern Indians.* Bureau of American
Ethnology, Bulletin 88. Washington, 1929.

————. "Religious Beliefs and Medical Practices of the Creek
Indians," *Bureau of American Ethnology, Forty-Second Annual Report,* 473-
672. Washington, 1928.

————. "Social Organization and Social Usages of the Indians of the
Creek Confederacy," *Bureau of American Ethnology, Forty-Second Annual
Report,* 23-472. Washington, 1928.

Frederick Jackson Turner. "The Diplomatic Contest for the Mississippi Valley," *Atlantic Monthly,* XCIII (1904), 676-91, 807-17.

————. "English Policy toward America in 1790-1791," *American
Historical Review,* VII (1902), 706-35, and VIII (1902), 78-86.

————. "The Policy of France toward the Mississippi Valley in the
Period of Washington and Adams," *American Historical Review,* X (1905),
249-79.

Arthur Preston Whitaker. "Alexander McGillivray," *North Carolina
Historical Review,* V (1928), 181-203, 289-309.

————. *Documents Relating to the Commercial Policy of Spain in the Floridas
with Incidental Reference to Louisiana.* Deland, Florida, 1931.

————. "The South Carolina Yazoo Company," *Mississippi Valley
Historical Review,* XVI (1929), 383-94.

————. *The Spanish-American Frontier, 1783-1795: the Westward Movement and the Spanish Retreat in the Mississippi Valley.* Boston, 1927.

William Marinus Willett. *A Narrative of the Military Actions of Colonel
Marinus Willett, Taken Chiefly from his own Manuscript.* New York, 1831.

Samuel Cole Williams. *History of the Lost State of Franklin.* Johnson
City, Tennessee, 1924.

INDEX

Abecootchee, Creek town, 108
Adair, James: book by, 9–10; praises
 Lachlan McGillivray, 9–10
Adkins, 21
Alabama River, settlement on, 69–70,
 104
Alabamas: depredations by, 34, 158,
 168–70, 179, 226–29, 232–34, 240,
 333; threatened, 247; to meet at
 Mobile, 327
Alexander James: threatens Creeks,
 200; influence of, 201
Algerians, 90
Allen, blamed for Red Shoes' death, 66
Allen, misconduct of, 286–87
Altamaha River, hunting lands on, 44,
 119
Altries, killed by Indians, 111
American Historical Association,
 Caughey as president of Pacific
 Coast Branch, xv
American Revolution, Bernardo de
 Gálvez's role in, xiv
Americans: encroachment by, 23, 66,
 90–92, 106, 163, 173, 271–72, and
 passim; westward migration of, 65,
 69–70, 236, and *passim;* designs on
 Indian trade, 73, 81–82, 84–87,
 90–93, 184–85, and *passim;* turbu-
 lent, 87; rumored attack by, 87–88,
 94–95; compared to Algerians, 90;
 invite Creeks to Galphinton, 95–99;
 English hostilities against, 99;
 McGillivray blamed by, 103;
 revengeful disposition of, 110;
 defeated by Creeks, 160–65, 167,
 172–73; settlers on Tombigbee
 endangered, 158, 227–30, 232–34,
 236; Creeks not to make war upon,
 319–20; Creeks dislike, 236, 340;
 defeated, 331–33, 336; influence on
 Chickasaws, 334, 336, 338. *See also*
 United States, Georgia, Cumberland
Ames, Fisher, quoted, 3

Anza, Juan Bautista de, Caughey
 research on, xiv
Apalache: Narváez at, 17; missions at,
 19; Panton's trade at, 25, 86, 89,
 153, 308–9; McGillivray visits, 100;
 threatened by Bowles, 209; Hevia
 sent to, 304
Apple Grove, described, 41, 53
Appleton, James Lamar, research on
 Treaty of New York, xx
Archivo General de Indias,
 McGillivray letters in, xiv
Assimilation, post-1950s arguments on,
 xviii
Atakabe Olactá, Chickasaw chief,
 338
Augusta: treaty of, xxii, 32, 105–7, 131;
 Indians invited to, 27, 62, 105;
 rumored attack, 112; hostages at,
 150
Ayllón, Lucas Vásquez de, 17, 18

Bahama Islands: occupied by English,
 19; reports from, 346. *See also* New
 Providence
Bailey, overtakes Alabamas, 169
Baird Bluff, 82
Baker, Mrs., Indian captive, 334
Ballard, charges against, 69
Ball play: mentioned, 14, 15;
 described, 41
Barber, Joshua, journey of, 179
Barnard, Timothy: carries letter, 214;
 punishes Wellbank, 347
Bear Creek, Americans to settle on,
 259, 336
Beards Bluff, trade at, 254
Beckwith, George, British agent, 43,
 277, 282
Bellew, letter carried by, 333, 345, 350
Belly, Richard, surrender demanded,
 137
Bernardo de Gálvez in Louisiana,
 1776–1783 (Caughey), xiv

Bertucat, Luis: expected at St. Marks, 155; praised, 164, 166, 167; seizes vessel, 166; at Mosquito River, 284

Bias, in Caughey writings, xviii

Bienville, Jean Baptiste le Moyne, Sieur de, 11

Big Fellow, Creek chief, 155

Black, Tom, carried letter, 254

Black drink, ceremony of, 39

Black John, loses horses, 215

Bledsoe, of Cumberland, 178

Bloodyfellow, Cherokee chief, 349-50

Blount, William: Cherokee treaty, 295; Tennessee Company, 318

Bolton, Herbert Eugene: career, xiii, xiv; Caughey as student of, xiv; as founder of borderlands history, xiv; turns to southwest history, xiv; at University of California, Berkeley, xiv

Bonamy. *See* Miller and Bonamy

Borderlands history: Bolton as founder of, xiii, xiv; value to study of Southern history, xxii

Bouchier, Captain, succeeds Davenport, 160

Bourbon County, planned by Georgia, 34

Bowles, William Augustus: brings presents to the Creeks, 35-36, 192-93, 196, 214, 241, 284; described, 36, 186, 192, 194-95, 202-3, 223; plans of, 36-37, 197-98, 204-5, 223, 224, 306; identity of his backers, 36, 191, 203, 205, 207; followers of, desert, 37, 208-9, 221; return of, 47, 296-97; reports of, 48; memorial to Floridablanca, 49, 302, 311, 313; seizes St. Marks, 49, 305-9, 311-12, 314, 319; goes to New Orleans, 50, 310, 312; imprisoned, 50-51, 313, 316, 318; papers of, 50, 322, 347; results of removal of, 51-52, 314, 316, 318-19, 327; trip to England, 296-97, 311; a threat to Panton, 297-300; escapes capture, 298-300; disturbs the Creeks and McGillivray, 298-301, 303, 322,

324-25; writes to O'Neill, 302; Hevia sent to capture, 304; McGillivray's leniency toward, 308, 316, 323; warns of plots, 310; life threatened, 311; director of the Creeks, 311; criticizes McGillivray, 311, 318; can be used against McGillivray, 317. *Correspondence,* writes to Carondelet, 310

Broad River, 111

Broken days, 104-5

Brown, Dee, and New Indian History, xviii

Brown, Jane, grateful to McGillivray, 325-26, 333. *Correspondence,* writes to McGillivray, 325

Brown, Thomas: describes Bowles' plans, 37, 203; McGillivray's salary adjusted with, 79; mentioned, 211, 221

Bruin, Peter Bryan, carries letter, 159

"Bully," 171; Bowles at house of, 222

Burgess, James, 6; Barnard with, 214; Bowles with, 222; proscribed by Bowles, 306

Cadillac, De Lamothe, 11

Calichies, Upper Creek, town, 119

California history, Caughey writings in, xiv-xv

California Supreme Court, rules loyalty oath unconstitutional, xv

Campo, Marques del, Spanish ambassador, 186

Carondelet, Francis Hector, Baron de, 22; seizes Bowles, 50-51, 313, 316; intrigue against McGillivray, 51, 307, 320, 339, 341-42; treaty with McGillivray, 51-52, 329-30; proposes Indian confederacy, 52, 313, 317, 326, 331, 343-44; arrival of, 295; described, 295; sends Hevia, 304; sends Olivier, 307, 320, 339, 341-42; McGillivray to visit, 321-23, 327-28; opposes Treaty of New York, 316-17, 326; increases McGillivray's salary, 330, 332; opposes a congress, 335; meets with

Indians, 349–51. *Correspondence,*
writes to McGillivray, 304, 307, 330,
331, 334, 337, 341, 343, 349; to Las
Casas, 313; to Panton, 316; Bowles
to, 310; McGillivray to, 318, 327,
332, 335, 344, 351; Olivier to, 320,
326, 328; Panton to, 353, 354, 355,
356; Milfort to, 357; White
Lieutenant to, 360
Carr, Tom, proscribed by Bowles,
306
Caswell, Richard, governor of North
Carolina, 161
Caughey, John: birth, xiii; parents, xiii;
college career, xiii; first job, xiii;
enrolls at UCB, xiv; dissertation,
xiv; refuses to sign loyalty oath, xv;
returns to UCLA, xv; writes on
school desegregation, xv; as editor
of *Pacific Historical Review,* xv;
death, xv; rejects miscegenation
arguments, xvii; extols McGillivray
as diplomat, xviii; biased language
in writings, xviii; writes McGillivray
biography, xxi
Caughey, Rudolph Weyerhaeuser,
xiii
Caupolicán, Araucanian chief, 4
Chake Thlocko. *See* Muscle Shoals
Charleston: described, 15; McGillivray
at, 15; founding of, 18; commissioners at, 96–97
Chatahochie River, 119
Chehawes. *See* Coweta
Cherokee River: Americans on, 109,
161, 172–73, 285, 292, 318; war on,
126, 172–73; French traders on,
killed, 155; forts on, 161; defense
on, recommended, 269
Cherokees: Mobile treaty, 25, 29;
Treaty of Hopewell, 28–29, 101–2;
Willett visits, 40–41; with Bowles at
London, 48; memorial of, 90–93;
attack Americans, 125, 232, 262,
353; bad behavior of, 134; lands
revert attacked, 201; confer with
Creeks, 230; decline treaty, 245,
295; confederation with Creeks, 313,

317, 326–44, 349–51, Panton visits,
321–22; to meet at Pensacola, 327;
meet Carondelet, 343–44, 349–51
Chetaws, Bowles among, 298
Chiaha, Lower Creek town, 108, 125
Chickasaw Bluffs, Americans at, 160,
292
Chickasaw Mingo. *See* Franchimastabe
Chickasaws: Treaty of Hopewell,
28–29, 102, 244; and Colbert, 68,
345; trade of, 74, 79, 83, 142,
161–62, 189, 352; memorial of,
90–93; Creeks among, 104, 106,
232–33, 240, 248; Davenport's
intrigue, 134, 159–60, 162; commissary for, 144; American fort, 159,
334–35; Nolan visits, 199–200; delegates arrive, 232; pro-American
conduct of, 266, 345; confederation
with the Creeks, 313, 317, 326,
343–44, 349–51; to meet at
Mobile, 327; invited to Cumberland, 332–33, 336, 338, 345; urged
to hold lands, 334, 337; meet
with Carondelet, 343–44, 349–51;
satisfaction demanded of, 348;
influence of Mountain Leader,
348–49
Chief Mingo, Chickasaw chief, 336
Choctaws: Treaty of Hopewell, 28–29,
102, 244; trade of, 74, 79, 83, 142,
161–62, 189; Americans among,
104, 122, 134, 160–62, 169; talk of,
to Creeks, 106; commissary for,
144; and settlers on Tombigbee,
226–28, 232; distrust of, 266; confederation with Creeks, 313, 317,
326, 343–44, 349–51; to meet at
Mobile, 327; invited to Cumberland, 332–33, 336; urged to hold
lands, 334; meet with Carondelet,
343–44, 349–51; Creeks attack, 351
Chovacla, favors peace, 126
Clark, George Rogers: described, 47;
rumored attack by, 87, 294
Clarke, Billy: leads Georgians, 110–12;
at Rock Landing, 251–52; urges
trade, 254

Hoghego River. *See* Cherokee River

Hollowing King, of Coweta, 123, 134; speech at Coweta, 33, 150, 151; letter to, cited, 37–38, 215; met by Willett, 41; speech of, 41–42; with Pickens, 253

Holstein River, Americans on, 160

Hopewell, treaties of, 28, 101–2, 244

Houston, John, governor of Georgia, 81, 84

Howard, Carlos, to New York, 43, 264, 270–77, 289; describes Bowles, 202; carries letter, 263, 277, 279; described, 264, 276; compares Spain and the United States, 271–72; describes St. Patricks, 281–82; describes negotiations at New York, 282–84. *Correspondence,* writes to McGillivray, 223, 270; to Quesada, 281; McGillivray to, 273

Huguenots, in Florida, 18

Humphreys, David, American commissioner, 39–40, 251–55; methods, 253; characterized, 260; report of, 260

Hundley, Norris, as Caughey student, xiii; on McGillivray's diplomacy, xviii

Hurons, 153

Hutchings (Anthony), surveyor, 147

Identity, McGillivray's ambivalence on own Creek, xxi

Indian Munny, carries letter, 66

Indian River. *See* Mosquito River

Indians: as central players, xviii; confederation of, 52, 161, 313, 343–44, 349–51; north of the Ohio, 99, 153, 316; O'Neill's plan for control of, 156–57; attitude toward trade and presents, 184–85, 194, and *passim;* mode of war, 201–2; traditional history, 360–61. *See also* Creeks, Cherokees, Chickasaws, Choctaws, etc.

Ingles, A., land speculator, 259, 280

Iroquois, 153

Irwin, Jared, Georgia commissioner, 130

Jackson, Andrew, campaigns of, 57

Jackson, Georgia general, 122

Jackson, James, 45

Jameeson, carries letter, 63

James, Benjamin: in American interest, 169, 247; overture to, 334; attempt to kill, 343; McGillivray writes to, 333

Jaudenes, Josef de, 43

Jefferson, Thomas, accompanies McGillivray, 276

Jenkens, fate of, 231

Jesuits, martyred in Florida, 18

Johnson, and murder of Laurence 231, 237

Johnson, Samuel, and St. Andrews Society, 279

Johnson, William, 9, 21

Johnston, boat captain, 222

Joseph, Nez Percé chief, 4

Joyce, merchant at Mobile, 172, 179

Karns, daughter of, scalped, 117, 124

Keeff, James, trader, 144, 158

Kentucky, separatist movement at, 178; connection with Canada, 178; Bowles approached by, 310

Kilikaski, Cussitah chief, 349

King, John, Georgia commissioner, 130

Kinnard, Jack, 6; to succeed McGillivray, 54–55, 355, 357; incompetence of, 55; at St. Marks, 287; carries letter, 303, 315

Knox, Henry: view on Creek treaties, xxii–xxiii; analyzes Creek problem, 39; host to McGillivray, 43–44, 276–78; seeks Creek trade, 44; criticized, 46; explains purpose, 254; actions of, 282; McGillivray's nephew left with, 283–84; orders to Seagrove, 315; Seagrove writes to, 323

Koasati, McGillivray's heritage from, xx

Kyalejie, Upper Creek town, 108

Land speculators: schemes of, 40, 52, 259–63, 266–70, 280–81; McGillivray opposed to, 40, 318. *See also* Yazoo

Lane, Timothy: quarrels with McGillivray, 34, 37, 154–55, 196; Spanish informant, 196, 198; punishment of, urged, 199, 211, 218, 220, 242

Langley, Linda, on McGillivray's ethnic heritage, xx

Language, Caughey's use of biased, xiii

L'Anse a la Graisse. See New Madrid

Lanzos, Manuel, absent from Mobile, 331, 333

Las Casas, Luis de. Correspondence, O'Neill writes to, 284; Miró to, 285; Carondelet to, 313

Laurence, murder of, 231–32, 237

Leonard, James, Georgia informant, 339–40

Leslie, John: knows Seminoles, 125; McGillivray visits, 138; Weatherford's debt to, 141; warns McGillivray, 217; introduces Howard, 264; commends Spain, 264–65, 273; McGillivray answers, 277; at St. Patricks, 281; notified about Bowles, 296; proscribed by Bowles, 306. Correspondence, writes to McGillivray, 263; to Quesada 338; McLatchy to, 151; McGillivray to, 205, 222, 254, 263, 280; Panton to, 359

Leslie, Robert, carries letter, 296; proscribed by Bowles, 306; writes to Panton, 305

Letters, McGillivray's; value of xxii; as significant source of American Indian history, xxiii

Lewis, Tom, describes Bowles, 299

Leyburn, James: critical review of McGillivray of the Creeks, xix; criticizes Caughey's lack of social history, xix

Lincoln, Benjamin, American commissioner, 39–40, 252–53, 255; report of, 260

Lincoln, Nebraska, xiii

Linder, John, Jr., 231 informs about Bowles, 212; estate of, 351.

Correspondence, writes to Favrot, 136; McGillivray to, 212

Lisk, 63

Little Ogeechee, 111

Little Prince, of the Broken Arrow: to succeed McGillivray, 54–55, 355; conduct of, 346–48; and Bowles' papers, 347

Little River: McGillivray at, 163, 329, 363; settlers on, 213; McGillivray may retire to, 300

Little Tallassie, 9, 197; described, 10, 61; Willett at, 41; Olivier resides at, 51, 320; McGillivray returns to, 52; Garcon sent to, 152

London, Bowles at, 48

Louisiana, Carondelet's policies in, 52; boundaries of, 67

Loveitt, James, proscribed by Bowles, 306

Lower Creeks: and Bowles, 36, 48, 186, 296, 298–301, 303, 322, 327; oppose peace, 38; neutrality of, 126; commissary for, 144; summoned to Coweta, 147; meeting among, 238; ask return of Bowles, 314; McGillivray to visit, 319; Olivier visits, 327; call on McGillivray, 344–47. See also Creeks

Loyalists: at St. Augustine, 63; proposed colony, 69–70

Loyalty oath: Caughey refuses to sign, xv; found unconstitutional, xv

Lucas, blamed for Red Shoes' death, 66

MacArthur, General, 62; McGillivray writes to, 71

McDonald, British commissary, 135

McFarlan, Indian victim, 343

McGillivray, Alexander: historical context at birth, xv; as Creek spokesman, xvi, xxi; as Creek trader, xvi; fluency in English, xvi; negotiates treaties, xvi, xxii; as cultural broker, xxi; surrenders land to U.S., xvii; death, xvii; estate, xvii; studies on life of, xvii; emotional

Sullivan, Stephen, interpreter, 360–62
Swan, Caleb: journey of, 44–45, 284; observations of, 45, 284; cited, 63, 66

Taitt, British agent, 212
Talapuches. *See* Creeks
Tallapoussies, 66; squander ammunition, 134
Tallassies, Creek town, 108; favor peace, 126; friendly to Americans, 136; attack Cumberland, 145; meet at Coweta, 151; turn against Georgia, 151, 154
"Talleyrand of Alabama," xvii
Tally, 69
Tame King, of Tallassie: seized, 32, 139–40; at Tuckebatches, 123–24, 127; favors Americans, 133, 136; speech of, 140; causes confusion, 197; influence of, 214
Tammany, Society of St., 43
Taska Etoka. *See* Franchimastabe
Taskiniahatkie. *See* White Lieutenant
Taylor, carries letter, 218
Telfair, Edward, 111
Tennessee Yazoo Company, grant to, 259, 318; to fortify Muscle Shoals, 291–92
Tensaw, settlers threatened, 34, 157, 158, 197, 228–29, 234; plot at, 158–59, 172; and Bowles, 211; settlers defended, 229–30, 233
Terrapin, Cherokee warrior, 245
Thlaycatska, Lower Creek town, 108
Thomson, Alcey, Indian captive, 324
Toclatoche. *See* Yntipaya Masla
Tolintoneche, presents to, 143
Tombigbee: rumored attack on, 34, 38, 158, 227–29, 232–34; plot at, 158–59, 227; settlers defended, 229–30, 233; fort on, 334, 336; hostilities on, 342
Tomopa Mingo, Creek chief, 342
Tonyn, Patrick; arrival, 67; letters, 68, 72
Toole, describes war, 111
Toopsa Táwah, marriage ceremony, 12

Toulouse, French fort, 11, 41
Toushatchie, Upper Creek town, 108
Trade, Indian: dependence of the Creeks upon, 8, 23–26, 64–66, 71–74, 115, 184–85, and *passim;* Indian attitude toward, 10, 184–85, 194; Spain provides, 23–25, 75–78, 82, 99, 142, 173, 180, 246; McGillivray's share in, 24–25, 65–67, 72–74, 77–78, 88–89, 248, and *passim;* role of Panton in, 24–26, 77–80, 120, 144, 161–64, 184–85 188, 206, 335, and *passim;* tariff of prices, 25; at St. Marks, 25, 72–74, 79, 82, 100, 142, 166–67, 206; rivalry of Panton and Mather, 25–26, 83, 85–86, 88, 172; methods, 62, 82; American offers, 44, 73, 81–84, 87, 90–93, 120, 254, 271, 285, 290–91; rivalry of Panton and Turnbull, 350, 352
Treaties: New York, xx; Pensacola, xxii; Shoulderbone Creek, xxii
Treaty making, McGillivray and, xvi–xvii
Tuckebatches: meeting at, 31, 107–9, 119–20, 123–24, 127–28; letter from, 170; among Chickasaws, 240
Turnbull, John: opposes Spain, 234; trader, 350, 352
Tuskatokah. *See* Franchimastabe
Tustunie Opoia, Lower Creek chief, 314
Twiggs, Georgia general, 122, 132

Uchees, thievery of, 158
Ugulayacabe, Chickasaw chief, 343
United States: boundaries, 21, 44, 52, 64, 67, 92, 96, 133, 135, and *passim;* critical period, 22–23, 65, 70, 81; dissolution of, predicted, 23, 70; proposes Creek treaty, 27, 95–97, 101–3; agents of, characterized, 27–28, 55, 253, 260; treaties of Hopewell, 28–29, 101–2; commissioners sent by, 32–33, 38–39, 147–51, 170–71, 174–75; new government of, 38, 200, 238–39, 254;

387

United States (*continued*)
negotiates at Rock Landing, 39–40, 251–58, 260; contests Georgia land grants, 40, 42, 259–62, 266–70; invites creeks to New York, 40–42, 256–58, 260–63; Spain's envoy to, 43, 91–92, 103, 134–35, 143, 272; Treaty of New York, 43–46, 273–78, 282–83, 290–91, 293; employs, McGillivray, 44, 54–55; and Indian trade, 44, 73, 81–84, 87, 90–93, 120, 254, 271–72, 285, 290–91; guarantees Creek lands, 46; pays the Creeks, 47, 299; and State of Muskogee, 50; proposes peace, 113, 174–76, 182, 200; policies of, 173, 244–46, 342; unable to restrain Georgia, 192; lands ceded to, 193; negotiates with Spain, 334, 337–38, 341–42, 344–45, 349. *See also* Americans
University of California, Berkeley (UCB), xiii; Caughey at, xiv
University of California, Los Angeles (UCLA), xiii; Caughey at, xiv
University of Texas: Caughey at, xiii; Bolton at, xiv
University of Wisconsin, Bolton at, xiv

Valdez, Antonio, orders from, 177
Vallin, Madam, message from, 249
Veler, padre at Pensacola, 172
Viar, Josef Ygnacio de, chargé at New York, 43, 272; write, to Quesada, 276
Villebeuvre, Juan de la, quoted, 343; at Natchez, 350
Virginia Yazoo Company, grant to, 260

Wackakay (Wakokay), Upper Creek town, 108; ammunition for, 150; to attack Chickasaws, 348
Walker, Abraham, 6; losses of, 168–69, 179, 229; overseer, 212
Walsh, Michael, 63
Walton, 231; describes Lower Creeks, 347
Walton, Emily (Caughey's mother), xiii

Walton, Georgia agent, 168–69
Ward, Charles T., review of *McGillivray of the Creeks*, xix
Ward, Robert David, research on Treaty of New York, xx
Warrior King, of Cussitah: quoted, 37–38, 215; restrains Bowles, 223
Washington, George: view on Creek treaties, xxii–xxiii; election of 38, 239; faces Creek problem, 39; sends Willett, 40, 258, 260–62; purposes of, 41–42, 260–64, 267, 270; receives McGillivray, 43, 276–77; signs Treaty of New York, 43, 45, 278; criticized, 46; notified from Rock Landing, 254; opposes Spain, 282; orders of, 315; talk of, to Choctaws, 331
Washington, Thomas, hanged, 292
Watson, Thomas D., on McGillivray and Creek sovereignty, xx
Weatherford, Charles, 6, 205; carries letter, 103, 199; in debt to Leslie, 140; punishment of, 140, 158, 218; release of, 167; Spanish informant, 212; Georgian informant, 339; sent to Philadelphia, 340
Webb, Walter Prescott, Caughey takes class from, xiii
Weekly, loyalist, 69
Welch, Robert, sent to Coolamies, 70; trader, 334
Wellbank, George: has Bowles' papers, 50–51, 322, 347; with Bowles, 224, 305–6; called to Bahamas, 346; influence of, 347–48; arrest expected, 350; flight of, 358
Weokey, Upper Creek town, 108; Mico of, commended, 155
Western History Association, Caughey elected president of, xv
Whitaker, Arthur: on McGillivray, xvii; criticizes Caughey biography, xix; debates Caughey on McGillivray role, 19
White, Edward, writes to McGillivray, 315; McGillivray writes to, 321

White, Enrique: McGillivray's host, 30; at Pensacola, 319
White, James, American commissioner, 32–33, 147–48, 174; at Coweta, 148–51
White, Nicholas, trader, 249
White Ground Indians, kill cattle, 147
White Lieutenant, of Okfuskee: complaint of, 55, 360–62; present for, 132; loyal to Spain, 360; denounces Seagrove, 360–61, writes to Carondelet, 360
Whitfield, George, carries letters, 175, 180–81, 183–84, 189, 215, 220
Willett, Marinus: goes to Creek Nation, 40–41; invites Creeks to New York, 41–42, 258, 260–62, 288; returns to New York, 43, described, 258, 260; signs treaty, 278
Williamson's Pastures, 111
Wind clan, 5, 62
Winn, Richard, American commissioner, 38
Woods, at Yazoo, 169
Wright, J. Leitch, on McGillivray and the Treaty of New York, xx
Wyandots, 153

Yaholla Mico. *See* Hollowing King
Yamassee Revolt, 19–20
Yazoo: land grants, 40, 42, 259–63, 266–70; company of, defeated, 46, 280–81, 288, 318; congress at, 160; Choctaw grant, 169, 268; Americans at, 320; trade not permitted, 350
Yellow Bird, Cherokee chief, 41
Yellow Hair. *See* McMurphy, Daniel
Yellow Water, Indians robbed at, 170
Yntipaya Masla, Creek chief, 114–17

Zéspedes, Vizente Manuel de: praises the Creeks, 30, 112–15; informed about Bowles, 37, 208–9, 221; furnishes passport, 89; letter for, 121; talk of, to the Creeks, 127–28; has confidence in McGillivray, 206; sends Howard to New York, 264, 270, 272, 277, 289; departure of, 276. *Correspondence,* writes to McGillivray, 112, 117, 143, 202; to Yntipaya Masla, 114; to Ezpeleta, 208; Panton, Leslie and Company to, 79; McGillivray to, 87, 124, 138, 141, 148, 162, 165, 221

CPSIA information can be obtained at www.ICGtesting.com
Printed in the USA
LVOW070028111211

258799LV00001B/322/P